Holland under Habsburg Rule, 1506–1566

Holland under Habsburg Rule, 1506–1566

The Formation of a Body Politic

JAMES D. TRACY

UNIVERSITY OF CALIFORNIA PRESS
Berkeley   Los Angeles   Oxford

NORTHWEST MISSOURI STATE
UNIVERSITY LIBRARY
MARYVILLE, MO 64468

University of California Press
Berkeley and Los Angeles, California

University of California Press
Oxford, England

Copyright © 1990 by
The Regents of the University of California

Library of Congress Cataloging-in-Publication Data

Tracy, James D.
Holland under Habsburg rule, 1506–1566 : the formation of a body
    politic / James D. Tracy.
        p.   cm.
Includes bibliographical references (p.
ISBN 0-520-06882-3 (alk. paper)
1. Holland (Netherlands : Province)—History.   2. Netherlands—
History—House of Hapsburg, 1477–1556.   3. Netherlands—History—
Wars of Independence, 1556–1648.   I. Title.
            DJ401.H64T73   1990
949.2′02—dc20   90-10856
                                                                          CIP

Printed in the United States of America

1   2   3   4   5   6   7   8   9

The paper used in this publication meets the minimum requirements
of American National Standard for Information Sciences—Permanence
of Paper for Printed Library Materials, ANSI Z39.48-1984∞

949.2
T76h

*To Patrick, Sam, and Mae, whose
willingness to be schooled in foreign
parts is now a part of this book.*

FEB 5 1992

Contents

Maps and Tables

Acknowledgments

Much of the research for this book was supported by a Fulbright grant from the Council for International Exchange in Brussels during my sabbatical in 1979–1980, and by a similar grant from the Council's office in Amsterdam the following summer, supplemented by a grant from the American Council of Learned Societies. Writing was made easier by two summer research grants from the Graduate School of the University of Minnesota. Maps were drawn by The Cartographic Laboratory (Department of Geography, University of Minnesota), and the index was done by John Jensen (Special Collections, University of Minnesota libraries). Along the way I have profited even more from the encouragement, advice, and example of friends and colleagues in the Netherlands. Hugo de Schepper (Catholic University of Nijmegen) initiated a rather inexperienced foreigner in the use of the rich collections at the Algemeen Rijksarchief in Brussels, and Jeremy Bangs (now at Plimouth Planation in Massachusetts) did the same for town archives in Holland. Juliaan Woltjer, emeritus from the Rijksuniversiteit te Leiden, was kind enough to give me a critical reading of the entire manuscript, in an earlier and much longer form, and began the necessary process of convincing me it was far too long. Wim Blockmans at Leiden and Henk van Nierop at the University of Amsterdam shared their expertise in pertinent areas where my own knowledge would not get me very far. Finally, I owe a special thanks to colleagues at Leiden who made me welcome during a teaching stint (spring 1987) and a subsequent shorter visit, especially Jan de Jongste, and not least to the students in my *doctoraal werkcollege,* who proved once again that nothing rejuvenates a scholar's enthusiasm so much as having others with whom to share it.

Introduction

The question of how it is that men have learned to govern themselves is one that must be posed anew in each scholarly generation. Certainly it is a question that has held special interest for American students of European history, perhaps because of a fascination with forms of government, a fascination rooted in American history. Americans of one scholarly generation made distinguished contributions to medieval English constitutional history, just as others of this current generation have illuminated the political and social history of the self-governing towns of Renaissance Italy and the free imperial cities of Germany.[1] This book will focus on the question of self-government at the level of a province, a form of political organization that is, roughly speaking, intermediate in complexity between the city-states of central Europe and the emerging national monarchies of western Europe.[2]

As late as the eighteenth century, serious political thinkers like Montesquieu and Rousseau did not believe it was feasible for men to govern themselves, save within the bounds of a small, face-to-face society, such as Rousseau's native Geneva,[3] or rural communes like the three "forest cantons" that were the original nucleus of the Swiss Confederation.[4] In the historical experience of ancient and medieval Europe, there was no reason to think otherwise. The city-states that were time and again the breeding ground of republican institutions might embrace large territories including other cities, but these territories were governed from and for the metropolis, so that other cities were subjects rather than partners in the state. As H. G. Koenigsberger remarks, the city-states of northern and central Italy never developed parliamentary institutions, in part because their civic patriotism could not be transformed into a wider patriotism.[5] City-states and rural communes could occasionally form unions among themselves, of which the Swiss Confederation was the most enduring example, but these federal bodies

1

lacked some of the essential attributes of a state since they never presumed to intervene in the internal affairs of component members.[6] Intermediate in size between the city-states and the large kingdoms of medieval Europe, there were of course provinces and principalities, many of which had parliamentary bodies; but these assemblies were always answerable either to a territorial prince or to provincial officials appointed by the king. In all of European history, there had never been such a thing as a self-governing province with an integrated structure of authority ruled not by a prince, but by a consensus among its component parts. To be more precise, there had never been such a thing prior to the Dutch Republic.

In the early Middle Ages, the portion of Europe now included within the boundaries of Belgium and the Netherlands was divided among a number of distinct principalities, each with its own dynasty. North of the linguistic frontier running roughly from Dunkirk to the Ardennes forest, Flanders and Brabant were mostly Netherlandish-speaking, whereas Holland, Zeeland, and Utrecht were wholly so. To the south, Artois, Hainaut, and Namur were French-speaking. During the course of the Middle Ages each of these territories developed similar institutions, including local parliaments or "states," and some of them formed dynastic unions among themselves. But it was only under the Dukes of Burgundy, a junior branch of the French royal house, that most of the territories of this region, while still preserving their separate institutions, were joined together under a single ruler.

Duke Philip the Good (1419–1467), third in the Burgundian line, put in place a number of unitary institutions for his Low Countries possessions, including a *Parlement* or sovereign court at Mechelen and a States General to which each of the provincial states or parliaments sent its deputies. But the harsh and ambitious rule of his son Charles the Bold (1467–1477) provoked a strong reaction towards greater provincial autonomy under his daughter, Mary of Burgundy, the last of her family. At Mary's untimely death (1482) the Burgundian Netherlands passed to her husband and successor, Maximilian I of Habsburg, leaving a foreign prince to face provinces that were already hostile to the pretensions of centralized authority. Maximilian and his Habsburg heirs had to move with great caution, even if their first objective was merely to rebuild the framework of centralized government to the point initially reached under Philip the Good.

The Burgundian-Habsburg dominion was thus one in which provinces and their parliamentary bodies, while still under princely rule, enjoyed an unusual freedom of action. Emperor Charles V, Maximilian's grandson and ruler of the Netherlands from 1514 to 1555, was largely successful in reestablishing the foundation of princely rule, thanks to an able government in Brussels led by his sister, Mary of Hungary. But his son and heir, King Philip II of Spain, was less inclined to take advice from Netherlands notables. He and his military governor, the Duke of Alba, rekindled a spirit of opposition in the provinces by pursuing to their logical conclusion the fiercely orthodox religious policies of his father. In 1572, angered by the King's fiscal policies, Holland and Zeeland launched a Revolt that gained the support of five other northern provinces and eventually culminated in Spain's recognition of the United Provinces, or Dutch Republic, as an independent nation (Treaty of Westphalia, 1648).[7]

The precise nature or form of the government that came into existence as the seven provinces waged their long war against Spain was confusing to outsiders, even to those who might now be counted among forerunners of the modern discipline of political science. For example, Johannes Althusius, in his *Politica Methodice Digesta*, lists the United Provinces and the Swiss Confederation under the same category of commonwealths, that is, the *consociatio foederalis,* or federated body politic. In fact, however, his description of the two republics betrays an important difference not given theoretical recognition. In both cases, following contemporary Swiss and Dutch writers, he describes the competence and composition of the two respective federal parliaments, the Swiss Diet and the States General. But in the case of the Netherlands, he goes on to provide equally detailed descriptions of the states or parliaments of the several provinces, each of which sent its deputies to the States General with carefully limited powers.[8] In other words, although many cantons in the Swiss Confederation were city-states dominated by a single urban center, all of the component provinces of the Dutch Republic were themselves federations in miniature, in which the decision-making power was shared among locally powerful constituencies. In previous centuries, some Low Countries provinces had developed a system of three estates, providing representation for the clergy, the nobility, and the towns. But there was no representation for the clergy in the officially Calvinist Republic; thus, its provincial assemblies were controlled either by the nobles, as in Guelders, or, as in Holland and Zeeland, by the cities that had voting rights.[9]

The house of Orange provided a certain executive authority since members of this family often held the antiquated title of *Stadtholder* in various provinces. But this title had to be granted by the provincial states, and there were long periods when the States of Holland, the most influential province, chose not to have a Stadtholder. Frederick Henry (1626–1647), who for a time governed through a committee of States General deputies, and Willem III (1672–1699) were the only Princes of Orange who ever enjoyed anything like the position of a monarch.[10]

Government in the United Provinces involved a process of devolution so cumbersome that foreign observers, accustomed to the efficiencies of princely cabinets, would sometimes shake their heads in disbelief. According to an eighteenth-century Orangist partisan, "This form of government is such that in matters of any great import two or three rogues can hinder the most salutary decisions taking place."[11] Important questions presented to the States General were referred to the states of the several provinces, which often gave their deputies strict instructions on how to vote, necessitating still another round of discussion at the provincial level since the States General required unanimity among the provinces on questions of taxation and many other issues. When one considers further that everything depended on the commercial wealth and naval strength of the single province of Holland and that the States of Holland sometimes required unanimity among its eighteen voting cities,[12] it is indeed puzzling that such a system of government could sustain the Republic in a conflict that lasted intermittently for over eighty years. On a theoretical plane, one might argue over whether sovereignty in the United Provinces resided in the

States General, or (as seems most likely) in the states of the several provinces, or even in the individual cities which voted in the latter.[13] In practice, however, the States of Holland and similar provincial bodies were self-governing; that is, they were competent to resolve by consensus of their members all important matters save those few that the States General managed to reserve for itself.[14] In sum, the Netherlands was the one corner of Europe where provinces might aspire to something approximating self-government, and Holland was perhaps the one province where traditions of republican government flourished most vigorously.

To date, scholars have given little attention to the evolution of provincial government in the northern Netherlands. Such questions are seldom discussed in English since the Dutch language has an undeserved reputation for being both difficult and obscure. That the political development at the provincial level has also been neglected by Low Countries scholars is perhaps to be explained by reference to two very different historical myths. First, the classic treatments of this period, whether at the hands of the great Belgian scholar, Henri Pirenne, or of K.J.W. Verhofstad in the Netherlands, start from premises favorable to the idea of national integretation. Thus both Pirenne and Verhofstad, each for his own reasons, tended to view Burgundian or Habsburg rulers as protagonists of a more modern and a more just political order in which hitherto dominant regions and social groups would be forced to accept some curtailment of their privileges. In this view, the provincial states are seen (with some justice) as fighting a rear-guard battle to protect the selfish interests of their constituents—that is, the nobles, the clergy, and especially the cities with voting rights. As champions of a retrograde "particularism," they might be characterized as "reprehensibly archaic," and are certainly not of great historical interest.[15]

A second and very different vision of Low Countries history, rooted in the struggle against Spain, presents the rebel provinces and their parliamentary bodies as champions of religious and political liberty, determined at all costs to fend off foreign tyranny.[16] This view is not wholly without merit, but it does tend to minimize the more selfish preoccupations of provincial elites and to maximize institutional creativity during the Revolt—that is, once "Dutch" history, properly so-called, had begun. In fact, a fair portion of the government apparatus that the rebels put to good use had been imposed on recalcitrant provinces by Habsburg rulers in earlier decades.[17]

It seems clear that the strengths and weaknesses of these two traditional interpretations of the history of the Low Countries are complementary. If it is reasonable to describe men and women rebelling against the Duke of Alba's strong-armed methods as fighting for religious and political freedom, it is equally clear that their whole conception of "liberties" (in the plural) was deeply imbedded in a medieval notion of special privileges for particular provinces, towns, and social groups.[18] If the United Provinces of the seventeenth century did indeed show a remarkable ability to govern themselves on the basis of a working consensus of their various elites, it was partly because elements of that consensus (such as management of a public debt) were already traditional, having been imposed on Holland and other provinces in the previous century. In short, Netherlands provinces of the sixteenth century, adapting to new circumstances partly by virtue of their traditional autonomy and partly by virtue of pressure from their Habsburg rulers, were undergoing what can be seen in retrospect as an apprenticeship in self-government. To describe that process, with special reference to the one province of Holland, will be the aim of this book.

For a number of reasons, Holland is the most interesting of the seven provinces that sustained a long rebellion against Spain. In the decades prior to the Revolt, Holland had been the only northern province whose wealth and importance bore any resemblance to that of the great southern provinces, Flanders and Brabant. For example, under Charles V, Holland's quota in the annual "ordinary subsidy" was roughly two-fifths of the quotas of Flanders and Brabant, whereas Zeeland and Utrecht, two other northern provinces which flanked Holland on the south and west, owed about one-third of Holland's quota.[19] Later, under the independent United Provinces, Holland was responsible for fifty-eight percent of the annual taxes voted by the States General, and three of the Republic's five admiralties were located within its borders. Dutch ship-building and the more important branches of Dutch commerce—the Baltic trade and the United East India Company—were concentrated even more so in Holland. In token of Holland's place in the Republic, the States General convened on a different floor of the same building in The Hague where the States of Holland had been meeting for centuries. If the house of Orange was widely believed by foreigners to exercise a princely role in Dutch politics and diplomacy, diplomatic residents in The Hague understood quite well that, more often than not, the man who served as Grand Pensionary of the States of Holland was the single most important person in the Republic.[20]

This volume will deal with the political development of Holland from the death of Charles V's father, Archduke Philip the Fair (1506), to the Protestant iconoclasm (1566) which shook the foundations of Habsburg rule in the Netherlands and caused Philip II to entrust these provinces to the Duke of Alba whose high-handed and arbitrary rule subsequently provoked the Revolt. In order to understand Holland's political development under Charles V and Philip II, it will first be helpful to have some sense of how Holland previously developed as a province and of how its political institutions (more generally, those of the Habsburg Netherlands) compare with those in the rest of Europe in the early sixteenth century. Accordingly, Chapter 1 will focus on the late Middle Ages, especially the Burgundian era, when the integration of the County of Holland into the larger Burgundian state depended on the active collaboration of patrician town governments. Chapter 2 will put into a European setting the relationship between the States of Holland, in which the leading towns were represented, and the Habsburg central government. The next three chapters will show how the States, under Charles V, gained experience and a measure of autonomy in managing some of the traditional concerns of government. Chapter 3 will describe how recurring invasions from the neighboring duchy of Guelders forged in the States a consensus for taking the offensive against Guelders, leading the deputies to demand, albeit with only limited success, a role in military affairs. Chapter 4 will show how Amsterdam, center of the Baltic trade, guided the States in a successful defiance of government policies inimical to the one branch of commerce on which the prosperity of the whole province depended. Chapter 5 will center on the process by which a government pressed by wars with France was forced to surrender to the provincial states effective control over the collection and disbursement of its most important revenues. Paradoxically, the States of Holland (and other provinces) acquired a solid credit rating, as the central government fell deeper into debt. Finally, the last two chapters will examine the issue that more than any other drove a wedge between Habsburg sovereigns and their loyal subjects in the Low Countries. In Chapter 6, it will be seen that the *placards* by which Charles V sought to "extirpate" heresy in his native lands necessarily infringed on the legal privileges of the towns and gave them a powerful incentive to stand together in defense of their rights. Chapter 7 will show how many of these strands of development were woven together during the early years of Philip II's reign, as a weak and impoverished government demanded obedience to the *placards*, while the provincial states, conscious of their fiscal and institutional strength, rallied behind the great nobles of the realm in a national campaign against them.

1
TOWNS AND PRINCES IN LATE MEDIEVAL HOLLAND

This chapter provides a historical context for the political institutions of sixteenth-century Holland, with special reference to
the relationship between the major towns and the Habsburg
government. It will first be useful to show how the growth of
towns in fourteenth-century Holland coincided with political
circumstances that made successive ruling dynasties dependent
on the towns for support. Philip the Good, Duke of Burgundy
(d. 1467), had the backing of urban patrician oligarchies and
laid the foundations for integrating the County of Holland into
a larger territorial state, although much of what he accom-
plished was undone in a reaction following the death of his son
Charles the Bold in 1477. In the last two decades of the fifteenth century, Holland went through a period of sharp economic decline, which proved to be only a temporary setback for
towns linked to the dynamic seafaring trades, but the beginning
of prolonged stagnation for towns primarily dependent on industry. As a consequence, the Habsburg successors of Holland's
Burgundian rulers found that the seafaring towns, especially
Amsterdam, were in the strongest position to bargain for what
they wanted.

THE GROWTH OF TOWNS IN FOURTEENTH-CENTURY
HOLLAND

The inhabitants of the medieval Low Countries shaped their
land by their own labor as few other peoples have done. Already
in the eleventh century, Frisian- and Netherlandish-speaking
communities were forming polder boards (*heemraadschappen*) to

9

organize the diking of rivers and the drainage of swamps and bottom land. In the twelfth century, princes formed higher polder boards (*Hoogheemraadschappen*) for the larger task of holding back the power of the sea. It was by placing themselves at the head of this reclamation movement that the counts of West Friesland consolidated their authority over districts lying between the IJ and the Maas, and formed what came to be known as the County of Holland, including West Friesland. By about 1300, Holland was protected by a network of drainage channels and dikes—including sea dikes along the Maas, the IJ, and the Zuider Zee—which must surely rank as one of medieval Europe's more impressive monuments to human collaboration and engineering skill.[1]

Holland's continuing struggle against storm and flood deserves to be better known to English-speaking readers,[2] and rural polder boards no doubt provided an appropriate symbol of the sturdy independence of village communities in this region.[3] But fourteenth-century Holland was remarkable also for another feature that is more important for the theme of this book: the relative importance of its towns. Unlike Flanders or Brabant, Holland had few towns of any consequence prior to the thirteenth century, but during the first half of the fourteenth century numerous small cities in Holland developed individual economic profiles and attracted migrants from the countryside. Dordrecht prospered as an *entrepôt* for the trade in German Rhine wine, whereas Rotterdam and Enkhuizen were important centers for the fishery that developed in Holland as schools of herring shifted their seasonal migrations from the Baltic to the North Sea. Leiden began importing the highly-valued English wool for its cloth industry around 1350, while Gouda, Haarlem, and Delft were already brewing the hop-flavored beer that had been available only as an import from northern Germany. Amsterdam's intrepid seamen soon found that eastern Baltic cities, though members of the Hanseatic League, were eager for a direct connection with the Low Countries that would enable them to bypass Lübeck's traditional control of the Baltic trade. The late H. P. H. Jansen, the leading student of Holland's late Middle Ages, estimated that in 1350 the seven leading towns together counted some 40,000 people, about a fourth of the province's population.[4]

Moreover, the cities began in the same period to assume a political role commensurate with their economic position. The dynasty of West Friesland, which had come to rule over the counties of Holland and Zeeland, died out in the direct line in 1299, and the fourteenth century witnessed transfers of power to two collateral lines: first the Avesnes counts of Hainaut (1299–1346), then the Wittelsbach dukes of Bavaria (1346–1428). In both cases, a succession crisis weakened comital authority and made the new rulers dependent on cooperation from assemblies of nobles and townsmen, similar to those forming all over Europe during the thirteenth and fourteenth centuries.[5] Unlike England or neighboring Brabant, Holland in the early fourteenth century did not as yet have a stable conception of parliamentary institutions. Moreover, representation was not necessarily tied to the province as a distinct unit, for the same principle operated both at a local level where peasants in Kennemerland and West Friesland had a practice of electing deputies for discussions with the count, and at a dynastic or regional level, as when, under the house of Avesnes, deputies from Holland, Zeeland, and Hainaut were convened as a body. Within this loosely defined framework, however, urban deputies gradually assumed a more prominent role, partly because the counts had need of the new urban wealth. Holland's fourteenth-century rulers were especially interested in freeing the traditional *bede* or subsidy from customary restrictions that limited its use to certain occasions. To do so, they needed the consent of the governed, and of the towns in particular.[6]

The role of the towns was decisive in what started as a family quarrel between the first ruler of the Wittelsbach dynasty, Count Willem V, and his mother, Margaret of Bavaria, and developed into a protracted civil war between two factions known as the Hoeks and Kabeljauws (Hooks and Codfish). The Hoeks, including most of Holland's noble families as well as the city of Dordrecht, backed Margaret, whereas Willem V and the Kabeljauws had the support of most towns, possibly because of their opposition to Dordrecht's "staple" privilege by which goods passing up and down the rivers had to be offered for sale in its market.[7] But Willem V no sooner began to consolidate his power than he showed early signs of the madness that in 1358 led to his being confined for the rest of his life. His younger brother Albert then governed for many years as *ruwaard* or protector, and was only recognized as Count of Holland after Willem's death in 1389. As Duke of Bavaria-Straubing, Albert was often absent from the Wittelsbach family's Netherlands possessions, but he effectively pacified Holland by appointing equal numbers of Hoek and Kabeljauw nobles to official posts and by reducing the dimensions of the Dordrecht staple.[8]

Under the balanced regime created by Duke Albert, Holland was an island of prosperity amid the general economic distress of Europe in the latter half of the fourteenth century. By about 1350, Hollanders were bringing North Sea herring to Skåne, the traditional market center for Baltic herring. Somewhat later, perhaps around 1400, they invented the *bus*, a vessel that permitted the catch to be cleaned and salted at sea while it was still fresh.[9] Amsterdam and other towns expanded their commercial interests from herring to wider contacts in the eastern Baltic, while the new industries of towns like Leiden (woolen cloth) and Gouda (brewing) flourished.[10] Since there was no comparable urban development in Hainaut, Duke Albert reversed the traditions of the house of Avesnes, and made The Hague the principal residence and administrative center for his Low Countries territories, while his son, Willem van Oosterbant, ruled in his name in Hainaut. Albert's prestige on the wider European stage is evident in the double marriage he contracted in 1385 with Philip the Bold, Duke of Burgundy (d. 1404), a younger son of the French royal house and ruler by marriage of Flanders and Franche Comté: Willem van Oosterbant wed Marguerite of Burgundy, and one of Albert's daughters married John the Fearless, the future Duke of Burgundy.[11]

Under Willem van Oosterbant or Willem VI (1404–1417), Holland faced yet another question of succession, since his only child, Jacoba of Bavaria, was a widow at the time of her father's death. Initially there were several claimants for the Avesnes–Wittelsbach inheritance and for Jacoba's hand, but in the end Jacoba was left on her own to face the invasion of Holland

(1425) by Duke Philip the Good of Burgundy whose mother had been a sister of Count Willem VI. For some time, Jacoba's supporters held out in Gouda and in the district around Alkmaar where peasants roamed through Kennemerland razing the castles of Kabeljauw nobles. (This peasant revolt in favor of a ruler who counted on Hoek support, together with the hostility that urban craftsmen often displayed for Kabeljauw patrician governments, helped engender a patriotic reading of Holland's medieval history common in the later Republic when the Hoeks were seen as the party of Holland's common folk and its ancient liberties, and the Kabeljauws were viewed as lackeys of Burgundian overlordship, little better than a foretaste of Spanish tyranny.) After three years of fighting, however, Jacoba bowed to the Duke of Burgundy and his Kabeljauw allies and signed a treaty acknowledging Philip the Good as her heir (1428). Holland thus became, as it had never quite been before, a province ruled from beyond its borders.[12]

HOLLAND'S TOWNS UNDER BURGUNDIAN RULE

When Philip the Good succeeded his father John the Fearless as Duke of Burgundy (1419), his Low Countries possessions were limited to the counties of Flanders and Artois. Within ten years, cashing in on opportunities arising from marriages arranged by his grandfather, he had added Brabant, Namur, Luxemburg, Holland, Zeeland, and Hainaut. Only in Holland was armed struggle required to make good his claim. In his newly won territories, the rule of this powerful prince witnessed the building of new institutions to bind them more closely together, but not a rude disruption of their separate identities. To be sure, Philip imposed penalities on the peasants of Kennemerland, loyal to Jacoba of Bavaria till the bitter end, and he garrisoned castles in Holland with "foreign" troops (that is, Walloons from his French-speaking lands), a novelty that would later be remembered as ominous.[13] But neither Philip nor his advisers seem to have entertained the idea of quashing local privileges merely because they were inconvenient to his purposes. The Duke asserted his will in this quasi-absolute manner only when confronted with rebellion, particularly rebellion by those of low status like the peasants of Kennemerland with their communal traditions, or, more often, by the turbulent and powerful guilds of populous cities in Flanders and Brabant. The revolt of the great city of Ghent (1451) was especially notable both for its gravity and for the severity with which it was suppressed.[14] But incidents of this kind had no bearing on Holland where (save at Dordrecht) craftsmen were not allowed to organize into guilds and had no formal voice in local government. It was under Philip's rule that most of Holland's towns acquired the privilege of choosing a given number (twenty-four to forty) of their richest and most notable citizens to form a town council to advise the burgomasters and *schepenen* (aldermen). In time, the term *vroedschap* (wisdom) came to be widely applied to these bodies in which membership was for life and replacement was by co-optation. Town councils of this type grew steadily more influential and were an important legacy of the era of cooperation between Philip the Good and Holland's Kabeljauw towns.[15]

Broadly speaking, Philip and his officials gave provincial institutions in Holland a more definite shape and brought them into closer conformity with prevailing practices in Flanders and Brabant. In 1428 Philip created the *Raad van Holland* (Council of Holland) and gave it a form that was to continue in effect until the Dutch Revolt. There were to be eight councillors, together with a presiding officer. Some of them had to be of noble birth; others had to be schooled in the law since one of the Council's chief functions was to hear cases that came from lower courts (those of the sheriffs or *schouten* in the towns and of the bailiffs or *baljuwen* in rural districts), either on appeal or (in rare instances) on "evocation" by the Council itself.[16] Philip also put in place a more formal structure for the process of representation. The treaty by which Jacoba recognized him as her heir (1428) is the first document to employ the term *Staten van Holland,* or States of Holland, a clear derivation from the French *états* (the provincial parliaments of the Low Countries will be discussed more fully in chap. 2). Late medieval counts of Holland had to seek the consent of their subjects, rural as well as urban, on a number of important occasions; a new ruler had to be acclaimed at various prescribed locations throughout the territory, not just in the towns, and requests for taxation were presented to rural as well as urban assemblies. During the course of the fifteenth century, however, these earlier usages faded into obscurity, and the "States of Holland" came to be regarded as the one body that represented the entire province. Within this body there was a definite tendency towards hierarchical organization. Many smaller cities continued sending representatives to the States well into the sixteenth century, but by about 1500 it was clear that only seven votes counted: one for the nobles as a corporate body, and one each of the six "great cities." In the order in which they voted, these were Dordrecht, Leiden, Haarlem, Delft, Amsterdam, and Gouda.[17]

Meanwhile, Holland's institutions were integrated into the wider Burgundian world. Philip the Good's interests were represented in Holland and Zeeland by a provincial governor or Stadtholder, usually chosen from among the great noble families of the French-speaking provinces—the same men for whom Philip created the Order of the Golden Fleece to bind them to one another as well as to their sovereign lord. The Stadtholder usually had a residence in Brussels where he could serve as a bridge between the plain-speaking Netherlandish burghers of his province and the nuanced milieu of a francophone court aristocracy. When residing in the territory assigned to him, the Stadtholder commanded the Duke's military forces, negotiated with the States on *beden* and other matters, and presided over the *Raad van Holland*.[18] It was also under Philip the Good that the existing monetary union between Flanders and Brabant became the basis for a common currency; thus, gold coins and monies of account throughout the Low Countries came to be reckoned in silver groats of Flanders or stuivers of Brabant— one stuiver was equal to two groats. (For purposes of simplicity, sums mentioned in this book will be given in Holland pounds of forty groats, corresponding to the unit of account most commonly used in the sixteenth century.) Finally, starting in 1463, the States of Holland and of other provinces were asked to send deputies to a larger assembly, the States General, at which taxes and other matters could be discussed.[19]

It was clear that Holland's incorporation into the Burgundian Netherlands would have important fiscal consequences. Already in the latter half of the fourteenth century the *bede* became simply an extraordinary subsidy which the prince requested as occasion demanded, without regard to the limits prescribed in feudal custom. Under Philip the Good, it came to be known as the *ordinaris bede*, collectible every year on the basis of an assessment of wealth, the *schiltal*, which was renewed periodically. In addition, *extraordinaris beden* were also requested for special needs (like the crusade Duke Philip swore in 1455 to undertake), though in this case the States had more latitude to reduce the amount or refuse altogether.[20] Higher levels of taxation did not go unnoticed, especially since town governments often met their quotas by raising the rates for the *accijnsen* or excises on beer, grain, and other items of common consumption, taxes which struck hardest at those least able to pay. Moreover, even at this time, as later under Habsburg rule, Hollanders had a natural tendency to exaggerate the extent to which their contributions supported the Duke of Burgundy's luxurious court and his ambitious foreign policy, and to underestimate the advantages Holland derived from its inclusion in a state that was one of Europe's great powers.

Perhaps the most interesting question along these lines concerns the role of the Burgundian state in the one external conflict that was of the greatest moment for Holland's economic future, the 1438–1441 naval war with the so-called Wendish cities of the Hanseatic League, that is, Lübeck and five of its neighbors. Denmark at this time controlled both the Copenhagen and the Malmö sides of the Øresund, linking the Baltic to the North Sea, and the Sound Toll was the crown's principal source of revenue. Lübeck, a major naval power, was strong enough to insist on exemption. Hence the Hollanders, in their efforts to break into the Baltic trade despite the determined resistance of Lübeck, had a potential ally in the King of Denmark. After a ten years' truce between Holland and the Wendish cities, war broke out again in late 1437, when Lübeck and her allies seized Holland's grain ships. In regard to their main objective—to gain the right to trade at will in the Baltic—the Hollanders emerged victorious, mainly because they had supported Erik of Pomerania against rival claimants to the Danish throne.[21] The cost of fitting out warships during these years was borne entirely by Holland in a manner that shows the breadth of engagement by Holland's towns and villages in the Baltic trade: on one occasion, twenty-two towns and a larger number of villages, mostly in northern Holland, were responsible for a total of sixty-eight warships. Philip the Good's role was limited to a series of symbolic actions that clearly identified Holland's cause as his own, including appointing a commander of Holland's fleet and banning sailing to the Baltic by merchants from other Netherlands provinces. He also empowered a deputation of leading Amsterdammers to back, in his name, whichever claimant to the Danish throne seemed most likely to win. By sealing off trade between the Wendish cities and the southern Netherlands, Philip helped ensure Holland's victory. The powerful merchant communities of Bruges and of the rising city of Antwerp, wealthier by far than Amsterdam, had long-standing connections with Lübeck and Hamburg, and it was scarcely in their interest to see these traditional trading partners undercut by competition from Holland. When Philip banned merchant shipping to the Baltic, deputations from Bruges, Antwerp, and other cities requested that they be exempt and that the Hollanders be required to respect neutral shipping, including vessels from Hanseatic cities not directly involved in the fighting. For their part Hollanders naturally opposed both requests. Philip threaded his way between the conflicting interests of his territories by reiterating the ban on shipping to the Baltic, while warning the Hollanders that neutral shipping must be respected.[22] In the past, competing mercantile interests of various Low Countries principalities had often been a cause of war. Henceforth, conflicts of this sort would be fought out in a struggle for influence at the ducal court.

Within ten years of Philip the Good's death, the edifice of centralization carefully built up during his reign came crashing to the ground when Charles the Bold, in the last of his many campaigns, was slain in a desperate assault on the well-fortified town of Nancy in Lorraine. Duke Charles (reigned 1467–1477) displayed tendencies that Richard Vaughan calls "absolutist or at any rate authoritarian," especially in regard to the claims of urban communes, both in the Netherlands and in other areas to which his territorial ambitions extended.[23] In the Netherlands, it was to be expected that a prince of Charles's temper would accel-

erate the formation of central institutions begun by his father. In
1471, Charles created a standing army in imitation of the French
model, the *compagnies d'ordonnance*, consisting initially of 1,250
"lances" of nine men each. In 1473 he established a *Parlement* at
Mechelen to hear cases from provincial courts like the Council of
Holland, either on appeal or by evocation. Under his firm hand,
deputies from the several provinces were instructed not to communicate with each other at meetings of the States General, but
only to give their answers to the Duke's requests.[24] Perhaps the
most striking feature of his rule was a steep rise in the level of
taxation, consistent with the needs of his wars against France, his
conquest of the duchy of Guelders (1473), and his less successful
campaigns along the Rhine. During Charles's reign, expenses of
the central government mounted from an annual average of
366,000 Holland pounds under Philip the Good to 693,000
pounds. Initially (1468) he obtained from the States General a
ten-year *ordinaris bede* for approximately 140,000 Holland
pounds per year. In 1473, this was replaced by a new levy of
roughly 600,000 pounds per year. Charles also breached the wall
of privilege that had hitherto sheltered clerical goods from taxation. Having conducted a census of ecclesiastical properties and
the dates at which they were acquired, he ordered (1474) a five-
percent levy on the value of all properties obtained in the last
twenty years. Many monasteries refused to pay, especially in Holland, but they yielded when the *Parlement* of Mechelen not only
rejected their suit, but threatened confiscation if they appealed
to the Pope. The States General balked at Charles's demands
only in 1476, when, contrary to promises that had been made, he
requested another *bede* while the one approved in 1473 was still
current.[25]

Despite Charles's autocratic tendencies and his record of conflict with towns elsewhere, his reign in Holland was remarkably
tranquil. When he was still known as Charles of Charolais, the
future Duke was already a familiar figure in Holland where
Philip had assigned to him as an appanage two island districts in
the Maas estuary, Strijen and Putten. Once he became Count of
Holland in his own right, Charles showed remarkable patience
with Dordrecht, which had for years refused to pay its assigned
bede, but now was given a nominal reduction of its allotment and

allowed to make up the difference by amortizing arrears. Amsterdam repeatedly raised large sums for the Duke through the sale of *renten* secured by domain revenues, while Holland and Zeeland together patiently bore a surprisingly high quota of 25.4 percent for the huge *bede* approved in 1473.[26] It may be that the prosperity of Holland's commerce under a pro-English regime made these heavy charges bearable. But one may also note that Charles's hostility to towns was primarily directed against the guildsmen who had rights of participation in magistracies throughout the southern Netherlands (including the principality of Liège), and who often displayed the fiercest attachment to local autonomy. Holland's town governments included no such troublesome elements (save at Dordrecht, where guild influence was waning), and the men of wealth and standing who made up the various *vroedschappen* could doubtless see some advantage in having a strong and vigorous prince.[27]

Reaction against Charles the Bold's wars and the taxes needed to sustain them began even before his sudden death on the field of battle. In order to extract from the various states promises of assistance against France, Mary of Burgundy, Charles's daughter and heiress, was obliged to promulgate a "Great Privilege" incorporating many of the states' demands for greater provincial autonomy. Among other things, the *Parlement* of Mechelen was abolished, the States General was given leave to convene at will, and Mary promised to make no war without consent of the States. Still further concessions were necessary at the provincial level. In Holland, for example, the six "great cities" were assured that none of them would have to pay any tax not approved by its own deputies; in other words, the principle of majority rule was abandoned. The States were also given leave to convene at will, and the power of the Council of Holland to evoke cases from local courts was restricted.[28]

Meanwhile, civil war in Holland broke out again, as leading Hoeks rallied urban commoners against the burden of excise taxes (*accijnsen*) decreed by their mostly Kabeljauw magistrates. By 1481 the Hoeks were forced out of Holland, but they had gained the support of the powerful city of Utrecht, which had long played a part in Holland's factional wars. Holland and the city of Utrecht now joined in a war (1481–1484) in which public credit counted for as much as gunpowder. Utrecht, the biggest city by far in the northern Low Countries, compelled its burghers again and again to subscribe to city annuities, or *renten*. But the "great cities" of Holland carried the day by pooling their credit to raise 200,000 in *renten* issued by the States of Holland as a corporate body, backed by domain revenues that the prince had entrusted to the States.[29]

Maximilian of Habsburg, the future Holy Roman Emperor, became Mary's husband in 1478; when she died unexpectedly in 1484, he became Regent for the couple's young son, Archduke Philip the Fair. Nourishing a quarrel of his own with France, Maximilian was eager to recover the lands that France had seized after the death of Charles the Bold (notably the Duchy of Burgundy), but the prospect of further war with France was unpopular in the Netherlands, especially in Flanders which had strong economic ties to France. Maximilian twice lost control of Flanders, and just as he was about to reduce this important province to his obedience, the fires of revolt spread to Holland, first to Rotterdam, then to the villages and small towns of Kennemerland and West Friesland, a traditional reservoir of support for the anti-Burgundian Hoeks. The insurgents, whose demand for "bread and cheese" gave the uprising a sobriquet, have been interpreted by one scholar as social rebels, and by another as marking the the final campaign in Holland's 150-year-old civil war.[30]

The most serious threat to Maximilian's position in the Netherlands developed farther to the east, in Guelders, where the young Duke Karel van Egmont, once ousted by Charles the Bold, returned in triumph, with French help. Backed by French gold, an independent Guelders could choke off commerce on the great rivers and force the Netherlands government to open a second front in any war against France. Maximilian recognized the danger at once, but he no longer had a free hand in the affairs of the Netherlands. Philip the Fair, now fifteen, was old enough to be acclaimed as ruler in his own right, in the traditional ceremonies when the new prince visited each province and swore to uphold its privileges.[31] Philip's closest advisers were servants and prominent nobles from the French-speaking provinces, like Guillaume de

Croy, lord of Chièvres. These men fully concurred with the States in their desire to avoid war with France—or with France's ally, the Duke of Guelders. Other leading figures at court—chiefly from noble families in the Netherlandish-speaking provinces, like the Nassaus, the Egmonts, and the Bergens—were more sympathetic to Maximilian's desire to press the issue in Guelders. Scholars disagree as to whether these differences represented a struggle between a "national" party (Chièvres and his allies) and Habsburg dynastic interest, or between groups of nobles who were, respectively, pro-French and pro-English, in keeping with the differing economic orientations of the French- and Netherlandish-speaking provinces.[32] In any case, once Philip's wife Juana became heiress to the kingdoms of Castile and Aragon (1501), owing to the unexpected deaths of two older siblings, even Maximilian had to admit that France must be placated in order to ensure a smooth Habsburg succession in the Spanish realms. Philip was able to claim the inheritance of his late mother-in-law, Isabella of Castile, only to be carried off himself a few months later by sweating sickness (1506). The problem of Guelders was thus left to be resolved by Philip's sister, Margaret of Austria, whom Maximilian appointed as Regent for his young grandson, the future Charles V.[33]

SEAFARING TOWNS AND INDUSTRIAL TOWNS

Holland during the reign of Charles the Bold seems to have attained a level of prosperity that was not to be equalled for some time. The most hopeful economic development in fifteenth-century Holland had been the growth of the Baltic trade, centered in Amsterdam. Although Netherlands ships had earlier sailed in ballast to the Baltic, for want of suitable cargo, Netherlands merchants were soon supplying sea captains with goods worth sending "east," that is, to the Baltic: sea salt from the Bay of Biscay, brought initially by Zeelanders to one of the ports on the island of Walcheren; English woolen cloth (or, to a lesser extent, cloths from Leiden and other Holland towns); wines from the Rhine and Bordeaux regions; and barrels of North Sea herring that had been cleaned and treated while still at sea, in

Holland's growing fleet of herring *busses*.[34] Trade created a demand for new ships, and by the later fifteenth century shipcarpenters had migrated from the estuaries and sand dunes of Holland to urban centers such as Haarlem, which in the 1480s was filling special orders for large ships from towns in neighboring provinces like Antwerp in Brabant. Some merchants were now branching off from the Baltic for "northern" voyages, to Bergen in Norway, which offered a market for some of Holland's humbler products like cheese and beer and provided the tall timbers needed for masts.[35] From the Baltic came pitch for the shipyards, amber, and Russian furs, but mainly grain, especially rye, the bread of the common man. Huge quantities of Baltic rye were stored in the attics of Amsterdam's patrician houses and traded in the open-air market on Warmoes Straat.[36] By 1497, the first year for which the Danish Sound toll register is extant, some two-thirds of the skippers paying the toll listed home ports in Holland, mostly in Amsterdam and in West Frisian ports like Enkhuizen and Hoorn.[37]

Other sectors of the economy were also profitable. The herring fishery, for example, was strong enough to absorb much of the province's surplus rural population. Although Flanders and Zeeland had herring fleets each with its own traditions, by 1477 Holland's was evidently the largest, having an estimated 250 busses and employing some 6,000 men.[38] Rural folk could also migrate to one of the "great cities," many of which had industries that were still growing through the early fifteenth century. For much of this century, Leiden profited from the troubles of the older centers of woolen cloth manufacture in the Low Countries, particularly in Flanders. Guilds of weavers and fullers were politically powerful in Ghent and other Flemish cities, but Leiden's cloth workers were never allowed to organize into guilds, which meant that wages remained relatively low, though still higher than in the countryside, since the urban cost of living was affected by *accijnsen* on beer and grain. N. W. Posthumus, the historian of Leiden's woolen industry, finds that prosperity peaked in the third quarter of the fifteenth century.[39]

Brewing was the other great industry of the era. Holland's brewing towns did not export to the Baltic, where north German beers were well established, but they did find markets closer to home. Haarlem shipped much of its beer to Zeeland, whereas Gouda and Delft, the other major brewing centers, concentrated on Flanders. Haarlem's industry seems to have peaked in the 1430s, when there were 100 active brewers. The industry in Gouda shows a similar pattern, while production in Delft continued on an upward curve for some time until the eve of the Dutch Revolt.[40]

The *binnenlandvaart* or inland waterway linked centers of domestic production to the seafaring trade. The route that was officially sanctioned (by the placement of comital toll stations) ran up the IJ to Sparendam where locks gave access to the Spaarne, thence to Haarlem and the Haarlemmermeer, and from there by the Oude Rijn to the Gouwe; at Gouda ships and barges passed through another lock into the Hollandse IJssel and so reached the Maas. Large caravels coming from the Baltic weighed anchor at Amsterdam where they were serviced by lighters that ferried goods to the city for transshipment on barges. Smaller cog ships, having shipped their masts, could pass directly through the lock at Sparendam and make their way to the Maas along Holland's inland waterways. F. Ketner, an authority on the fifteenth-century *binnenlandvaart*, emphasizes the importance of moving goods to or from the Baltic. In the 1430s merchants of the Hanseatic League began negotiating for group rates with masters of the comital toll stations, at Sparendam and Gouda for fresh water, and at Geervliet on the Maas for salt water. The route through Holland was especially favored during the Hanseatic boycott of Bruges (1451–1456), and traffic soon exceeded levels that had been reached prior to Holland's war in the Baltic with Lübeck and her allies (1437–1441). As measured by the revenues of annual farm contracts for the Gouda toll, traffic roughly doubled from about 1441 to 1481, while the increase at Sparendam (though starting from a smaller base) was even greater.[41]

The surprisingly high quota that Holland paid in the *beden* of Charles the Bold's reign no doubt bears some relation to its prosperity. For a *bede* of 500,000 pounds in 1473, Holland and Zeeland together were assessed for 25.4 percent, or as much as Flanders and more than Brabant. In the sixteenth century, Holland's quota was three times higher than that of Zeeland, so that if the same proportion obtained under Charles the Bold, Holland would have been responsible for 19.05 percent of the total *bede*. By contrast, Holland's quota for an *extraordinaris bede* of 1523 was 13.33 percent, while the quotas for Flanders and especially Brabant were slightly higher than those under Charles the Bold.[42] The political influence of the various provinces at court was surely a factor in the determination of *bede* quotas, but one has to assume that government financial officials, in the 1470s as in the 1520s, had an accurate notion of the burden each province could bear.

The clearest indication of the sharp economic decline that began around 1480 is provided by Leo Noordegraaf's study of prices and wages in Holland between 1450 and 1650. During this long period, the most dramatic increase in prices came between 1480 and 1482, when grain prices rose nearly 500 percent. Noordegraaf notes that 1480 marked the beginning of a stretch of rainy years, as well as the beginning of renewed civil strife. That poor weather conditions and political turmoil were responsible for the severe shortages in the period between 1477 and 1494 is indicated in both the price of goods and the testimony of chroniclers.[43] Indeed, the Utrecht War of 1481–1484 imposed an unprecedented strain on Holland's fiscal resources; the issue of *renten* for which the States of Holland stood surety—just over 200,000 pounds—was gigantic for a period in which the annual *ordinaris bede* was only 60,000 pounds.[44] Villages in Holland at this time had the capacity to contract corporate debts through sales of *renten* "on the common body of the village," and it seems that it was the fiscal pressure associated with the Utrecht War that first compelled many villages to enter the credit markets.[45] Certainly this war and its consequences for the regional economy are worthy of further study.

Wars and bad harvests come and go, but the problems afflicting Holland's woolen cloth industry were enduring and deep-rooted. The reputation of Leiden's cloth depended on the exclusive use of high-quality English wool, but after 1480 Leiden's drapers were denied access to the English wool staple at Calais because of their credit problems. Eventually, the city had to interpose its own credit, pledging (1493) its most important *accijns* revenues for repayment of what Leiden drapers owed at Calais. Imports from Calais declined steeply during the 1490s. Worse, by the time Leiden's debts were finally settled (1505), the supply of wool reaching Calais was beginning to be limited by English export restrictions since Tudor monarchs were encouraging domestic production of woolen cloth.[46] Meanwhile, consumer taste was changed considerably by the introduction of lighter combination fabrics such as kerseys from England and says from Armentières and other towns in the southern Low Countries. Thanks to the use of Spanish wool, production levels for Leiden cloth were maintained at the high levels of Charles the Bold's reign, or even slightly increased, until a steep decline set in after 1530. Already by about 1500, Leiden's drapers abandoned the expensive practice of making commercial voyages to the Baltic and resigned themselves to selling at cut rates to Amsterdam's Baltic exporters. Leiden's cloth industry was not to recover its former prominence until the early years of the Revolt, when Protestant say-weavers from Hondschoote in Flanders migrated en masse to Leiden.[47]

Holland's export breweries also encountered new kinds of competition in the latter part of the fifteenth century. For a time, towns like Haarlem and Delft profited by developing their own version of the strong beer imported from Germany, whereas Gouda specialized in a brew that was lighter and cheaper. It was only a matter of time before other towns tried to capture the local market for themselves, in part by imposing higher excise taxes on beer from Gouda or Delft, just as these towns had done with German beers. Because of such difficulties, Gouda's production gradually declined from a peak of 370,000 barrels in 1480 to only 47,000 in 1571, on the eve of the Revolt.[48] Delft's brewing industry seems to have done reasonably well into the middle decades of the sixteenth century. In Haarlem, beer production reached 5,000 to 6,000 "brews" per year in the 1430s (each brew yielding thirty to forty barrels), and remained at this level until decline began in the 1530s. Haarlem seems to have been more successful than Gouda at finding new markets for its beer, particularly in Waterland and

West Friesland. But domestic consumption was falling during the second half of the fifteenth century, even though Haarlem's population was rising from an estimated 7,500 in 1398 to 12,213 in 1496. J. C. van Loenen believes that purchasing power in the city was falling mainly because of continuing increases in the *accijnsen* that the city government levied on both the production and the consumption of beer.[49] In turn, the *accijnsen* were being raised to keep up with higher *beden* under Charles the Bold and during the period of turmoil after his death. Thus the costs of warfare were being passed on to urban commoners.

The troubles of the cloth and brewing industries are documented in the *Informatie* or revision of the *schiltal* assessment for 1514. One has to take with a grain of salt information that local officials provided in order to reduce their *bede* quotas, but there seems no reason to doubt the reality of substantial decline in these areas, either in total production or in the number of producers, as reported by town after town. Thus Haarlem reported seventy-five brewers, half as many as there had been ten or twelve years before, while Delft said there were forty brewers fewer than there had been only three years previously. (Since production levels remained steady, one may assume a process of concentration in the brewing industries of both towns). As for woolens, Haarlem reported an annual production of 800 or 900 half-bolts, as opposed to about 2,000 ten years earlier, whereas Gouda's production declined during the same period from 1,050 to 700 cloths. In smaller towns like Naarden or The Hague, which specialized in lighter or cheaper fabrics, the reported decline was much more precipitate.[50]

Towns engaged in the seafaring trades presented the commissioners with the same kinds of arguments used by other towns, in order to demonstrate their poverty. Thus Dordrecht's Rhine wine trade had allegedly dwindled to insignificance because wine merchants farther up the Rhine had established branch offices in Antwerp, with which they now traded directly. Enkhuizen reported that since 1497, conflicts in the Baltic had caused losses (in ships and goods) of 66,050 pounds; Hoorn reported losses of 12,000; and Amsterdam (counting the ships burned by a

Guelders army in 1512), 210,000. As to ocean-going vessels, Dordrecht had but two hulk-ships, as compared with eighteen or twenty some years previously, while Hoorn had only four or five ships sailing to the Baltic as compared with twelve or thirteen.[51] In these cases, however, the claim of poverty is belied by the financial picture that emerges as the commissioners examine city treasury records, where possible for a period of five years running. The wars of the 1480s and 1490s had imposed a great fiscal burden that the towns (like the villages just mentioned) met by selling *renten* secured by the full faith and credit of the city treasury. In 1494 all six of Holland's great cities obtained from Philip the Fair's government a one-year postponement for payment of interest on town *renten*. But the *Informatie* indicates that some towns had regained solvency far more rapidly than others. Leiden had more hearths than any other city in Holland (3,017), but of these only 1,113 were inhabited by persons able to contribute in the taxes whereby the city collected a small percentage of everyone's wealth. (Levies of this kind were often made by town or village authorities, and the most common rate seems to have been one percent, or a hundredth penny.) Leiden's annual income (26,672 pounds) was somewhat in excess of its annual *renten* charges (20,503), but the surplus vanished when one took into account other regular expenses, such as the *ordinaris bede,* and interest payments on the so-called "*renten* of the common land,*" that is, those sold by the States of Holland during the Utrecht War. Worst of all, Leiden had a staggering total of 128,130 pounds in old debts, mostly consisting of unpaid *renten* interest from former years. No wonder, then, that the fiscal tutelage that all of the great cities had to accept during the 1490s was in Leiden continued right down to the time of the Revolt; unlike other towns, Leiden had to suffer the indignity of having its treasury records periodically examined by government commissioners in order to obtain yet another postponement for payment of some of its debts.[52]

Haarlem's financial position was not much better. The city's population in 1514 (2,714 hearths) was greater than it had been in the prosperous years of Charles the Bold, but slightly over half its residences were either inhabited by people too poor to pay taxes or empty altogether. A hundredth-penny tax levied in 1496 indicated a taxable wealth of 433,400 pounds, but Haarlem's average annual income (19,390 pounds) was smaller than for any of the other great cities, and the level of annual *renten* interest (16,400) left little room for *bede* payments or for the ordinary expenses of running a city. Its arrears amounted to 92,287 pounds. Delft and Gouda were in slightly better shape. Gouda's population had declined severely (1,694 hearths in 1514, as opposed to 2,800 in 1477), but its unpaid debts (23,386) were small in comparison to those of Leiden and Haarlem, and there was a comfortable margin between the annual income of the city treasury (23,377 pounds) and its obligations to pay annual *renten* interest (13,746). Delft had 2,733 hearths in 1514, second after Leiden, and the number of poor is not given. Nothing is said about old debts, and income from a hundredth-penny tax levied in 1508 indicates 536,400 pounds in taxable wealth.[53]

In Dordrecht and especially Amsterdam, city officials were not able to conceal the fiscal sedimentation of a vigorous local economy. Dordrecht had refused to participate in the previous revision of the *schiltal*, the *Enqueste* of 1496, so that there are no figures from earlier years for purposes of comparison. For a town with a relatively small population (1,500 hearths), it had a large annual income (29,460 pounds), to go with the smallest total of *renten* interest reported for any of the great cities (12,060). Amsterdam's income was even larger (33,666 pounds), and its population had grown impressively since 1477, from 1,869 hearths to 2,532, of which only one-fourth are described as poor or clerical. There were debts dating from prior to the city's reorganization of its finances in 1499, but the text gives a blank here instead of a figure. Between 1505 and 1507 Amsterdam levied a thousandth-penny tax ten times, and the total income produced (equivalent to one hundredth-penny) indicates a taxable wealth of 1,018,200 pounds. As if sensing that this figure would be out of line with what was reported for other towns, the *burgermeesteren* offered an explanation: in a merchant community like others, they said, citizens exaggerate their taxable wealth, in order to improve their credit.[54]

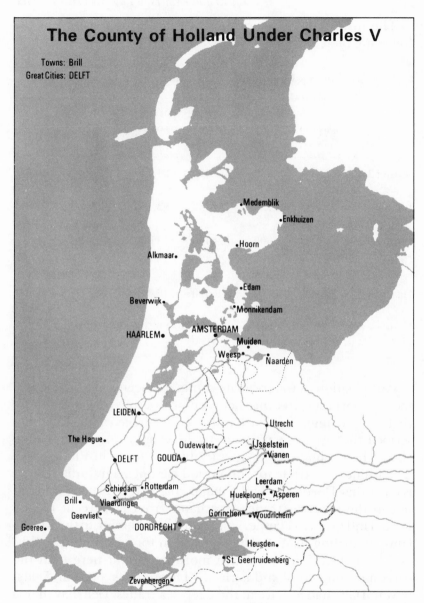

The County of Holland Under Charles V

Towns: Brill
Great Cities: DELFT

Medemblik
Enkhuizen
Hoorn
Alkmaar
Edam
Beverwijk
Monnikendam
HAARLEM
AMSTERDAM
Muiden
Weesp
Naarden
LEIDEN
Utrecht
The Hague
Oudewater
IJsselstein
Vianen
DELFT
GOUDA
Leerdam
Schiedam
Rotterdam
Huekelom
Asperen
Brill
Vlaardingen
Gorinchen
Woudrichem
Geervliet
Goeree
DORDRECHT
Heusden
St. Geertruidenberg
Zevenbergen

Map 1. County of Holland under Charles V

The information just presented can be summarized in the following table:[55]

Table 1. The Six Great Cities of Holland in the 1514 *Informatie*

	hearths (1477)	hearths (1514) [poor]	average income (in pounds)	average renten interest	arrears	taxable wealth
Amsterdam	1,869	2,532 [833]	33,666	24,744	?	1,018,200 (1505/7)
Delft	N/A	2,733	28,733	23,406	N/A	536,400 (1508)
Dordrecht	N/A	1,500	29,460	12,060		
Gouda	2,800	1,694 [554]	23,377	13,746	28,386	N/A
Haarlem	2,526	2,714 [1,470]	19,390	16,400	92,287	433,400 (1496)
Leiden	N/A	3,017 [1,904]	26,672	20,503	128,130	

Participation in water-borne commerce seems to be the single most important difference between prosperous towns and those that are struggling. Dordrecht's *burgermeesteren* in 1514 described the city as living from trade, even as they complained about the decline of the city's traditional trade in Rhine wine. The Rhine wine trade for this period has not been studied, but it is clear that Dordrecht had a major role in the riverine trade, if not in the overseas trade. Merchants from Dordrecht moved Rhineland grain to Flanders and North Sea herring to the Rhineland; according to W. S. Unger, trade in foreign cloth (English) and beer (German) was much more important here than the corresponding local industries.[56] Through its port of Delfshaven, Delft had a share in the deep-sea trades. Delfshaven was built in 1389, when the city obtained permission to dig a channel from the river Schie to the Maas, so as to have an outlet for its trade that would not be dependent on the rival towns of Schiedam and Rotterdam. In 1514, the commissioners learned from the *burgermeesteren* of Rotterdam, not Delft, that Delfshaven was home to a respectable fleet of twenty herring busses. Through Delfshaven there were also Delft firms that traded in the Baltic, at least at a later date.[57] Amsterdam is clearly a case apart, since most of the Holland ships passing through the Sound were based either in Amsterdam itself or in the nearby regions of Waterland and West Friesland. Noordegraaf points out that revenues for the town crane, directly linked to the volume of goods brought to the wharves, increased by 400 percent between 1496 and 1514.[58]

Toward the other end of the fiscal scale, Gouda and Haarlem participated in the benefits of the seafaring trades only indirectly, because of the privileged position each enjoyed along the Holland *binnenvaart*. Leiden, which was not an obligatory port-of-call along the inland waterway (the route from Haarlem to Gouda entered the Oude Rijn upstream from Leiden), was the only city wholly dependent on manufacturing, and it was also the poorest of the great cities, despite having (in 1514) the largest population.

In sum, Holland was a province in which one-fourth of the population lived in towns in the fourteenth century; by 1514, it was more than half.[59] Neither figure is likely to have been exceeded in many other regions of Europe. Though numerous, towns were relatively small, and they also presented a relatively simple social structure since they were ruled by a self-perpetuating patrician elite, with little or no participation from craft guilds. Patrician governments owed their position, at least in part, to a tradition of loyal cooperation with the Wittelsbach and Burgundian dynasties, which in turn depended on the towns—especially the six with voting rights in the States—to meet the demands of a growing governing establishment and an increasingly ambitious foreign policy. Somewhat surprisingly, this pattern of cooperation was not disrupted by the imperious demands of the fisc under Charles the Bold, possibly because of Holland's underlying prosperity at the time. But as Holland was visited with severe economic difficulties in the last two decades of the fifteenth century, some of the great cities were rendered incapable of contributing materially to the government's needs, whereas those whose economies remained vigorous found themselves in a much strong position. Thus was established a pattern of fiscal negotiations with the States, which remained substantially in force until the time of the Revolt and which will be an important theme in subsequent chapters of this book. Simply put, Gouda and Leiden were concerned only to pay as little as possible, whereas Dordrecht and especially Amsterdam were wealthy enough to offer what the government asked and to bargain for what they wanted.

2
THE STATES OF HOLLAND AND THE HABSBURG GOVERNMENT

Like the provincial parliaments of other Netherlandish-speaking provinces in the Habsburg Netherlands, especially Brabant and Flanders, the States of Holland represented the interests of the towns to an unusual extent, and enjoyed a degree of political influence that was arguably without parallel elsewhere in Europe during the sixteenth century. The other side of the coin was that the central government of the Netherlands was relatively weak, since it depended on the good will of the towns for money to fend off invasion, and thus had little opportunity for implementing some of the more exalted notions of princely authority that were current at the time. The power of the purse, however, did not necessarily give the States the upper hand since they were themselves divided and inconsistent. The States of Holland could be a motley collection of ambassadors from mutually suspicious towns, each bargaining for its own narrow interests, or a parliament truly representing, as the deputies claimed, "the common body of the land."

THE STATES OF HOLLAND AMONG EUROPE'S PARLIAMENTS

In the history of other civilizations there is no analogue to the parliamentary institutions that appeared all over Latin Christian Europe, from the British Isles to the Crusader states, and from Iberia to Poland, roughly between 1100 and 1400.[1] The classical tradition of English constitutional history presents a clear line of development from the feudal *magnum consilium,* which advised the king on important matters, to parliament in a proper sense, which began only when the king's need for revenue induced him to summon representatives of the commons, including the towns—for no prince could introduce the then novel principle of taxation without the consent of the realm. For bodies that reached this latter stage, Otto Hintze distinguishes between two "ideal types" of parliamentary structure, a "two-chamber" institution found in England, Scandinavia, and eastern Europe, and a "three curia" (or three estates) system to be seen in France, Germany, parts of Italy, and Iberia.[2] But in the Low Countries (not discussed by Hintze) leagues among the towns of a given principality may be as old as the Anglo-Norman *magnum consilium*. Hence scholars here are less likely to reserve the term "representative institutions" to assemblies that have the power to consent to taxation.[3]

Still another difference worth noting is that members of the English Parliament "represented" their constituencies in a different way than the deputies to many continental parliaments. Once elected, members of Parliament had a general mandate to vote as they saw fit on whatever issues might arise. In England the granting of full powers to deputies can be documented as early as Edward I's writ of summons for the "model parliament" of 1295. Over 200 years later, direct pressure from Charles V induced the towns of Castile to grant "full powers" to their deputies to the Cortes, but only after the revolt of the *Comuneros* had been put down.[4] In the Low Countries, by contrast, no question could be put to a vote unless it had been raised either in the writ of summons or at a previous meeting, and deputies had an explicit charge (*last*) instructing them how to vote on each issue. In the estates of Piedmont-Savoy, which worked in the same way, deputies were called "ambassadors" and indeed functioned like ambassadors, rather than "representatives."[5] Likewise, deputies to the States General of the Netherlands operated under instructions from their provincial states—which were sometimes so strict that a sharp-tongued minister of Duke Charles the Bold was prompted to ask if the deputies were also told how many times they could drink during the course of a journey.[6]

These differences raise a more general question about the precise way in which any medieval or early modern parliament can be said to "represent" the whole territory for which it speaks. At least on the continent, it was common to say that deputies represented "the land," that is, a territory understood by its inhabitants to be a *communis patria*. The fundamental work on this point was done by Otto Brünner, who argued (from Austrian and south German evidence) that a *land* was a community of landholders, living under a common law, who may or may not have been ruled by a single prince. Thus the territorial estates (*landstände*) should be understood as the *land* acting as a corporate body.[7] Brünner's argument does not work everywhere, even for the German-speaking territories—for example, in East-Elbian Germany, *land* meant a territory ruled by a single lord, not a territory with a common law. But Peter Blickle's impressive study of the smaller territories of south Germany confirms the broad applicability of Brünner's argument for a link between representation (*landschaft*) and the existence of a self-conscious community; for Blickle, *landschaft* means "the subjects of a given lordship, organized as a community and acting as a corporate body."[8]

These important questions of terminology have yet to be fully explored by Low Countries historians, but preliminary indications do seem to bear out Brünner's contention that there was no representation unless there was first a *land* to be represented. To be more precise, the term *land* was often used for small dependencies of a single feudal lord, such as the *land van Stein* in Holland, near Gouda, whereas *gemeen land* or *communis patria* referred to the whole of a territory. During the fourteenth century there were regular meetings of the "Four Members of Flanders," that is, the cities of Ghent, Bruges, Ypres, and the federation of small towns and rural communes known as the Franc of Bruges. At these meetings, *gemeen land* or *communis patria* referred to the rest of Flanders, that is, all the other towns and rural communities. By the fifteenth century the Four Members had appropriated these terms for their own use; they now claimed to represent or speak for the *gemeen land* of Flanders.[9] Just as the pace of urbanization and political development in medieval Holland was slower than in Flanders, the term *gemeen land* seems to have appeared quite a bit later here, but it was certainly in use by the late fifteenth century, when the

States of Holland sold what were called *gemeen lands renten* to finance the Utrecht War.[10]

The States of Holland sources clearly did speak for the province as a whole in the creation of *renten* debt (see chapter 5); by action of the States, *renten* were sold "on the common body" (*lichaem,* or *corpus*) of the land. *Gemeen lands renten* created a corporate liability in the sense that merchants from any Holland town could have their goods seized for non-payment of interest in towns outside Holland, like Bruges or Antwerp.[11] But just as the issuance of *renten* by the States was relatively new in Holland, dating only from the Utrecht War, so too was the idea that Holland was a *lichaem,* capable of acting (through the States) in a corporate way. As late as 1514 a Dordrecht jurist, Meester Floris Oem van Wijngaerden, argued that Dordrecht and neighboring South Holland formed a *lichaem* that had nothing in common with the rest of Holland; even if Holland too was a *lichaem,* as Dordrecht's opponents contended, "the members are so diverse that one cannot be outvoted by the others."[12] Even in the towns, where magistrates had long been accustomed to pledge the faith and credit of the community through the issuance of *renten,* the basic metaphor of the body politic had not yet found a universal language. Thus Amsterdam's *vroedschap* resolutions of the 1490s speak of loans being contracted "on the belly (*buyck*) of this city," rather than "on the body of the city," the usage which was even at this time spreading from the towns to the villages.[13] One has the impression that the pressures of war-time finance were inducing local authorities at various levels—from village elders to the States of Holland—to presume to act in behalf of their constituencies in new ways, and to find a new, corporate[14] language to express the powers they claimed. For if Holland was indeed a *lichaem,* there could be no question of the States' right to act in ways by which all Hollanders would be bound.[15]

In effect, the States were a meeting ground for contrary pressures. On the one hand, Habsburg officials (and, no doubt, many creditors) wanted to deal with a small number of deputies who could speak authoritatively for the entire province. On the other hand, the deputies had a natural desire to share as widely as possible the responsibility for decisions to which either the government or fellow Hollanders might object. Thus even though the government recognized only the six "great cities" as having voting rights, the States sometimes requested postponement of a particular issue until deputies from the smaller cities could be summoned, so as to have a "broader mandate" (*breeder last*) for the final decision.[16] Also, although the town governments to which deputies were answerable were clearly oligarchical in character, magistrates had an uneasy awareness of their accountability to fellow townsmen, and it was not unusual for deputies to vote against a subsidy proposal on the grounds that "the common man" would not tolerate it.[17]

For students of Low Countries history, the parliamentary typology that makes the most sense is the one proposed by W. P. Blockmans. Most assemblies, including the English Parliament and many of the French and German estates, were dominated by their noble or clerical deputies; these bodies met infrequently, and were primarily concerned with fiscal and political issues. A second category includes mainly the Low Countries parliaments, plus a few others; these assemblies met frequently, and were often concerned with economic issues, as befits a fundamentally urban constituency. Differences in the frequency of meetings are indeed striking. The Four Members of Flanders met 4,055 times between 1386 and 1506, for an average of 34 times per year, and the States of Brabant met 1,601 times between 1356 and 1430, for an average of 21 times per year. In Holland, the States convened 21 times per year between 1525 and 1529, and 13.5 times per year between 1542 and 1563. By contrast, the English Parliament was in session 73 times between 1384 and 1510, and the Cortes of Castile met 93 times between 1390 and 1520. The number of meetings is not a guide to how many days per year a parliamentary body was in session—for example, sessions of the English Parliament averaged seven months (1450–1520), whereas meetings of the provincial states of the Netherlands on their home ground usually lasted only a few days (delegations sent to court for negotiations with the Regent and her officials might have to remain in Brussels for a month or two). But frequent meetings are a good indicator of the degree to which parliamentary deputies were subject to the control of their principals.[18]

For present purposes, one might broaden Blockmans's "urban parliaments" category by looking at a few other parliamentary bodies that resemble those of the Netherlands in some respects, even if they may not meet the criteria Blockmans suggests. Piedmont's estates have certain structural affinities with those of the Netherlands, while Württemberg in Germany and Aragón in Iberia each enjoyed a certain historical reputation as a bulwark of parliamentary "liberties."[19] In Piedmont, the Cisalpine portion of the Duke of Savoy's lands, the estates convened frequently; and town deputies—controlled, as in the Netherlands, by a strict mandate—played an especially prominent role.[20] In Württemberg, nearly fifty small towns with voting rights made the urban chamber of the *Landtag* or territorial estates more influential than it was in most other German principalities.[21] In Spain under the crown of Aragón (including the kingdoms of Aragón and Valencia and the county of Barcelona), towns had a strong position in the *Corts*. During the sixteenth century the *Corts* convened infrequently, once every five or six years, and thus was quite unlike the Netherlandish parliaments. Nonetheless, economic concerns figure prominently in the long list of *furs* or statutes of the *Corts* which the crown customarily approved at the end of each session.[22] For Aragón and Piedmont there is a further point of comparison with the Netherlands: in both realms the estates of various territories convened as a "states general," while preserving their separate identities. In Aragón the estates of the three principalities mentioned above usually convened together as the *Corts General,* but they deliberated and voted separately; in Cisalpine Savoy, the estates of Piedmont, Val d'Aosta, and the marquisate of Saluzzo could meet either separately or jointly as the *Stati Generali* of Piedmont. Like the Habsburg Netherlands, these polities were, in Otto Hintze's phrase, "monarchical unions of corporate states," in which the natural centrifugal tendencies of each province were anchored in a separate representative assembly.[23]

During the first half of the sixteenth century, a hypothetical omniscient observer of European political institutions might have singled out the parliamentary bodies of Aragón, England, the Low Countries, Piedmont, and Württemberg as having the most authority in their respective commonwealths. Yet by the end of the century the *stati* of Piedmont had disappeared, and the authority of the *corts* of Aragón and the estates of Württemberg had considerably diminished. In Piedmont, Duke Emmanuel Philibert lost his lands in a French invasion in 1536, and recovered them again only in 1558, after having served as Philip II's Governor-General in the Low Countries. Possibly because he had seen enough of parliaments while in the Low Countries, he declared that the *estats* of Savoy and the *stati* of Piedmont were now abolished, and proceeded within a few years to raise the level of the subsidy by 500 percent.[24] Meanwhile, both the *corts* of Aragón and the estates of Württemberg transferred much of their power to standing committees. In Württemberg, standing committees that (among other responsibilities) collected and disbursed revenue were created during the Habsburg period (1519–1534), and revived in 1554 when the Duke had to call upon the *Landtag* for help with his debts.[25] In Aragón, the separate principalities of Catalonia and Aragón each had a tradition of naming powerful committees to handle business between sessions, and in the sixteenth century the *Corts General* did the same, electing a permanent committee that, during the long intervals between sessions, had considerable authority in the collection and disbursement of funds and in the appointment of government officials.[26] Blockmans argues persuasively that committees of this type tend to escape the control of their parliamentary principals, becoming more like organs of the territorial government.[27]

In part, the contrast between Aragón or Württemberg and the provincial states of the Netherlands was dictated by geography, for it was much easier for town deputies to shuttle back and forth to a central meeting place in tiny Holland (roughly 2,000 square miles) than it was in Aragón or Württemberg. In any case the Netherlandish parliaments never permitted their rulers the luxury of dealing with smaller and more malleable permanent committees. The States of Holland had no standing committees prior to the Revolt, and even the development of *ad hoc* committees was fairly rudimentary.[28] Since none of the cities with voting rights was more than a day's travel from The Hague,[29] where the States traditionally convened, there was no real pressure to create a substitute for frequent meetings. Government commissioners seldom gained approval of what they wanted at the first or even the second session and often had to make a circuit of the towns for direct discussions with the magistrates. One cannot imagine a structure of representation more calculated to keep power in the hands of the deputies, or rather, in the hands of the patrician colleges of burgomasters and town councils to whom they reported for instructions.

Yet the survival of parliamentary institutions did not depend only on their structure. This was, after all, the age in which princes were shaking off the constraints imposed on them by representative assemblies during the late Middle Ages, the heyday of parliamentary authority. Already in 1439 the Estates General of France had voted the usual taxes without attaching to them the usual time limit, so that the French king henceforth enjoyed a unique freedom to tax his subjects without first obtaining the consent of their representatives.[30] In Castile, the Cortes held monarchs of the early fifteenth century accountable for how they spent war subsidies, but by the time of the Catholic kings, growing royal influence in the election of urban deputies gradually eroded the prerogatives of the Cortes. To be sure, Charles V and his *Flamengo* entourage did manage to provoke a celebrated uprising by demanding a subsidy for his coronation at Aachen (as King of the Romans, 1520), but once the revolt of the *Comuneros* was put down, Charles found the Cortes pliant, and free of awkward questions about how the king spent his subsidy income or where he fought his wars.[31] Meanwhile, political thinkers in France and elsewhere were at work on a theory of princely "absolutism," aided by conceptions of sovereign power found in Roman law and possibly by a practical sense that representative assemblies stood for a self-serving and outmoded parochialism.[32]

In such an era, parliamentary bodies continued to flourish only where they offered the prince something he could not do without and could not otherwise obtain. For example, at the time of the Reformation prince and parliament had to act in concert to abolish the traditional rights of the Church, both in England and in a number of Germany's secular principalities; in both cases scholars believe that parliamentary bodies, by giving sanction to these great religious changes, enhanced their own authority.[33] The help of parliamentary bodies was equally indispensable to princes attempting to cope with the novel phenomenon of government debt. In many of the secular principalities in the Holy Roman Empire (including Württemberg), creditors demanded better assurance of repayment than the prince himself was able to supply. The only remedy was for the *Landtag* to assume responsibility for his debts, which also meant taking over the collection and disbursement of his revenues.[34] The provincial states of the Netherlands performed a similar role for their Habsburg rulers, except that the debt in question exceeded that for a number of the major German principalities put together. Moreover, the Netherlands parliaments took a uniquely[35] active role in managing the debt, by issuing low-interest *renten* in their own name, so that the capital raised could be used by the government to pay off high-interest bankers' loans (see chapter 5). In other words, the Netherlands provincial states, already distinguished by a structure that gave urban magistrates an unusual degree of influence in affairs of state, had fiscal responsibilities that made them even more indispensable to their ruler than similar bodies were in other territories.

For a variety of reasons, then, Netherlands town magistrates were in a peculiarly strong position to wield the power of the purse. Thus the custom by which such bodies attached formal conditions to their consent to a subsidy was consistently observed in the Netherlands during the sixteenth century, after it had gone out of fashion in Castile and before it became common in England. Under Henry VIII, Charles V's contemporary, English Parliaments passed the king's subsidy requests without delay, "for Commons did not yet realize what great leverage their control over supply gave them."[36] By contrast, the States of Holland routinely wrote conditions of various kinds into the *accord* by which they agreed to a *bede;* this act, known as the *acceptatie* after it was signed by the Regent, provided at the very least a basis for complaint if the States felt their stipulations were not being met. To be sure, Charles V in person flatly refused to "bargain" with his subjects in the States of Holland.[37] Yet Charles was usually absent from the Netherlands (this may have been the real key to the success of the states), and no one who spoke in the Emperor's name commanded the same respect he did. Thus Margaret of Austria, as Regent of the Netherlands, recommended postponing the redress of grievances until after taxes were voted, but was not able herself to put the idea into practice.[38]

The conditions attached to a *bede accord* often had to do with matters of war and diplomacy. In the late Middle Ages it was not uncommon for parliaments to set limits to the prince's ability to conduct foreign policy, often in the form of a requirement that he not make war without consent of the estates. But such restrictions were largely swept away by about 1500; in the Netherlands, for example, clauses to this effect in the 1477 Great Privilege were among those abolished in 1494.[39] The new emphasis on princely power had become a received doctrine by the early seventeenth century, when James I's Lord Treasurer tersely informed Parliament that declaring war was part of the king's prerogative.[40] Such claims would probably not have been formally disputed in the Netherlands. Nonetheless, by setting conditions and restrictions, the states repeatedly hedged in the ruler's war-making power. Like the Württemberg *Landtag*, the states of Holland were able to negotiate military unions with other Habsburg lands in time of war.[41] Like the *Corts* of Aragón, they mandated certain allocations from subsidy income for defense of the sea lanes.[42] Like the *Stati Generali* of Piedmont, they made stipulations as to where troops paid by a subsidy would be stationed.[43] They were also able to insist on the removal of an infantry commander whom they distrusted and to extract promises that the troops they paid for would be used to invade enemy territory instead of merely defending the frontier (see chapter 3). There are as yet no comparative studies of parliamentary involvement in military policy, but one suspects that the Netherlands provincial states intervened in military affairs more extensively than similar bodies did elsewhere.

Finally, the Dutch-speaking parliaments of this era are distinguished by a rich documentation, as befits bodies that played important roles in their respective territories. Sources are of five basic types. Official summaries of the acts or "resolutions" of the States of Brabant and Holland and of the Four Members of Flanders are extant from the sixteenth century. The best known record of this kind is the *Resolutiën van de Staten van Holland,* which begins in 1525; the first six volumes (through 1560) were published in 1751, and the whole series (289 volumes, through 1795) was in print by the end of the eighteenth century.[44] A second class of sources owes its existence to the fact that the annual accounts of town and local treasurers include a section that scrupulously records travel expenses, including monies paid to deputies attending meetings of the provincial states. Even the briefest entries of this kind will usually list dates and places of the meeting, and some towns or other jurisdictions had a tradition of including capsule summaries of the purpose or results of the meeting as well. For the Four Members and the States of Flanders, there are now seven imposing volumes, covering the period from 1384 to 1506, in which materials of this kind are collected and edited by Blockmans, Prevenier, and Zoete.[45] This basic work remains to be done for the States of Brabant and Holland, although the first volume of a new series of documents for the States of Holland to 1433 has just recently appeared.[46] Minutes of the town councils or *vroedschappen* in several Holland towns provide a third kind of source for what was decided or proposed at *dagvaarten* or meetings of the States. *Vroedschap* resolutions for Gouda (relating to the States) and Amsterdam (to 1550) have been published, but those of Haarlem give the fullest description of the *dagvaarten*.[47]

The rarest but perhaps most interesting kind of source is the *Memoriaalboek* or travel diary of the town secretary, or (a more grandiose title) town pensionary, a paid official who was often empowered to speak for the town. When the States of Holland sent a delegation to Brussels for discussions with the central government, it usually included the pensionaries of two or three towns (see chapter 5).[48] Travel diaries for four such officials have survived: Andries Jacobszoon (1523–1538) and Aert Sandelijn (1548–1564) of Amsterdam, and Willem Pieterszoon uyten Aggar and Jacob de Milde (1531–1558) of Leiden. These documents give a running account of the *dagvaarten,* slanted ever so slightly in the interests of a single town. Andries Jacobszoon's *Memoriaalboek,* spiced by the author's personal opinions, also provides rare glimpses of private conversations between government officials and Amsterdam's deputies.[49] Finally, the views of government commissioners who negotiated with the States can be gathered from the correspondence of leading court figures closely involved with Holland and of the Council of Holland in The Hague, which represented the government at the local level. Two names merit special mention here: Antoine de Lalaing, Count of Hoogstraten, who served as Stadtholder or governor of Holland from 1522 to 1540, and Lord Gerrit, Lord of Assendelft, First Councillor of the Council of Holland from 1527 until his death in 1555.[50] It will now be helpful to look more closely at the government which these men served.

THE HABSBURG GOVERNMENT IN ACTION

For the complex of territories that Charles V inherited from his Burgundian ancestors (minus the Duchy of Burgundy itself, reabsorbed by France in 1477) there was neither a commonly agreed-on name nor a unifying princely title. Each province had a traditional compact between rulers and subjects, like the famous *Blijde Inkomst* or *Joyeuse Entrée* in Brabant, which every new ruler had to swear to uphold.[51] When Prince Charles came of age at fourteen (1514), he too had to be recognized separately in each province—as Count of Artois, Duke of Brabant, Count of Flanders, Count of Hainaut, Count of Holland and Zeeland, Count of Luxemburg, and Count of Namur. Charles made his tour of Holland in June and July 1515, passing through five of the six great cities, plus The Hague (the administrative capital) and Rotterdam.[52]

Two years later (September 1517) Charles took ship for the kingdoms of his maternal grandparents, Ferdinand and Isabella, where he spent most of his adult life. In the years that followed, Charles spent a total of fifty-five months in the Netherlands on five different sojourns, the longest being from June 1520 through May 1522, from January 1531 through January 1532, and from September 1548 through May 1550.[53] In the long intervals of his absence, Charles entrusted the Netherlands to the women of his family.

Margaret of Austria, his aunt, named Regent by Maximilian I in 1506 when Charles's father died, continued in office until 1514 when Charles came of age. On his departure for Spain in

1517, Charles called on Margaret to resume her former position, and the widowed Duchess of Savoy served loyally until her death in 1530. (For her residence Margaret preferred Mechelen to Brussels the traditional capital; thus, Mechelen was the seat of government during these years.) Charles then turned to his widowed sister, Mary Queen of Hungary, who had lived in relative seclusion after her husband was killed in the battle of Mohacs (1526). Though Mary lacked Margaret's political experience and self-confidence, once in office, she grew in stature and presided over what must be seen in restrospect as the high point of Habsburg authority in the Netherlands, the period just prior to the disastrous Habsburg-Valois War of 1552–1559. When her brother abdicated (1555), she too submitted her resignation as Regent.[54]

Like the Dukes of Burgundy, the Habsburg Regents of the Netherlands were advised by a Privy Council and a separate Council of Finance. The great nobles who served on these councils (along with legists, or "men of the long robe") often held simultaneously positions as governor or stadtholder of one of the provinces; the great families were slowly fusing into a national aristocracy, and their support was the *sine qua non* for a strong regency. The French-speaking provinces produced a disproportionate number of these families, including such names as Croy, Lalaing, and Montmorency. The Dutch-speaking provinces were represented by the Nassaus (lords of Breda in northern Brabant), the Bergens (lords of the market town of Bergen-op-Zoom in northern Brabant), the Marquis of Vere (Zeeland), scion of an illegitimate branch of the house of Burgundy, and the Egmonts of Holland, who had been leaders of the pro-Burgundian Kabeljauw faction. (The Brederodes, though they were reckoned to control as much as one twelfth of the land in Holland, were never accorded the same political recognition, perhaps because of their role as leaders of the anti-Burgundian Hoek faction.)[55] The Grand Council of Mechelen, established by Charles the Bold and then, after the political debacle of 1477, reestablished in 1504, served as the high court of the Netherlands, hearing some cases in the first instance, but usually on appeal from lower courts.[56]

The Emperor maintained a voluminous correspondence with

the Netherlands, especially with Mary of Hungary, most of which remains unpublished.[57] But the only time that Charles V was principally occupied with the internal affairs of the Netherlands was in 1531, during the transition from Margaret of Austria to Mary of Hungary. The Emperor insisted that Mary must not bring with her the humanist advisers, prominent in her entourage in Budapest, whose orthodoxy he suspected. Since Margaret's latter years had been troubled by quarrels among the great nobles, Charles instructed his sister on how to keep these important men at peace with each other, and he bade her not to act without their advice.[58] To improve the process of deliberation, Charles also divided the former Privy Council into two bodies: a Council of State in which the great lords provided counsel on war and diplomacy, and a Secret Council in which "men of the long robe" dealt with internal affairs of the realm (1531). Jean Carondolet, Archbishop of Palermo, served as President of both Councils until his death in 1540, and Lodewijk van Schore, a *doctor utriusque juris* from the University of Leuven, was particularly effective in this dual capacity (1540–1548).[59] Thereafter the two functions were split, possibly because of a growing work load. Under Schore, and particularly under his successor as President of the Secret Council, Viglius Zuichemius van Aytta (1549–1573), this body assumed an ever larger role, both judicial and administrative.[60]

In each province the Regent and her Councils relied on a local apparatus of government that also dated from the Burgundian era. The *Raad van Holland* in The Hague was given a new administrative statute by Charles V in 1531. As before, the Council was to have eight salaried members or "councillors ordinary" (including a presiding officer), chosen from among Hollanders or Zeelanders who were of noble birth or had law degrees. Since the Council invariably included men from some of Holland's most prominent families, like the lords of Assendelft or the Duvenvoirdes of Warmond, it was respected for its ability to represent the interests of the province; these were men whose family honor rested on a tradition of service to the prince, but they were never a faceless panel of bureaucrats slavishly devoted to his wishes.[61] Besides the councillors ordinary, there were (unsalaried) councillors extraordinary. The larger *Hof van Holland* also included secretaries ordinary and extraordinary, process-servers (*deurwaarders*), and messengers. There was also the *Rekenkamer van Holland,* whose auditors supervised a separate fiscal bureaucracy. All told, there were some 200 Habsburg officials, high and low, resident in The Hague. In addition, there were over 100 judicial officers scattered throughout the province, usually sheriffs in the towns and bailiffs in rural districts, most of whom employed subordinates. Counting all who were directly appointed by Charles V as Count of Holland, the province had about 1.5 government officials per 1,000 inhabitants.[62]

Since the fourteenth century, two very different conceptions of princely power had coexisted in the Netherlands. One view, most clearly expressed in contractual agreements like the *Blijde Inkomst* of Brabant, regarded the prince as the protector of the rights and privileges traditionally enjoyed by his subjects, whether in an individual or a corporate capacity. In the late Middle Ages, when parliamentary bodies throughout Europe were successfully asserting their claims to share in the authority of the prince, this was the most widespread understanding of the idea of the state. As Maurice Powicke has said of England in the period before the Reformation, it was "a theory of the state . . . as a self-directed organism held together by a common regard for customary rights and obligations." Koenigsberger finds a similar understanding of the state in Piedmont-Savoy, where "communes and nobles relied on rights which were anterior to those of the crown." In this framework, according to Otto Hintze, "even the power of the ruler appears as a privilege, a 'prerogative'."[63]

The other concept of the state stems from the revival of Roman law with its notion of a sovereign power on which all other rights depend. In fourteenth-century Holland, this view found expression in the *De Cura Reipublicae* of Philip of Leiden and in the writings of his mentor, Geraard Aelwijnszoon, both of whom provided legal justification for revocation of privileges by the counts of the Avesnes or Wittelsbach lines. Sixteenth-century Habsburg officials were certainly aware of the Roman law discussion of princely authority, and some of them knew Philip of Leiden's work; the first edition of *De Cura Reipublicae,*

published in 1516, was dedicated to Meester Vincent Corneliszoon van Mierop, a Hollander who was to become an important member of the Council of Finance under Mary of Hungary.[64] Similarly, one finds among the papers of Lodewijk van
Schore an autograph memorandum supplying legal citations to
support the proposition that "In time of need, secular princes
may impose taxes on churches and ecclesiastical persons, who
may not excuse themselves from this exaction by any privilege."
H. G. Koenigsberger describes an occasion when Schore's predecessor, Jean Carondolet, put emissaries from Holland to the test
by asking if the Emperor did not have a right to abolish the
privilege they had come to defend; wisely, the Hollanders said
they hoped to offer practical arguments for their position, not
to dispute "about the powers of princes."[65] In 1543, when Mary
of Hungary tired of resistance by the States of Holland to a new
tax on exports, she imposed it "by the Emperor's absolute
power," and no one was bold enough to claim the Regent had
no right to act as she did.[66]

But the fact that Charles V's officials were aware of such doc-
trines, and could sometimes put them into practice, does not
imply any settled policy of making the Emperor "absolute" in the
Netherlands by abolishing the privileges of his subjects. For example, during Charles V's reign there were only three cases in
which the government imposed a *bede* on a province without the
consent of the states, and in each case the same or comparable
beden had already been approved by other provinces. Writing in
the nineteenth century, when the patriotic school of Dutch historiography tended to project the tyranny of the Duke of Alba back
into earlier decades of Habsburg rule, Robert Fruin asserted that
Viglius and Granvelle (Philip II's most trusted adviser) were "disciples of Philip of Leiden." But Viglius the statesman still awaits a
proper study, and Granvelle's biographer concludes that although he was a "zealous champion of the absolutist and state-
church ambitions of the crown" under Philip II, he was "careful
and gradual" in his approach to the curtailment of privileges.[67]

The roots of a certain ambivalence among Habsburg jurists
about the powers of the prince can be seen in the legal opinions
of Niklaas Everaerts (1462–1532), then a law professor at the
University of Leuven, and later President of the Council of Hol-

land (1509–1528) and then of the Grand Council of Mechelen (1528–1532):

> It would be wicked to say that [the opponent of Everaerts' client] was unjustly deprived of his rights by Duke Charles [the Bold], the fount of justice. . . . Presumption is always in favor of the justice of the prince himself, to such an extent that if the prince command something contrary to divine law, such as the hanging or murder of someone whose trial is still under way, or similar things, he must be obeyed.

> [The prince is bound by the terms of a compact made with his subjects] not least because God, who is King of kings and Lord of lords, is bound by His compacts.[68]

If Everaerts were a political theorist, he would have to reconcile the apparent conflict between these two texts. But as a practicing lawyer he was free to choose whichever concept of princely authority suited the circumstances of his clients. Similarly, government officials trained as lawyers could also employ different concepts of the state, depending on the needs of the moment, or on the particular traditions of the offices they held. For example, when the States of Holland had an important privilege to defend, deputies expected a favorable hearing from the Grand Council of Mechelen, but not from the Secret Council; the former body had a record of upholding privileges granted by past rulers, but the Secret Council, which met regularly with the Regent, was necessarily attuned to her wishes.[69] In The Hague, there are occasional indications that the Chamber of Accounts, sworn to watch over the prince's revenues, was not so well disposed toward existing privileges as the Council of Holland, whose members were in the habit of remonstrating with Brussels if they felt the needs of the province were being overlooked.[70] All of these officials served the prince, but they were not bound by any single notion of what his majesty's service required.

At a more personal level, there may be some doubt about the degree to which members of the official hierarchy really did serve the interests of the prince. Great nobles feuded among themselves for influence at court,[71] and could on occasion flatly refuse to obey a direct order from the Regent.[72] Stadtholders struggled with the Regent for effective control of the machinery of government in their respective provinces.[73] Moreover, the loyalty of most government officials was at least intermittently compromised by the widespread practice of influence-buying. To put things in perspective, Koenigsberger points out that money collected in this fashion might be regarded as compensation for the financial risks that officials were expected to incur as part of their service to the prince. Alain Derville describes the practice by which towns curried favor with powerful men at court as a form of patronage, a practice to be distinguished from those seen as unambiguously disreputable, such as bribing a judge in a criminal case or extorting money from a town by threatening to attack its privileges.[74] Nonetheless there are indirect indications that influence-buying was in bad odor, at least among those who had to pay the bill. Payments were usually made not in cash, but in valued commodities, such as wainscoting (*wagenschot*) or barrels of French wine.[75] Gifts were sometimes refused by particular individuals,[76] yet by means of gifts, wealthy persons could obtain cancellation of a fine imposed by their town court, or prevent the Council of Holland from passing sentence of death on a kinsman convicted of treason.[77] Towns and corporate bodies like the States of Holland could expedite their requests in the same way.[78] Men who were themselves members of the inner circle described this process as "making friends at court," but plain-spoken burghers in the States referred to it as "corrupting the great lords."[79]

In the end, the policy of the Habsburg government was given shape and coherence not because its officials shared a common conception of princely authority or because they served their prince with a saintly selflessness, but because of imperatives dictated by the geopolitical situation of the Habsburg Netherlands. Lacking any defensible frontier against France in the south or against Guelders in the northeast, and dependent on commercial intercourse with all parts of Europe, the ten (eventually seventeen)[80] provinces were a realm made for peace. In the larger scheme of dynastic politics, however, decisions that led to war were made in Paris or Valladolid or even in smaller capitals allied with the great powers. The Netherlands were but a pawn or at most a rook in the struggle for hegemony between Habsburg and Valois, which erupted into full-scale war six times between 1515 and 1552. Much against the will of the Regents, who hoped the Netherlands might remain neutral in Franco-Spanish wars,[81] it became the overwhelming priority of this government to maintain field armies in time of war and especially to find money to pay the troops so they would not prey on the Emperor's own subjects.

The government's financial problems and the resulting fiscal negotiations with the States of Holland will be the subject of chapter 5. Here it will suffice to note that while revenues roughly quadrupled during the reign of Charles V,[82] government indebtedness on the Antwerp exchange increased by a factor of about sixty to one.[83] Thus fiscal officials like Holland's Receiver for the *beden* sent their receipts directly to the counting house of one or more great firms in Antwerp,[84] and the bankers themselves took an active interest in the revenues by which their loans were secured. In compensation for important loans, bankers might acquire the administration of important domain revenues like the Antwerp toll[85] or the import license for alum, a mineral vital to the woolen cloth industry.[86] Provincial merchants—and their spokesmen in the states—complained, with reason, that the government was violating its own strictures against monopoly by entering into some of these arrangements.[87] But the "great purses" were a source of life's blood, and the government could ill afford to be scrupulous about how it obtained the ready cash that kept mercenary armies from ravaging the lands they were meant to defend. In the end, the government could escape the clutches of the bankers only by becoming still more dependent on the states, through the creation of a funded debt (see chapter 5).

Financial difficulties do not seem to have diminished the government's ability to dispense effective justice. As measured by case load, there was (until the 1550s) a steady increase in the number of suits brought before the Grand Council of Mechelen, especially on the part of plaintiffs in more distant regions.[88] But the regulation of economic activity in the perceived interest of justice, considered a normal function of government, was hobbled by the need for striking bargains either with the great bankers of Antwerp or with the provincial states. In the traditional view, widely shared among ordinary folk, "monopolies" were held responsible for a whole range of economic ills, including exorbitant prices for consumers and the business failures of honest tradesmen.[89] Fiscal officials cast covetous eyes on "the great and excessive monopolies that merchants practice."[90] Yet for practical reasons one had to make exceptions for the "great purses" that supplied the government with credit, just as Charles V in Germany had to shield the Fuggers from the effects of anti-monopoly initiatives in the imperial Diet.[91] In Holland, the government seems to have had success in legislating more against grain dealers who bought up commodities in advance of the harvest than against manufacturers employing new techniques that drove smaller operators out of business. The reason is that grain dealers (who feared competition from larger firms in Antwerp and elsewhere) were represented in the States, whereas small manufacturers threatened by what they saw as predatory business methods were not.[92] A sensible government could neither permit the Hollanders to ship grain to France or other lands at war with the Netherlands merely to obtain a higher price,[93] nor allow the shippers of this one province to pare their costs by evading regulations concerning armaments that had to be carried while sailing routes endangered by privateers.[94] Yet because of the importance of the shipping interest in Holland, it was almost impossible to force compliance on such matters. Government officials were right in believing that they alone could speak for the interests of the Low Countries as a whole, as distinct from the interests of one or another province. But in a state with the peculiar history and political structure of the Habsburg Netherlands, the real question was whether the government, however well-intentioned, was strong enough to prevail against a determined assertion of provincial interests.

ECONOMIC RIVALRIES AMONG THE TOWNS

In the early years of Charles V's reign, it was far from clear that towns voting in the States had a common conception of what Holland's interests were, much less a willingness to subordinate local concerns to any larger objective. On one point there was no doubt: the States of Holland did not necessarily have the same interests as the central government. Since 1480 the States had had an Advocate of the Common Land, whose function was the same as that of a town pensionary; that is, he was empowered to speak on behalf of the States in discussions with agents of the central government. The Advocate also kept a private record of the acts of the States, although no such records are extant prior to the tenure of Aert van der Goes (1525–1543).[95] The States voted in 1525 to remove Van der Goes's predecessor, Meester Albrecht van Loo, because he had accepted a post from Charles V as Count of Holland and because, it was argued, no man could serve two masters. It was also in 1480 that the Receiver for the *Beden,* an official of the prince, was authorized to collect smaller sums that would be employed by the States for purposes of their own. Such levies were collected according to the *schiltal,* but were called *omslagen,* perhaps to distinguish them from the *beden.* Monies from the *omslagen* were used to pay for travel expenses of non-noble deputies or for incidental political expenses such as influence-buying at court. Beginning in 1509, *omslagen* were collected by a separate Receiver for the Common Land; this official remained for some time a princely appointee, but gradually came to take his orders from the States (see chapter 5).[96] The distinction between officers of the prince and officials of the States was still somewhat uncertain; for example, the nobles who took part in the States' deliberations were, until the 1550s, men who also served the prince in the Council of Holland or some other important office.[97] Nonetheless, the tendency towards greater autonomy of the States as an institution seems clear enough.

The Advocate's task was to speak for the *gemeen land,* but in fact any consensus the deputies might achieve was in constant danger of being undermined by private discussions between government officials and individual town magistracies. Many of the objectives that town governments pursued could be obtained only by face-to-face negotiations of this kind. For example, every city wanted to keep its *bede* payments as low as possible, and deputies willingly traded their consent to new taxes for an increase in the *gratiën* or rebates for their town. By the 1520s, Leiden, Gouda, and Delft were aware that Dordrecht and Haarlem enjoyed *gratiën* of sixty-six percent on the *ordinaris bede,* and were demanding the same for themselves. For *extraordinaris beden,* in which both the amount of the *bede* and the level of *gratie* were less fixed by custom, government commissioners had notable success in collecting affirmative votes by making generous offers of *gratie.* It was nothing more or less than the classic strategy of *divide et impera.*[98] The travel diaries of town pensionaries offer unique glimpses into these behind-the-scene deals. In impoverished Leiden, a *gratie* that reduced the city's interest payment on States of Holland *renten* by as little as twenty-eight pounds was duly noted by the pensionary. But wealthy Amsterdam had more important fish to fry than reducing its *ordinaris bede* liability by a mere two or three thousand pounds.[99] Amsterdam's Andries Jacobszoon comments bitterly on the "auricular confession" in which deputies from individual towns were summoned to meet "apart" with the Regent's commissioners: charmed by the "holy water" of rebate promises, "every city looks out for itself, without thinking about the welfare of the *land.*"[100]

In addition to the divisive issue of rebates, there were deep-rooted economic conflicts which pitted town against town and caused one or both parties to seek intervention by the government. Examples of such rivalries are legion,[101] but there are two conflicts, or rather series of conflicts, that stand out from the rest. The first and more obvious was the Dordrecht staple, a tenacious legacy of the fourteenth century. In 1505 Gorinchem brought suit against the Dordrecht staple before the Grand Council of Mechelen, joined by thirteen cities and three seafaring villages. As the legal action dragged on for years, Dordrecht expanded its claims to cover newly developing branches of the river trade. Skippers from Brill had prospered in recent years by picking up sea salt in Zeeland for delivery in centers of the herring fishery like Rotterdam and Schiedam, without first proceeding upstream to call at Dordrecht. In 1520 Dordrecht seized two salt ships from Brill and, just to make the point clear, had its warships draw up in hostile array before the harbor of Brill. To add insult to injury, in a case separate from the one before the Grand Council, the Council of Holland found that Dordrecht had acted within its rights against Brill.[102]

In 1527 Dordrecht's gunboats seized a grain ship bound for Schoonhoven on the Lek and stationed four warships at the mouth of the Lek to prevent further evasions of its staple rights. When the Council of Holland summoned both parties to The Hague, Dordrecht evidently did not appear, but Schoonhoven was joined by supporting delegations from many cities, including Amsterdam. On the recommendation of the Stadtholder, Hoogstraten, the plaintiffs sought out Niklaas Everaerts, President of the Council of Holland, who was then in Mechelen. Everaerts urged the plaintiffs to appeal to the Emperor through the Grand Council of Mechelen, for the staple privileges were indeed "contrary to all natural right, and therefore null" (*contra omnem equitatem naturalem, ergo nul*). In effect, Everaerts was suggesting that the Emperor's *potestas absoluta* could be invoked to provide a remedy where positive law worked an injustice. But the President of the Grand Council told the Hollanders nothing could be done unless an action were brought—notwithstanding the fact that the action brought by Gorinchem in 1505 was still pending. It continued in that state even during Everaerts's tenure as President of the Grand Council (1528–1532). Tribunals like the Grand Council, which were instructed to settle disputes amicably if at all possible, had a deep aversion to rendering a verdict that could seriously damage vital interests of one party or another.[103]

Meanwhile, new occasions for dispute continued to arise. In 1539 tensions between Dordrecht and Rotterdam reached the point that grain ships from Amsterdam, passing down the Hollandse IJssel towards Rotterdam, were armed and manned with troops, to defy Dordrecht's "outlyers." Rotterdam's claims, like those of Gorinchem and Brill, were backed by many towns and villages throughout Holland. But when the Grand Council finally did pronounce judgment (October 1540), it was favorable to Dordrecht on all points, except that goods coming down the IJssel were declared to be free of the staple. This decision did not settle every question—for example, Dordrecht complained of evasion by Amsterdammers importing Rhine wine by way of the Zuider Zee—but the staple henceforth had to be accepted by all as a basic fact of Holland's legal and economic life.[104] On this important issue, *potestas absoluta* had proven to be a weak reed.

The other major issue that divided Holland's towns had to do with the flow of goods north and south along the inland waterways. As indicated in the last chapter, much of the traffic between the Maas-Scheldt estuary and the Baltic passed through Holland, and the *binnenvaart* was also a highway for local commerce: "wool ships" and "eel ships" and "salt ships" served the needs of consumers and industries within Holland, as did water barges (for breweries) and others loaded with turf dug for fuel.[105] The volume of traffic is suggested by an account that survives for the period from May 1542 through April 1543, according to which 6,126 toll-paying ships or barges passed through the Gouda lock; over the whole year, excluding winter days when the channel was frozen solid, an average of nineteen vessels per day passed through, not counting those with goods for which no toll was collected. At the Sparendam sluice, the northern point of entry for the *binnenvaart*, officials reported in the 1550s that as many as sixty to eighty ships and barges might be waiting to enter the lock at one time, a volume of traffic that made it necessary to begin issuing numbered lots to skippers to avoid disputes. Cities that maintained large fleets for the inland waterways included Amsterdam, Dordrecht, Gouda, and Haarlem; for example, according to the 1514 *Informacie,* Amsterdam had eighty-three *binnenvaarders;* Dordrecht, one hundred and forty.[106]

Since the fourteenth century, the official route for such traffic had been marked out by stations of the Holland Toll—notably at Sparendam, Gouda, and Dordrecht. The lock at Sparendam, cut into the dike along the IJ, was rebuilt in 1518 after being destroyed by a Guelders army. Twenty-two feet across, the new lock could accommodate thirty vessels between its doors. To help protect the vulnerable IJ dike, the outer doors were set in a foursquare frame; thus, cog ships (including some coming directly from the Baltic) had to ship their masts before passing through. Haarlem had offered to build, at its own expense, a wider lock with doors open at the top, but the *Hoogheemraadschap* of Rijnland, representing the interests of landowners threatened by flooding, insisted on a sturdier and safer construction. From Sparendam the route went up the Spaarne to Haarlem, thence across the Haarlemmermeer either to Leiden or to a point farther up the Oude Rijn, along the Gouwe and through the lock at

Gouda into the IJssel, which flowed into the Merwede not far below Dordrecht.[107] But if this axis of traffic ran roughly north-northwest by south-southeast, the axis of commercial vitality in the Low Countries lay along a line running north-northeast by south-southwest, from Amsterdam (east of Haarlem) to Antwerp and its out-ports or to Bruges, both of which were reached by crossing the Maas estuary downstream from Dordrecht. Towns like Delft and Rotterdam lying at some remove from the legally privileged route had good reason for seeking a more direct connection with Amsterdam.

The stage was thus set for a series of conflicts in which towns along the established *binnenvaart* fought tenaciously to hold back route changes apparently dictated by the commercial development of the region. Each side found allies readily enough. Defenders of the old *binnenvaart* enlisted the cooperation of farmers of the Holland Toll who in turn called upon the Emperor's revenue officials to enforce a long-standing ban on the use of alternate water routes. Gouda and Haarlem repeatedly cited the provisions of this ordinance, reissued several times during Charles V's reign, which guaranteed them the privilege of controlling the *binnenvaart,* much as traffic along the great rivers was regulated by the Dordrecht staple.[108] Proponents of innovation relied on the aid of men who held rights of low justice in Holland's rural judicial districts or *ambachten;* a willing *ambachtsheer* could find or allege justification for making improvements in the inland waterways that were not prohibited by the Emperor's ordinances.[109] The *Hoogheemraadschap* of Rijnland was also involved because any change in the flow of water had implications for drainage and flood control; for example, land farther downstream might be endangered if a local *ambachtsheer* replaced a "fan sluice" door, which rotated on a water-level horizontal axis to let water out, with a "wind-up" sluice door that permitted passage of barges.[110] Basically, however, it was a battle between towns— Gouda, Haarlem, and Dordrecht—dependent on the traditional route, and others—Amsterdam, Delft, and Rotterdam— that could profit from new connections. Leiden, lying just off the traditional route, could support either side, depending on the circumstances.

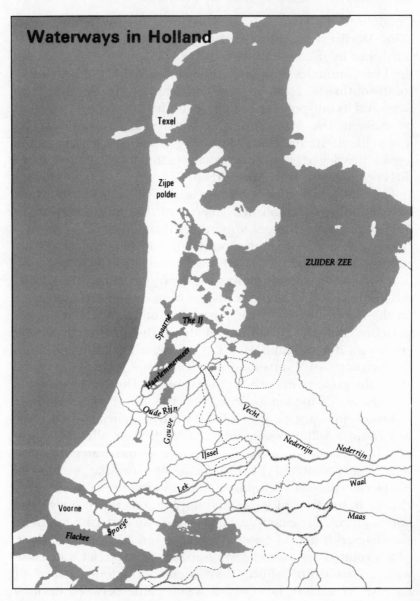

Map 2. Waterways in Holland

Between 1492 and 1565, disputes of this kind are recorded for at least eight places around the "ring of Rijnland," from Sparendam on the IJ dike to the Zijdewijnd dike that divided the *hoogheemraadschappen* of Rijnland and Delfland. At several of these points dams or sluices were rebuilt and torn apart frequently over the course of the decades, often after a band of armed men appeared on the dike to smash to pieces whatever in their view infringed on the privileges of their town.[111] Despite the "bearing of arms" sometimes accompanying such demonstrations, there were never any actual battles. Hence these little-known disputes lack the whiff of gunpowder that lends drama to the long battle over Dordrecht's staple rights. Yet they are no less indicative of deep fissures in the urban economy of Holland. In both cases, commercial innovations was pitted against a dogged defense of entrenched privilege. Invoking the power of the prince to right the wrongs of the past, legal briefs on one side appealed to the "common law" freedom of trade,[112] whereas those on the other side were content to rest on the positive law created by the actions of former princes. In both cases, the defenders of free trade and productive innovation repeatedly suffered a double indignity, defeated first by the *force majeure* of their opponents (the gunboats of Dordrecht or lock-smashing sorties by the men of towns like Haarlem and Gouda), and then in verdicts rendered by the courts. Finally, the losers represented in both cases Holland's dynamic seafaring trades (the Baltic commerce of Amsterdam, the herring fisheries of the Maas ports), whereas the victors represented more retrograde sectors of the provincial economy. Dordrecht had no role in the Baltic trade; by the end of Charles V's reign, Rotterdam was beginning to challenge its traditional supremacy on the north bank of the Maas.[113] Haarlem and Gouda were, with Leiden, heavily involved in the industries that had flourished until the mid-fifteenth century, but had steadily declined ever since. The fact that the defenders of traditional privilege won the legal battles does not mean they won the war; in fact, the frequent reissue of the ban on non-traditional inland waterways suggests that innovators and entrepreneurs were still busy devising ways to evade the rules. But both the nature of the conflict and its apparent outcome do raise a question as to how towns with such differing interests could ever form a common front.

THE INTERESTS OF HOLLAND

The answer to this question lies in the fact that there were outside the province forces and powers which could do more harm to Holland's towns than they could ever do to each other. First, the Duke of Guelders could throttle Holland's commerce by choking off the great rivers in the south, while his freebooters watched the Zuider Zee channels by which ocean-going ships passed to and from Amsterdam. Since the government persistently viewed the Guelders wars as a minor part of the larger struggle with France, Holland's towns had to stick together if they were to use the power of the purse to focus attention on their problems (see chapter 3). Second, despite the differences among the towns, Holland's economy was integrated in two important ways: almost every town and village had at least an indirect stake in the Baltic trade, and the province as a whole formed one of several regional satellites around the great commercial and financial hub of Antwerp. Holland by itself, even if united, was not strong enough to withstand a direct challenge from its rivals in the Baltic, and there was also a danger that fiscal policies at home could undercut its competitive position. A threat in either of these two spheres required persuading the Habsburg government to take the right sort of action, and Hollanders had no leverage for moving Brussels to their will unless they could speak with one voice (see chapter 4). Further, the war taxation of Charles V's reign set in high relief urban grievances against the traditional exemptions of the clergy and the nobility, especially the feudal enclaves (seven towns and some thirty-seven villages) that were "outside the *schiltal*" and thus did not contribute to the *beden*. Since the towns were pitted in this case against families like the Egmonts and (later) the Nassaus, here too they had no hope of prevailing unless they pooled their strength (see chapter 5). Finally, the draconian provisions of Charles V's heresy laws posed a direct challenge to some of the most cherished privileges of the towns and threatened at times to provoke riots among the burghers; here too, magistrates learned that they could protect the privileges of their town only by trying to protect the privileges of all (see chapter 6). All of these themes become tangled up together in the first ten years of Philip II's reign, when a government seriously weakened by war finance (and by a devolution of credit-worthiness to the provincial states) attempted once more to stoke the fires of persecution (see chapter 7).

Some of these conflicts may create the impression that Holland's towns stood for a "modern" conception of social and economic life, in which everyone might trade freely and no one would enjoy special privileges. To see how misleading such an impression is, one need only take note of how the twenty-five "walled cities" of Holland joined together to obtain a ban on rural industry (*buitennering*). In Henri Pirenne's classic presentation of pre-industrial economic development in the Low Countries, government and entrepreneurs were allies in knocking down the barriers to cheaper and more efficient production posed by the manifold regulations of urban guilds. In many respects Pirenne was correct: the new cloth industries of the sixteenth century flourished in smaller towns that had no guilds, and high government officials were certainly familiar with the argument that "trade must be free."[114] But in Holland, unlike the Flanders that Pirenne was more familiar with, towns large and small pooled their political influence to seek relief from rural competition, especially in brewing and cloth-weaving. In 1529, the six great cities voting in the States made a ban on rural industry a condition for their consent to an *extraordinaris bede*. But nobles voting in the States, who stood to profit from economic growth in the villages, resisted the proposal, and the promised ordinance was not issued. Hoogstraten offered to help, but expressed doubt as to whether feudal enclaves (areas not subject to the jurisdiction of the Council of Holland) could be comprehended within the proposed ban. Finally the cities decided to "make friends" with the influential Lodewijk van Vlaanderen, lord of Praet, who was at this time one of the small circle of councillors travelling with the Emperor. On 11 October 1531 the cities got what they wanted—a prohibition against the practice of brewing, weaving, leather-working, masonry, or any other industry (*nering*) outside the walled towns. A few months later, the States voted a special *omslag* of 30,000 pounds, presumably to be paid by the towns only, as the cost of this cherished privilege; since the Council of Holland supported the position of the nobles on this question, no member of the Council would sign the authorization for this *omslag*, and the Advocate of the Common Land had to do it himself. The ban did not mean that rural industry in fact came to an end. Apart from the feudal enclaves, which were indeed not covered by the ban, the *ambacht-sheren* also had to be contented one way or another, either by buying out their claims to operate or license rural industries, or by having the city itself acquire title to the *ambachtsheerlijkheid* of adjacent districts.[115] But it would certainly not be right to represent Holland's urban economy in this period as the springboard for a modern form of commercial capitalism. Pirenne saw urban protectionism as a function of the political influence of artisan guilds in the great cities of the southern Netherlands. Holland's magistrates may have had patrician pedigrees, but in their determination to suppress competition from the countryside, they were blood brothers to the weavers and fullers of Ghent.[116]

There is a unifying thread in the arguments made by urban deputies to the States, but it lies in the medieval principle of privilege (insofar as the towns benefited from it), and not in the modern idea of free trade. Given Amsterdam's long battle against the Dordrecht staple, it might seem that the merchant communities of these two cities present a textbook between a medieval regulated trade and a modern spirit of enterprise. As will be seen in chapter 4, however, the real defense of Amsterdam's precious freedom of trade in Baltic grain lay not in legal or pragmatic arguments, but rather in a privilege that was granted in 1495 by the cash-starved Maximilian I, exempting Amsterdam from duties on foreign grain. However much Amsterdammers might wish to appeal to the power of the prince to overturn "unjust" privileges (like the Dordrecht staple), they surely realized that the same power could be turned against their vital interests.[117] In the early years of Charles V's reign, no one could have predicted whether the government might succeed in playing on the divisions among Holland's towns to make itself stronger, or whether the towns might develop a cohesion among themselves that might effectively limit the government's influence within the province.

In fact, no body politic ever achieves a perfect union. Even in the most stable commonwealth, there are faults and fissures which wisdom of hindsight can always point to in "explaining" whatever schism or bifurcation that the confluence of events may bring about. In the case of the Habsburg Netherlands, Pieter Geyl has pointed out that to observers in Charles V's reign, the most important line dividing the Dutch-speaking provinces would have been between the urbanized areas in the west (Flanders, Brabant, Holland, and Zeeland) and the more rural eastern provinces, some of which had only recently come under the rule of the Netherlands government. But since the division that occurred after 1572 between north and south, patriotic Dutch writers found reasons for believing that even under Habsburg rule Hollanders were different, more independent of spirit than Flemings or Brabanders.[118]

To speak of Holland's towns as developing, already under Charles V, a spirit of resistance to Habsburg rule would be to fall into the trap Geyl so well describes. But one can speak of habits of action that tend to be repeated simply because people find it easier to do so. A major argument of this book is that Charles V's reign in Holland witnessed the development of important habits of cooperation among the towns and nobles represented in the States. The point is not that the members of Holland's political elite reached, by ripe deliberation, the sage conclusion that there was strength in union. Rather, pressure from external foes, combined with energetic action by the Habsburg government, induced the towns to begin collaborating in new ways. The end result of this process was a States of Holland more capable of speaking for the province as a whole and more confident in dealing with the problems that governments had to face, backed by an administrative machinery of their own and a strong credit rating. The fact that such provinces had come to exist by the time of Philip II's reign did not mean that the Revolt was necessary or inevitable. Had there not been such provinces, however, it is hard to imagine how the Revolt could have succeeded.

3

THE GUELDERS WARS

During the sixteenth century and the first half of the seventeenth century, as Europe's great powers fought each other for control of Italy, then plunged into a long era of religious conflict, more and more states adopted for their own use the professional standing armies first developed in France. Field armies grew in size by several magnitudes, from the 10,000 England's Henry IV led into battle at Agincourt (1415), to the 30,000 France's Charles VIII led across the Alps (1494), to the 100,000 or more commanded by Tilly or Wallenstein in the Thirty Years' War. Since the proportion of wealth that princes extracted from their subjects grew apace with these changes in the character of warfare, military expenditures promoted greater centralization of political power in the hands of the prince and his officials. In Perry Anderson's words, "war was the forcing house of absolutism." This "military revolution" confronted sixteenth-century Europeans with a momentous political choice.[1] They could avoid dependence on a military establishment, by attempting to revive the civic militia; Machiavelli's Florence embarked on this path, but the militia's flight before a Spanish army (1512) showed only how difficult it was to recreate an institution that was tied to the waning city-state culture of the late Middle Ages.[2] Alternatively, they could accept the practical necessity of relying on professional troops and swallow the consequences by surrendering more and more power to the prince who served as commander and paymaster.

This chapter will show how the States of Holland found a way of managing military affairs that might be seen as an alternative to this dilemma. Burghers in Holland and other Low Countries provinces were still expected to maintain military equipment in good order and to rally to arms when summoned by the town bell. Yet the States were under no illusions about the chances of Holland's burghers standing in an open field against professional troops. Instead, the States endeavored to maintain civilian influence in military affairs by using their power of the purse to influence the way in which wars were fought.

In what follows, it will first be useful to examine the deep suspicions with which Charles V's subjects viewed the constant incursions into their territory by the Duke of Guelders—as if certain great nobles in the Netherlands deliberately fomented wars they did not intend to win, merely to enhance their own power and that of the prince. This climate of suspicion, indicative of the inexperience of commoners in matters of war and diplomacy, actually strengthened the position of the States as they bargained with officials over war subsidies, for deputies were able to argue persuasively that the war had to be fought in such a manner as to lay to rest popular mistrust of the government. Even if troops were not in fact employed as the States had wished, deputies were brought in on the discussion of military finance and military organization, in order to gain their confidence and their consent to taxation.

THE GUELDERS WARS AND THE "COMMON MAN" IN HOLLAND

Leonardo Bruni, humanist and chancellor of republican Florence, remarks at one point that when the armies of a republic lose a battle, citizens will sooner believe they have been betrayed than that they have been beaten.[3] The process by which human beings attribute sinister motives to those who rule over them has seldom been addressed by historians, perhaps because the phenomenon is too commonplace, or because scholars prefer to avoid the nettlesome task of deciding which suspicions are worth taking seriously and which are not. But there are no good reasons for thinking that princes were ever so fiendishly clever as (for instance) Erasmus makes them out to be, when he suggests that rulers deliberately provoke each other to war in order to have an excuse for taxing their subjects.[4] It is true that

sixteenth-century rulers could find reasons for thinking that
war was "not altogether a bad thing." As J. H. Shennan says of
Charles V's political testament, the old Emperor believed that
war "kept soldiers occupied and prevented them from causing
trouble at home; people paid their taxes more readily in war-
time and formed the habit of paying."[5]

War was also seen as providing a certain tension that was
needed for the health of the body politic. For example, Guillaume Budé, the great French humanist, suggested that the
blessings of peace were not unmixed: "Yet peace also brings
forth a hesitant and sluggish sense of security, which usually
gives birth to luxury and laziness, whence come torpor and
shameless pleasures."[6] Despite the fact that it was sometimes
jurists, "men of the long robe," who argued for war while noblemen with military experience counselled against it, nobles were
commonly thought to encourage their princes to enter into conflicts in which the nobles themselves found employment. During ceremonies to celebrate the Peace of Cambrai, ending hos-
tilities between France and the Habsburg lands (1529), the
chamber of rhetoric of the French town of Amiens put on a play
about how wars were ended. While merchants and peasants
plead for peace, Mars objects; when the parties appeal to Lady
Nobility, she explains that peace is difficult because the nobles
are nourished by war. The conclusion is that only God can bring
war to an end.[7]

Suspicions of this kind were no doubt enhanced by the special circumstances of the Habsburg Netherlands in its long conflict with the Duchy of Guelders (1493–1528). To begin with,
the Emperor Maximilian was always seen as the foreigner who
entered into his Low Countries inheritance by marriage, and he
did hope to employ the wealth of the Low Countries to help
finance his projects elsewhere in Europe, even if he had little
success in doing so.[8] In addition, the usages of war made combat a matter of life and death for the ordinary peasant or towns-
man, but not for rival noble commanders. Noble commanders
on both sides regularly made private truces with one another
(*stillsaeten*) to exempt their own lands from the ravages of campaigning. Netherlands peasants who lived outside the enclaves
of feudal jurisdiction thus bore the brunt of enemy attacks,

The Habsburg Netherlands in 1555

GRONINGEN
Groningen
FRIESLAND
Drenthe
HOLLAND
Haarlem · Amsterdam
OVERIJSSEL
· Deventer
Leiden
The Hague · UTRECHT GELDERLAND
Gouda · · Utrecht
Delft · Arnhem ·
Dordrecht · Nijmegen
· 's Hertogenbosch
ZEELAND
Middelburg · Gelderland
BRABANT
Sluys
· Bruges Antwerp ·
· Nieuport
Ghent · Mechelen ·
FLANDERS · Leuven LIMBURG
Ypres · · Brussels
ARTOIS
Tournaisis
HAINAUT NAMUR LIÈGE
Cambrésis
LUXEMBURG

20 10 0   20   40 Miles

Map 3. The Habsburg Netherlands in 1555

and when the Duke of Guelders' mercenaries chanced to fall within their grasp, their vengeance was swift and sure.[9]

In addition, Guelders was ideally located to conduct "exploits" into the Netherlands provinces of Holland and Brabant—that is, to inflict damage on the subjects of Charles V.[10] The Duke's lands bestrode three branches of the Rhine important to Holland's commerce—the Waal, the Lek, and the Nederrijn. To the south, it adjoined Holland's fertile southeastern salient along the Maas. To the north, its coastline was a springboard for harrassment of the merchant shipping that threaded its way to Amsterdam along well-marked channels through the Zuider Zee shallows. In between, Guelders was separated from Holland by the down-river portion of the episcopal principality of Utrecht (later, the province of Utrecht), but this did not prevent Karel van Egmont's armies from striking through into central Holland.[11] Facing an invasion from Guelders almost as soon as she assumed office as Regent (1506), Margaret of Austria found the problem compounded by the fact that the States General consistently refused to vote funds for the war, just as they had done under Charles's father, Archduke Philip.[12] After a brief interval of personal rule by the young Archduke Charles (1514–1517), Margaret resumed the regency just in time to witness the enemy's most stunning success in thirty-five years of campaigning. The Black Band, a feared mercenary army now in the service of Guelders, crossed from Friesland and cut a swath of destruction down the length of Holland; before returning to Guelders, they sacked the small town of Asperen with a brutality that impressed itself vividly on the minds of contemporaries.[13] The modern historian of this conflict finds that Margaret and Maximilian were quite reasonable in demanding stern measures against Guelders and that critics of this policy, among the nobles and in the States General, were naive to think that Karel van Egmont could be controlled by maintaining good relations with his patron, the King of France. But what struck contemporaries was the inability of the seemingly powerful Habsburg state to protect its subjects from the depradations of a robber-baron princeling. As an English envoy in Brussels remarked in 1516, "Even now the prince [Charles] is in the Low Countries, and the Duke of Guelders takes his subjects prisoner."[14]

Moreover, the secret nature of diplomacy was bound to cause suspicion in a regime in which ministers of the prince had to offer some explanations to the parliamentary bodies that granted new taxes, but did not wish to explain everything. When Habsburg officials met with the Bishop of Utrecht at Schoonhoven (November 1527), the States of Holland were told the Bishop had offered his lands to the Emperor in return for protection against Guelders, but that no final agreement was made since the Regent had no authority to accept such an offer. Amsterdam's Andries Jacobszoon rightly scoffed at this evasion: "I don't believe a bit of it, because they were there together in Schoonhoven for a whole week." Deputies grudgingly admitted on another occasion that they could not expect to be privy to all of the Emperor's "mysteries," but they would no doubt have been shocked by some of the schemes concocted by clever and ambitious officials for expanding Habsburg dominion. (For example, in 1535 there were contacts between emissaries of the radical Anabaptist kingdom of Münster [1534–1535] and Habsburg officials who saw in the Anabaptist uprising a chance to grab the Bishop of Münster's lands.)[15] Even the more ordinary and reasoned processes of statecraft involved strategic thinking that was difficult to grasp from the more local vantage point of the states. In his *Historia Brabantiae Ducum* the Leuven humanist Hadrianus Barlandus suspects a sinister motive for the inaction of a Habsburg commander and his 2,500 *landsknechten* while a Guelders army sacked the town of Tienen in Brabant (1507). In fact, Rudolf von Anhalt, a respected commander, was under orders from Margaret of Austria to avoid a direct engagement until he had more troops.[16]

All of these circumstances may help to explain why Charles V's Netherlands subjects mistrusted their government. Yet it is a surprise to see how matter-of-factly sensible men like Barlandus and Erasmus can talk about devilish intrigues mounted by princes against their own subjects. Indeed, one might be tempted not to believe they meant what they said, were it not for the fact that equally sensible and learned men a generation or two later spoke in the same matter-of-fact way about the reality of witchcraft. One must not underestimate the fears of ordinary

people about the mysterious world of power politics or discount
the capacity of intellectuals to spin such fears into theories so as
to give them the appearance of rationality.

Sources for political opinion in the Habsburg Netherlands for
the first two decades of the sixteenth century are sparse and
indirect. For debates within the states, there are only the brief
summaries of States General meetings edited by Gachard,[17] and
a similar compilation at the provincial level, the "Roet Boek van
de Staten van Brabant," which is extant from 1506.[18] For Holland in particular there are several chronicles or histories, including three by friends of Erasmus: *Hollandiae Gelriaeque Bellum*, a
narrative of the 1507–1508 campaigns by Willem Hermans, an
Augustinian canon of the congregation at Steyn (near Gouda) to
which Erasmus had also belonged;[19] the *Divisie Chronyk*, a compilation attributed to Cornelis Geraerts (called Goudanus or
Aurelius), another monk of the same order, which covers Holland's medieval history down to 1517;[20] and the *De Rebus
Batavicis Libri XIII* of Reynier Snoy, a physician of Gouda.[21]
Rather more interesting and seemingly better informed than
any of these works is the unpublished "Historie van Hollant"
(1477–1534) by an anonymous author who clearly had close ties
with Amsterdam and who reports on religious matters with a
detail that suggests a clerical hand.[22]

These authors are by no means unanimous in assigning
blame for the depradations Holland suffered in the Guelders
wars. The point of Hermans's narrative is that the seige of the
strategic castle Poederoy (1508) failed because Holland's towns
were squabbling among themselves, "as in the fables: the frog
and the mouse were having a fight; the crow, watching from on
high, snatched up both warriors and tore them to pieces."[23]
Cornelius Aurelius, in a Latin verse essay on the ancient Bata-
vians, apostrophizes Holland in a similar vein:

> But though you have such power on land and sea,
>   it is to be regretted
> That Guelders alone diminishes your praise,
> For does it not seem that, by the great sluggishness
>   of the Senate [i.e. the States],
> All your ancient glory has ebbed away?[24]

Elsewhere in the same work Aurelius has letters to his "patrons," including one who was a member of the Council of Holland, and it seems likely that his views on Guelders reflect the outlook of Habsburg officials in The Hague.[25] Holland's leading commander in these campaigns was Floris van Egmont, Count of Buren and lord of IJsselstein, whom Reynier Snoy portrays as the innocent victim of destructive jealousy among other nobles.[26] Since Snoy (like Hermans and Aurelius) had ties with Gouda,[27] it may be that all three writers represent the clear hostility to Guelders that one finds in the regions most often subject to direct attack, that is, northern Brabant ('s Hertogenbosch) and southern Holland (Dordrecht and Gouda). But the "Historie van Hollant" blames Holland's problems on the government and its commanders, and occasional references in discussions within the States General suggest that similar views were not uncommon.

Floris van IJsselstein, a military hero for Reynier Snoy, was apparently the object of widespread suspicion. Since Karel van Egmont was a distant cousin of the Holland Egmonts, IJsselstein's leading role in the Guelders wars might be attributed to family jealousy. Thus in March 1512 he complained to the Regent that deputies from Delft and Amsterdam undercut his appeal to the States of Holland by "coming into your presence crying for peace." Some months later, Thomas Spinelly, an English agent in the Low Countries, reported that the Hollanders were willing to raise funds for 1,200 *landsknechten*, should the Duke of Braunschweig command them, but would do nothing for IJsselstein.[28] The anonymous author of the "Historie van Hollant" recognizes in many instances that it was IJsselstein's timely intervention that raised a seige or beat back an invading force,[29] yet on other occasions he represents IJsselstein as deliberately refraining from pressing home the attack. In the fall of 1504, IJsselstein withdrew his army south of the Maas to 's Hertogenbosch, even though the weather was still fair, thus permitting Guelders to make forays into Holland; in 1508 his faint-hearted counsel stayed the brave Rudolf von Anhalt[30] from storming the town of Weesp after it had been taken by the enemy; and he played the same role at Venlo in 1511, where a combined Anglo-Netherlands army eventually had to break off its seige.[31]

Conversely IJsselstein is blamed by this anonymous writer for
starting up the war against Guelders after the Peace of Cambrai
(December 1508) by his incursion into Guelders territory the
next spring.[32] As the chronicler reads them, IJsselstein's inten-
tions were to prolong the fighting. Though other "lords" also
advised Anhalt against storming Weesp, it was IJsselstein, "so
the common rumor went," who spoke as follows: "Let the Hollanders have experience of war, until we get the bottom ones
out of the chest."[33] Theodoricus Velius, a seventeenth-century
chronicler of Hoorn, reports a similar rumor for 1517, when
the Black Band passed under the walls of Hoorn in the course
of its destructive foray: "Lord Floris van IJsselstein stood with
the lord of Wassenaar and other nobles on the north bulwark,
and as the enemy passed by, said to those around him, 'This is
not the way it was said.' Hearing these words the burghers
misunderstood them, and suspected the lords of having known
about this attack in advance."[34] It was thus not just IJsselstein
whom some evidently mistrusted, but other great lords as well.
According to the "Historie van Hollant," Anhalt left Holland
after the dilatory seige of Weesp "because he could see that
what the old lords were doing here was nothing but foolishness,
and there was no honor to be gained."[35]

The devastating invasion of Holland by the Black Band (1517)
was the occasion for special recrimination against those deemed
responsible. The author of the "Historie van Hollant" calls attention to the fact that Haarlem was one of the places where
Stadtholder Hendrik van Nassau had stationed cavalry as a defensive measure. Since Haarlem was remote from Guelders and
Friesland, whence invasion might come, "many people won-
dered" why cavalry had been posted there. But once the invasion
came, "it gave testimony that the lords of the Court had known
very well what the lord of Guelders would do, and that the whole
business was planned."[36] When Nassau's (including a detach-
ment of the Black Band that had chosen to remain "Burgundian") were giving chase to the Black Band, they arrived at Amsterdam's Haarlem gate and sought passage through the city to
shorten their way. The burgomasters were amenable to this proposal, but citizens gathered at the Haarlem gate and prevented
its being opened to the mercenaries. Without doubt, says the

anonymous chronicler, what the burghers feared would indeed have come to pass if the *knechten* had been let in, "for, as some of the *knechten* later admitted, had they gotten within the gates they would have at once cried out, 'Guelders, Guelders' "![37] Even as Asperen was being sacked, Erasmus, then in Brussels, provided an account of the invasion in a private letter to a close friend. Unlike the anonymous chronicler, he was unaware that Nassau had posted troops in various towns. He blamed the government for not even allowing the towns of Holland to defend themselves, much less providing for their defense, and predicted that the mercenary band responsible for the sack of Alkmaar would be allowed to escape unpunished. Rather, they were themselves the chosen instrument to punish Holland for its refusal to accede to government requests for a second *bede* to cover the costs of Prince Charles's journey to Spain: "Since the Hollanders grumbled about this, the storm was loosed on them by design; everyone understands the trick, but it is not safe to speak." When the members of the Black Band were in fact released some months later, after being surrounded and forced to surrender, Erasmus was not surprised.[38]

Another major invasion from Guelders some years later seems to have provoked similar suspicions in Holland. When Maarten van Rossum occupied The Hague (March 1528), instead of sacking the city, he extorted from its burghers the sum of 28,000 pounds, roughly twenty times its quota in the *ordinaris bede*. Two later chroniclers, Lambertus Hortensius of Amsterdam and Pontus Heuterus of Delft, assert that Van Rossum's assault on The Hague was carried out by agreement with Margaret of Austria, whose intention was to induce the Hollanders to be more generous in granting new taxes (the accounts seem to be independent of each other, since each writer gives a different reason for reaching this conclusion). D. S. van Zuider, the scholar who in 1911 published a comparison of these two accounts, notes cautiously that he has found no information in the archives to confirm the allegations of Heuterus and Hortensius.[39] Here, it is possible to recognize the stories related by Heuterus and Hortensius as elements in a persistent political myth: when Hollanders suffer defeat, they are not beaten by the enemy, but betrayed by their leaders.

Such extreme suspicions of the government were by no means confined to Holland. In April 1509, when Margaret of Austria was again trying without success to pry some money loose from the States General, Maximilian received reports about "certain secret damned devils who are making the deputies believe that lord Floris van IJsselstein and I are not content with the Peace made at Cambrai and that we two are trying to break it—unlike their beloved idol, the aforesaid Karel van Egmont, who will be well content to keep the peace if no one gives him occasion to break it."[40] In 1512 Margaret complained of her constant difficulties with the States of Brabant, in which two of the great cities, 's Hertogenbosch and Antwerp, were willing to support the war against Guelders, while the other two (Brussels and Leuven, which lay farther from the usual theater of action) were "unmanageable." Certain wicked spirits, she writes, "say that I ask only to have war and destroy them, as you did before, and many other evil words tending to arouse the people. What is worse, on Good Friday night they were so bold as to post secretly certain notices on the church door of this city [Mechelen?], to my derision and scorn."[41] Such people could not be reasoned with; they could only be humored. One way to deal with the states, often employed by Margaret, was to offer peace to Guelders on favorable terms, with the understanding that the states would grant subsidies once peace was concluded.[42] Another way, suggested by Maximilian, was to send a commander-in-chief whom the states trusted (Duke Heinrich of Braunschweig), while offering the states a chance to name the captains who would serve under him.[43] It was a measure of the government's desperation that deputies to the states, mere laymen in military affairs, were invited to play a role in important decisions. It remains now to be seen how the States of Holland responded to such invitations in the 1520s, when the campaigning against Guelders was renewed.

THE STATES OF HOLLAND AND
THE MANAGEMENT OF WAR

During the 1520s the Habsburg government finally made headway against Guelders. Between 1521 and 1523 an army commanded by Jan II van Wassenaar, scion of one of Holland's oldest families, occupied and subdued the hitherto independent province of Friesland, thus depriving Guelders of an important base of support, while vindicating a claim to the lordship of Friesland which dated back to the medieval counts of Holland. In 1527, an invasion by Karel van Egmont prompted the Prince-Bishop of Utrecht to surrender both parts of his territory to Charles V; thus by the Treaty of Schoonhoven (November 1527) Utrecht and Overijssel became Habsburg provinces. An ensuing campaign into Guelders forced the childless Duke to recognize Charles V as the heir apparent for his own lands (Treaty of Gorinchem, October 1528).[44]

Holland made important contributions to these successful campaigns, as can be seen from the following table:[45]

Table 2. Total *Beden* Voted by the States of Holland, 1519–1533

	(*Holland pounds of 40 groats*)	
	Amount Consented	Net (*with* gratie *subtracted*)
1519	106,604	93,720
1520	96,888	81,872
1521	**209,771**	**177,074**
1522	**305,450**	**255,218**
1523	**271,853**	**248,870**
1524	125,000	97,172
1525	160,000	114,839
1526	80,000	60,789
1527	80,000	58,638
1528	**460,222**	**373,188**
1529	100,000	68,264
1530	220,900	192,883
1531	95,500	65,800
1532	131,500	104,900
1533	120,000	(91,148)

Spending for the Guelders wars was concentrated in the four years for which figures are printed in bold (1521–1523, 1528); in both columns, totals for these four years are roughly equivalent to totals for the other eleven years covered. What Holland contributed in 1528 would not be matched or exceeded until the great military crisis of the 1550s. From these figures one may conclude that the States (at least in Holland) were no longer unwilling to support the war. It seems reasonable to infer that years of punishing raids all along the frontier had finally overcome the disunity in Holland that Willem Hermans lamented in his account of the siege of Poederoy. But if Hollanders understood the need for a united front against Guelders, they still did not necessarily trust the government which fought the war on their behalf.

Hoogstraten and the Council of Holland would have preferred to guard against the hit-and-run tactics of Karel van Egmont by creating a permanent military force to stand watch along Holland's frontier. (Hoogstraten himself commanded one of the *bandes d'ordonnance* that made up the small standing army of the Netherlands, but it was not stationed in Holland.) Several times during the 1520s the States were asked to organize a 1,000-man militia, or a call-up system in which every tenth man from the towns and every fourth man from the villages would report for duty whenever the church bell or town clock sounded the tocsin. But deputies could recall earlier occasions when mercenary companies stationed in the province failed to prevent hostile incursions. Burghers and peasants could not be expected to stand in the open field against *landsknechten* with nothing to lose, and besides no one could be found willing to serve "for less than six, eight, or ten stuivers" per day—at a time when the going rate was between three and four stuivers per day for German *landsknechten* (infantry) and eight stuivers for a cavalryman.[46] These reasons for rejecting the militia proposal were not without merit, but the result was the discussions about war taxation invariably took place in the aftermath of a raid from Guelders that left people in some part of Holland angry and frustrated.

In these circumstances the deputies and their fellow townsmen could support new *beden* for the purpose of avenging what the Hollanders themselves had suffered. Yet from the government's point of view, an army once raised might serve more useful purposes if it were not risked in the hazard of battle. This conflict of perspectives could only exacerbate the climate of suspicion that already existed. In Jacobszoon's *Prothocolle*, deputies often excuse their unwillingness to approve war subsidies by referring to widespread popular mistrust of the government. When the States consented (3 October 1523) to a sale of *renten* that would raise 80,000 pounds, they were told the money was needed to invade Guelders, which was the only way to make Karel van Egmont cease his depredations in Holland. But three weeks later, Hoogstraten and his men were still camped, as before, near the town of Gorinchem. Far from invading Guelders, Hoogstraten forbade the men of Gorinchem to improve their defenses by razing houses outside the walls. Hence "the common talk is that had no bede been promised, peace would have been concluded by now."[47] In fact, this guess was not altogether amiss, even if "common talk" put the cart before the horse: peace was not delayed in order to obtain a new *bede*, but the *bede* was viewed by the Regent as a means of bringing Guelders to the bargaining table. The States were not told that Margaret of Austria had rejected (8 October) Hoogstraten's proposal to invade Guelders, since there was not money enough for such an undertaking; an invasion was in any case inopportune so long as it remained unclear whether the Duke of Guelders might be willing to come to terms. Backpedalling from what he had promised the States, Hoogstraten responded to the Regent by falling into line with her wishes: "the worst agreement we could get would be better than the best war we could manage."[48]

Some months later (28 December) Hoogstraten defended his conduct at Gorinchem and asked approval of a revised budget[49] for the 80,000-pound *bede*. But the deputies insisted on allocating the money according to the budget they had approved when they consented to the sale of *renten*. Moreover, the folks back home had found new reasons for thinking the government was not serious about prosecuting the war: "The common man cannot understand, and murmurs greatly, because the men of Guelders crossed the Vaert [a channel running south from

Utrecht] and came into our land just after our people withdrew from the Vaert, the houses were burned in Naarden two or three days after the 80 horse [stationed there] were called away to Brabant; whence comes great murmur . . . among the people, so that an uprising is to be feared."[50] In one of the private conversations Jacobszoon records, an Amsterdam burgomaster put things succinctly to Jean Carondolet, Archbishop of Palermo and President of the Privy Council: people will refuse further support for the war "because they believe things are still being done the same old way. This infamy cannot be purged and extirpated from the human heart except by carrying the war (*exploicterende*) into the land of Guelders; seeing this, people will give the hearts out of their bodies."[51]

Confronted with such arguments, officials like Carondolet and Hoogstraten, desperate for new *extraordinaris beden*, had no choice but to promise what the deputies seemed to want, even if they had no authority from the Regent to make such promises. Hoogstraten had to deal with "great murmuring in Holland" because his troops had remained inactive at Gorinchem, despite the attack that had been promised when the States agreed to the 80,000-pound sale of *renten*.[52] While this sale was still proceeding, the government broached the idea of a further subsidy for campaigning during the following spring and summer. In Mechelen on 31 December, Margaret of Austria, known to her subjects as the Gracious Lady, spoke in French to deputies from Holland. Guelders must be invaded, said the Gracious Lady, but the Hollanders must help themselves, as in case of fire, since Brabant and Flanders were expending their resources for the defense of Hainaut and Artois, which had been ravaged and burned by the French.[53] In the world of statecraft, matters were never so simple as one made them out to be in public speeches. But Margaret was (as she wrote Charles V) "embarrassed as to how I shall content" the frequent deputations she received from the States of Holland: "What they most complain about is that they always pay under cover of war, but one does not use their money to make war." The Regent's experience with the Hollanders was a textbook example of the maxim proposed by her shrewd and trusted adviser, Mercurino Gattinara, as one of his "ten commandments for war": "Seeing all their sacrifices end in a truce, peoples will not resign themselves to more [sacrifices], for they believe the semblance of war is a pretext for taking their money." On this occasion (31 December 1523) Margaret herself promised the Hollanders an attack against Guelders, and both IJsselstein and Hoogstraten privately recommended an attack to the Regent. Yet Margaret believed it more important to conserve the resources of the Netherlands for a spring offensive against France.[54]

Publicly, Margaret encouraged the States of Holland to discuss a Union with Antwerp and 's Hertogenbosch, the two "great cities" of the States of Brabant that had consistently supported the war against Guelders.[55] She perhaps had in mind a campaign of plunder, as Hoogstraten had at one point suggested, rather than a full-scale invasion. Meanwhile, keeping her options open, she pursued the possibility of discussions with Guelders.[56] In the States of Holland, negotiations for a new *bede* were held up because the Hollanders, sniffing the truth, learned that Habsburg commanders had been ordered not to attack (*exploicteren*) while representatives from Guelders were in Gorinchem to discuss a truce. Having received assurances on this point, the Hollanders agreed to the Union and approved another *extraordinaris bede* of 80,000 pounds, but it was in fact not to be spent for a new campaign since Guelders and the Netherlands signed a one-year truce in June 1524.[57]

The *bede* discussions in 1523 and 1524 show that the States of Holland lacked the leverage to set effective conditions on how the troops they paid for would be used. The Stadtholder and even the Regent simply made whatever promises seemed necessary and then set military policy as they thought best, without much regard for the will of the States. It is hard to imagine how the rulers of the Netherlands could have conducted themselves much differently, since they could not permit the wishes of a single province to become paramount. For the Netherlands as a whole, France was a more dangerous enemy than Guelders, even though Hollanders might not think so.[58] Also, since the deputies usually represented the extravagant fears of the populace without claiming these fears as their own, government officials may have felt they had some room for maneuver, assuming that the deputies, wiser in the ways of the world than the common man, would understand why certain promises could not be kept. Bargains were more likely to be kept when deputies spoke for themselves and for the concrete interests of the towns they represented.

During the Frisian campaign of 1522–1523, the States were in effect presented with a choice between Holland's short-range and long-range interests. Holland had not supported either the Habsburg government's redemption of its claim to Friesland (pawned to a German prince) or the confiscation of goods from Guelders and Friesland, the immediate *casus belli* in 1522.[59] But once Guelders had joined forces with the anti-Habsburg resistance in Friesland, threatening to make the Zuider Zee a hostile lake for Holland's commerce, Hollanders gave strong support to the war effort, especially to Wassenaar's siege of Sloten, the last fortress held by the "Guelders Frisians." When the States approved a 40,000-pound sale of *renten* in March 1523, the formal acceptance of this *bede* by the Regent stated that all of Holland's cities wished the money to be spent for the campaign in Friesland where (the deputies complained) the war had been badly managed until now.[60] Evidently in hopes of drawing Wassenaar back to Holland, a band of "Guelders Frisians" crossed the Zuider Zee in September and conducted a raid through Holland from north to south while Hoogstraten's deputy, Castre, did nothing to stop them. According to the "Historie van Hollant," all of these events occurred because of "some at Court who do not love Holland," and would have been sorry to see the war in Friesland brought to a successful conclusion. In the States, deputies grappled with the more concrete question of how best to allocate Holland's *bede* revenue. Together with some smaller towns, four of the six great cities (Delft, Gouda, Haarlem, and Leiden) reversed their previous decision, arguing that funds still coming in from the 40,000-pound sale of *renten* should be used for "putting out the fires at home," that is, for defending Holland itself. But Amsterdam, with a vital interest in making the Zuider Zee safe for its commerce, took a longer view, insisting that the fires in Friesland were more important. In the end, it was Amsterdam's reasoning that prevailed. When the States consented to a second and larger sale of *renten* for 80,000 pounds (3 October 1523), they stipulated that the war in Friesland must go forward, and that "robbers' nests" or pirate bases along the Zuider Zee must also be cleared out.[61]

The outcome of this discussion is indicative of Amsterdam's influence in the States. Voting members of the States spoke in a fixed order, and each one had a distinctive and reasonably consistent profile in sources of the 1520s. The nobles were inclined to give the government what it wanted (though not at the price of infringing on their own fiscal privileges), and they also represented the interests of rural taxpayers, opposing efforts by the great cities to minimize what city-dwellers would have to pay.[62] Dordrecht spoke after the nobles, and first among the cities; its deputies continued the city's tradition of support for government requests, though somewhat less loyally than the nobles did.[63] Haarlem, speaking second, had made (prior to 1518) a secret agreement to the effect that a large portion of its *bede* quota would be remitted if Haarlem provided the necessary third vote whenever two other cities agreed to a new *bede* (three towns plus the nobles made a majority of four votes).[64] Delft, speaking third, was the first city in Holland to adopt the poor law reform pioneered by Ieper (Ypres) in Flanders;[65] its deputies declaimed repeatedly against the inequity of a system of taxation in which the wealthy paid little and against the inequity of the *schiltal* assessment, in which Delft itself had the highest quota.[66] Leiden (speaking fourth)[67] and Gouda (speaking last)[68] complained incessantly of their blighted industries (brewing and woolen cloth, respectively), and almost always had to be brought round by private negotations after a majority of the States had already agreed to a *bede*. (The government insisted that unanimity was not required for a binding consent, but in practice towns threatened to withdraw their consent unless all of the others agreed to pay.)[69] Amsterdam, speaking fifth, had a certain tactical advantage because it would often be the second city (after Dordrecht) to vote affirmatively on a *bede* request; thus, the conditions it attached to its consent had a good chance of being taken seriously. Haarlem's secret agreement with Nassau could not have been enforced for very long (after a time, the city's favorable rebate level could be defended simply as a

matter of custom), but the pattern of consent to *bede* requests in
the 1520s shows a certain regularity: it often happened that the
nobles and Dordrecht consented first; Amsterdam consented
after the kind of private discussions that Jacobszoon records,
and Haarlem added the needed fourth vote. Special commissioners would then be sent to Delft, Leiden, and Gouda to extract their consent.[70]

As a price for their cooperation with the government on the
Frisian war, Amsterdam's deputies demanded access to government *bede* accounts. Ruysch Janszoon, perhaps the most influential figure among Amsterdam's burgomasters at this time,[71]
wanted to know how money from the 40,000-pound sale of
renten (approved in March 1523) was actually being spent.
Willem Goudt, Receiver for the *beden* in Holland, agreed to
show him his accounts, but Ruysch Janszoon was not pleased
with what he found, for (as was the usual practice) the expense
items in Goudt's accounts were mostly in the form of quittances
(*décharges*) from government officials, with only vague indications as to what they did with the credits that Goudt had provided. In fact, harrassed fiscal officers of the Habsburg government regularly used *bede* income to pay off old debts, while
raising new loans to cover the needs for which a given *bede* had
been requested.[72] Hoogstraten assured Ruysch Janszoon that
the accounts of the Treasurer of War (from whom Goudt had
décharges) would show how monies from the 40,000-pound sale
of *renten* were indeed expended for the war in Friesland; further, he said, money from the new 80,000-pound sale of *renten*
was badly needed, for the States of Brabant, having other commitments elsewhere, could not afford to maintain more than
1,000 *knechten* in Friesland. Unwittingly, Hoogstraten had given
Ruysch Janszoon the proof he needed that something was
amiss. According to Janszoon's information, which Hoogstraten
did not dispute, if Wassenaar had only 3,200 *knechten* in Friesland and if Brabant supported 1,000 while the pro-Habsburg
Frisians paid for another 1,500, what had happened to Holland's 40,000 pounds? "I know very well where the money has
gone," said Janszoon, "to purge old scars and wounds of debt,
for the Friesland garrisons, whose wages the Emperor should
be paying from his domain revenues."[73]

At the next meeting (25 October 1523), the States tried to get Hoogstraten to agree that, as a further condition for their consent to the 80,000-pound *bede,* Wassenaar would be ordered not to dismiss his troops so long as Sloten held out. Speaking in Hoogstraten's behalf, the *Audienceur,* Laurence Dublioul, told the deputies it was not in the Stadtholder's power to make such decisions. But Dublioul did invite the States to name a committee to oversee disbursement of the 80,000 pounds.[74] Soon afterwards, Sloten surrendered to its besiegers, and Friesland became a Habsburg province. This happy conclusion to the Frisian campaign did not prevent a bitter and protracted discussion in the States over the budget (*staet*) for the 80,000 pounds currently being raised through a sale of *renten.* A new budget submitted to the States included (as Ruysch Janszoon had suspected) a large sum, more than 30,000 pounds, for "old debts" in Friesland, and another 16,000 pounds to reimburse Hoogstraten for money he had raised against his own credit to hire troops (these were evidently the men that were supposed to invade Guelders, but did not). The States at first insisted on striking out both items, but agreed after six weeks of wrangling to accept the 16,000 pounds for Hoogstraten and 12,000 for old debts in Friesland. In the interim Hoogstraten had a sharp exchange with Aert van der Goes, then pensionary of Delft, who told him he would not be reimbursed for troops that had done Holland no good. "I know some of you do not want me as Stadtholder of Holland," Hoogstraten retorted, "but whether you like it or not I shall remain Stadtholder so long as it pleases his imperial majesty."[75]

It must have been galling for a man of Hoogstraten's stature to wait upon the pleasure of Holland's burghers to have his loan repaid. The States had apparently asked to have him as their Stadtholder,[76] and it certainly made sense to have a man with Hoogstraten's influence at Court take a personal interest in Holland's welfare. But now Delft's pensionary insulted him, and the Amsterdammers refused to credit his word that the Zuider Zee would be included in the truce (June 1524) with Guelders. Believing that they had even sent a secret mission to the Emperor in Spain to plead for his removal as Stadtholder, Hoogstraten retaliated by threats and bluster: the truce with

Guelders, he told the Amsterdammers, "is not so strongly made
that I do not know how to break it."[77]

By this time the Stadtholder had gotten his money back, but
there were further indignities to be endured at the hands of
the States. Since Hoogstraten spent most of his time in
Mechelen, as a member of the Privy Council and head of the
Council of Finance, he appointed the lord of Castre, a Brabant
nobleman, as his Deputy Stadtholder for Holland. Mistrusted
by the States, Castre certainly did not give the impression of
being an effective commander. He did nothing to stop the raid
that Guelders forces mounted from Friesland (September
1523). When Hollanders feared another invasion during the
following winter, Castre, who had withdrawn to the south,
suggested opening sluice gates to flood the countryside—a
comment that prompted Dordrecht's deputies to say Hollanders would do better to keep their *bede* money and defend themselves. When Castre appeared before the States, it was to say
he dared not return to his Walloon mercenaries without
money, and when he faced a Guelders army in battle, he was
beaten (Vianen, May 1524). Hence when the truce with
Guelders was extended for another year (June 1525), Amsterdam's delegation to the States suggested saving 1,800 pounds
by cancelling Castre's appointment.[78]

Castre's position in Holland became an urgent matter when
war with Guelders was renewed late in 1527, owing to the an-
nexation by the Habsburgs of the ecclesiastical principality of
Utrecht. The States of Holland were not privy to these "mysteries" of statecraft, but they were quick to recognize the strategic
importance of having a Habsburg Utrecht as a buffer between
Guelders and Holland. By March 1528, Holland had entered
into a Union with northern Brabant for a spring offensive, in
support of which the States agreed to a new issue of 80,000
pounds in *renten*.[79] Doubtless in keeping with Hoogstraten's
wishes, Margaret of Austria provided Castre with a letter of
appointment as commander of infantry for the invading army.
But it was at this time that Maarten van Rossum marched
through Holland and occupied The Hague. Castre, stationed
with a detatchment of troops in Leiden, sent instructions to bar
the dike roads leading towards Haarlem and Amsterdam,

should Van Rossum attempt to exit Holland by going north; he would see to it that the enemy did not escape via Leiden. In fact, Van Rossum did pass by way of Leiden and crossed unharmed into Utrecht.[80]

The States plainly told Hoogstraten that because of assault on The Hague and because of his pleurisy, Castre commanded no respect among Hollanders who rallied to arms at the sound of their town bell. In turn, Hoogstraten painted the Amsterdammers as disloyal, accusing them of supplying victuals to the rebel town of Utrecht. Amsterdammers surmised that Castre had been told all, for he "smiled broadly" at them, and said he would personally stuff into a sack and drown anyone caught supplying Utrecht with victuals. "Do it, lord," replied an Amsterdam burgomaster, Meester Pieter Colijn, "we ask it of you."[81] On 14 April, deputies from fifteen cities met to consider having a Captain-General for Holland. By way of Pieter Colijn, Wilhelm von Renneberg, a Rhenish nobleman whom the Bishop of Utrecht had appointed commander of his cavalry, sent word that he too lacked confidence in Castre. The States then fixed on Renneberg as Castre's replacement to command the infantry that Holland would fund. To reach their goal, the States appointed a committee to set about going over Hoogstraten's head to other members of the Regent's Privy Council. Pieter Colijn, with deputies from Dordrecht and Gouda, held conversations with Erard de la Marck, Prince-Bishop of Liège and an important Habsburg ally; Jan van Bergen, lord of Bergen-op-Zoom in Brabant; Adolph of Burgundy, lord of Vere in Zeeland and hereditary Admiral of the Netherlands; and Floris van IJsselstein, who, as Captain-General of the whole army, supplied the necessary letters of appointment (for Renneberg) and dismissal (for Castre). Hoogstraten had to accept a fait accompli.[82]

On still another issue, Hoogstraten and IJsselstein found Margaret of Austria and the States lined up against them. When the States approved the 80,000-sale of *renten* in February 1528, their agreement stipulated that in this war there must be no more *stillsaeten* or private truces with the enemy by vassals of the Emperor.[83] *Stillsaeten* were not the exclusive privilege of the nobles, for towns and even villages could enter into these agreements on their own. But the great nobles' use of *stillsaeten* was, for urban deputies in the States, a major test of whether these powerful men "belong to the body of Holland" and are therefore obliged "by natural law" to share in the burdens of defense.[84] Margaret of Austria promised the States to do her best to abolish the practice. Yet it was no easy task for the Regent to lay down orders to the men who commanded her armies. When Hoogstraten ordered an embargo on trade with towns in Utrecht that were in rebellion against their Prince-Bishop, the Council of Holland had to point out that no embargo could succeed while towns of Charles V's vassals—including Culemborg (which Hoogstraten ruled in his wife's name) and Montfoort—continued their trade with the enemy.[85] Hoogstraten made a counter-proposal to the States: his wife's town of Culemborg, even though it was a fief of the Duchy of Guelders, would nonetheless cease trading with the enemy if the States would agree to station 700 or 800 foot-soldiers within its walls.[86] Since the towns and villages that made up feudal enclaves did not pay in the *beden*, using *bede* money for their defense was a sensitive issue. When the States were asked to pay extra for placing 1,000 *knechten* in the vassal towns of south-eastern Holland, the nobles agreed at once, "since we are all together members of one *lichaem*." But urban deputies will have recalled that the nobles showed less enthusiasm for the notion of Holland as a common body when it came to exemptions from taxation. In this case Dordrecht supported the proposal, but the other five great cities said they had no instructions for discussing it.[87]

While Hoogstraten and the States argued over private truces, the war against Guelders went well for the Habsburg cause on several fronts. Towns in Overijssel declared for Charles V; Bishop Henry of Bavaria subdued rebels within the city of Utrecht; IJsselstein and others captured several Guelders towns on or near the Zuider Zee. But Tiel, near Holland's southeastern frontier, held out stubbornly against IJsselstein's besieging army.[88] During these months the States of Holland approved several additional *extraordinaris beden*,[89] and deputies continued to raise the question of *stillsaeten*. Even as his army lay before Tiel, IJsselstein as Count of Buren concluded special truces for Buren and other portions of his lands that lay within the Duchy of Guelders. Again Margaret of Austria promised not to permit any *stillsaeten*, but members of her Council told the deputies that the city of 's Hertogenbosch in Brabant, always a staunch foe of Guelders, had requested IJsselstein to make these arrangements, so he would agree to undertake the siege of Tiel. IJsselstein himself said the same thing when he appeared before the States, but noted that the agreement involving Buren was due to expire soon and would not be renewed.[90] But within a matter of weeks Tiel surrended, and Guelders submitted to terms so that effective enforcement of the ban on *stillsaeten* was left to Margaret of Austria's successor as Regent, Mary of Hungary.

Attempts by the States to bend the government's war policy to their will cannot be called a great success. Government leaders did agree to stipulations that troops raised be used to attack Guelders, but Margaret of Austria did not allow agreements of this kind to interfere with her perceptions of how the Netherlands (not just Holland) might best be defended. The States were able to dedicate to Friesland much of the income from *beden* approved to support Wassenaar's campaign there, but in this case Holland's interests and the government's were the same. Margaret and her advisers surely welcomed the opportunity to add another province to the Habsburg dominions. In the case of *stillsaeten* the Regent and the States were also in agreement, but here the *bede* agreement clauses that Margaret endorsed and tried to implement had little real effect since the "great lords" were not easily dislodged from the traditional practice of protecting their own lands in this way. The one instance in which the States were able to assert their will against direct opposition—the dismissal of Castre—again points to the powerful position of the great nobles. It was only with their cooperation that Castre was ousted.

Yet this cooperation with the great lords may also be indicative of what the deputies learned from the Guelders wars. As it happened, there was no further land warfare within Holland's borders until the time of the Revolt. But there were occasions (as will be seen in the next chapter) when the States turned to the great lords in order to get military orders written to their satisfaction. By the 1520s, and no doubt a good deal earlier, the

States had learned the advantages of nurturing a close relationship with these powerful men. Just as the city of 's Hertogenbosch engaged IJsselstein's self-interest by promising to support his private truces if he agreed to besiege Tiel, the States of
Holland secretly offered him 1,200 pounds if he would capture
the rebel city of Utrecht.[91]

Deputies had also learned to discuss military strategy in
terms that the great lords might approve. Much of the pressure
for an offensive against Guelders came from the fear and anger
of common folk, but one of the conversations Jacobszoon records (within the *vroedschsap* of Amsterdam) suggests that urban elites had their own well-considered reasons for an
aggresive strategy: "If war comes, let it be offensive and not
defensive, for in a defensive war the well-being of the land is
wasted, and there is no profit to be gotten."[92] The speaker
seems to mean by "profit" the same thing that Maximilian I
meant by "exploits" of war; in other words, money is better
spent if it brings results, by forcing the enemy to terms, than if
it merely attempts to prevent what probably cannot be prevented anyway—that is, damage to one's own territory. There is
in fact a certain resemblance between the States' demands for
an offensive against Guelders and the pleas that Maximilian
reiterated, mostly in vain, during the reign of his son, Archduke Philip. Under the pressure of repeated raids from
Guelders, the Hollanders seem to have become belated converts
to the strategy that the Emperor had advocated and that the
men who fought under him would have appreciated.

Finally, the deputies gained some practical experience of
what had to be done, off the field of battle, to support and
maintain an army. Upon the invitation of government officials,
the States appointed from among their number commissioners
of muster, whose job it was to make sure that mercenary commanders actually enrolled the men for whom they were being
paid.[93] They inspected the accounts of the Receiver for the
beden, and in order to keep money free for the current campaigns they wished to support, they bargained with some success about which of the government's old debts might be
charged to the accounts of Holland's *beden.*[94] Perusal of these
accounts led to questions about the Treasurer of War's accounts,

and in 1528 the Council of Holland wrote Hoogstraten that the States would not approve a further *bede* unless the Treasurer of War or his clerk came to Holland to render account of how previous subsidies had been spent.[95] Discussions of this kind were no doubt facilitated by the fact that at least a few of the deputies were men with some military experience who could deal without embarrassment with professional commanders.[96]

Thus civilian deputies were by way of gaining some experience in the arts of managing a war, not because of their own stature as merchants or landowners, but because they represented the common body of the land. If popular suspicion of the government was invariably exaggerated and misplaced, it was a creative error, stiffening the resolve of the deputies to be firm in their negotiations with government commissioners. For their part, officials could not deal directly with popular fears, but they could and did respond to the climate of suspicion by taking into their confidence those who claimed to speak for the common man. Poised between the anxieties of their fellow townsmen and the fiscal needs of the government, deputies dealt with both by moving, somewhat timidly, into areas that had formerly been the exclusive preserve of the great lords.

4

HOLLAND'S SEAFARING TRADES

Holland was nothing if not a seafaring province. Its ocean-going commerce had three main branches: the North Sea herring fishery, the original foundation of Holland's maritime prosperity; the "westward" trade, which brought salt from France (later Spain) for use in preserving fish; and the "eastward" trade, which brought herring, salt, and manufactured goods to the Baltic in return for grain and raw materials. The westward trade was of great moment for Netherlands shipping—for example, "250 great ships" from the Low Countries were reported taking on salt near La Rochelle in 1546[1]—but it will be mentioned only in passing here since Holland contributed many of the ships involved, but not much else. Merchant capital for this trade came from Antwerp, and its focal point was in the ports of nearby Walcheren Island in Zeeland. In these circumstances, the States of Holland had little to do except to lodge repeated but vain protests against war-time regulations that required west-bound merchantmen to carry double the usual armament or to sail in convoy.[2]

One would expect the provincial States to be more assertive on behalf of the maritime trades in which Holland investors had a greater stake, and indeed they were. But efforts to provide the herring fleet with adequate protection against the depredations of French warships and Scottish privateers were hampered by the persistent refusal of three of the great cities—Gouda, Haarlem, and Leiden—to provide any funds for this purpose. The Baltic trade was a different matter since it contributed in various ways to the well-being of the entire province, even the industrial towns. Thus Amsterdam was able to rally other members of the States in fending off repeated efforts by the government to impose a duty on the re-export of Baltic grain. To maintain a favorable balance of power in the Baltic, the States, again led by Amsterdam, organized two war fleets against Lübeck; with the cooperation of the great nobles, they also frustrated government plans to intervene against a claimant to the Danish throne whom the Hollanders favored, but Charles V did not. Thus at least in regard to what was later called the "mother trade" in the Baltic, the States were able to articulate clearly and defend effectively what was perceived as the interest of Holland.

DEFENSE OF THE HERRING FLEET

Contemporary sources suggest that Holland had a fleet of approximately 315 herring busses by 1552, and 400 in 1562, nearly equal to or perhaps somewhat greater than the combined fleets of Flanders and Zeeland. These vessels ranged in capacity from twenty to forty *last* (a measure of volume equal to about eighty-five bushels), with an average crew of fourteen. An account for the *lastgelt* tax for 1550, apparently the only such account that has survived, indicates a catch of 17,000 *last*, which would have had a market value in the range of 650,000– 700,000 pounds.[3] Each bus represented a sizable investment, a tempting target for the enemy in time of war, especially if laden with its catch. The merchantmen of Normandy and Brittany could easily be refitted for privateering, and during Charles V's reign in the Netherlands France also experimented with the use of its Mediterranean-based galley fleet against foes in or along the North Sea. Herring busses faced an additional danger as they followed the herring on their annual southward migration along the east coast of Scotland and England. Scotland, France's traditional ally, had its own herring fishery, and Scottish freebooters could give attacks on Netherlands busses a color of patriotism.[4]

From the standpoint of the Habsburg government, every merchantman or herring bus taken by the enemy in the North Sea was a visible blow to the Emperor's *reputacion*.[5] But if Flanders had a tradition of using warships to convoy its fishing fleet,

Holland apparently did not. For its fishermen and the investors who backed their voyages, defensive measures were worse than useless if slender profit margins were jeopardized without affording real protection. To pay for warships to protect the herring fleet, the government demanded a *lastgelt* on the catch, arguing that those who benefited from a service must pay for it. Towns and villages that maintained fleets of herring busses had meetings among themselves,[6] but they would not vote for a *lastgelt* unless the States also voted a contribution, to show that their cause was Holland's cause. But in the States, towns that had no profit from the herring fishery balked at approving *omslagen* or special levies for this purpose. Thus in 1522 a majority in the States (three cities plus the nobles) approved an *omslag* for warships, but three other great cities—Gouda, Haarlem, and Leiden—flatly refused to pay their quotas.[7] Even among those who supported such levies, it was feared that warships did no good, and the States refused a request for a similar *omslag* in 1524, alleging that there had been no "profit" in previous war fleets and that it was better to let busses sail at their own risk.[8]

Absent an agreement on funding warships, the government was willing to allow the herring fleet to put to sea under the protection of "safe conducts" issued by the King of France. But Hollanders wanted no part of safe conducts unless they were made available to all interested parties. Experience suggested that wartime trading licenses of this kind, whether for the herring fishery or for trade in commodities like salt or wine, gave certain "great purses" (including government officials) a chance to control the market. For example, when deputies from Zeeland proposed using safe conducts for the herring season of 1528, Andries Jacobszoon noted in his travel journal that only the "Admiral of the Sea" (Adolph of Burgundy, lord of Vere) would profit from this arrangement.[9]

After an interval of calm following the Peace of Cambrai (1529), war broke out again in 1536, and the appearance of French warships off the coast of Holland prevented the herring fleet from sailing. The States grudgingly approved an *omslag* of 6,000 pounds to help fit out men-of-war. But the warships returned after barely a month at sea, having expended all the funds that had been raised, and would not put to sea again until more money was found. This venture left Hollanders more convinced than ever that warships could not protect herring busses.[10] The next year, the Admiral of the Sea, determined to make Holland recognize his authority, demanded twenty-five stuivers per crew member for the fishing licenses that he had obtained from the French crown. But in return for the States' consent to a desperately needed *extraordinaris bede*, Mary of Hungary promised that Holland would get several hundred safe conduct certificates free of charge. As the traditional sailing date drew closer, however, Hollanders learned that the Admiral would not release any safe conducts, despite the Regent's promise. Little Schiedam, wholly dependent on the herring fishery for its livelihood, paid the Admiral 850 pounds for fishing licenses for its busses. Even so, one of them was subsequently seized by Breton warships, causing Hoogstraten to fear "commotion" in Holland. Eventually, one hundred safe conducts were delivered to Holland and quickly used up.[11]

During the last decade of Mary of Hungary's regency, Scottish privateers terrorized the North Sea; they were known to find safe harbor in French ports, and the government of young Mary Queen of Scots was considered too weak to restrain its subjects even if it wanted to. A petition to the Habsburg government by Antwerp merchants (1551) claims that Scots and other pirates had taken ships and goods worth about 1,600,000 Holland pounds over the previous eight to ten years.[12] In 1547 Mary of Hungary convened deputies from the three fishing provinces to discuss Scottish piracy. There was considerable sentiment in favor of safe-conducts, said to be cheaper and more effective than naval armaments, but the Queen would not hear of safe-conducts negotiated with a weak Scottish government. In the States of Holland, Amsterdam rejected the *omslag* demanded by the fishing towns, on the grounds that warships were of no use to the Baltic fleet. Since three other great cities (Gouda, Haarlem, and Leiden) always voted against money for warships anyway, there was now a firm majority in the negative. At this point the Queen showed her mettle. She issued orders prohibiting any herring bus or merchantman from sailing until the three martime provinces should agree on an acceptable plan for naval defense. Under duress, deputies from the three provinces proposed pooling their resources to create a common Netherlands war fleet, with a total tonnage of 1,625 *last,* allotted according to the size of the respective herring fleets; thus Holland's share would be 750 *last,* or 45,000 pounds of a total budget of 100,000.[13] Maneuvering this proposal through the States of Holland required Assendelft to use all his negotiating skill on deputies from Amsterdam, who could not believe that the same men-of-war could protect merchant ships bound for the North Sea as well as herring busses. Similar arrangements were made the following year, but in 1549 Amsterdam's objections could not be overcome, and it was thus impossible to obtain the necessary four votes in the States.[14] Only towards the very end of Mary's regency were the government and the States able to work out their differences. Responding to long-standing requests from the States, the Regent agreed to release funds from the *ordinaris bede* to help pay for an annual war fleet. Meanwhile, her chief naval strategist, the humanist Cornelis de Scepper, had drafted a plan which recognized the truth of Holland's contention that warships could do little to protect herring busses scattered widely over the fishing grounds; Scepper proposed that a large squadron of warships should patrol on station off the Maas estuary, while swift *jachten* (yachts) maintained communication with the herring fleet. Under these terms, Holland agreed to provide eight warships, in a fleet of twenty-five sail that was intended to protect all branches of Netherlands trade in the North Sea.[15] The development of this new strategy for naval defense was no small accomplishment, but most of the credit should go to the leadership provided by Mary of Hungary and her officials, not to the fragmented States of Holland.

THE STRUGGLE FOR FREE RE-EXPORT OF BALTIC GRAIN

Merchant capital for the Baltic trade came increasingly from Amsterdam, and many of the skippers for the "eastbound" or Baltic trade were based either in Amsterdam or in the villages of Waterland, just across the IJ. But its benefits and implications ramified throughout the province, more so than any other commercial activity. The West Frisian ports of Hoorn and Enkhuizen had a stake in the Baltic trade, as did Delft because of its harbor,

Delfshaven. The shipping industry, centered in villages north of the IJ, was directly dependent on the need for "eastwarders." Holland shipwrights could produce forty caravels a year, to maintain an ocean-going fleet estimated at 400 vessels, not counting herring busses.[16] Officials from Brussels apparently viewed arguments in behalf of the Baltic trade as reflecting only the selfish interest of Amsterdam, for they seemed puzzled when other members of the States, sometimes even the nobles, lined up behind Amsterdam. When Leiden's deputies to the States were asked by government commissioners why they supported Amsterdam's position on the Baltic grain trade, they replied that if the Easterlings (north Germans) brought their grain to England instead, they would not be bringing Leiden cloths back home.[17] The herring fishery also depended in part on Baltic markets; herring was caught and processed on busses from Enkhuizen or Schiedam, packed into barrels at Haarlem and sold to Easterling merchants from the wharves near Amsterdam's Haarlem gate.[18] As for towns like Gouda and Dordrecht, traffic along the *binnenlandvaart* that was so vital to them would have been far less were it not a link between Antwerp and the Baltic.

One must distinguish at the outset between the underlying vigor of Europe's Baltic trade and Holland's strong yet precarious position in that trade. The single most important source of information on the flow of trade is the toll register for Denmark's Øresund, the channel passing from the North Sea into the Baltic between the then Danish province of Skåne (now part of Sweden) and the island of Fyn. Westward voyages through the Sound as recorded in the register rose from a combined total of 2,017 for the first two years on which information is available (1497 and 1503) to annual averages of 1,853 for 1537–1539 and 2,410 for 1557–1559. For 1497 and 1503 together, Netherlands shipping accounted for 70 percent of the west-bound voyages, and ships based in northern Holland accounted for 78 percent of this total. Though rising steeply in absolute numbers, Netherlands voyages over these decades declined as a percentage of the total, to 52 percent in 1557–1560, while shipping from the Wendish cities, including Lübeck and Hamburg, increased dramatically on a percentage basis.[19]

One can thus envision trade between north Germany and the

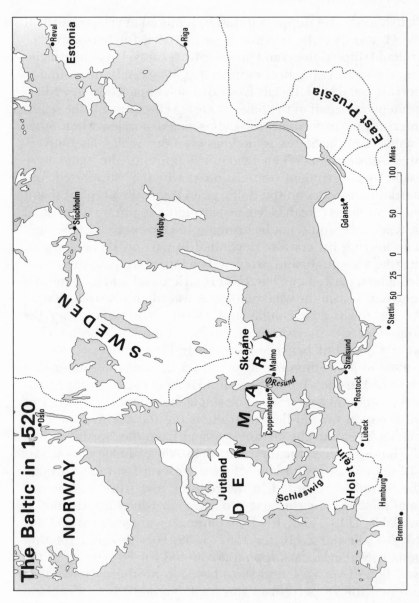

Map 2. The Baltic in 1520

Netherlands as a series of overlapping arcs. Holland vessels entering the Baltic called mainly at Danzig and other towns in Prussia and Livonia—towns that in the fifteenth century had welcomed an alternative to shipping their goods by way of Lübeck and Hamburg. Lübeck skippers sometimes called at Amsterdam—indeed, one of the inns for north German merchants on Warmoes Straat was called Lübeck Arms. More likely, they eschewed the *binnenlandvaart* through Holland and chose the more dangerous but nonetheless traditional route through the English Channel to the Scheldt estuary, thence to Bruges where the Hanseatic League had long had its staple. As for Germany's North Sea ports, Bremen seems to have specialized in bringing grain from its own Weser valley hinterland to Amsterdam. Hamburg's ships might first enter the Baltic to take on grain, then choose among three possible destinations: Amsterdam, Bruges, or Antwerp.[20]

There is no series of data that permits comparison of the relative volume of traffic along these various arcs, but from arrangements made for the dowry of a Danish king, one can see how contemporaries judged the participation of various Lowlands provinces in the Baltic trade. When Christiern II (1513–1523) married Isabella of Austria, one of Charles V's sisters (1514), he was promised a dowry of 350,000 Holland pounds. But dowry installments were not paid, and when Christiern seized Holland ships in the Sound (1519), the Netherlands government agreed to have payment of the dowry secured by the *ordinaris beden* of four provinces. Holland was assigned payments of 20,000 per year; Brabant, 11,000; Zeeland, 10,000; and Flanders, 9,000. This apportionment recognizes the unique importance that the Baltic trade had for the entire province of Holland—it alone had all of its "great cities" individually assessed—but it also shows that Holland's stake in the total Netherlands Baltic trade was reckoned at less than half.[21]

In effect, Holland had potential rivals within the Habsburg Netherlands as well as in the Baltic, and its place in the Baltic trade depended on trading habits that were by no means fixed. If the Netherlands government imposed fiscal exactions on the vital grain trade, north German merchants might decide to

avoid the Netherlands altogether and take their goods elsewhere. Lübeck, always hostile to Holland, could at times induce
the King of Denmark to close the Sound to Netherlands shipping, or, worse still, to ships from Holland, while allowing those
of Brabant and Zeeland to pass unmolested. Closer to home,
the great merchant-bankers of the southern Netherlands might
wish to contract in the Baltic for large grain purchases to be
shipped directly to Antwerp or even to more distant markets,
such as Lisbon, thus bypassing Holland and its *binnenlandvaart*.
One way or another, there were few years in which the States of
Holland did not have cause for concern.

Officials in Brussels could hardly be blamed for regarding
Holland's Baltic trade as a resource for the entire realm. Jean
Ruffault, the Treasurer-General, argued that Amsterdam's privilege for the free re-export of grain (granted by Maximilian I in
1495) must be set aside in order to ensure supplies for the other
Netherlands provinces. Margaret of Austria twice forbade Hollanders to export any grain except by purchase of a special
license, or *congie*, but both times the edict was soon withdrawn.
Yet the patient Ruffault, so Andries Jacobszoon claimed, admitted to a personal stake in plans for a *congie*.[22] Moreover, Flanders and Artois, which had their usual sources of grain cut off
in time of war with France, had special access to Charles V in
Spain, since the two Netherlands members of his council there
were Lodewijk van Vlaanderen, lord of Praet (descended from
an illegitimate line of the old counts of Flanders), and Adrien
de Croy, count of Roeulx and Stadtholder of Artois.[23] In
Mechelen, Margaret of Austria was persuaded that the traditional liberties of Holland's commerce were an affront "to the
sovereignty of the Emperor in his native provinces."[24] Thus
while Ruffault drafted plans for administering the *congie*, the
Regent proclaimed (January 1527) a ban on all grain exports
until officials could be appointed to take inventory of existing
stocks and collect the export license fees.[25]

Ordered by the Regent to publish the ban on grain export,
the Council of Holland took the risk of delaying publication in
order to summon, on its own authority, a special meeting of the
States. Haarlem seemed unwilling to oppose the Gracious

Lady's will, but Delft and Dordrecht deferred to Amsterdam, as the other cities usually did on such matters. On this occasion one of Amsterdam's burgomasters outlined the dire consequences of a *congie:* if the new edict were published, prices for spring grain in the Baltic would immediately jump, and rich speculators could drive prices still higher by buying up export licenses to control the market.[26] The States sent a delegation to Mechelen where Jean Carondolet, President of the Privy Council told them that although it had cost him much "trouble," the Regent had agreed to drop the idea of sending commissioners to Holland to take inventory of its grain stocks. A year later, however, Commissioner Jan Pelt arrived in Amsterdam demanding access to grain stored in the attics of patrician houses. But this was a time when the government desperately needed funds for a spring offensive against the Duke of Guelders and his allies. In return for the States' agreement (February 1528) to raise 80,000 pounds by a sale of *renten*, both Hoogstraten and Margaret of Austria gave assurances that Hollanders would be "contented" in the matter of the export licenses. Thus when Jan Pelt began actual collection of the *congie* at Dordrecht a few months later, an embarrassed Stadtholder sought to excuse himself by an analogy that fisher folk might understand: "the court is like an eel." The real problem, he said, was that the Emperor was not about to surrender a levy that promised to yield 60,000 pounds a year.[27]

Pelt was apparently ordered to suspend operations for the duration of the current war, but once peace with France was concluded (November 1529), he renewed his collections on the Maas, and, for the Amsterdam trade, stationed agents at the "sea gates" where ships passed from the Zuider Zee channels into the North Sea.[28] Meanwhile, Frans de Wet, Receiver for the Zeeland Toll and a sometime Haarlem burgomaster, obtained from the Privy Council a new interpretation of his prerogatives, permitting him to tax incoming goods belonging to foreign merchants unless intended for consumption in Holland—for example, sea salt and French wine intended for re-export to the Baltic. Hoogstraten believed the Hollanders might have grounds for an appeal to the Grand Council of Mechelen, since the Privy Council made its decision without hearing their side, but he himself would not support such an appeal: "it were better for the Emperor to have no beden in Holland than for the cities to continue in the freedom from tolls they have hitherto enjoyed." While Frans de Wet "pestered" certain sea captains, who wrote to Amsterdam for "solace and support," a delegation from Holland failed even to obtain a copy of the new regulations. Aert van der Goes, Advocate of the State, had apparently presented their request in a manner that the Privy Council deemed "bitter."[29]

Just at this time, the States were being asked to "anticipate" payment terms on two *extraordinaris beden*, which meant raising by various means a sum in excess of 100,000 pounds. Andries Boelens and Cornelis Bennink, two of Amsterdam's leading merchant-statesmen, told Hoogstraten that their colleagues would not consent to these requests without concessions on both the *congie* and the Zeeland Toll. At this assertion the Stadtholder flew into a rage: "Who do you think you are? I will take a plank as thick as my hand is long, and lay you out flat as one of these boards in the floor"! But the men of Amsterdam knew from previous experience of the Stadtholder's "hard words"[30] that one had to wait for the calm that followed a storm. To obtain the votes he needed in the States, Hoogstraten had to agree to have a commissioner of inquiry appointed to collect information concerning the likely effects of a *congie* (see the following paragraph);[31] he also persuaded his colleagues on the Privy Council to remand the Zeeland Toll dispute to the Grand Council, which, as expected, eventually decided in Holland's favor. The States helped out by agreeing to "corrupt" Treasurer-General Ruffault, who was seen to be Frans de Wet's chief ally in the Privy Council and who was apparently contented by a gift of 1,000 pounds.[32] (In such cases, it was usually the Stadtholder who advised the States on who should receive "gratuities"; the money came from the *omslagen* that the States regularly collected for their own purposes.)[33]

Meanwhile, Jan van Duvenvoirde, lord of Warmond and a member of the Council of Holland, collected testimony from forty-eight individuals knowledgeable about the Baltic trade, including Antwerp financiers and merchants from Baltic cities. His report, published in 1922 by P. A. Meilink, is an impressive argument for Holland's case. Time and again, Warmond's informants reported that merchants in the cities that sent grain to Amsterdam—Danzig, Hamburg, and Bremen—were extremely sensitive to novel fiscal exactions and were even now avoiding Low Countries ports. For example, at the mere rumor of a *congie*, twenty-eight Bremen grain ships were said to have sailed for England, not Holland.[34] Easterling merchants were also taking occasion to sail directly to Lisbon. Ordinarily, it was cheaper to move goods to Iberia by way of the Low Countries, for Netherlands skippers who might otherwise go in ballast to take on salt in the Bay of Biscay were glad to offer low rates so as to have a cargo for their outbound voyages.[35] Now, however, Baltic skippers were taking on Netherlands pilots, even at double the normal wage, for the unfamiliar waters south of the Scheldt estuary. This willingness to venture into unknown seas is understandable in light of the impact an export license fee would have on the slender profit margins of the Baltic trade. For a *last* of rye (eighty-five bushels) costing some twenty-five pounds, merchants might expect a profit of twenty-four stuivers (1.2 pounds) upon delivery in Antwerp, after paying six stuivers in toll fees on Holland's inland waterway. But the *congie* would mean a surcharge of eighteen stuivers. Hence no less a personage than Erasmus Schetz, one of Antwerp's premier merchant-bankers, found it worthwhile to hire three large vessels in Middelburg (Zeeland) to go in ballast to Bremen and thence bring grain directly to Lisbon.[36] More than a dozen of Warmond's witnesses testified to another transaction in which the King of Portugal's factor in Antwerp sent the Portuguese humanist, Damião de Gois, to the Baltic to take delivery on 1,500 *last* of rye bound direct for Lisbon.[37] One has the clear impression, doubtless intended by Warmond (a loyal Hollander), that Holland's middleman role in the grain trade was at risk.

To help steer Warmond's report through the Privy Council, Hoogstraten coached Aert van der Goes on how to speak "graciously and humbly" to the great lords,[38] but only Charles V himself could decide the issue. When the Emperor arrived in Brussels (February 1531) to inaugurate the regency of his sister, Mary of Hungary, there was discussion within the States of Holland about requiring abolition of the *congie* as a condition not merely for a new *extraordinaris bede*, but even for renewal of

the current *ordinaris bede*. Yet this was the occasion on which the
Emperor appeared in person to order his subjects in Holland
not to "bargain" with their sovereign; rather they should grant
unconditionally what was asked and "trust" in his love and affec-
tion for them.[39] With an Emperor who spoke in this fashion one
did not quarrel. But Hoogstraten was busy behind the scenes
distributing gratuities to Francisco de los Cobos and Nicholas
Perrenot, lord of Granvelle, the two most influential members
of Charles's inner circle. Care was taken to ensure that a
speaker of Dutch would be present when Warmond's report
was discussed in the newly formed Council of State, and a map
was prepared so that the Emperor might see how ships sailed
"out and around" from Amsterdam. As a result, the question
was remanded to the Grand Council of Mechelen, which in this
case too pronounced in favor of Holland's established privileges
and thus against the *congie*.[40]

In 1535 Mary of Hungary issued a new ban on grain export,
though the Council of Holland again refused publication. This
time, hoping to take advantage of well-known divisions within
Holland, Treasurer-General Ruffault caused to be inserted in
the Grand Council's 1531 decision a clause providing that only
Baltic grain was exempt from export duties, not the grain that
came from the Rhineland to be exported via the Maas. In response, Hoogstraten advised the States to "make friends" with
IJsselstein's son, Maximiliaan van Egmont, the young Count of
Buren, and Reynier van Nassau, the young Prince of Orange.[41]
The States also drew up a memorandum explaining that if north
Holland lost its seafaring trade, the Emperor would not have at
his disposal, in time of war, the 400 ocean-going ships of Amsterdam and Waterland, a fleet more numerous, it was said, than the
combined fleets of England, France, and Brittany.[42] Once the
great lords had been properly "corrupted" (a term used in the
States, not by Hoogstraten), the Council of State took up the
issue. President Jean Carondolet confronted Ruffault with his
alteration of the 1531 Grand Council decision (no light matter
for an official of the Habsburg state), and Orange told Philippe
de Lannoy, lord of Molembaix, that he and his colleagues on the
Council of Finance would "regret it" if they did not deal with
Holland as the majority of the great lords wished. When Mary of

Hungary was to communicate to Charles V the Council of State's favorable decision, Hoogstraten and Buren insisted on seeing a copy of the letter before it was sent. Simultaneously, the States of Holland drew up a list of those to be rewarded: 400 *wagenschot* of fine lumber (wainscoting) for Hoogstraten and Orange, and smaller amounts in wood or cash for five others.[43] The key to the victory of the States on this occasion was their success in appealing to powerful men like Buren and Orange as *ingelande*[44] or landowners having a personal stake in Holland's well-being. This common front against the *congie* marked the beginning of an era of good feelings between States and great lords, whose cooperative efforts the same year sought to prevent Holland from being harmed by the government's Copenhagen project (see the following section).

Some years later, political circumstances permitted Ruffault and the Council of Finance to try the *congie* yet again, albeit under a different name. Charles V's personal appearance in the Netherlands to suppress a rebellion by the powerful city of Ghent (1540) allowed the Regent and her Councils to act with unwonted firmness when other towns proved refractory. Moreover, Lodewijk van Schore, an able administrator with an exalted conception of princely prerogative, had recently succeeded Carondolet as President of both the Secret Council and the Council of State.[45] In Holland, the influential Hoogstraten (d. 1540) had been replaced as Stadtholder by the still young and inexperienced Reynier van Nassau. Also, the great cities may have been more divided among themselves than usual because of the recent (and long-delayed) verdict by the Grand Council in favor of the Dordrecht staple; for whatever reasons, Dordrecht's deputies broke precedent by refusing (at least initially) to join the other five cities in opposing an export duty on grain. At the same time, Amsterdam's long-time ruling faction (including men like Cornelis Bennink and Ruysch Janszoon) had been replaced by a rival group, the so-called Hendrik Dirkisten, who were not only inexperienced but perhaps a bit scornful of the normal ways of doing business at court.[46] Thus when Holland's great cities were told (November 1540) that an exit fee (*exue*) would henceforth be levied on the re-export of "eastern" grain, the States could think of nothing better to do than to forward to the Queen a formal protest delivered to the Amsterdam city hall by merchants from Danzig and Hamburg, adding a comment of their own: "The Easterling is by nature a hard man, and above all others loves freedom in his trading. . . . He will altogether not abide any new impositions." To deliver this message, the States sent a delegation "upcountry" to hold discussions with the Regent and her Councils, but did not distribute gratuities to the great lords. The deputies sought help from the Prince of Orange, only to learn that the Queen had forbidden him to meddle in this matter.[47]

Amsterdam now sent its own officials to Antwerp and Zeeland to duplicate the kind of information that Warmond had collected in 1530. But "certified" reports that 150 Easterling grain ships had already bypassed Holland during the current sailing season were not sufficient to forestall the moment that Amsterdam had long dreaded. On 2 October 1541 a collector for the grain *exue,* whom the city fathers had managed to hold off for two months, called at the house of a prominent grain dealer to begin his inquest about grain exported from Amsterdam since the November edict. The collector was told the man he sought was not at home, and when he returned that evening, as announced, a riot broke out, forcing the burgomasters to open one of the town gates to permit the Emperor's tax collector to escape with his life. Amsterdam claimed that this untoward disturbance was provoked by "unknown louts," but the government had information naming eleven men as participants in the riot, including several prominent merchants and grain dealers. While Schore drafted a letter listing the penalties Amsterdam must suffer "to repair the injury done to the Emperor," a delegation from the States, hoping still to discuss the grain *exue,* was refused a hearing in the Secret Council, owing to the "shameful treatment" meted out to his majesty's tax collector. But all was not lost. After distributing wine worth 420 pounds to six great lords, the States worked out an agreement by which the Emperor would be compensated for his "interest" in the grain export fee by a special extra payment of 25,000 pounds, of which Amsterdam paid half. Meanwhile, friends at court had already told Aert van der Goes that no second collector would be sent to Amsterdam, since (understandably) no one could be found to take the job. In the end, the *exue* plan was defeated not by any great political skill on the part of Amsterdam's newly installed ruling faction, but by fierce devotion to the city's privileges on the part of ordinary men and women who filled the streets on the night of 2 October and nearly killed the Emperor's tax collector.[48]

Nonetheless, Mary of Hungary's government refused to abandon its efforts to subject the vital grain trade to some centralized control. In 1545 because of a scarcity in the southern provinces, the export of foreign grain was again prohibited. This time the nobles broke the usual unanimity of the States in opposing such measurers, as Dordrecht had briefly done in 1540. But with help from Granvelle, who was rewarded for his efforts, the States received permission to bring suit before the Grand Council, that stalwart upholder of lawful privilege. Meanwhile, the grain measures of Delft sat patiently in prison rather than providing the information required of them according to the Queen's edict. In the chambers of the Grand Council in Mechelen, government attorneys tried for over a year to prevent Warmond's report of 1530 from being accepted as part of the documentation. When the Grand Council finally ruled in Holland's favor once again (1548), the States seemed to take the result for granted;"for the honor of Holland" they refused to authorize anything more than the usual token gratuities for members of the Grand Council. But Amsterdam subsequently called attention to the fact that the States had not received their official copy of the judgment. As late as 1555, pertinent sacks of documents were still being held by the Secret Council, despite letters patent commanding their release to the secretary of the Grand Council, whose duty it was to engross the official copies of a judgment.[49] Clearly, there were those close to the Regent who continued to view Holland's commercial liberties as inimical to the Emperor's prerogatives, even if they were unable to translate their wishes into law.

HOLLAND'S STAKE IN NETHERLANDS BALTIC POLICY

If the *congie* was a grave threat to Holland's Baltic trade, the possibility of an alliance between Denmark and Lübeck was even worse. Holland first gained a secure footing in the Baltic trade by supporting the king of Denmark in a naval war against Lübeck (1438–1441),[50] and Denmark continued to play a pivotal role in Holland's commercial success. When Lübeck declared war against Denmark in 1509, King Hans obtained promises of help from Holland, and Lübeck soon declared the Sound closed for Holland shipping. Following a meeting with representatives from Zeeland and Antwerp, the Hollanders obtained permission from Margaret of Austria's government to levy a *lastgelt* or tonnage tax in order to arm ships of war. In the spring of 1511 four Holland warships accompanied a large fleet that was convoyed through the Sound by Denmark's admiral, Jens Helgersen Ulfstand. On the way back, however, a fleet of 250 sail—including grain ships that had wintered in the Baltic—was attacked by Lübeck's war fleet near Hela, at the mouth of the Vistula; the four warships were driven off, and some fifty grain ships were seized. This was the worst disaster suffered by either side in over a hundred years of naval warfare in the Baltic: Hoorn's losses were estimated at 20,000 Holland pounds; Amsterdam's, at 100,000. Hollanders did not again brave Lübeck's blockade of the Sound until the Wendish cities signed a ten-year truce in 1514.[51]

Denmark's new king, Christiern II (1513–1523), was married to Charles V's sister, Isabella, but devoted more attention to his mistress, the daughter of Sigbritte Willemsdochter from Amsterdam. Even after the girl died, Sigbritte remained on the scene as Christiern's chief financial adviser, convincing him that Denmark could prosper if, like Holland, it tamed the power of its nobles and clergy. Encouraged by the burgomasters of Copenhagen and Malmö, Christiern also sought to boost the trade of his own towns at the expense of foreigners. Lübeck and Danzig, often at odds, now concluded an alliance against Denmark. Meanwhile, Christiern provoked rebellion in Sweden by arranging the murder of nobles opposing him. In Denmark nobles backing his uncle, Duke Frederik of Holstein, forced him to take ship for exile in Zeeland (April 1523).[52] Already in June 1522, Lübeck had declared the Sound closed to Hollanders, and Danzig agreed to bar them from its port. The States of Holland sought immediate reprisals against Lübeck goods, but even after the government—over the objections of Bruges and other Flemish cities—announced a ban on sailing through the Sound, Amsterdammers complained that Lübeck could still market its goods in the Netherlands by means of ships bound from Hamburg to Bruges.[53] Hollanders proposed forcing the Sound and eventually did so (June 1523) when twelve warships provided protection for a fleet of 130 merchantmen.[54]

It now remained to establish relations with a new government in Denmark where Frederik of Holstein (soon to be King Frederick I) was *de facto* ruler. Already by August 1523, Amsterdam's pensionary had returned from a mission to the Baltic, reporting that both Denmark and Lübeck were prepared to re-open the Sound if they received promises that the Netherlands would not support Christiern II. Margaret of Austria now sent an emissary to join negotiations in the Baltic, though he was primarily interested in a vain effort to secure succession rights for Christiern II's son. Hence the pensionaries of Antwerp and Amsterdam gave their personal assurance (July 1524) that the Netherlands would not back any re-conquest effort by Christiern II, and peace was confirmed when Margaret of Austria approved their action some months later.[55]

Seven years later Christiern II, grown weary of exile, raised troops in Germany and appeared before Amsterdam, demanding payment of the arrears that Holland still owed him from his late wife's dowry. Having extorted from the States of Holland what he needed to outfit a war fleet, he set sail for Norway (October 1531), where he and his supporters laid siege to a castle outside Oslo.[56] For Lübeck, Christiern's return to Scandinavia was a chance to revive the old alliance with King Frederik I against the Hollanders. Lübeck had just passed through a period of social and religious upheaval in which the Lutheran Reformation swept to victory and the power of the staunchly Catholic patrician oligarchy was broken. Jürgen Wullenwever, an influential leader of the popular movement, now rallied the populace for a determined effort to recover Lübeck's old trading privileges, at Holland's expense. Frederik I for his part had no enduring *casus belli* with Holland, and the Schleswig–Holstein nobles who were his original supporters included many friends of Holland, men who traded directly with Netherlands merchants at makeshift harbors on the North Sea coast. But so long as Christiern II's return to the throne seemed possible, Lübeck's naval might was invaluable to all who feared him; thus, Frederik I endorsed a temporary ban on Netherlands shipping through the Sound, and Danzig agreed to detain in its harbor the ships that waited through the winter to carry back spring grain.[57]

The Netherlands government was kept apprised of these developments mainly through Amsterdam's contacts in the Baltic.[58] Poppius Occo, factor for the Fuggers, had had close dealings with Christiern II and corresponded with leading figures in Holstein and Lübeck.[59] Cornelis Bennink, who (with Ruysch Janszoon and Allert Boelens) was the leading figure among Amsterdam's burgomasters in this period, was on friendly terms with the Holstein nobleman Melchior Rantzau, King Frederik I's closest adviser.[60]

Lübeck warships now cruised the Baltic and the North Sea deliberately seeking out vessels from Holland, while allowing those from Zeeland or Brabant to pass unmolested. In May several Holland merchantmen were captured off the island of Texel at the entrance to the Zuider Zee and off Dunkirk in Flanders.[61] Since no merchant would sail to the Baltic under these circumstances, Amsterdam convened a special meeting of leading Baltic shippers, from Amsterdam itself and from the seafaring villages of neighboring Waterland. The States of Holland accepted this group's proposal to fit out for war sixty merchant vessels initially financed by Amsterdam and Waterland. In June, Mary of Hungary decreed the confiscation of all Easterling goods in the Netherlands, save for those of a few towns still considered friendly.[62] But in Copenhagen in July, the Netherlands delegation, including Cornelis Bennink, was able to conclude a renewal of the 1524 treaty with Denmark. Almost at the same time, Christiern II surrendered to a superior force in Norway, upon the understanding that he might still negotiate to recover some of his lands. Instead, at the insistence of Lübeck, he was clapped into imprisonment in Schleswig where he had only enemies. At the news of these events, grain prices in Amsterdam fell from forty-six to twenty-four pounds per *last* of rye.[63]

Here the conflict might have ended, had it not been for Wullenwever's determination to continue the struggle against

Holland with or without Danish help.[64] In order "to chastise Lübeck," Amsterdam and Waterland proposed to the States of Holland that thirty warships be fitted out at a cost of 60,000 pounds over four months. The nobles accepted this proposal, but the other cities did not: this must be the Emperor's war, not Holland's, so other provinces would have to contribute too. Hoogstraten suggested that owners might lend their ships to the government until arrangements could be worked out, but "Amsterdam cum sociis" said they would rather see their seafaring trade destroyed. By 24 April 1533 an agreement was worked out: while Amsterdam and Waterland chose the best thirty of their merchantmen to be equipped for war, the States would "anticipate" a sum of 12,000 pounds from the next *ordinaris bede* term and send a delegation "upcountry" (to Brussels) to seek the rest of the money that was needed. Furthermore, this agreement was contingent on Mary of Hungary's naming a Supreme Commander for the fleet to make it clear this was indeed the Emperor's war.[65]

As the month of May wore on, however, the Council of Holland grew alarmed at what might happen if the project for a war fleet fell through. As Assendelft wrote Hoogstraten, seamen at Enkhuizen were already displaying "insolence" because of the delay, whereas certain deputies to the States believed that "the delay [came] from your Excellency's being too hesitant to release the Emperor's money." Reporting on a 29 May meeting at which the States renounced their agreement to provide 12,000 pounds for the fleet from *ordinaris bede* funds, the Council reminded Hoogstraten that no Supreme Commander had been appointed and that the thirty-day period for which merchant ships were to be held for war fitting had elapsed. Furthermore, people were greatly suspicious that other provinces might be able to conduct business as usual while Holland suffered: if Holland's ships were taken while those of Flanders and Zeeland were let go, "it would cause in this land a great uproar, from which a great commotion and rebellion [were] likely to arise."[66] (The Council's fears about the popular mood were not idle; as will be seen in chap. 6, it was during this period of Baltic war, with seafaring employment scarce and bread prices high, that a revolutionary Anabaptist movement swept across Holland.)

To this urgent plea the Queen at last responded by naming a Flemish nobleman, Geraard van Merkeren, as Supreme Commander. At about the same time, the Council of State authorized Hoogstraten to make financial arrangements for the war fleet "at the least cost."[67] As usual, there was no ready cash in government coffers. Hoogstraten had to give his personal bond to Antwerp bankers for a loan in excess of 35,000 pounds, so he and Merkeren could bring 30,000 in cash to Holland as earnest money from the government.[68] Since estimated costs for the fleet had risen, Hoogstraten asked the States for 50,000, but they at first refused. So long as Lübeck goods were being sold openly in Flemish markets, deputies would not be convinced that the government was treating this as the Emperor's war. But on 20 August owing to what Aert van der Goes called Hoogstraten's "hard work and tricks" in private discussions with the delegations from each town, the States consented to a 50,000-pound *extraordinaris bede*. Appearing with Merkeren before the Amsterdam *vroedschap*, Hoogstraten told the Supreme Commander that his orders were to "punish Lübeck." The fleet sailed out from the Zuider Zee on 12 September.[69]

After this protracted debate, the results of Merkeren's voyage were anticlimactic. While his fleet lay in the Sound, smaller vessels took a few prizes near Lübeck, but twelve ships returning from Bergen in Norway were able to enter Lübeck's harbor without incident. Ter Gouw credits the account in the "Historie van Hollant," according to which Merkeren, once in the Sound, revealed secret orders from Hoogstraten instructing him only to open the Sound (permitting Holland ships that had been trapped in the eastern Baltic to return) and not to attack Lübeck; thus, it was at Merkeren's command that the twelve ships from Bergen were allowed to pass by unscathed. It will be recalled from the last chapter, however, that the "Historie van Hollant's" version of events is often warped by a deep suspicion of the Regent's advisers. Two officers whom Merkeren sent to report to Hoogstraten told a significantly different story. Merkeren did have instructions that he disclosed to his captains only in the Sound, but they were to return to Holland by 15 October. Much to Merkeren's disappointment the twelve vessels did escape, thanks to a shift in the wind.[70] This account is far the more credible of the two, but it also leaves something out. At the time of Merkeren's voyage, the Netherlands government was engaged in promising negotiations with the Danish Rigsrad and with Christiern III, eldest son and likely successor of the recently deceased Frederik I. As had happened in the Guelders wars, the government's cautious military strategy, intended to keep open doors that might lead to peace, was at cross purposes with the Hollanders' straightforward desire to "punish" their enemies. The following spring, Cornelis Bennink again formed part of a Netherlands delegation to the peace talks sponsored by Hamburg at which Lübeck eventually agreed to a four years' truce.[71]

Even though Lübeck's latest campaign against Amsterdam had ended, Baltic affairs were still in turbulence because Frederik I's death left the succession to the Danish throne unsettled. Noble members of Denmark's Rigsrad (including Melchior Rantzau) favored the candidacy of Christiern III, but the bishops did not, since Christiern as Duke of Holstein was an avowed partisan of the Lutheran Reformation. Another possible candidate was Count Christoffel of Oldenburg, who claimed to represent the interests of his imprisoned cousin, King Christiern II, and who quickly gained the support of Lübeck. In the ensuing Counts' War, Christoffel gained control of Copenhagen, while Christiern, elected by the Rigsrad majority, controlled Jutland.[72] Amsterdam favored Christiern III because of ties with men in his entourage and because he seemed the likely winner.[73]

Charles V, however, still had dynastic plans for Denmark. Following the death of his beloved nephew, Christiern II's son, the Emperor allowed himself to be won over by the ambitious schemes of an exiled Swedish prelate and partisan of Christiern II, Johann von Weeze, Archbishop of Lund. Frederick of Wittelsbach, brother of the Count Palatine, was to wed Christiern II's young daughter, Dorothea, and assert a claim to the Danish throne by right of his wife. Despite a long and thoughtful letter from Mary of Hungary expressing serious reservations about this plan, the Emperor pushed ahead, and the marriage was solemnized in May 1535.[74] Since Lübeck had by now abandoned him, seeking another candidate more amenable to its wishes, Christoffel of Oldenburg declared that he was holding Copenhagen for the Count Palatine and sought help from the

Netherlands. Accordingly, in February 1536, Mary of Hungary asked the States of Holland for a fleet that would convey the Count Palatine and his troops to the relief of Copenhagen. Hoogstraten argued that the success of the Count Palatine was in Holland's interest, since Christiern III had allied with both Lübeck and the Duke of Guelders. But Hollanders were not worried about Christiern III. It must have been a rare token of Christiern's underlying good will that Cornelis Benninck had received (and passed on to Assendelft) the original copy of a letter from the Duke of Guelders to Christiern. In May 1536, Christiern himself wrote to assure Amsterdam that he would protect Holland's rights in the Sound if Holland did not send a fleet to the aid of his enemies.[75]

In any case, the States fended off requests for the use of Holland's precious ocean-going fleet. First, they insisted that Mary of Hungary call a meeting of the States General. Then, after several more discussions, they agreed to let Holland ships be used, provided that all expenses were borne by the Emperor and that the ships were fitted out in Zeeland at the home port of Adolph of Burgundy, lord of Vere and hereditary Admiral of the Netherlands. The States further insisted that Vere's command of the fleet be by special commission from the Queen, not by right of his office as Admiral, for Hollanders had always contested the Admiral's rights over their shipping.[76] But by this time a more formidable obstacle had arisen. Meynert van Ham, commanding 3,000 troops in the service of Guelders, Christiern III's ally, occupied the town of Appingedam in Groningen and threatened to attack Holland if the fleet sailed for Copenhagen. To deal with this problem, Mary of Hungary ordered Hoogstraten and Maximiliaan van Egmont, the young Count of Buren, to cross the Zuider Zee and attack Meynert van Ham's position with their *compagnies d'ordonnance* currently stationed in Holland. But the States, aided by the Council of Holland, persuaded both great lords to disregard the Queen's orders since the departure of these troops would leave Holland exposed to a possible attack from Guelders.[77]

Meanwhile, reports reaching Holland indicated that Christiern III was tightening the noose around Copenhagen and that the fall of the city was imminent, if it had not already occurred.

Hence Mary of Hungary sought to resolve the impasse in the only way possible, ordering the 3,000 foot soldiers or *knechten* hired by the Count Palatine to march off to Appingedam to help the Stadtholder of Friesland subdue Meynert van Ham. This campaign was a success, but the Count Palatine, who was just arriving to take command of his troops, must have marvelled at the strange ways of the Netherlanders. Because Holland refused to be associated with the campaign against Christiern III, merchant ships were being refitted for war at Vere (in Zeeland) while the *knechten* awaited embarkation at Harlingen (in Friesland). Worse still, Adolph of Burgundy had difficulty collecting artillery for the fleet because Holland's towns, ordered to deliver up their own artillery pieces, were instead (so the Admiral complained) dumping them into the sea. Finally, because Hoogstraten and Buren refused to use their own *bandes* to deal with Meynert van Ham, the Count Palatine's *knechten* had been sent inland even farther from the ships. The Count then had to bring his men across the Zuider Zee and pay them extra wages for the long march through Holland to Dordrecht whence they were to be ferried across to the ships waiting in Zeeland. By this time, however, the Netherlands government had received definitive word of Copenhagen's surrender, and there was nothing to do but pay the *knechten* once again so they would be content to depart in peace.[78] After this waste of scarce government funds, Mary of Hungary begged the Emperor to dismiss her as Regent.[79] But the Queen, who had advised against the Copenhagen project, had no reason to be ashamed over its failure. The political constellation of the Habsburg Netherlands was such that when the great lords joined forces with the provincial states, as they had on this occasion, the government was rendered impotent.

In protecting Holland's Baltic interests, the States spoke with a unanimity only rarely disturbed by divisions between seafaring and manufacturing towns or by animosities relating to the Dordrecht staple. The States spoke with wisdom, on behalf of the dynamic seaborne economy of the Netherlands, as against the short-sighted fiscal goals of Treasury officials, or Charles V's ill-considered schemes for placing a new king on Denmark's throne. When the seagoing trades were divided among themselves, as in conflicts between the Baltic traders of Amsterdam and herring fishers of the Maas estuary, their fractiousness no doubt reassured government officials that such subjects needed, after all, a firm hand from the top. But when the vital Baltic trade provided the basis for a firm consensus on Holland's interests, the provincial States were able, with some help from the great lords, to display the confidence and effectiveness of a body that was used to self-government.

5
HOLLAND FINANCES UNDER THE CONTROL OF THE STATES

Fiscal issues were always at the heart of discussions between the States and the central government, and it was in this area that the institutional autonomy of the States increased most dramatically during the reign of Charles V. The Emperor's wars with France made his officials in the Netherlands desperate for new funds and thus willing to agree to an arrangement, long sought by the deputies, guaranteeing that the money would be spent for the purpose intended. In this way the provincial states gained control over the collection and especially the disbursement of revenue. Moreover, because much of the new money for the government's needs was in the form of funded debt managed by the provincial states, Holland and other provinces established a solid credit rating, even as the government in Brussels fell into a veritable penury.

The fiscal power of the States was not without important side effects in Holland. In particular, the instruments of the new provincial public debt—*renten* issued and funded by the States— were an attractive investment opportunity for the narrow circle of men who repeatedly served as town magistrates and deputies to the States and thus had less time to devote to business. This pattern of investment was part of a larger picture in which leading deputies were becoming less like their merchant constituents and more like the Habsburg officials with whom they regularly dealt. In addition, higher levels of taxation meant that some groups in Holland had to pay a good deal more. Political realities were such that the States could not force the government to tax privileged enclaves under the jurisdiction of the great noble, and would not tax Holland's commercial wealth. As a consequence, the extra burden was borne by those who were already paying more than their share, that is, the peasantry and the urban commons. Thus, even as the States acquired new sources of institutional strength, the deputies began to lose touch with the "common body of the land" that they claimed to represent.

THE STATES GAIN CONTROL OF HOLLAND'S FISCAL MACHINERY

The Habsburg-Valois wars that punctuated Charles V's reign were progressively more expensive, owing to changes both in fortifications and armaments and in the size of armies, all of which can be seen in retrospect as part of Europe's "military revolution." In the Netherlands, the annual cost of waging war in the 1550s was twice what it had been in the 1540s, and seven or eight times what it had been in the 1520s. Since the last of these wars was also the longest (1552–1559), one can understand why the governments of both Spain and France had to seek relief from their creditors before it was over.[1] The traditional *beden* were not much help in meeting rising military expenditures, because their value was reduced by the rebates (*gratiën*) enjoyed by towns with voting rights in the provincial states. The practice of having the states issue *renten* against future *bede* receipts led to a further diminution of disposable income because most of these annuities were not retired on schedule, owing to other claims against the *bede*. Thus by the 1540s, Holland's *ordinaris bede* of 100,000 pounds was reduced by about 30,000 pounds for *gratie* to the six great cities, and 22,000 for annual interest on the still unredeemed portion (about two-thirds) of *renten* that had been issued by the States between 1515 and 1533. When war with France broke out again in 1542, Mary of Hungary's government was able to push through some new forms of taxation, including a *morgental* or acreage tax on land and a ten percent tax on income from *renten* (except those issued by the states) and real property. These measures helped, but not enough. The alternative was credit, of which there was a seemingly inexhaustible supply among Antwerp's community of merchant-bankers. During Charles V's reign, government borrowing on the Antwerp exchange seems to have increased by a factor of about sixty to one, but the bankers demanded as much as twenty-two percent interest for government loans, and they were extremely cautious about whose word they would accept as a guarantee of repayment. Promises from members of the Habsburg family were definitely not good enough. Instead, creditors insisted on personal bonds (*obligations*) first from the great lords (like Hoogstraten) who made up the Regent's Council and then from the receivers who collected *bede* revenue in the provinces. By the 1550s, even the promises of these important men were no longer sufficient. In the end, the Habsburg state kept itself afloat by shifting an important part of its indebtedness to the provincial states, which were still able to find buyers for their *renten* at rates as low as 6.25 percent.

Starting in 1542, Holland and other provinces issued a new series of *renten* funded not by the *beden*, but by new taxes collected and disbursed by the states. In Holland, these *renten* were retired more or less on schedule, and the system was expanded dramatically during the last Habsburg–Valois war (1552–1559). During these years Holland's public debt mounted to 1,236,000 pounds, a sum about twelve times greater than the annual *ordinaris bede*, yet because of careful management by the States, roughly half of this total had been retired by 1566.[2] The states thus created an effective means to relieve some of the pressure on the Habsburg treasury and incidentally to make the provinces more credit-worthy than their sovereign.

In the early modern era collectors of revenue owed to princes often found themselves harried by payment orders from many different sources, amounting to sums vastly in excess of their receipts. Thus, effective control of revenue was in the hands of whoever established the pecking order by which conflicting claims were settled.[3] In Holland, the Receiver for the Emperor's *beden* was appointed by the Council of Finance, and looked to this body for direction about what his priorities should be. Everyone seemed to be agreed that the holders of *renten* issued by the States—especially those who lived outside the province—could not be trifled with;[4] therefore, other claimants had to fight for what was left of *bede* receipts after interest payments were made. Foremost among these claimants, the States stipulated in the formal document by which consent to a *bede* was given how the money was to be spent. Apparently the States would not agree to a *bede* without seeing a projected budget, or *staetgen,* which then became part of the agreement, at least as far as the States were concerned.[5] That these written conditions were not taken lightly in Brussels is shown by repeated efforts on the part of government commissioners to get the States to consent "simply," that is, without restrictions.[6] Even apart from such agreements, the States believed they had an implicit contract with their sovereign to make *bede* funds available for defending the province when invasion threatened.[7] Yet when wolves came to the door, the cupboard was always bare.

The Emperor's loyal officials often had claims of their own against his *bede* income. Like Hoogstraten and the other great lords who gave counsel to the Regent, men such as Assendelft (President of the Council of Holland) were routinely expected to interpose their personal credit between the prince and his creditors. For example, Assendelft took out a loan in Amsterdam in 1531 to help expedite the departure of Christiern II's warships. In addition, his majesty's humble subjects, like the brewers and grain dealers of Amsterdam, provided supplies on this occasion and were usually willing to accept a promissory note from a Hoogstraten or an Assendelft.[8] Not unreasonably, all such creditors expected repayment from Holland's *beden;* after all, what were these subsidies for, if not for the defense of the land?

The claims mentioned thus far reflect local priorities that were not necessarily those of the Habsburg state. Although the provincial states harbored the constant suspicion that the dynasty was milking its Low Countries possessions to support ambitions elsewhere, the truth seems to be that Spain contributed far more to the defense of the Netherlands than the Netherlands did to any other Habsburg enterprise.[9] The real problem was that the government viewed provincial subsidies as resources for its general needs, especially as sureties for its recurring loans in the Antwerp exchange. By order of the Council of Finance, Holland's Receiver for the *beden* would be issued a *décharge* or quittance in return for a personal bond or *obligatie* that one or more bankers would then accept as surety for a loan. Thus as money for a *bede* flowed into the Receiver's office in The Hague, it was loaded onto carts and sent under armed guard to Antwerp in repayment for the loan.[10] In this way, funds that Hollanders intended for local needs were transmuted into the life's blood of the larger Habsburg state. During Willem Goudt's long tenure as Receiver for the *beden* in Holland,[11] interested parties found again and again that his commitments in Antwerp took precedence over everything else.

During the 1530s, deputies were dismayed to learn that discussions about the use of *bede* receipts were moot because the money had been "spent" before it was collected. In 1531 the States consented to an *ordinaris bede* of 80,000 pounds per year for the next six years. When Holland was asked in 1532 to "anticipate" payments due in 1535 and 1536, the deputies refused, alleging that money might be needed for a struggle against Lübeck in the Baltic. They were then told that Charles V had "levied the ordinaris bede by loan for two years [1532 and 1533], and took the money with him, for resisting the Turk." Goudt explained to disbelieving deputies that even the money earmarked for redemption of *renten* in those years was "ewech" (gone), although it had not been collected yet. Assendelft contended that the Emperor had a right to take one-third of the receipts from a *bede* "in cash" (that is, for two of the six years), but the deputies naturally disagreed.[12] Finally, rather than anticipating the money due in 1535 and 1536, the States agreed to raise 28,000 pounds by issuing *renten* to be redeemed from the receipts of those years. In June 1535, however, Goudt reported that these *renten* could not be retired on schedule since receipts for the last two years of the *bede* had already been spent. The following June, when there were fears of an invasion, deputies got a look at Goudt's own budget summary for 1536 and did not like what they saw. Hoogstraten and the Council of Holland joined in remonstrating with Goudt that the money should have been held for defense of the land, in keeping with the terms of the consent by the States. But Goudt insisted there was no money left and that he had done nothing but follow his instructions from the Council of Finance.[13] In fact, the Council of Finance and the Regent consistently backed the arrangements Goudt had made in Antwerp, even if it meant postponing the claims of a Hoogstraten or an Assendelft for reimbursement, or disabusing Hoogstraten's successor, Reynier van Nassau, of the idea that *bede* receipts could be used for improving Holland's defense.[14]

These disputes over how revenues were to be spent indicate a tension fundamental to the political structure of the Habsburg Netherlands, a hard-to-categorize polity in which formerly independent provinces were (so it might have seemed) slowly being welded together into a single realm by the press of external circumstances as well as by the firm hand of Habsburg rule. That the subjects of this government thought of themselves as "Burgundians" or "Netherlanders" is not always clear,[15] not even for the small political elite of each province. What is clear is the strength of provincial feeling, as evinced in 1537, when the States of Holland steadfastly refused an *extraordinaris bede* for the defense of far-away Artois, threatened by a French invasion. The excuse alleged by the deputies on this occasion—that Artois had not come to Holland's aid during her recent troubles in the Baltic[16]—need not be taken too seriously since each province no doubt had a vivid memory of the sins and transgressions of its neighbors. The Regent thus had to be circumspect about using Peter's money to defend Paul. In April 1543, when Leiden's pensionary, Jacob de Milde, spread a rumor that 50,000 pounds from the Holland *beden* was being used for the defense of Maastricht, Mary of Hungary ordered the government's confidant in the Council of Holland to find out who told De Milde the money had been used for Maastricht.[17] Meanwhile, when the States agreed in 1542 to new forms of taxation, they refused to entrust the collection of this money to Willem Goudt and named instead a man of their own choosing who angered the Regent by refusing to involve himself in the government's loans in Antwerp. As a result, Goudt was left without a "receipt" to cover an *obligatie* he had signed for 50,000 pounds plus interest.[18]

The government and the States might have continued struggling over such issues, had not the balance been tilted towards the States by a third party, the Antwerp banking community. By now, the bankers knew that even a man of Hoogstraten's stature could not count on timely reimbursement from the revenues of the province entrusted to his care. They surely knew too that *rentemeesterbrieven*[19] (the promissory notes of local collectors like Goudt) were being charged to "the next *bede* consented," not just to future years of a current *bede*.[20] Lenders thus sensed a need to get still closer to the subsidies that provided the government with its major source of revenue. Already in 1537, Mary of Hungary sent instructions that if the States of Holland were not willing to "anticipate" the 1538 payment for a current *bede*, they should at least send "letters" on the later payments which could be used to obtain a loan in Antwerp. Before responding to the Regent, Assendelft expressed his puzzlement to Hoogstraten: "I do not understand what letters the aforesaid States could send, other than the act of consent [for the *bede*], which the Advocate tells me has been delivered long since." In Flanders, where credit markets were more sophisticated, towns and castleries were issuing letters of obligation on future *bede* payments as early as 1544. In Holland, the States began endorsing *obligatiën* for *bede* receipts of the entire province in 1553.[21]

By this time, deputies were demanding that revenue be collected by the States' own agents, not by a Receiver for the *beden* who took his orders from the Council of Finance in Brussels. Apparently since the Utrecht War of 1481–1484, there had been a separate revenue office in The Hague, that of the Receiver for the Common Land, who was initially charged with managing the "common land *renten*" issued during the war. Subsequently, this official collected the (usually) small levies or *omslagen* that the States needed for purposes of their own such as the salary of the Advocate or gratuities for the Emperor's officials. The Receiver for the Common Land was appointed by the sovereign, but during Charles V's reign the office gradually became more answerable to the States. For example, after 1530, payments from the *omslagen* were made by authorization of the Advocate, not, as previously, of one of the members of the Emperor's Council of Holland. Heyman van der Ketel (1539–1545) may have been the first Receiver for the Common Land appointed upon the recommendation of the States. Connections between those who served the sovereign and those who served the States were still very close—Van der Ketel's father was Meester Vincent Corneliszoon van Mierop, an important member of the Council of Finance—but there was a clear tendency toward institutional autonomy.[22]

With the introduction of new forms of taxation and a new series of provincial *renten,* the States demanded a greater role for the Receiver for the Common Land. Thus it was Heyman van der Ketel, not Willem Goudt, who collected the money realized from the first two issues of the new series of *renten* in 1542 and 1543. At first, the shift from one collecting agent to another was a mere formality; for example, Van der Ketel took 31,000 pounds from the first of these *renten* sales and gave it to Goudt for payment of one of his debts in Antwerp, even though the States had instructed him not to use any of his receipts for this purpose.[23] Perhaps because Van der Ketel came from a family that served the government so loyally, the States did not again call upon him for the collection of money for *extraordinaris beden,* whether by sales of *renten* or by other means. Instead, they turned to Vrank van der Hove, who in 1545 succeeded Van der Ketel as Receiver for the Common Land. In Van der Hove the States found a man willing to serve only one master; for example, at their direction, he used money from the new taxes that were meant to fund *renten* to make up Holland's arrears in a recent *extraordinaris bede.* More importantly, upon instructions from the States, he refused to give government auditors unrestricted access to precious data on wealth-holders contained in local accounts for the tenth penny on the income from *renten* and real property.[24]

Van der Hove's successor, Aert Coebel (1546–1563), presided over a major expansion in the responsibilities of his office. With the renewed outbreak of war in 1552, the States demanded that all *extraordinaris beden* be collected by the Receiver for the Common Land, even if the money was to be raised by the traditional *schiltal* assessment rather than by one of the new methods introduced in the 1540s. Thus, the Receiver for the *beden,* Jacques Grammaye, was left with nothing but the *ordinaris bede,* which in these years had a nominal value of 100,000 pounds, but a net value of only 48,000 after deductions for rebates and for interest on the old series of *renten.*[25] By contrast, between the beginning of the war in 1552 and Charles V's abdication at the end of 1555, Coebel collected *extraordinaris beden* with a nominal value of approximately 1,200,000 and a net value only slightly less.[26]

Because the States now controlled most of Holland's revenue through the Receiver for the Common Land, Antwerp bankers turned to the States for assurances on their loans to the government. Using funds from an *extraordinaris bede* of 300,000 pounds approved by the States in April 1553, Coebel made payments of 93,000 to various Antwerp firms, including the factor of the Fuggers, for loans originally contracted by Grammaye. Later that year, he began making payments on *obligatiën* issued by the States, as indicated in the following table:[27]

Table 3. Payments to Antwerp Bankers by Aert Coebel, 1553–1555 (in Holland pounds)

Bede *approval date*	*Nominal sum*	*Payments on* obligatiën
October 1553	100,000	42,000
October 1554	200,000	91,478
December 1554	200,000	183,000
May 1555	200,000	180,000

The bankers were thus dealing directly with the States, bypassing the Emperor's fiscal bureaucracy. Meanwhile, the unfortunate Grammaye reported a total of 596,000 in "unfruitful *décharges*," that is, quittances for promissory notes that he had delivered to the bankers, but for which there were no revenues in sight.[28]

If the States had initially a good reputation in the eyes of lenders, they surely improved it by careful management of the new *renten* debt. The States had decided in 1544 to fund the new issues by combining an "impost" or excise on beer and wine in the towns with a *morgental* or acreage tax in the countryside. In the 1540s and for the much larger issues of the 1550s, the Receiver for the Common Land collected and disbursed these levies according to the instructions of the States. After a shaky start and several increases in the rates, the combined impost and land tax kept interest payments current. Diversions of money from this fund to other purposes were at first not very common because for everything he collected Coebel had to account to a joint committee that included auditors from the Emperor's Chamber of Accounts in The Hague as well as deputies appointed by the States.[29] As will be seen in chapter 7, however, the steady flow of money into the office of the Receiver for the Common Land would eventually give the States a freedom of action which a cash-starved government did not possess.

HOLLAND'S MAGISTRATE ELITE AS INVESTORS IN RENTEN

One of the striking features of the new provincial debt that was created in Holland after 1542 is that, by and large, the biggest investors were the same men who, as deputies to the States approved creation of the debt and oversaw its management. Before examining *renten* investments more closely, it will first be helpful to consider who the deputies were.

Between 1542 and 1562 there were 285 *dagvaarten* or meetings of the States convened by the central government, an average of 13.5 per year. This total does not count the numerous occasions when smaller delegations were sent to Brussels to give the States' response to a *bede* request or to conduct other business. For most meetings a town sent two or three deputies, but sometimes it was considered sufficient to send the pensionary by himself—for example, to hear a *bede* "proposition," which did not require an immediate response. The extent to which towns relied on their pensionaries to represent them in these discussions may be seen from the following comparison:

Table 4. Trips to *Dagvaarten* by Pensionaries as Percent of All Trips, 1542–1562

Dordrecht	Haarlem	Delft	Leiden	Amsterdam	Gouda
43%	49%	46%	52%	43%	9%

The low figure for Gouda is due to the fact that this town dismissed its pensionary in 1545, apparently as an effort to save money. But all the other cities—even Leiden, which struggled the most with its debts—found it necessary to have two pensionaries on the payroll. The pensionary's growing importance in town life was part of a larger process of bureaucratization of urban institutions, visible somewhat earlier in the southern provinces of the Low Countries. Just as the pensionary's responsibilities expanded, men with the title "Meester," denoting a legal degree, began to appear more frequently on the magistrate rolls.[30] In the States of Holland, the elder statesmen were pensionaries like Leiden's Meester Jacob de Milde who attended 196 meetings during this period or Haarlem's Meester Lambrecht Jacobszoon who attended 181. These men were still employees of their town governments—only Amsterdam's Meester Adriaan Sandelijn seems to have become a member of the *vroedschap*, while still serving as pensionary[31]—but their counsel cannot have been without influence in shaping the instructions on which they acted in the States.

If there were two deputies, one would likely be the pensionary, and the other a member of the college of burgomasters. It often happened that the same burgomaster attended several meetings in a row, and in some cities, like Amsterdam, the college of (four) burgomasters rotated by quarter in attending the *dagvaarten*.[32] The burgomaster could be accompanied by one of his colleagues, or by a member of the *vroedschap* or of the college of *schepenen*, but the deputation of these lesser officials seems to have become less common over time. As a rule, the magistrates who most often represented their towns were the ones most frequently elected burgomaster. Among the six great cities, there were notable differences in the degree to which the responsibility of serving as deputies was concentrated among a few individuals. It should be reiterated that government in all these towns was oligarchical: membership in the *vroedschap* was for life, and a man was usually not elected burgomaster unless he was also a member of the *vroedschap*. Nonetheless, there are various indices of representation at the *dagvaarten* which suggest that the formation of an oligarchy-within-the-oligarchy was more advanced in some towns than others. The following table compares the six cities in terms of (a) the total number of trips by magistrates, not counting pensionaries; (b) the number of magistrates who served as deputies; (c) the average number of trips per magistrate deputy; and (d) the trips by the five magistrates most often chosen as deputies, as a percentage of all trips by magistrates. Towns are ranked according to their place in the last column, which is the sum of each town's ranking in the other four columns.[33]

Table 5. Magistrate Deputies at *Dagvaarten,* 1542–1562

	Number of Trips	Number of Deputies	Average Number of Trips	Percent of Trips by Top Five Magistrates	Sum of Rankings
Amsterdam	322	26	12.4	58%	7
Gouda	434	42	10.3	65%	9
Dordrecht	322	30	10.7	57%	10
Leiden	245	34	7.2	60%	15
Delft	299	42	7.1	43%	19
Haarlem	246	42	5.9	45%	20

Gouda's high ranking in the fourth column is due to nearly constant attendance at the *dagvaarten* by just a few men. Jan Dirkszoon Hoen, who attended 103 meetings, must have been Holland's most traveled magistrate. In 1546 Hoen was a leading brewer, with a total number of "brews" which ranked second among eighty-three practitioners of the city's most important trade. He began the first of his thirteen terms as burgomaster a few years later (1548–1565), and it was during this period that he also attended the *dagvaarten* including, at one stretch, twenty-eight consecutive meetings. Hoen seems to have made a career in politics, and the same might be said of Witte Aertszoon van der Hoeve (five times burgomaster, fifty-four *dagvaarten*), Jan Gerritszoon Hey Daems (sheriff from 1548 to 1552, forty-one *dagvaarten*), and Jan Willemszoon Moel (nine times burgomaster, thirty-five *dagvaarten*). Two of these four magistrates, Hoen and Hey Daems, were apparently the sons of men who had served multiple terms as burgomaster.[34] At the other end of the attendance scale, Gouda and Haarlem had a large number of men— nineteen—who attended only one meeting of the States; in Gouda, even a "Pieter Gerritszoon the priest" was called into service. One may infer that except for the few who were willing to make of it something like a profession, taking time for the business of the province was an unwelcome duty to be shared among as many men as possible.[35] But the assiduous attendance of these few men did not necessarily win Gouda an influential voice within the States. Gouda spoke last at the meetings, and the *vroedschap* resolutions for this period indicate a strategy of returning negative answers to *bede* requests as long as possible, until the consent of other towns left no choice. Christopher Hibben's fine study, *Gouda in Revolt,* shows a town which, left to its own devices, avoided innovation of all kinds like the very plague, a practice that seems to have been followed also during the Habsburg period.[36]

Dordrecht's leading deputies came from families distinguished in the service of the city or the Emperor. Arent Corneliszoon van der Mijle, who served twenty-one times as burgomaster between 1542 and 1572 and attended forty-eight *dagvaarten*, followed his father and grandfather in the same office. His first cousin once removed, Damas Philipszoon, was town treasurer for fourteen years and a frequent attender of *dagvaarten* in the previous generation, and this man's nephew, Wouter Barthoutszoon, a participant in twenty-four *dagvaarten*, was Van der Mijle's contemporary in the magistracy. Pieter Jacobszoon Muys was something of an exception, since after a great flood in 1423 his family had moved to the smaller town of Schiedam where they provided two generations of burgomasters, until Pieter Jacobszoon returned to Dordrecht where he was *schepen* sixteen times (1539–1568) and attended forty *dagvaarten*. Jacob Oom came from a family whose members had been magistrates in Dordrecht since the 1380s; he was among the twenty children of a late fifteenth-century burgomaster, served in that capacity himself in 1556 and 1558, and attended thirty-three *dagvaarten*. Heyman Adriaanszoon van Blijenburgh served as sheriff and burgomaster, was treasurer for seventeen years and a participant at thirty-one *dagvaarten*. Descended from the lesser nobility in the thirteenth century, his ancestors included a leading burgomaster and a military commander of the fifteenth century. As a final example, Willem Blasius Bucquet, the son of Charles V's Master of the Mint at Dordrecht, attended thirty *dagvaarten*.[37] This sort of linkage between magistrates and comital officials—including the sheriff, who also appeared often at *dagvaarten*—was noticeable in Dordrecht; one is reminded of the fact that while tenacious in asserting its own privileges, this city was usually more willing than the others to grant what was asked by the prince.[38]

Among delegations from the six great cities, Dordrecht's deputies were the most tinged with blue blood, Gouda's and Amsterdam's the least.[39] Delft, along with Haarlem and Leiden, falls somewhere in between. For Delft, a chance survival of lists of potential officeholders in 1553 provides some clues as to the business interests of leading deputies to the States. Jan Sasbout Dirkszoon, a participant at forty-four *dagvaarten* and a burgomaster twenty-four times between 1532 and 1562, is identified as "rentenier, formerly a brewer." As with the equivalent French term, a *rentenier* was in the first instance an investor in land.[40] Jan Dirk Herpertszoon, burgomaster twice in the 1550s who attended twenty-five *dagvaarten*, was also a *rentenier*, but still did "some business as a merchant." A bit farther down the attendance list, the same description was given for Huygh de Groot, a participant at sixteen *dagvaarten*, who served eight times as burgomaster. De Groot's father had been burgomaster fourteen times, and his grandson was the famous Hugo Grotius. Although not mentioned in the 1553 lists, Cornelis Janszoon Cruyser attended twenty *dagvaarten* and served as burgomaster four times between 1558 and 1561. Frans Duyst van Voorhout, a member of an important clan that combined city magistrates, farmers of comital domain revenue, and lesser nobles, was four times burgomaster in the 1560s and a deputy at twenty meetings; earlier, he was a *rentenier* and served as Bailiff for the rural district of Delfland. Michiel Janszoon Camerling, who was at twenty *dagvaaarten*, was the only "brewer" among Delft's leading deputies even though this industry was still of great importance for the city.[41]

For present purposes, the "sum of Rankings" (table 5) among urban delegations to the States suggests a particularly interesting contrast between the neighboring cities of Amsterdam and Haarlem. To begin with, Amsterdam's college of four burgomasters was somewhat more independent of other magistracies than were their counterparts in other cities. In Amsterdam, three new burgomasters were chosen each year by the "old council," which consisted of all former burgomasters and *schepenen,* and which had no other function besides this election. The three new burgomasters then chose an "old burgomaster" from among their retiring colleagues. By contrast, in Haarlem and in Leiden, burgomasters were elected by the *vroedschap,* in conjunction with the outgoing *gerecht* (burgomasters and *schepenen).*[42] Accordingly, Amsterdam's executive college had less need to report to the larger *vroedschap.* Thus Haarlem's *vroedschap* received detailed reports on what was discussed at each *dagvaart,* and it was the *vroedschap* that decided how to proceed. In Amsterdam, the *vroedschap* assumed this role only in time of crisis, as in 1542, when the city was being forced to surrender its practice of selling "apart" when *renten* were issued by the States.[43]

As one might expect in these circumstances, Haarlem's magistrates made fewer trips to the *dagvaarten* then their colleagues in other cities, and the few who went frequently still travelled less often than leading magistrates elsewhere. Burgomaster Joost van Hillegom was the leader with twenty-eight trips, and Meester Gerrit Hendrikszoon van Ravensberg, a frequent burgomaster after 1557, had twenty-three. In Amsterdam, however, the strong college of burgomasters became the focal point for a series of ruling factions. S. A. C. Dudok van Heel has shown that for periods of roughly forty years, the college of burgomasters was effectively controlled by successive groups, each consisting of a small number of interrelated families.[44] Between 1535 and 1538, in the wake of an armed uprising by revolutionary Anabaptists, the ruling faction that included Ruysch Janszoon and Cornelis Bennink was replaced by another led by Meester Hendrik Dirkszoon, which came to be

known as the "Dirkisten." The Dirkisten then remained in
power until 1578, though not without provoking serious internal opposition, resulting in the *Doleantie* which seventy burghers submitted to the central government in 1564, and which
will be discussed in Chapter 7. What is of interest here is that
the five men whom the *Doleantie* accused of concentrating
power in their hands were with one exception the same men
who represented Amsterdam most often at the *dagvaarten*, as
the following table shows:[45]

Table 6. Amsterdam Burgomasters and Deputies, 1542–1562

	Number of Times as Deputy	Terms as Burgomaster	Named in 1564 Doleantie
Pieter Kantert Willemszoon	59	12	yes
Joost Sijbrandszoon Buyck	44	8	yes
Meester Hendrik Dirkszoon	35	10	yes
Dirk Hillebrandszoon Otter	27	7	yes
Klaas Doedeszoon	23	7	no
Sijbrand Poppiuszoon Occo	14	4	yes
Klaas Gerrit Mattheuszoon	12	5	no

During the twenty-one-year period in question, these seven
men filled sixty-three percent of the possible slots as burgomaster and made sixty-six percent of the trips to *dagvaarten* by
all Amsterdam magistrates. Certainly in this case, frequency of
attendance at the meetings of the States reflected a comparable measure of influence in the councils of government at
home.

Among buyers of Holland *renten* after 1542, men invested
more than women did; and town magistrates, together with
Habsburg officials in The Hague, invested significantly more
than did other men.[46] If one makes a further distinction between magistrates in general and those who were prominent as

magistrate-deputies to the States, it is clear that the latter were especially noteworthy as buyers of Holland *renten*. As a rule, the magistrates who attended *dagvaarten* were more likely to purchase *renten* than their stay-at-home colleagues. In the following table, magistrate-deputies are first treated as part of the general class of magistrates, then for the two cities where the largest purchases were made, they are separated from their colleagues who were magistrates but not deputies. For this purpose, calculations are limited to the period 1553–1562, since magistrates were sometimes forced to buy *renten* before 1553.[47]

Table 7*a*. *Renten* Purchases (in pounds) by Burghers of the Six Cities, 1553–1562

	Buyers	Total Purchases	Average Purchase
Deputies	48	107,881	2,248
All magistrates	105	171,369	1,632
Other laymen	417	206,137	494

Table 7*b*. *Renten* Purchases by Magistrates in Amsterdam and Delft, 1553–1562

	Buyers	Total Purchases	Average Purchase
Deputy-magistrates	24	64,705	2,696
Other magistrates	36	49,996	1,389

Moreover, those magistrates who attended the *dagvaarten* most frequently were likely to be the largest investors. During the period in question, twenty-eight men appeared twenty times or more as deputies; of this number, sixteen bought *renten*, for a total of 54,408, or an average of about 3,400. By far the largest buyer of Holland *renten* was Gerrit Hendrikszoon van Ravensberg (22,568), who appeared twenty-three times as a deputy for

Haarlem. His purchases are excluded from the following table, so as not to skew the results:

Table 8. *Renten* Purchases by Deputies, 1553–1562

	Number of Deputies	Number of Buyers	Total Purchases	Average Purchase
Amsterdam	24	12	31,542	2,629
Gouda	31	10	7,526	753
Dordrecht	21	5	8,308	1,662
Leiden	24	3	1,332	444
Delft	28	16	33,253	2,078
Haarlem	27	5	3,352	670

The cities that stand out in this summary are Amsterdam and especially the smaller and less wealthy Delft, where magistrates as well as deputies had a quite unusual appetite for *renten*.[48]

In sum, the closer one gets to what may be described as an elite among the deputies, the more one finds men who invest impressive amounts of their own money in the new debt that they themselves managed as deputies to the States. The fact that these men were withdrawing funds from other unspecified uses and putting them into *renten* has both an economic and a social meaning. There was surely some disinvestment from productive activities, though not so much as one might think, because many investors bought *renten* as a means of providing security to their children; for this purpose the most obvious alternatives were other kinds of *renten*, like those which town governments issued for their own purposes.[49] Where there was disinvestment, it seems more likely to have occurred in declining industries, less so in the vigorous commercial sector or among men active in land reclamation projects. One must also take seriously the possibility that men who devoted as much time as many deputies did to affairs of state were choosing a manner of life rather than a form of investment. One could become a politician in the same sense that one might become, for instance, a farmer of government revenues. In either case, money invested in Holland *renten* was safe and probably of some political benefit. In his study of Florentine patricians of the early fifteenth century, Gene Brucker finds that leading magistrates were set apart from other Florentines not by their wealth or their business interests, but by a conscious choice to devote themselves to the affairs of the city, a choice reflected also in exhortations to invest in the public debt.[50] Holland's patricians have not left for posterity a record of their thoughts that might compare with the *pratiche* of Renaissance Florence. Nonetheless, one may reasonably credit them with the same variable combination of *amour propre* and civic-mindedness that always has drawn men to politics.

The social importance of *renten*-buying by the deputies is that this form of investment was part of a larger process by which leading patrician families became assimilated to the lower ranks of Habsburg officialdom. If one defines the boundaries of social groups by a combination of intermarriage, shared occupational interests, and shared investment habits, it seems that government officials and town magistrates were in the process of fusing together as an office-holding elite, whereas Holland's traditional noble families remained sharply distinct from both. The men who served the Emperor at the Hof van Holland in The Hague (and their womenfolk) were the largest per-capita purchasers of Holland *renten* all through the reign of Charles V. By contrast, nobles were prominent among buyers for the first series of Holland *renten* between 1515 and 1533, but not for the second series, especially after the practice of constraining wealthy Hollanders to buy was dropped in 1553.[51] Henk van Nierop shows that, after about 1550, nobles were also withdrawing from their traditional share of comital offices in The Hague. (The fact that nobles were often leading investors in the reclamation projects that gained momentum about this time could help to account for both tendencies.)[52]

Much of the prosopographical work for Holland's official families remains to be done, but it will likely be found that vacancies left by the nobles were filled from patrician families like the Sasbouts of Delft and the De Jonges of Dordrecht, many of whom continued to be represented at city hall as well as at the Hof van Holland. Delft's leading deputy to the States during the period discussed above was the prominent burgomaster, Jan Sasbout; his brother Joost Sasbout had been Councillor Ordinary in the Council of Holland until 1543, and his son Jan Janszoon Sasbout, also a magistrate, was Delft's second-leading buyer of Holland *renten*.[53] One son of Dordrecht's Arent Corneliszoon van der Mijle became Castellan of Gouda, and another became President of the Council of Holland.[54] As for intermarriage, Holland's nobles maintained their distance from commoners, as Van Nierop's discussion of endogamy shows, but official and magistrate families regularly contracted marriage connections, as if among social equals. In Haarlem, Meester Gerrit Hendrikszoon van Ravensberg, the leading investor in Holland *renten*, was married to a daughter of Meester Vincent Corneliszoon van Mierop of the Council of Finance.[55] In Dordrecht, the second wife of Heyman Adriaanszoon van Blijenburgh was a daughter of Meester Vincent van Droogendijk, Auditor in the Chamber of Accounts; Blijenburgh's second cousin, the prominent city treasurer, Damas Philipszoon, was married to a daughter of a Councillor of Friesland.[56] In Amsterdam, two of Meester Hendrik Dirkszoon's sons married daughters of Meester Reynier Brunt, the Procurator-General (chief prosecutor) at the Court of Holland.[57]

The men who represented their cities most often at the *dagvaarten*, and the men who represented the sovereign in Holland, were thus drawing closer together. Those trained in the law—like most officials and an increasing number of magistrates—were used to representing conflicting interests in a way that need not entail personal animosity. Furthermore, officials based in Holland were usually natives of the province and habitually remonstrated with their superiors in Brussels over instructions they deemed contrary to Holland's interests. Hence deputies could be at ease with the "lords" who spoke for the prince, because both parties shared important common goals, such as the protection of Holland's grain trade.[58] Finally, the deputies were by way of becoming lords themselves; they contracted for a vast new debt; they funded it by levying taxes as they saw fit; and for enforcing collection of these taxes, they had at their disposal the full judicial apparatus of the Hof van Holland.[59] Appropriately enough, it was near the end of Charles V's reign that the deputies began to style themselves *mogende heren,* or "mighty lords."

ALLOCATION OF HOLLAND'S FISCAL BURDEN

In their capacity as "mighty lords," the deputies decreed unprecedented levels of taxation that fell most heavily on the peasants and on urban commoners. In order to understand why the fiscal burden was allocated in this way, it will be helpful to look first at two categories of property that for political reasons could not be taxed: 1) towns and rural districts lying within feudal enclaves held by the more important nobles; and 2) the commercial wealth of the towns.

Feudal Enclaves

In Holland, as elsewhere, the clergy had privileges that the States attacked repeatedly and with some success, but ecclesiastical wealth could not be more than a secondary issue in a province which had few important monasteries and where land owned by ecclesiastical corporations seldom exceeded ten percent in any given village. The same might be said of the personal privileges of the nobility, for Holland's 200 noble families, though important as landholders, were not a dominant presence in the economy of a province that in 1514 had an estimated population of 275,000.[60] Instead, the major obstacle to any equitable system of taxation in Holland was the private jurisdiction of the great lords. *Morgental* accounts from the middle decades of the sixteenth century suggest a total of about 300,000 *morgen* of land in Holland (1,055 square miles), of which approximately twelve percent consisted of lands "outside the *schiltal*"—that is, they were not liable to the *beden* because they were part of feudal enclaves.[61] In addition, the Count of Egmont, whose nine villages in Kennemerland had been assessed for 3.15 percent of the *schiltal* valuation in 1514, was granted a privilege in 1522 exempting these lands from all future *beden,* provided only that he and his heirs paid the trea-

sury 800 pounds a year.[62] Roughly speaking, then, fifteen percent of the landed wealth in Holland lay beyond the tax collector's reach. Private lords also controlled seven small towns
located in Holland's southeastern corner.[63] The sovereign or his
Regent claimed on occasion to draw on a reserve of power
(*potestas absoluta*) in order to "derogate from" or overturn privileges deemed contrary to the general good. This authority was
sometimes used against the towns,[64] and deputies to the States
could not understand why it might not also be used against the
holders of feudal enclaves, especially for forms of taxation not
based on the *schiltal.*

Yet the Habsburg state in the Netherlands was founded on
the cooperation of the great nobles who in their capacities as
Stadtholders and military commanders were expected to help
maintain the loyalty and obedience of the provinces where their
own lands were concentrated. Only a few men had this kind of
status in Holland. Floris van IJsselstein (d. 1539) and his son
and successor as Count of Buren, Maximiliaan van Egmont
(d. 1551); Lamoraal van Egmont, son of Jan IV, Count of Egmont; Reinout van Brederode (d. 1556), and his son and successor Hendrik; members of the Nassau family, including Hendrik
(d. 1538), his son Reynier, who died in the Emperor's campaign
in the Rhineland (1544), and their distant cousin Wilhelm
(henceforth William of Orange), who came from his German
homeland to claim Reynier's inheritance and acquired important holdings in Holland by marrying the heiress of Maximiliaan van Egmont; and, finally, Philippe de Montmorency,
Count of Hornes, who married into the other branch of the
Egmont family.[65] The importance that Charles V attached to
such men may be gauged from his patient and detailed correspondence with the young Reynier van Nassau, who briefly succeeded Hoogstraten as Stadtholder of Holland.[66] When Charles
V was dangerously isolated at Regensburg just before the beginning of the first Schmalkaldic War, it was Maximiliaan van Egmont who led a Netherlands army across Protestant Germany to
bring him support (1546).[67] Since the same men controlled much
of the land in Holland's feudal enclaves, efforts by the States to
have these areas taxed faced a formidable political obstacle.

The issue was of long standing,[68] but became acute in the

1540s when new forms of taxation were introduced and the previously exempt lands were supposed to be included. Since the States doubted that money would actually be collected in these areas, they inserted in their acts of consent to the new *beden* clauses providing that the rest of Holland would not be liable for sums not paid by the *pretense vryen* or "self-styled free" lords.[69] There are occasional references to sums being paid, either by voluntary agreement with a particular lord, or by time-honored methods of constraint (placing local magistrates under arrest). In fact, between 1543 and 1556, a total of 98,598 pounds was collected from lands held by the "three personages" most prominent among Holland's exempt lords: William of Orange, Count Lamoraal of Egmont, and the Count of Hoorn. It is equally clear, however, that these great men waged a stubborn legal battle to maintain their privileges intact and never permitted their subjects to surrender a stuiver, except under protest.[70] For example, when the magistrates of Maximiliaan van Egmont's town of Leerdam refused to pay the tenth penny on real property and *renten* income, the Council of Holland had them placed under house arrest in The Hague. But the Count of Buren, "neglecting his government" (as Stadtholder of Friesland), came to The Hague and insisted on sharing the fate of his loyal subjects. The Council, fearing reproach, let everyone go.[71]

The Grand Council of Mechelen issued a "provisional verdict" condemning those who claimed exemption to pay what was asked, pending a final resolution of the validity of their claims. After the death of Maximiliaan van Egmont (1551), William of Orange pursued his late father-in-law's claims before the Grand Council, as did the Count of Hornes. The States expected their case before the Council to be defended by Holland's Procurator General, but this official seemed unwilling to go against the great lords, despite an admonition from the Emperor.[72] In April 1553, the States consented to a tenth penny on real property income, as part of an *extraordinaris bede* of 300,000 pounds. In November, Holland's delegates sought the help of Viglius Zuichemius van Aytta, Schore's successor as President of the Secret Council. The act of consent for the 300,000-pound *bede* stated that the Emperor agreed to a "derogation *de motu proprio*" from any privileges that might obstruct the collection of the tenth penny from all persons of whatever condition. Thinking this clause might not be sufficient, the Hollanders wanted a *derogatie particulier* naming the Count of Egmont by name, but Viglius said the Emperor would never grant such a thing without giving Lamoraal van Egmont a hearing. He did admit that the Egmont privilege of 1522 applied only for *beden* collected by the *schiltal*, not for all *beden*. By the end of Charles V's reign, the nobles in the States were taking the same line as the towns, suggesting that *gratie* for *beden* collected by the *schiltal* should be made up from the exempt areas, but the issue was still in doubt.[73]

It thus became a question for Philip II, the new King of Spain and Count of Holland, who came to the Netherlands in late 1555 to take charge of the campaign against France. By August 1556 the States must have had an inkling how the King would decide, since calculations were being made as to how much would have to be returned to the "three personages" if their claims were vindicated. On 7 September, Philip announced that Orange, Hornes, and Lamoraal van Egmont were absolved of all *bede* liabilites past or future. Counting sums that had to be repaid as well as sums that were never collected, the total loss to the King's treasury was reckoned at 190,000 pounds.[74] Even so, it might have been a small sum to pay for the friendship and loyalty of such important men, were it not one of the ironies of Low Countries history that these three personages would become, in the King's mind, his great enemies. Twelve years later, Orange was in exile, leading a fledgling revolt; Hoorn and Egmont, protesting their loyalty to Philip, had been placed under arrest by the iron-fisted Duke of Alba and were beheaded in the Groote Markt of Brussels.

Commercial Wealth

In general, the government's efforts to tax Holland's commerce were not much more successful than its attempts to impose a *congie* on the re-export of Baltic grain (see chap. 4). The new taxes introduced in 1543 included a hundredth penny on the value of all goods exported from the Netherlands and a tenth penny on commercial profits. But Holland resisted both, apparently more so than the other provinces did. Mary of Hungary had to impose the hundredth penny "ex potestate absoluta Imperatoris" ("by the Emperor's absolute power") because the States would not accept it; even then, the edict was not published in Holland for some months, and when it was, Amsterdam's port officials refused to cooperate with the collector.[75] Holland was also the only province to insist on modifying the tenth penny on commercial profits, to make it instead a tenth penny on the assumed profit (1:16) of mercantile inventory. More than six months after the States had agreed to the tax in this form, the Queen complained that it was still not being collected. By November 1545, only about 1,200 pounds had actually been collected from the tenth penny on mercantile inventory. The tenth penny on commercial profits was collected again in Flanders and Brabant,[76] but in Holland it was not even proposed to the States.

The next major effort to tax the activities of Holland's merchants came in 1549, in the form of a four-year tax on imported wine consumed in the Low Countries, a tax intended to pay for warships to patrol the North Sea.[77] From the start, the wine tax failed to live up to expectations. In July 1550, the first sailing season when the new system was to be in effect, the States were told that the promised warships had not materialized because there was as yet no revenue to pay for them. The tax-evading skills of wine importers in the Low Countries are suggested by the decline of receipts over the first two years as indicated in the following table:[78]

Table 9. Receipts (in pounds) from Wine Tax, 1550–1552

	In Holland	*From Other Provinces*
January 1550/1551	11,608	41,685
April 1550/1552	3,124	15,554

Receipts cannot have improved in subsequent years because war with France broke out again later in 1552. In August,

Viglius admitted to deputies from Holland that money collected on wine consumed in Holland would not fit out a single warship, "indeed, not even a *jacht*." (For purposes of comparison, it might be noted that the wine excise farm in Amsterdam yielded the city 6,960 pounds for 1552; but this levy the farmer could recoup by collecting from tavern keepers, not from wine merchants.) After four years, a summary of the wine tax accounts shows a net deficit in excess of 59,000 pounds, representing sums borrowed that were not covered by the receipts.[79]

Combining all efforts to tax what one treasury official called "the great and excessive monopolies that merchants practice," it seems that roughly 40,000 pounds were collected in Holland between 1543 and 1554. During the same twelve years, Holland's net *bede* contributions, not counting deductions for *gratie* and *renten* interest, amounted to 2,235,705 pounds. In other words, direct taxes on mercantile activity (not counting what was paid for commercial properties in the tenth pennies on real estate) yielded a sum equal to only 1.8 percent of the taxes collected in Holland.[80]

In the absence of tax records from other provinces, one cannot tell if, for example, Flanders and Brabant were any different, but there are indications that Holland was peculiarly stubborn in fighting off taxes in commerce. If so, it was no doubt because the States of this province were so composed as to provide no real counterweight to the influence of the cities with voting rights. The States of Brabant had a clerical first estate,[81] as well as an influential noble estate; in the all-important third estate of the States of Flanders, known as the Four Members, one of the four votes was cast by the Franc of Bruges, a corporate entity representing the small towns and rural communities of West Flanders.[82] By contrast, the college of nobles in the States of Holland had only one of the seven votes. As for the six great cities, each had dominant economic interests, and the deputies who represented these towns, however their own wealth may have been invested, were expected to uphold and defend these interests. Every town hall had a locked chest containing privileges granted by previous rulers, and if these were not sufficient to fend off danger to a town's economic well-being, deputies in the States were expected to employ whatever arguments might work. For example, "free trade" could be defended by citing arguments from "natural law" or by adducing the practical experience of towns that prospered by allowing foreigners to trade without restrictions.[83] Some of these discussions in the States, if studied more closely, might be of considerable interest for historians of economic thought; but the point here is that Holland's urban deputies, by a combination of legal reasoning, judicious bribes, and plain stubbornness, were just as successful as the great lords were in shunting the burden of taxation off onto someone else.

Since money had to be gotten somehow and could not be obtained either from the merchants or from the feudal enclaves, one obvious alternative was to look more closely at taxes on land. In the 1515 *schiltal* assessment, Holland's rural areas were assigned only 42.25 percent of the *ordinaris bede*, whereas twenty-five cities, including the six great cities, were asked to pay 57.75 percent. In light of recent work on Holland's prosperous agrarian economy, the rural assessment seems low, and there could be some truth in claims made by urban deputies that the towns were given high quotas in 1515 to make up for the rebates they habitually received. From the accounts of levies of the tenth penny on *renten* and real property income, beginning in the 1540s, it seems the towns had only about thirty percent of such investment in Holland. To bring the urban share up to the percentage represented by the 1515 *schiltal* (57.75 percent), one might assume that characteristically urban assets (mercantile inventory, part-ownership shares in ships, etc.) amounted to nearly as much as all investments in the countryside, but this assumption seems unlikely.[84] If there was any initial imbalance in favor of the countryside, the States, dominated by the great cities, more than took care of it during Charles V's reign. Towns with voting rights steadily increased their own rebates, and pressure from the government to make good what was lost through rebates sometimes led to still higher burdens for country folk. To take but one example, in 1543 the States agreed to a 75,000-*schiltal* levy to be paid in the full amount, that is, with no deduction for *gratiën*. To gain the great cities' consent to this novelty, the government had to allow them the *gratie* they would have gotten if the face value of the levy were 100,000, or approximately 24,000, the amount that the countryside would have paid in a levy of 60,000. Hence to get the full 75,000, Holland's villages had to be assessed for quotas consistent with a levy of about 135,000, nearly twice as much as the sum to which the States had agreed. Noble deputies insisted that they had not consented to this nefarious scheme, and when village magistrates went to the town halls of Haarlem and Amsterdam for an explanation, "the burgomasters said, '[the collectors] are asking too much,' and they said nothing about their *gratiën*."[85]

Many of the *extraordinaris beden* to which the States consented after 1543 included a *morgental*, or a tenth penny on income from *renten* and rural property. By making a few assumptions,[86] one can construct a rough estimate of the portion of net *bede* income (after subtraction for rebates) collected from the countryside.

Table 10. Portions of Holland *Beden* Paid by Town and Country, 1543–1560

	Towns	Countryside	Total
Ordinaris bede (schiltal)	449,647	550,755	1,000,402
Extraordinaris bede (schiltal)	381,911	449,056	830,967
Tenth penny	147,222	339,784	487,006
Morgental	—	249,227	249,227
Totals	978,780	1,588,822	2,567,602

In other words, the proportionate real contribution of Holland's countryside (sixty-two percent) and towns (thirty-eight percent) was almost exactly the reverse of what both were assessed in the *schiltal* of 1515—that is, forty-two percent and fifty-eight percent, respectively.

Taxing the land more heavily was not altogether unreasonable, in light of indications that there was a new impetus for reclamation projects after about 1550. *Morgental* accounts show new land being added outside the dikes,[87] and there was also considerable investment in the building of sturdy new dikes and retaining walls at sensitive points. At Hondsbosch (Petten), north of Haarlem, such a dike was constructed to guard newly reclaimed land in the Zijpe polder, and the important sluice at Sparendam was rebuilt for the first time in stone in 1566. The technique for draining inland lakes by attaching pumps to windmills, although not used extensively until after 1600, was also developed during these years. Even apart from improvement of the land, the spread of a new type of mixed farming, described by Jan De Vries, made the coastal regions of the northern Netherlands attractive to investors from the wealthier and more urbanized provinces to the south.[88] Major investors included members of the great nobility, both in Holland[89] and in the southern Netherlands, as well as Antwerp merchants[90] and Holland magistrates. For example, Heyman Jacobszoon van Ouder Amstel, burgomaster and sheriff of Amsterdam during the 1530s, made extensive purchases of domain land put up for sale.[91] Among those who controlled Amsterdam's college of burgomasters during the 1540s and 1550s, Dirk Hillebrandszoon Otter owned fishing rights near Edam, and Joost Buyck and Geraard Klaaszoon Mattheus were said to be the only non-local owners of land near the village of Egmond Binnen.[92]

In the taxation of land, the important question was whether the "mighty lords" of the States were taxing wealth-holders like themselves, or the peasants who were their leaseholders, and their debtors on the private *renten* market.[93] In this respect, there was an important difference between the *morgental* and the tenth penny. In collections of the tenth penny, the owner was usually expected to pay two-thirds; the "user," only one third. In practice, the peasant paid the collector the full ten percent that was due and then recovered two-thirds of the amount by deducting it from what he owed his landlord or his *rentenier*. By contrast, the *morgental* in Holland was collected "at the burden of the user." Used periodically, the tenth-penny tax raised large sums, but the *morgental* became the more regular feature of the new taxation system, especially for the purpose of keeping up annual interest payments on the *renten* debt created after 1542.[94]

As for the towns, the most practical way[95] to extract more revenue (as distinct from investment, in the form of *renten* purchases) was to create provincial excises to go with the *accijnsen* that towns had been collecting from their inhabitants for centuries. Traditionally, a wealthy town like Amsterdam paid its *bede* quotas directly from *accijns* revenue, whereas a poor town like Leiden depended on *accijnsen* to fund the town *renten* it made its burghers purchase in order to meet its *bede* quota. Since higher excise taxes had been known to cause riots in Low Countries towns, magistrates were not eager to see provincial excises added on top of their own.[96] When the States agreed to an "impost" on beer and wine to help fund *renten,* the rate was only two stuivers per barrel of domestic beer. By contrast, as of 1520, Leiden was charging its inhabitants eight stuivers per barrel, whereas Haarlem charged ten.[97] In the 1550s, the cities still collected considerably more from beer drinkers than the province did:[98]

Table 11. Beer Excise Income for 1556

	Urban	Provincial
Amsterdam	42,156	8,940
Leiden	9,727	3,300

In theory, provincial excise taxes were supposed to be paid by everyone, but whether privileged persons in fact paid them is not clear. Members of the Council of Holland certainly did not,[99] and no doubt most of the money came from ordinary consumers. It was thus the urban commons, along with the peasantry, who funded annual interest payments on States of Holland *renten* held by patrician investors.

The inequity of this arrangement, apparent to contemporaries, did not pass without discussion in the States and in the correspondence of government officials. A deputy from Rotterdam, complaining of how the small cities were "deceived" when their quotas were set higher to make up for the rebates of others, told the great cities that "they could all go to a thousand devils." Even those who benefited from *gratie* acknowledged it to be "an ungodly thing." The men of Delft went so far as to suggest that because of *gratie* "God decrees that this land remain burdened by wars."[100] But none of the other cities took Delft's complaints very seriously because everyone knew that Delft had the highest quota in the *schiltal* of 1515, and thus had the most reason for seeking a new basis for taxation. In fact, any pleas for greater justice in the allocation of burdens could be interpreted as special pleading.[101] Each party to the discussion had a clear vision of the inequity of all special exemptions—except its own, which were of course based on immemorial privileges from the ruler or sanctioned by "natural law" or both. Government officials, from Meester Vincent Corneliszoon to Mary of Hungary herself, were determined to have "equality" in taxation, yet Viglius would not oppose the exemptions enjoyed by his friends and colleagues in the Council of Holland.[102] Everyone agreed that some ways of raising new revenue might be more fair than others. For example, Delft's deputies invoked the authority of the New Testament and the "Emperor Octavian" on behalf of a province–wide *capitale impositie*, or one percent capital levy of the kind that towns commonly imposed on their own burghers.[103] Yet everyone recognized that, as the Council of Holland once commented, if such a proposal was indeed "fairest," it was also hard to achieve; for without the spirit of community still expected to prevail within town walls, who would estimate the value of his own property correctly?[104]

One might well wonder why ordinary Hollanders did not rebel against an increasingly heavy burden of taxation widely perceived as unfair. Representing the authority of the Habsburg state, the Council of Holland worried a good deal about potential rebelliousness among the peasants, especially in Holland north of the IJ where memory of late medieval peasant rebellions may have lingered.[105] Members of the Council knew about the "Bread and Cheese" uprising in this region in the 1490s, and they may have known about the local Receiver for the *beden* who was murdered in 1497 by the villagers of Callants Oog, north of Alkmaar—a crime that had never been pun-

ished.[106] Thus in January 1537, Assendelft warned Hoogstraten that it might cause a revolt if there was yet another
extraordinaris bede in which the cities received *gratie* but the countryside did not. In May 1544, the Council told the Queen that
"the common folk will murmur" at the *extraordinaris bede* (described above) in which village quotas were set nearly twice as
high as they should have been for the face value of the subsidy.[107] As for the "mighty lords" of the States, they surely understood that their standing in the eyes of the government derived from the fact that they were perceived as representing, in
a milder and more manageable form, the anger and ill humor
of the populace. Could they retain the trust of the "common
man," as they increasingly took on the functions and attributes
of a government whose motives remained deeply suspect? The
truth is that their authority, like that of the government, hung
by slender threads of tradition and grudging obedience.

6

"NO MORE FOR THE BUTCHER'S BLOCK": HABSBURG HERESY LAWS AND HOLLAND'S TOWNS

The enforcement in Holland of the government's heresy laws time and again provoked legal and constitutional conflicts. More often than not, these conflicts pitted the magistrates of individual towns against Habsburg officials, especially Stadtholder Hoogstraten (1522–1540) and the Council of Holland. The States entered the discussion only at times when it seemed that the privileges of all towns were endangered by the government's actions. Yet the importance of these occasions is not to be measured solely by their frequency, for it was, as much as anything else, the perception of common threats to their privileges which brought Holland's towns together in the decades prior to the Revolt.

From previous discussion,[1] it will be apparent that efforts to curtail the economic privileges of a town like Amsterdam or Haarlem could easily provoke a riot. The threats that Charles V's heresy laws posed for burghers[2] of these towns were, potentially, even more explosive. It was not that Protestants were numerous in Holland before the Revolt. Luther's disciples in Holland were mostly driven out by the persecution of the 1520s, as were the "sacramentarians"[3] who denied the Real Presence of Christ in the Eucharist. The Anabaptists of the 1530s were strong in numbers, but among them only the followers of Menno Simons survived the downfall of the revolutionary Anabaptist kingdom of Münster in nearby Westphalia. Calvinism was destined to rule in Holland, but its beginnings here cannot be traced before 1566, and its adherents were still a tiny minority when they assumed leadership of the Revolt in 1572. The government's real problem was that there were large numbers of Catholics who viewed its legislation regarding heresy not only as an infringement on town privileges, but also as a means of propping up the hated privileges of the clergy.

As in other parts of Europe, the late Middle Ages in the Low Countries witnessed an extraordinary efflorescence of lay piety. Almost every major Low Countries town had its *beguinage* or *baghijnhof*, an enclosed courtyard for a religious community of women who took no vows and could return to private life whenever they wished.[4] The Brethren and Sisters of the Common Life, founded in Overijssel in the late fourteenth century, were another distinctive feature of this region; they too took no vows although they had close connections with certain monastic congregations.[5] Lay piety was expressed also in good works, many of them carried out under the aegis of civic responsibility. Characteristic of the Low Countries are the enclosed courtyards or *hofjes* for the use of the poor, of which the earliest surviving examples in Holland or Utrecht date from the fifteenth century.[6] Other urban charitable foundations, each with its lay board of male or female directors, included hospitals, homes for the aged poor, and endowments created for the purpose of distributing food to the poor who lived at home.[7] Every church had its board of *kerkmeesteren*, or churchwardens, likewise appointed by the city government; and large urban parishes had separate bodies for particular purposes, as well as numerous confraternities centered on specific devotions.[8] For those who craved deeper spiritual nourishment there were various Netherlandish editions of parts of the Bible,[9] as well as devout literature emanating from circles influenced by the Brethren of the Common Life, like the celebrated *Imitation of Christ* (ca. 1426), and vernacular treatises offering guidance in the discipline of mystical prayer.[10] These various movements were not necessarily supported by a consciously lay theology, but there were popular preachers, like the Franciscan Jan Brugman, who excoriated the vices of the clergy in their sermons. If lay piety had its theoretician, it was surely Erasmus of Rotterdam, whose *Enchiridion Militis Christiani* (1503/1504) called for a spirituality based on devout reading of Scripture and the Fathers, not on monastic "ceremonies."[11]

The emancipation of lay religion from the tutelage of the clergy was encouraged by a deepening critique of the special privileges of the clerical estate. Just as the States of Holland attempted to subject clerical property to taxation,[12] legal battles arose in the towns, for example, to force cloisters to pay a share of the maintenance costs for town walls and fortifications.[13] Among several urban riots against excise taxes in the 1520s, it seems the most severe was at 's Hertogenbosch in Brabant where popular resentment was directed specifically against the members of a wealthy and exempt ecclesiastical corporation, the collegiate chapter of St. John's Church.[14] It was because of the tax exemptions enjoyed by cloisters that town councils in Holland struggled all through the fifteenth century to prevent the building of new cloisters within their walls, and with good reason. By the beginning of Charles V's reign, Amsterdam had within its walls nineteen cloisters—sixteen for women and three for men; thus, approximately one-third of the land area could not be taxed.[15] Guildsmen and laborers resented competition from cloistered religious who did not have to pay excise taxes for the materials they used, such as the cloth-weaving sisters of Leiden and Delft or the nuns of St. Barbara's convent in Amsterdam who did washing and starching.[16]

Given lingering conflicts of this sort and the large number of men and women supported by religious establishments of one kind or another,[17] it is easy to understand why Luther's teaching evoked an immediate and sympathetic response in Holland as in so many other places.[18] Yet it would be a serious mistake to think of lay religion of the pre-Reformation era as pointed only towards ideas that lay in the future. Holland had few Benedictine monasteries,[19] but it was thickly settled with communities of the newer religious orders, especially the Franciscan friars who had seventeen houses in the province, all but one of which joined the Observant or reform branch of the order founded in the late fifteenth century. Each friary had a *terminus* or boundary within which its members preached, and the wandering friars enjoyed great popularity as preachers during the fourteenth and fifteenth centuries. Many of the famous preachers of the era were Franciscans, including the above-mentioned Jan Brugman.[20] Lay imitation of the ritual observances of monks and friars, criticized by Erasmus, must have been popular, to judge from surviving books of hours of lay folk, as well as from the practice of having seven of the canonical hours (*zeven getijden*) sung in parish churches.[21] The fourteenth and fifteenth centuries were also an era of new miracles and pilgrimage sites, the well-springs of age-old popular devotion. In particular, a number of Eucharistic miracles were reported in the Low Countries,[22] including several like the one in Amsterdam in 1345 or 1346, in which a priest was said to have brought communion to a sick man who immediately vomited the host into the hearth fire where it was subsequently discovered intact and unharmed among the embers.

With permission from the Bishop of Utrecht, the city fathers built a pilgrimage chapel on the site, known as the Heilige Stede or Holy Place. By the sixteenth century the Heilige Stede was more richly endowed than the city's two parish churches combined. Devout Amsterdammers gathered in this church on Wednesday evenings to hear vespers sung by a select choir of priests.[23] Humanist priests and scholars, many of them friends of Erasmus, provided a more articulate defense of traditional religion. In Delft, Cornelis Muys delved into fourteenth-century sources to write a biography of the pious priest whose women followers had founded the convent of which he was chaplain. In Amsterdam, Alardus Amstelredamus sometimes preached at the Heilige Stede and wrote treatises celebrating the miracle that it commemorated.[24]

Amsterdam's religious history in the late fifteenth and early sixteenth century features a series of sharp conflicts between civic-minded opponents of clerical privilege and defenders of traditional devotion. In 1462, on behalf of his own congregation, the Observant Franciscans, the preacher Jan Brugman led a successful campaign to breach the city's ban on new cloisters.[25] Between 1496 and 1513, the *vroedschap* fought a long and ultimately futile battle to prevent the building of a convent for the Poor Clares, the female branch of the Franciscans, who were ardently supported by Imme van Diemen, wife of Jan Bennink, the Sheriff of Amsterdam from 1495 to 1509. In order to be able to remove Bennink as Sheriff, the city lent 2,000 pounds to Maximilian I and obtained in pawn his right of appointing the

Sheriff; but Bennink was subsequently appointed a Councillor Extraordinary of the Council of Holland, in which capacity his influence in behalf of the Poor Clares was brought successfully to bear.[26] Finally, in 1531, there was opposition to the city government's decision to build a cloth hall "on hallowed ground," that is, at the angle between the north transept and the nave of the Heilige Stede. On the night of 31 May, 300 women gathered at the site and heaved timbers into the foundation pit to obstruct further construction.[27] The four ringleaders were assessed large fines by the *gerecht* (city court), which they eventually had to pay, despite the fact that they had enough influence to obtain an audience with Charles V in Brussels.[28]

One must not assume a direct connection between these conflicts and those of the Reformation era; for example, in the 1530s, the elderly Jan Bennink was considered a leading backer of certain Amsterdam preachers whose orthodoxy was suspect.[29] There were, however, some elements of continuity. Many humanists (if not all) were critical of the wealth and power of the Church, and many turned up also among Luther's early disciples in Holland. There were no doubt a great many Hollanders, not just among the educated elite, who shared Erasmus's opinion, ca. 1520, that Luther's principal crime had been to strike "at the crown of the Pope, and the bellies of the monks."[30] On the other side, the mendicant friars who had been in the forefront of late medieval devotion were also Luther's staunchest foes and the principal targets of anti-clerical rioting; Amsterdam's Dirkist magistrates, who came to power in 1538 with the intention of dealing more sternly with heretics, were close kin of the leaders of the 1531 "women's uproar" at the Heilige Stede.[31] In a town like Amsterdam, then, the prevailing opinion held that the clergy were quite wealthy and quite powerful enough, without having the added protection that the Emperor's heresy laws afforded them; still, a smaller but influential segment of opinion was determined to defend the cherished traditions of late medieval Catholicism.

Heresy was interpreted by the government as treason against God, or *lèse-majesté divine*, meaning that, just as for ordinary treason, normal procedures did not apply and normal privileges had no validity. This implicit abrogation of their privileges the towns necessarily resisted, some more forcefully than others. Caught in the middle, the Council of Holland tried to obey the Regent's orders, while preserving its own sense of due process. In what follows, it will be convenient to consider this many-sided conflict over three successive periods: the government's repression of dissent in the 1520s, both before and after Charles V's efforts to establish a territorial inquisition were thwarted by resistance from the States of Holland; the revolutionary Anabaptist movement of the 1530s, which led the towns and the government to bury their differences only as long as was necessary to suppress what was seen as a danger to the social order; and continuing friction during the remainder of Charles V's reign, when the government's continuing determination to treat heresy as a deadly crime was widely at variance with the more tolerant views of the towns and the States.

REPRESSION OF DISSENT IN THE 1520S

In Worms, where the princes of the Empire showed an ominous sympathy for Luther's defiance, Charles V issued the first edict or *placard* that prescribed "loss of life and property" for any of his Netherlands subjects who dared to print Luther's books or even read them. All who violated the terms of the edict were said to be "liable to the charge of *laesa majestas* (treason) as well as my indignation and the penalties declared above" (8 May 1521). The notion of heresy as treason against God, *laesa majestas divina*, dated from the early thirteenth century and was roughly contemporaneous with the establishment of episcopal courts of inquisition for the prosecution of heresy under Pope Innocent III (d. 1215). This definition justified the contention—a novel one at the time—that heresy was like civil treason a crime punishable by death. Convicted heretics were thus "remanded to the secular arm" for execution since Church courts did not have power of life and death. In the sixteenth-century Netherlands, zealous Habsburg officials believed, as the Emperor had stated in his 1521 *placard*, that any privileges or ordinary legal procedures that stood in the way of prosecuting the crime of *lèse-majesté divine* must now be considered null and void.[32]

In April 1522 Charles gave a special commission for the prosecution of heresy in his Low Countries provinces to Meester Frans van der Hulst, a member of the Council of Brabant who had distinguished himself as a foe of clerical privilege. A few weeks later the same authority was given to Meester Joost Lauwerijns, President of the Grand Council of Mechelen. The commissioners were to be assisted by several clerical inquisitors, including the Carmelite friar Niklaas Baechem van Egmond. Just before sailing for Spain in May, Charles summoned Dordrecht's Meester Floris Oem van Wijngaerden, a friend of Hulst, and "expressly commanded" him, under oath, to combat the spread of heresy. Erasmus, a member of the theology faculty at Leuven through 1521, regarded Lauwerijns as a man of moderation, but viewed the other inquisitors (especially Baechem who once denounced Erasmus to his face from the pulpit of St. Peter's church in Antwerp[33]) as fanatics ready to attack every novelty as heresy.

In Holland, Hulst's first target seems to have been Cornelis Hoen, an advocate before the Court of Holland, known in Reformation history because of his Latin treatise proposing a symbolic interpretation of Jesus' words at the last supper, "This is my body," which may have had some influence on the Swiss Reformer, Ulrich Zwingli.[34] Hoen is said in one source to have been an "old man" in 1523. His humanist learning, praised by Erasmus, seems to be confirmed by a citation from St. Jerome's *Epistulae* in a legal opinion that he provided for Amsterdam (December 1522) concerning a man accused of homosexuality. Hoen's friends were outraged by his arrest in February 1523. Even the cautious Erasmus wrote to a friend in the household of Pope Adrian VI that Hoen was "a good man, as I understand," and that he was "called a heretic because he dared to argue with" the inquisitor, Niklaas Baechem.[35]

Not satisfied to have his man locked up in the Voorpoort of The Hague, the prison attached to the Hof van Holland, Hulst had Hoen brought under guard to St. Geertruidenberg, still in the county of Holland, but south of the Maas. This action provoked a "great hue and cry" in the States of Holland, owing to the privilege *de non evocando* by which Hollanders were exempt from trial outside the borders of the province, exception being made only for crimes reserved to the prince, like treason (*lèse-majesté*) and counterfeiting. This privilege, like some others, was

granted first to individual cities and then (1452) to the whole
province. Subsequently, the Great Privilege of 1477 reinforced
the judicial autonomy of the towns. Even if most of its provisions were officially withdrawn in 1494, it seems to have been
widely believed in Holland that no burgher would have to stand
trial except before his own town court, at least in the first instance. Thus even though St. Geertruidenberg was technically
still within the borders of the province, Hulst was seen as violating the privileges of Holland. To judge from Margaret of Austria's response, the petition from the States also alleged that
persons had in the past been tried for heresy before the Council
of Holland (meaning that heresy was not one of the reserved
cases in which the privilege did not apply), and that Hulst had
departed from the Emperor's commission by not associating
Joost Lauwerijns and a Councillor of Holland in his inquiries.
Margaret ordered that Hoen be brought back under guard to
The Hague, there to be questioned by Hulst, Lauwerijns, and
one of the Councillors of Holland.[36]

Shortly thereafter (June 1523), Hulst obtained for himself a
papal commission as inquisitor for the Netherlands, allowing
him to behave as if he were no longer bound by the limits of his
office as imperial commissioner for heresy. Even the Emperor,
stout foe of heresy though he was, agreed with Margaret that
Hulst should not be allowed to exercise his papal commission.[37]
But one night in early August, Oem van Wijngaerden, acting
under instructions from his friend Hulst, drew up in front of
the Voorpoort with a wagon and a band of armed men, intend-
ing to take Hoen and another prisoner to Gorinchem. He was
prevented from doing so because the prisoners lodged an appeal and the jailer refused to release them to Oem van
Wijngaerden. Once again a storm of protest was loosed in the
States. But from Gorinchem Hulst flung defiance at his enemies: his power was from the Pope, not the Emperor, and he
intended to prosecute offenses dating not just from the *placard*
accompanying his commission from Charles V (April 1522), but
from the papal bull excommunicating Luther (June 1521). In
the States, while Oem van Wijngaerden defended his actions as
a sworn servant of the Emperor and the Pope, Meester Huych
van den Eynde, pensionary of Delft, poured vitriol on the ab-

sent Hulst, "a bigamist, a murderer, and a traitor to the father-land." Margaret granted the States an *acte* stating that no one would be prosecuted for offenses prior to issuance of the Emperor's *placard;* Hulst claimed that this document was a forgery, and the States were not satisfied until the Audiencer, the head of Margaret's chancery, came in person to assure them of its genuineness. Meanwhile, Margaret had ordered Hulst to cease his activities in Holland altogether, and a few months later she persuaded Charles V to withdraw his commission.[38]

By inducing the Regent to remove Hulst, the States had won an important victory since Charles V would not again attempt to create a tribunal specifically for the purpose of prosecution for heresy. Instead, this task devolved to the secular courts at the provincial level and to the ecclesiastical courts. Holland lay within the diocese of Utrecht, and the diocesan "official" (prosecutor) occasionally did turn his attention to charges of heresy in Holland, but, in keeping with *de non evocando,* he was obliged to conduct his inquiries in Holland.[39] The real struggle was between the Council of Holland in The Hague and town governments determined to shield their burghers from unlawful prosecution.

Meanwhile, the Protestant movement had quickly spread beyond the narrow circle of clerics and scholars who were early converts to Luther's ideas. A. C. Duke finds in the sources for popular religious dissent in the 1520s "disconcertingly few references" to Luther's cardinal doctrine of justification by faith, but a real passion for Scripture in the vernacular: between 1522 and 1530 there were twenty-two Dutch editions of the New Testament including several translations from Luther's Bible. People met in one another's homes to read and pray over the Bible, although these meetings seem at first to have supplemented rather than replaced the mass.[40] Under pressure from the Council of Holland, towns passed laws banning secret conventicles of this kind, and offenses against these ordinances or against the Emperor's *placards* sometimes came before the town court or *gerecht,* consisting usually of up to seven *schepenen* and a few burgomasters, presided over by the sheriff. Punishments were similar to the less severe penalties customarily employed for crimes like blasphemy or disrespect to religion, such as participating in a procession or making a pilgrimage; more serious offenders would have to spend days or weeks locked in the town jail, on bread and water.[41]

By contrast to these traditional measures, the Council of Holland did not shrink from the death penalty provided for in Charles V's *placard* of 8 May 1521. During the 1520s, most people convicted of heresy by the Council were sentenced to exile or to the performance of ecclesiastical penance. But two particularly stubborn and articulate defenders of the new gospel were publicly burned at the stake in The Hague: the priest Jan Pistorius of Woerden (1525), and Wendelmoet Klaasdochter (1527), a housewife of Monnikendam. The courageous demeanor of both of these victims of the *placards* was vividly described in anonymously printed eyewitness accounts, which helped create the new literary genre of Netherlands Protestant martyrology.[42]

By contrast, the towns seemed in some cases unwilling to take any action against local dissidents. In April 1525 the Council summoned representatives of the towns to The Hague to discuss "the abuses of the Lutheran sect," which "grow worse from day to day, the longer it goes on"; the cities were "not doing their duty to correct the same, as an example to others," failing which they had better consider "how to excuse themselves before the Gracious Lady [Margaret of Austria]." A year later, Everaerts told Amsterdam's deputies of an interview in which Margaret described "Lutherye" in Holland—especially in Delft, Amsterdam, and Hoorn—as a worse threat than the Hoek and Kabeljauw wars had been, "beseeching me with tears in her eyes that we take action to remedy things."[43] Already in 1524 the Council had asked Sheriff Jan Hubrechtszoon of Amsterdam for a written explanation for his handling of certain heresy cases. The sheriff and magistrates of Monnikendam were also upbraided for their inaction in the face of repeated and reliable testimony on Lutheran activity among local clergy and laity. Even in Haarlem, which was not among the towns frequently mentioned as centers of heresy, the magistrates would neither "punish sufficiently" the burghers who attended conventicles, nor allow commissioners from The Hague to do so, alleging that this would be an infringement on their jurisdiction.[44]

As the last example suggests, one of the sources of friction between the towns and Charles V's provincial government in The Hague was a difference of opinioń over the Council of Holland's competence in cases of heresy. If those who offended against the Emperor's *placards* were indeed guilty of *laesa majestas,* then the Council had jurisdiction in the first instance, any and all privileges to the contráry notwithstanding. But if *de non evocando* guaranteed the burghers of each town the right to be tried only before their own *gerecht,* as the men of Haarlem argued during the debate over Frans van der Hulst, the Council had no right to summon to The Hague the burghers of Haarlem or any town to face heresy charges.[45] As was usual when vital questions of principle were at stake, neither side wanted to push the issue to a painful clarity.[46]

The most interesting case occurred in Amsterdam (December 1526) where "Jan Zijvertszoon the crippled book-seller" was found in possession of books forbidden by the *placards.* Sent to the Council in The Hague for instructions, Andries Jacobszoon was told that Amsterdam must follow the *placards,* according to which such an offense was punishable by death or at least exile. Instead, Amsterdam's *gerecht* sentenced Zijvertszoon to two months on bread and water in the St. Olaf's gate prison. The Council cancelled the verdict and took the unusual step of summoning to The Hague not only the accused, but also Amsterdam's college of *schepenen,* to explain why they had not punished him according to the *placards.*[47] Jacobszoon's travel journal shows that the city had prepared a careful defense against the summons, based on the fact that the *placard* of 1521 contained a conventional reference to "discretionary punishment" (*arbitrale correctie*), meaning that local courts could mitigate the prescribed penalties according to the circumstances of the case. No less a personage than Joost Lauwerijns, President of the Grand Council of Mechelen, had assured the Amsterdammers that their interpretation of the *placard* was correct in this respect.[48] But Everaerts and the Council in The Hague were not moved by these arguments, partly because they had evidence that the *schepenen* would have punished Zijvertszoon according to the *placard,* had it not been for the intervention of the burgomasters then sitting with the *gerecht.* Jacobzoon and one of the burgomasters then went to Mechelen to appeal to Hoogstraten and Lauwerijns, but received only a letter that they were required to deliver unopened to the Council in The Hague. Finally, burgomaster Hillebrand Janszoon Otter promised to abide by the *placard* in the future: if the summons to the *schepenen* were dropped, "we will be good children." Cornelis Bennink, present as one of the *schepenen* for 1527, immediately added a qualification: "saving the privileges of the city." As for Jan Zijvertszoon, after serving his sentence in St. Olaf's gate, he is known to have been active in Amsterdam as a book-dealer and printer as late as 1535.[49]

This incident shows the crown's judicial officers and the magistrates of Holland's most important city groping towards accommodation in a sensitive area where the meaning of the privilege *de non evocando* had yet to be clarified—that is, the Council's jurisdiction over heresy cases in the towns. In June 1528, when the Procurator General summoned certain burghers to The Hague on heresy charges and when their attempt to deny the validity of the summons was rejected, Amsterdam appealed to the States for support. In the initial discussion the men of Delft asserted that "in all privileges we ought to support one another, even if it means sending to Spain." At the next meeting the States agreed to uphold Holland's privileges by supporting "in the name of the *land*" those charged with heresy by the Council of Holland. The crucial point, in the deputies' view, was that everyone had the right to be tried in the first instance before his own town court.[50] That this formulation still allowed for the appellate jurisdiction of the Council will not have escaped anyone's notice.

The Council too could be accommodating, in a different way. In 1528 the Council was confronted with a self-taught shoemaker from Dordrecht, Cornelis Wouters. Rather than recanting his views on the Eucharist, Wouters was "prepared to endure a painful death to make his strong faith known to the people." In this case the Council urged Hoogstraten to accept clemency on pragmatic grounds: strong measures hitherto employed "have not been as effective as one might have expected, but we have found by experience that incarceration has brought to repentance" men who would have "gone into the fire for their beliefs, had they been permitted." Hoogstraten may have accepted this argument, because Cornelis Wouters was kept in prison, at least for a time, rather than being sent to the stake.[51]

From these compromises one might have constructed a prudent policy for the suppression of religious dissent, like that of Elizabethan England or of the Spanish Netherlands toward the end of the sixteenth century when Protestant pastors were hounded across the northern frontier and life was made difficult for ordinary believers, although executions were kept to a minimum.[52] But such fine tuning in the machinery for enforcing uniformity of belief was not yet possible. On the one side, the Protestant movement was vigorously expanding and developing new varieties. On the other side, men like Hoogstraten and Reynier Brunt were sworn to uphold the Emperor's policy in all its rigor, and they knew very well that those who claimed to be making progress against heresy by gentler methods were either concealing the truth or deceiving themselves. The Amsterdam humanist, schoolmaster, and accused heretic, Jan Sartorius, was brought "to repentance" through incarceration, or so the Council of Holland claimed. Sartorius did indeed recant a few times, but eventually fled to Germany where he had a long and productive life as a Protestant theologian.[53] In April 1528, in the midst of sensitive discussions about financing the Utrecht War (see chap. 3), Hoogstraten told the Amsterdammers in private that he knew how "lazy" Sheriff Jan Hubrechtszoon was in prosecuting "Lutherans," and he threatened to take out a loan in Antwerp so as to redeem the Emperor's right to appoint the sheriff of Amsterdam.[54]

It may have been in response to frustrations of this kind among zealous officials that Charles V issued a new *placard* (October 1529) removing from all courts—both the town *gerechten* and the provincial councils—the customary right of using their own discretion to determine the severity of punishment (*arbitrale correctie*). Henceforth, each offense against the *placards* was punishable by death, and judges were explicitly instructed "to govern themselves according to the wording (*teneur*) of this ordinance."[55] The new policy had an immediate impact at the Court of Holland where Cornelis Wouters, the Dordrecht shoemaker, was brought out from prison to be executed. In the cities, however, it was business as usual. For example, according to information which Hoogstraten received a few year later, a certain Long John the lumberman was summoned before the Amsterdam *gerecht* in 1530. Having acknowledged that he had prevented a dying woman from receiving the last sacrament of the Church and then officiated at a burial service at which "Lutheran" hymns were sung, he was told by one of the burgomasters, Heyman Jacobszoon van Ouder Amstel, to go home and keep quiet.[56]

Possibly the government was not too worried about men like Long John. In the prevailing theory of society, the wealthy and the learned were expected to keep "the little folk" in line. Charles's religious policy had succeeded in driving into exile most of the educated men who would be the natural leaders of any dissident movement.[57] But the sequel would show how ordinary men and women, poring over the scriptures without benefit of learned guidance, developed a theology more radical than Luther's and far more dangerous to the established order.

MELCHIORITE ANABAPTISM IN HOLLAND

The revolutionary variety of Melchiorite Anabaptism that spread into the Netherlands from the "kingdom" of Münster (1533–1535) has been described by a number of scholars,[58] and many of the pertinent sources have now been published.[59] Of interest here is the way in which well-founded fears of insurrection apparently rallied town magistrates to the government's view that heresy was indeed akin to sedition—but only for as long as the danger of actual uprisings continued.

When Mary of Hungary assumed the Regency of the Netherlands, Charles V had doubts about the orthodoxy of her advisers,[60] and it may have been to reassure her brother that Mary reissued (October 1531) the draconian *placard* of 1529, prescribing the death penalty without exception for all listed offenses.[61] Meanwhile, one of Melchior Hoffman's disciples, under torture in The Hague, was revealing the names of ten of his male coreligionists in Amsterdam. Giving perfunctory notice to Amsterdam's authorities, the Council sent armed men to hale the accused out of their beds in the middle of the night and bring them for trial to The Hague where they were all beheaded on

5 December. By Charles V's command, their severed heads were to be placed on stakes outside Amsterdam, but when the Council's servants arrived bearing their grisly burden, the Sheriff and his men refused an order to help them in their task. Ruysch Janszoon, one of the burgomasters that year, demanded to know whether the victims "had rejected God." Meester Pieter Colijn, another of the burgomasters, promised that Amsterdam would deliver "no more people to the butcher's block." Historians are well advised to avoid ascribing motives to men and women long dead, but even a few such comments, scattered here and there in the sources for this period, are enough to create the strong impression that many Netherlanders were revolted by the inherent cruelty of Charles V's religious policy. The next time the minions of the law came from The Hague, meaning to arrest some fifty men and women whose names had been supplied by those recently executed, they found that all had fled the city, apparently after receiving warnings "from the house of the Sheriff."[62]

Hoogstraten, the government's Argus-eyed Stadtholder in Holland, apparently carried with him a portfolio of letters from the Council of Holland dealing with heresy. Many of these letters are from two zealous *poursuivants* of heretics, Procurator General Reynier Brunt and Councillor Guilleyn Zeghers,[63] but, interestingly enough, none are from First Councillor Assendelft, a humane aristocrat who saw Anabaptism as a religion of desperate folk who turned to it "partly out of poverty" and who doubted that it would attract any people of the more respectable sort, that is, those whom the government would have to worry about.[64] Modern historians would see a spectrum of religious opinion in the Low Countries during these years, running from out-and-out Protestants to "Counter-Reformers."[65] But Hoogstraten's informants did not make fine distinctions; there was, for example, the hyperzealous curate from Rotterdam who wanted the schoolmaster investigated because he used *The Colloquies* of Erasmus as a text. By contrast, Erasmus was an honored correspondent of Assendelft and other Councillors, and the States of Holland once voted him a birthday gift worth 200 pounds, in recognition of "the honor which he has brought to the fatherland."[66]

Thus if Hoogstraten and his correspondents were alarmed by the early spread of Anabaptism, others were not, at least not for a while. In Amsterdam, where leaders of the ruling party actively sponsored the careers of reformist preachers who denounced many Catholic practices,[67] the burgomasters were also reported to be maintaining informal contacts with leaders of the local Anabaptist community. Allert Boelens, one of the leaders of the current ruling faction, was seen in the company of the Anabaptist bishop, Jacob van Campen, and is said to have had dinner with Jan Beukels, soon to be the ruler of the Anabaptist kingdom of Münster, as he journeyed to the Westphalian city from his home in Leiden.[68]

Beginning in March 1534, however, authorities at all levels had a succession of bad scares. Later confessions make it clear that just as the Anabaptist movement was starting to grow in numbers, the pacifist convictions of the original Melchiorites were under severe challenge by emissaries from Münster like Meester Gerrit van Campen, a surgeon who told of visions occurring in Münster, including one in which a man descending from heaven opened his palms from which blood gushed forth. This was, he said, a sign that God had given his faithful the sword.[69] Meanwhile, for quite different reasons, the Council in The Hague had warned Hoogstraten of the possibility of insurrection, owing to the prolonged cessation of the Baltic trade, the effects of which would be especially severe among the "tough and evil-tempered" folk of northern Holland.[70] Both of these ominous developments converged in the fact that the priests accused of heresy and other suspect persons tended to move north in the Low Countries, farther from the centers of power in Brussels and The Hague. Thus in Holland the northern districts of Kennemerland, Waterland, and West Friesland became catch-basins for religious dissenters.[71]

City governments were reluctant to credit rumors of plots and conspiracies, until people all over Holland were seen selling their property, as if preparing for a journey.[72] The Council in The Hague soon had the text of a circular letter, supplied by Amsterdam, announcing that the faithful, unable to live free "under the dragon of this world," were to meet at noon on 24 March at the Berchklooster in Overijssel, for a journey to Münster. Thirty ships were reported to have sailed from Monnikendam in north Holland on 21 March; these must have accounted for the twenty-seven ships held on arrival at Genemuiden in Overijssel, near the Berchklooster. Five other ships were prevented from leaving Haarlem, and six were similarly detained in Amsterdam, including five that had come from Sparendam. The contemporary estimate that 3,000 persons were on the ships at Genemuiden may be high, but it is clear that the authorities suddenly had thousands of people on their hands and did not know what to do with them. With the government's permission, the Council of Holland proceeded to punish "leaders and baptizers," and let the rest go.[73]

Late in April a priest saw a woman carrying armor through the streets of Amsterdam late at night, and the next day a letter arrived from the Stadtholder of Friesland, warning of "two ships full of rebaptized heretics" said to be headed for Amsterdam. After the burgomasters met with the *vroedschap,* the civic militia companies (*schutters*), and "some others from among the men of substance (*Rijkdom*)" were summoned to the upper room of the town hall where they swore to "live and die by the city." Only then was the town bell rung to call the burghers to assembly. The city's desire to protect its own (that is, enrolled burghers, as distinct from mere residents) was evident in the decree that "every Anabaptist who is not a burgher" was ordered to be out of the city by 5:00 P.M., at which time the burgomasters and the *schutters* began a search of suspect houses and boats that eventually netted some fifty persons. Within a week, Hoogstraten arrived in Amsterdam to conduct his own interrogations, which lasted six days. In the ensuing weeks, fifteen male Anabaptists were excuted by city authorities, thereby breaking a precedent. Among the first to feel the sword of urban justice was the Münster prophet, Gerrit van Campen.[74] When Hoogstraten next returned to Amsterdam in October, he was finally able to appoint a sheriff who was "sincere" or reliable in religious matters. When two more Amsterdammers were arrested, however, a large, angry crowd gathered in front of the Franciscan friary where Hoogstraten was lodging, and came again the next two nights. Their aim was to prevent burghers from being hauled out of bed in the middle of the night, as had happened in 1531, and they would not leave until a draper apparently respected by the crowd was able to give them the assurances they sought.[75]

Meanwhile, the return of seafaring men on the Baltic and fishing fleets coincided with a dramatic increase in sectarian activity in north Holland. The Bailiff of Beverwijk reported that Anabaptists were preaching and baptizing in the open, and the Bailiff of Kennemerland dared not enter the town of Monnikendam because it was too "infected" with heresy. In January 1535 Assendelft warned Hoogstraten that "if we lose a single piece of land, I see the whole province gone." By this time, in response to urgent appeals from the Council, Hoogstraten's nephew, Escornaix, was on his way north with 300 Walloon mercenaries. But things were apparently not so bad as they seemed, for on 25 February Assendelft gave thanks to God that he had been able to lead a contingent of Escornaix's men into Monnikendam "without a battle." The expensive mercenaries were soon dismissed; they were ineffective at catching heretics because, in a landscape of villages laid out lengthwise along waterways, men on horseback could not prevent people from escaping in small boats at the sound of their clatter along the dike.[76]

In Leiden, some fifty Anabaptists collected weapons and gathered in two houses (including one owned by Jan Beukels) to wait further instructions. Being warned of a plot, the burgomasters rallied the *schutters* and surrounded the houses; those within resisted, and canon had to be brought up next day (24 January) to force their surrender.[77] During the same week, Delft's Meester Huych van den Eynde sent an urgent message to The Hague: a former servant of his, having repented of her heretical beliefs, had come to him with information about the "3,500 brethren" among whom she had been living in Amsterdam. Once granted immunity, at Van den Eynde's request, she told of a recent gathering of thirty-two "teachers" from places as far away as Deventer in Overijssel at the Half Moon in Sparendam. In mid-January the faithful in Amsterdam were asked to fast for three days and "pray the Lord God for victory."[78] Two weeks later, on the night of 13 February, twelve men and women shed their clothes at the command of a "prophet" and ran naked through the dark streets of Amsterdam, crying "Woe!" and "Revenge!" Saying they had been "commanded by God to proclaim the naked truth," they still refused clothing about a week later when Assendelft saw them: "they jump up and down like wild folk, and it is to be feared that some are possessed by the devil."[79] The first actual attack, in late February, came in Friesland where a party led by the Münsterite emissary Jan van Geel stormed the monastery of Oldeklooster; it was recaptured after a week's siege, but Jan van Geel escaped to fight another day.[80]

By April Geel was in Amsterdam, which he seems to have visited once in January as part of a bizarre scheme to grab the Bishop of Münster's lands for Charles V by making a bargain with the besieged Anabaptists. Pieter van Montfoort, a minor Habsburg official who was Geel's dupe in the affair, obtained a safe-conduct for him. In early May, when Geel and others were seen purchasing arms, Meester Pieter Colijn assured his fellow burgomasters that there was no cause for alarm. But on the night of 10 May, Colijn and others had a rude shock. Magistrates and others of the *rijkdom* feasting at city hall barely had time to escape as forty armed Anabaptists led by Geel stormed the building with cries of "Strike them dead!" As the *schutters* began gathering in arms before the occupied city hall, Meester Pieter Colijn, "being fiery," insisted on leading a premature counter-assault in which he and others were killed. Next morning the burgomasters brought up artillery and did the job properly.[81] Since only about half of the attackers were Amsterdam residents, one must assume that most of the city's settled Anabaptist community stayed home, along with Bishop Jacob van Campen. But in the wake of insurrection, the city's *gerecht* made no fine disinctions; everyone who knew about the plan and did not report it to the authorities was deemed to have forfeited his or her life. Of sixty-two executions during 1535 by the city, forty-six came in the wake of the 10 May attack on city hall.[82]

From what has been said, it may seem that magistrates and government officials buried their differences during the period of crisis as well as during the repression that followed. In fact, all they really agreed on was that those who engaged in sedition made themselves liable to the death penalty. The main continuing source of conflict was that officials in Brussels seem to have been the only ones who fully accepted the principle, stated in the *placards* of 1529 and 1531, that every infraction of the stated provisions was punishable by death. Everyone who actually tried people for heresy at the lower levels, including even so zealous a prosecutor as Reynier Brunt, favored some form of mitigation.[83] In February 1534 the Council in The Hague sent one of its members, Meester Abel van Coulster, to Brussels with a convincing plea for trial amnesty:

> [Many are] simple folk of dull mind, who would not have gotten anything into their heads except for sermons telling them they could be saved through rebaptism; now, seeing they have been seduced and deceived, they are so heartsick and penitent they scream and howl, some like wild crazy folk, running off and leaving wives and children behind. To execute all such men with the sword seems harsh, and would also cause great uproar in the land, since, the way people of small estate marry among one another, they have many friends and relatives.

The Regent and the Council of State proved amenable to the argument that Holland must not be "depopulated" by strict enforcement of the law, and a *placard* of 27 February gave repentant Anabaptists twenty-four days to make themselves known. Before this time had elapsed, still greater numbers of people were caught up in the net of the law through participation in the "journey" to Münster. A new clemency ordinance in April, renewed in May and June, extended the amnesty provisions for additional periods. It seems, however, that few people presented themselves for absolution.[84]

Furthermore, local courts often dealt in a lenient way with people whose circumstances did not fit the provisions of the clemency ordinances. In December 1534 Amsterdam's *gerecht* heard the case of an impenitent woman whom burgomaster Ruych Janszoon released, contrary to the wishes of the new sheriff, "because she is a dumb simple woman and sick in body as well." Somewhat later, Brunt caused her to be rearrested and drowned, as the *placards* provided for female heretics.[85] Cities also disregarded the provision that no one with a prior conviction for heresy could qualify for amnesty. Assendelft believed that the cities were generally unwilling to execute penitent Anabaptists, despite the Queen's wishes. In March 1535 Pieter

Colijn informed Assendelft that Amsterdam had beheaded sixteen men in two days, but still had in prison one man and seven women, "concerning whom the schepenen make great difficulty, because [the prisoners] may wish to repent." Brunt complained that the *gerecht* "reserved" or postponed sentence in these cases even though he and Assendelft had expressly commanded them to enforce the law.[86]

If the cities were disobedient, it was in part because the Council of Holland had set a bad example. In May 1534 the Council had sent the Queen and the Secret Council a list of nine "reserved" prisoners, with an explanation in each case as to why it would be "harsh" to sentence them to death. The Council would be willing to answer for its discretion "before God and the Emperor"; indeed, had the Queen and her Council been on the scene, "they too would have been moved by the poverty and misery of the prisoners to do the same thing." The answer from Brussels was uncompromising: "We sharply command you in the Emperor's name to proceed with the executions at once." Nonetheless, Assendelft and the Council wrote separately to Hoogstraten, reminding him of his personal promise of amnesty to one prisoner, and in the end at least some of those on the list were allowed to do penance.[87] In subsequent months, the Council received instructions from Brussels to stop using the Emperor's need for galley slaves as a reason for not sentencing sturdy heretics to death, and not to send heretical priests to ecclesiastical courts, which could only impose ecclesiastical penalities: "for *lèse majesté* there is no remand [*renvoi*] to Church courts."[88]

In effect, both the Council and the town courts attempted to preserve the legal usage of *arbitrale correctie*, despite the fact that it was expressly ruled out by the *placards* of 1529 and 1531. On one side of the conflict was a traditional and deeply rooted sense of due process, and on the other was the relatively novel principle that permitted the prince to override existing customs and privileges, as in the mandate (April 1535) by which Hoogstraten was given "absolute power" to proceed "by extraordinary means" in the prosecution of heresy in Holland. Among Habsburg officials in Holland, the Procurator General could be expected to represent the government's view most faithfully, and it was Reynier Brunt who laid a number of disputed questions before the Secret Council in May 1535, just prior to the uprising in Amsterdam. On each point, the Council's judgment stripped away any legal basis for mitigation of the *placards:* penitent Anabaptist women were to be executed, despite what the Council of Holland said; if the *schepenen* of Delft insisted on using *arbitrale correctie* in heresy cases, they should be summoned to The Hague to answer for it. The fact that certain persons were under age at the time and forced to participate in sectarian activity by their parents was no excuse; and there must be no tolerance in cases of *lèse majesté* and sedition either for urban privileges or for the claim that feudal enclaves are exempt from appellate jurisidication.[89]

In the aftermath of sedition, actions by which the future trouble-makers were treated leniently rather than harshly punished came to be seen in a sinister light. This atmosphere of recrimination provided a context for the change of ruling factions that took place in Amsterdam between 1536 and 1538. The college of *schepenen* was the point at which the government could most easily shape a town magistracy to its liking, because *schepenen* were appointed by the Stadtholder usually upon nomination by the *vroedschap* of twice the number of men needed. In January 1535 Brunt and Assendelft tried unsuccessfully to get the names of "sincere" men on the list for Amsterdam's annual *schepen* nominations. The next year, with the Anabaptist uprising still fresh in mind, Brunt and Assendelft found the *vroedschap* willing to advance the nomination date by a few weeks, contrary to the city's privileges, and for the first time in Amsterdam's history the seven new *schepenen* were all men who had never held the office before. Two of these men were married to leaders of the "women's uproar" of 1531 in defense of the Heilige Stede, and three others (Klaas Doedeszoon, Klaas Gerrit Matteuszoon, and Pieter Kantert Willemszoon) became leading magistrates of the Hendrik-Dirkist ruling party. Other "sincere" (i.e., orthodox) men were named *schepenen* in 1537, including Meester Hendrik Dirkszoon, and by 1538 the new men were numerous enough in the "old council" of former magistrates to effect a change in the composition of the crucial college of burgomasters.[90]

At a different level, the Council itself came under suspicion because the councillors had risked the wrath of their superiors by advocating clemency. Thus Hoogstraten asserted, just after a party of Anabaptists "driven by the spirit" had attacked a village near Leiden (December 1535),[91] that "one can now see the fruits of grace periods granted formerly." Some time in 1536 or possibly 1537, Meester Vincent Corneliszoon was sent from Brussels to The Hague with a list of questions demanding an explanation of the Council's leniency in specific cases. For example, why did the Council allow the notorious Jan Sartorius to live peacefully in Naaldwijk where known heretics consorted with him regularly, despite the fact that he himself had twice been punished for heresy? Why had they disobeyed orders by remanding a sacramentarian priest to the ecclesiastical judge in Utrecht? And why had they done the same for two women of the village of Pijnacker?[92] In October, the Queen sent Dr. Lodewijk van Schore, member and future President of the Council of State, to inquire again about the issues Meester Vincent had raised, especially those regarding the sacramentarian priest and the two women of Pijnacker. In its defense, the Council replied that it had sentenced more heretics to death than any similar body in the Netherlands had done. As for the prisoners in question, while they admitted to heretical beliefs, they had not committed any of the offenses specified in the Emperor's *placards*, and the Council asserted, as Joost Lauwerijns had done ten years earlier, that "cognizance of matters of faith belongs to the spiritual judge," not to civil authorities.[93]

Two years later the Queen herself visited The Hague, on a tour of the northern provinces. While the trusted Councillor Guilleyn Zeghers was commissioned to check up on heresy trials in the towns, Hoogstraten presided over an inquiry touching on the activities of Zeghers's brethren in The Hague. One of the accusations against a chaplain in the parish church of The Hague was that Councillor Abel van Coulster had "instigated" him to relate in a sermon how he had "scolded" a Franciscan for attacking the name of Erasmus; the same preacher was alleged to have boasted that "the Council and especially Lord Assendelft are for him, so that he had no fear of being arrested." The chaplain was cleared, but warned not to mention Erasmus in his sermons, lest his congregation be "scandalized." Coulster had to answer to allegation that he did not believe in Purgatory, and Assendelft was charged with "not being sincere in his conscience." Assendelft retorted that his accuser knew very well where he went to church and how much income he had assigned to masses for his ancestors.[94] Assendelft's problem was that, in this climate of suspicion, one could be Catholic yet not be Catholic enough.

Under these circumstances, neither the Council[95] nor town courts[96] had much leeway for refusing to proceed according to the *placards*. But one ought not presume that the real eagerness of civic authorities to ferret out religious dissenters lasted much beyond the rebellious episodes of 1535. Even in Amsterdam, where the new Dirkist ruling party followed a consciously orthodox line in religious matters, there were few executions during the tenure in office of Sheriff Cornelis Wouter Dobbens (1536–1542), despite his reputation for being "sincere": four Anabaptists in 1537 and six members of the church-robbing splinter group known as Battenburgers in 1540. The latter, as Mellink notes, were executed in the manner prescribed for criminals, not heretics.[97] It was in any case only a matter of time before local officials recognized that the pacifist teachings of Menno Simons were gaining the upper hand among the survivors of Münsterite Anabaptism. In May 1539 the Sheriff and *gerecht* of Haarlem sent the Council a detailed report of their interrogations, under torture, of fifteen recently captured Anabaptists: "We do not find from them that they are out after anyone's property or [the prince's] authority." They know nothing about the followers of Jan Battenburg, the church-robber, rather, "they say they are only seeking God with an upright heart."[98] Hoogstraten would no doubt keep up the pressure to treat Anabaptists as Anabaptists, regardless of such heretical subtlety, but his influence was not to last much longer. His death on 2 April 1540 marks the effective end of the period of intense persecution in Holland. .

LAX ENFORCEMENT OF THE PLACARDS, LINGERING DISPUTES

Between 1540 and 1555 the government of the Netherlands certainly had enough other things to worry about besides the enforcement of heresy laws. The *placards* were reissued six times between 1544 and 1550, and at the Council of Holland's suggestion the government had over one hundred copies printed to facilitate posting in all the customary locations.[99] But there is hardly any mention of heresy in the correspondence for these years between Brussels and The Hague—a correspondence that was in any case diminished, because, until William of Orange, no Stadtholder played such an active role in the province as Hoogstraten did. Reynier van Nassau (1540–1544) was preoccupied by his military responsibilities, and Lodewijk van Vlaanderen, lord of Praet (1544–1547) hardly set foot in Holland. Maximilian of Burgundy (1547–1558), the Marquis of Vere and hereditary Admiral of the Netherlands, insisted on being consulted, but was not very effective in dealing with the States, perhaps because Hollanders continued to reject the Admiral's claim to authority over their shipping.[100] Government officials may have persuaded themselves that the Anabaptist sect had indeed been "extirpated," and it is also possible that Charles V's dalliance with ecumenical discussions in Germany[101] made the prosecution of dissenters seem less urgent. Certainly the "permission for Lutheranism" that Mary of Hungary granted the Marquis of Vere some time prior to 1542—lest foreign merchants be scared away from his port city[102]—suggests some relaxation of the tense atmosphere of the 1530s.

Serious efforts were made to stop the publication and dissemination of heretical books, especially after Leuven theologians drew up an early index of forbidden works in 1546. Even the library at the Court of Holland had to be purged, lest condemned books fell into the wrong hands; the Council was given a list of titles, with orders to send these books to one of the inquisitors, the Leuven theologian Ruard Tapper, for his examination.[103] Equally dangerous were the often satirical plays by "rhetoricians" (*rederijkers*), of whom even small cities had a guild. In the 1530s, copies of allegedly scandalous plays were collected from Naaldwijk and Amsterdam. *Rederijkers* from various towns held one of their annual competitions at Brill in 1544 and again at Rotterdam in 1545. In 1546 the Queen wrote Leiden ordering the city not to permit such a competition; the *rederijkers* had actually planned to gather in Gouda instead, but the Castellan there managed to prevent the plays from being performed and sent copies to Brussels. In 1551, after being informed of another competition planned for Naaldwijk, the Queen ordered the Council not to permit it.[104]

Meanwhile the Council continued its trials of Anabaptists and other accused heretics. The *Register of Criminal Sentences*, extant from 1538, shows a return to the more lenient pattern of the early 1530s:[105]

Table 12. Sentences for Heresy by the Council of Holland

	Death	Banishment
1538	1	1
1539	1	3
1540	2	6
1541	2	2
1542	3	1
1544	4	3
1545	4	6

After 1545 there were no further sentences of any kind for heresy until 1558. It may be noted that suspicion about the Council's religious loyalty still lingered in Brussels. In February 1545 Bauduoin Le Cocq arrived in The Hague with a commission of inquiry from the Secret Council. Having seized the person of Herman Pieterszoon of Delft, a priest whom Hoogstraten had interrogated in 1539, Le Cocq found in his chambers "certain papers written in his hand and containing heretical opinions." Pieterszoon admitted having conversations about Scripture with "important persons" and with Assendelft's chaplain, whom Le Cocq found it worthwhile to question. Le Cocq was also told there were many suspect persons in Waterland, just north of Amsterdam, and he recommended preceeding in this region "by extraordinary means," such as were used in punishing the rebellion of Ghent in 1540.[106] For whatever reason his advice was not followed.

In the towns too there was a definite slackening of interest in heresy trials. In Gouda there had been few signs of heretical activity, and indeed in the 1520s there were manifestations of popular opposition to heresy. But when five Anabaptist women were seized in 1544 on the basis of information from Leiden, two were tried and executed, and the jailer led an escape by the other three. In Amsterdam there were only four executions under Sheriff Willem Dirkszoon Baerdes between 1544 and 1550, and none after 1553. Anabaptists arrested here in 1549 insisted under questioning that they were peaceful, and Woltjer thinks the Sheriff was convinced, even though there was a "monster trial" in 1552 in which dozens of self-confessed Anabaptists were interrogated.[107]

It was also indicative of a new climate that the States of Holland again began to be more assertive in discussions about heresy laws. During the Münsterite Anabaptist crisis there were few discussions about heresy in the States.[108] In 1544, however, the States came to Amsterdam's aid on a more fundamental issue that many thought had been won in the 1520s, the privilege *de non evocando*. The Council of Holland had summoned a certain Janne (Johanna) on heresy charges, and Amsterdam refused to deliver her, alleging she should be tried before the town court. In Brussels, Lodewijk van Schore insisted that the crime of *laesa majestas divina* was involved, and at a subsequent meeting the deputies were told that the Emperor would not allow a local court to assert its jurisdiction in the matter. When the States' petition to the government was rejected, with a further argument about *laesa majestas divina,* the deputies found this reasoning "dark and obscure." Janne was then summoned to stand trial before the Grand Council of Mechelen—a clear violation of *de non evocando*—but the final disposition of her case is not known.[109]

The most important case during this period was that of Engel Willemszoon or Angelus Merula, the 70-year-old pastor of the village of Heenvliet, a feudal enclave under the jurisdiction of Johan van Cruningen. In June 1553 the Council ordered the lord of Cruningen to deliver him to the Voorpoort in The Hague. The Council agreed that sending the prisoner to Utrecht to stand trial (before the inquisitor, Franciscus Sonnius) would not be a violation of *de non evocando* because Utrecht and Holland were "more or less the same province." But Merula appealed for help to the States, which after consideration of the matter rejected the Council's reasoning and would not permit him to be sent to Utrecht. After further negotiations it was agreed that another inquisitor, Ruard Tapper, would come to The Hague to interrogate Merula, who would pay his expenses. Notes taken by his nephew show Merula's willingness to stake his life on the doctrine of justification by faith, and after his martyrdom this interview was to be memorialized in a satiric *Apotheosis of Ruard Tapper*. At the time, he agreed to recant and was sentenced to imprisonment in a monastery. When Leuven was chosen as the place of his confinement, the Council "dared not" allow him to be taken out of Holland without telling the States, and on this point the States were adamant: if they did not accept the Council's reasoning about Utrecht, much less would they permit a Hollander to be sent to Brabant. But Amsterdam's deputies noted that if the place of punishment had been specified in the sentence, the States would not have been able to oppose it. Merula was in fact confined at various places in the southern provinces, and, having retracted his recantation, died on his way to the scaffold in 1558.[110]

This case shows that the issues which had made the trial of Cornelis Hoen a *cause célèbre* had never really been resolved. If the States were confident that *de non evocando* meant that accused heretics should stand trial before their local court in the first instance and not at all outside Holland, the government persisted in viewing *laesa majestas divina* as a crime to be dealt with by "extraordinary means." When heresy genuinely seemed akin to sedition, the towns were willing to collaborate with the Council of Holland in suppressing it, but when this crisis had passed, the government lacked the will or the capacity to impose its view of the law on its subjects in Holland. The resulting ambiguity could not endure long, if only because of the inherent dynamism of the religious movements of this era. In the southern Netherlands, if not yet in the north, Calvinism was by the 1550s gaining and organizing adherents more successfully than the Lutherans or Anabaptists had been able to do. Meanwhile many of the Catholic majority were frustrated by the entrenched power of unworthy or fractious priests,[111] whereas others were frustrated because the campaign against heresy was not successful. The answer to both problems, it seemed, was to reestablish the Church hierarchy in the Netherlands in such a way as to give bishops more authority over clergy and laity alike. When Philip II activated (1561) long-discussed plans for the formation of new bishoprics in the Netherlands, the problem of the enforcement of heresy laws would once again come to the fore.

7
HOLLAND UNDER PHILIP II, 1556–1566

Philip II was to be the last Count of Holland. During his reign Holland's history was more closely tied to events at the center of the realm than ever before. Despite his reputation as the protagonist of absolute monarchy,[1] Philip's initial instinct was to govern his lands in the Low Countries through the advice and consent of his subjects. For a brief period, the active collaboration of noble and burgher elites in the tasks of government brought the various provinces closer than ever to functioning as a nation with a common sense of purpose and identity. Having come to the Netherlands to take possession of his father's lands, Philip remained for four years because of the ongoing war with France. Duke Emmanuel-Philibert of Savoy, driven out of his own lands by France, served both as commander of the King's armies and Governor-General of the Netherlands. In hopes of overcoming resistance by the provincial states[2] to higher taxes, Philip accepted Savoy's proposal to have deputies from the various provinces "communicate together" in the States General, instead of merely stating the opinions of their principals, as they usually did at such meetings. In this way, it was hoped, the deputies might come up with their own means for fighting a war while combating the crown's enormous debt, now estimated at 9,000,000 pounds. After four months of interprovincial negotiation, in which deputies from Brabant took the lead, the States General presented a proposal that Philip II accepted in January 1558: 2,400,000 pounds would be raised through sales of *renten* by the provincial states, and the States General would borrow an additional 2,400,000 on the Antwerp exchange; to pay off this loan, and to provide for garrisons along the frontiers,

800,000 pounds would be raised each year for nine years. All monies were to be collected and disbursed by receivers responsible to the provincial states—like Holland's Receiver for the Common Land—and they in turn reported to a Receiver General appointed by the States General.[3]

When the Treaty of Cateau-Cambresis (April 1559) finally concluded the last Habsburg-Valois war, Savoy returned to his ancestral lands, and Philip II transferred the government of the Netherlands to a new regent, Margaret of Parma, Charles V's illegitimate daughter. Like Mary of Hungary, she was to be advised by a Council of State that included the greatest nobles of the realm, such as William of Orange and Lamoraal van Egmont. In light of later events, there were rumors, not now credited by historians, that Philip secretly instructed her to rely on the advice of only three members of the Council: Antoine Perrenot, Bishop of Arras and lord of Granvelle, the man most trusted by the King; Viglius van Aytta, President of the Council of State; and the Count of Berlaymont, President of the Council of Finance.[4] Philip did instruct Margaret to deal with the States General "in the old manner rather than the new," that is, not to allow the deputies of the separate provinces to communicate together. (The nine-years' *bede* had not worked well, and new arrangements were negotiated with the states of individual provinces in 1560.)[5]

Philip also gave Margaret special instructions for the maintainance of the Catholic religion. Like his father, he insisted that the courts enforce the *placards* without mitigation. As he prepared to sail from Zeeland for Spain, Philip ordered Margaret to deal with heretics under arrest in Middelburg "in such wise that the world may understand that I do not intend any equivocation in this matter."[6] Yet Calvinism was now flourishing in the southern provinces, especially in Flanders and in French-speaking areas adjacent to the frontier.[7] The northern provinces, if not yet infected by this new heresy, were also farther from Brussels and notoriously hard to control. Willem Lindanus, a doctor of theology from Leuven and a native of Dordrecht, had received a commission in 1557 to investigate heresy in Friesland where his efforts provoked spirited resistance from both the States of Friesland and the Council of Friesland. As delicately as she could, Margaret kept Philip informed of the stages of Lindanus's retreat, until he received permission to retire to his position as dean of the chapter church of St. James in The Hague.[8] More effective repression of heresy was certainly one reason why Philip embraced the idea of creating new bishoprics in the Netherlands. Plans drafted by a secret committee appointed by the King were approved in Rome in May 1559, and the finished text of a papal bull erecting the new dioceses was ready for issue in May 1560. Because the papal chancery wanted a fee of 10,000 pounds, which the impoverished government in Brussels could not pay, the publication of *Super Universas* was delayed until March 1561.[9]

Once the secret was out, it sparked furious controversy. Orange and Egmont's letter of protest to the King (July 1561) marked the beginning of the celebrated rift in the Council of State between Granvelle and a few loyalists on one side and most of the great lords on the other.[10] Popular opposition focussed on plans to strengthen the Church's campaign against heresy: *Super Universas* provided that two of the nine canons foreseen for each new diocese would have papal commissions as inquisitors. The upper clergy objected to the fact that the new dioceses would be funded from the revenues of existing monasteries; their voice was strongest in the States of Brabant where twelve important abbots made up the first estate. In the same body, William of Orange was spokesman for the nobility represented in the second estate, which feared an erosion of the ecclesiastical benefices that traditionally supported the younger sons of noble families. Finally, among the great cities that made up the third estate in Brabant, powerful Antwerp insisted that a stronger inquisition would ruin its trade with foreigners. The King's decision (April 1563) to suspend efforts to install a bishop in Antwerp signalled a prudent retreat. Bishops were accepted *pro forma* in some cities, including Haarlem in Holland, but even here they would not have power to reform the clergy until the iron-fisted Duke of Alba made credible threats to use force to break the resistance of privileged ecclesiastical corporations. The more immediate effect of these appointments was to strengthen the influence, in Brussels and Madrid, of those obsequious clerics who had faithfully supported the

King in his determination to "extirpate" heresy and who were now rewarded with bishoprics. Lindanus, for example, was eventually named Bishop of Roermond in Guelders.[11]

Within the Council of State, opposition focused on Granvelle who had been named Archbishop of Mechelen and primate of the Netherlands in the King's ecclesiastical reorganization. After several months of contention over various other issues, the great lords in the Council wanted the States General to be convened to discuss the affairs of the realm. But since Margaret was prevented from doing so by Philip's express orders, she summoned instead a chapter of the Knights of the Golden Fleece (May 1562). Orange took the occasion of their presence in Brussels to convene an informal meeting at his palace, on the site of the present Royal Library, from which Granvelle and Viglius were pointedly excluded. These discussions led to formation of a "league" against Granvelle, embracing most of the great nobles. Finally, Orange, Egmont, and Hornes announced in a letter to the King (March 1563) that they could not continue sitting in the Council of State so long as Granvelle was there. To emphasize the point, all three quit Brussels, and Orange and Egmont traveled together to Holland.[12]

After delaying for the better part of a year, Philip II at last instructed Granvelle to retire from the Netherlands (February 1564), for a temporary absence that proved permanent. After his departure, it was no longer possible to avoid full-scale discussion of the *placards* in the Council of State. None of the great nobles had embraced Protestantism at this time, not even Orange, but it is not too much to say they spoke for a national revulsion at the continuing ferocity of the persecution. In Antwerp, for example, the executioner barely escaped an angry mob after he had hastily dispatched his latest victim, a Calvinist minister who had formerly been a Carmelite friar in England. In December 1564 Egmont was dispatched to Spain with a formal request for the King to mitigate the *placards*, especially in regard to the death penalty. Egmont came back with the impression that he had gained his point, but in fact Philip would allow only the appointment of a "committee of theologians" to discuss the matter. This group proposed some mitigation of the *placards* for youthful offenders. During the summer, while Brussels awaited

Philip's reply, many of the lesser nobles, including some who were now Calvinists, held meetings in the principality of Liège to discuss what to do if the King refused even this concession. Philip's decision, expressed in the famous letters from Segovia Wood (October 1565), was that the *placards* must be enforced according to the letter, with no shadow of mitigation. What Geoffrey Parker has called the "First Revolt" of the Netherlands, which began when several hundred lesser nobles formed a union or "Compromise" among themselves to oppose the *placards* (December 1565), and continued with a wave of iconoclastic fury that swept across the Netherlands in August 1566.[13]

This chapter will examine the continuing strength and the growing autonomy of Holland's provincial institutions in the years when the authority of the central government virtually collapsed under the troubled regency of Margaret of Parma. The contrast is most evident in the fiscal sphere: at a time when the government could not even pay the salaries of its officials in The Hague, there was a steady stream of cash passing through the hands of the Receiver for the Common Land, permitting the States to provide "gratuities" for helpful officials in Brussels or The Hague, in transactions that were sometimes not recorded in the accounts to which government auditors were given access. At the same time, new leaders in the Council of Holland and in the pivotal city of Amsterdam seemed to lack the effectiveness of their predecessors. But after 1563, once he took a real interest in the affairs of Holland, Stadtholder William of Orange brought the States into an effective alliance with the great lords. Finally, active persecution of heretics had practically come to a standstill in Holland by the time of Philip's departure for Spain. Efforts to bring the Council of Holland as well as local magistrates to account for their laxity proved only that Margaret's weakened government altogether lacked the power to enforce laws that her subjects believed to be cruel and contrary to their privileges.

CREDIT-WORTHY PROVINCE,
IMPECUNIOUS GOVERNMENT

After 1560, the government's annual *bede* revenue from Holland consisted of 37,500 pounds for garrison wages and a net yield of

48,000 from the *ordinaris bede,* almost all of which was pledged to recurring expenses.[14] Domain finances in Holland were in such a woeful state that the Councillors Ordinary of the Council of Holland went for nearly three years without receiving a stuiver of their annual salary.[15] In effect, then, the government had no disposable income from this important province. Yet the States consistently refused Margaret of Parma's requests for *extraordinaris beden.*[16] Holland's economy in these years was adversely affected by complications overseas, including the succession of the Protestant Queen Elizabeth I in England (1558), and the Seven Years' War of the North, a struggle for supremacy in the Baltic between Denmark and Sweden (1563–1570).[17] But these troubles did not prevent the States from levying two tenth-pennies (1561, 1564) to help retire provincial debt; these payments were in addition to the approximately 100,000 pounds per year from the impost and land tax that was used to pay interest on the debt.[18] One may say that the States called on Holland's taxpaying capacity for servicing provincial debt, but not for addressing the needs of the central government.

Owing to the expanding activities of the provincial bureaucracy, the States built an "office of the Common Land" (1558–1560) next to the Dominican cloister in The Hague.[19] Just as towns had strongboxes with multiple keys to guard copies of their cherished privileges, the States now had in their new office a strongbox for provincial accounts and for privileges of the Common Land, with keys held by the Advocate, by a member of the King's Chamber of Accounts, and by two deputies, one for the towns and one for the nobles.[20] During the same period meetings of the States were beginning to be called by their own officials, rather than by the Council of Holland. As ad hoc committees (*gecommiteerden*) were created to oversee various aspects of the new fiscal system, Aert Coebel, Receiver for the Common Land, summoned the deputies on his own authority, apparently in 1554. When Jacob van den Eynde, the former pensionary of Delft, became Advocate of the States in 1560, he did the same.[21] More and more, the States were becoming a self-conscious and self-regulating "body," like a municipality on a grander scale.

This growing institutional autonomy of the States did not

pass without challenge. As they administered provincial taxes and provincial *renten*, deputies expected their decisions on disputed questions to be enforced by the judicial apparatus of the Court of Holland with its messengers and process-servers (*deurwaarders*). Some members of the Council were apparently disturbed by the fact that these lesser officials, representing the prince's authority in Holland, would now be expected to take orders from an assembly of his subjects. In February 1555, Willem Snouckaert, one of the Councillors Ordinary, presented the government with a sixty-seven-point indictment of alleged fiscal mismanagement by the States. The key issue was whether the Council had judicial review over fiscal decisions by the States. The Council (not just Snouckaert) claimed authority to intervene in this process, for example, by insisting on revision before promulgating tax decrees of the States as having the force of law, or by releasing the magistrates of a given locality from house arrest if it seemed they had been wrongfully detained. For their part, the deputies viewed the Court of Holland (and hence the Council) as having no role other than that of an enforcement agency in the States' levy of taxes. They even attempted, albeit without success, to prevent Hollanders who felt themselves aggrieved by the States from appealing to the Grand Council of Mechelen. When Holland assented to its share of the nine-years' *bede* (1558), the States made it one of their conditions that the Council in The Hague comply with and carry out the fiscal decisions of the States. The States evidently had some success in exerting pressure on the Council through the central government because in March 1562, the Council formally promised to carry out orders issued by the States in regard to revenues of the Common Land.[22]

Snouckaert's bill of particulars also charged that the Council and the Chamber of Accounts were not kept informed about the revenue-gathering activity of the States because Coebel was slow in rendering account and because the States did not furnish the Council with copies of their *Resolutiën*. More importantly, according to "common report" Coebel and his clerks were guilty of serious improprieties: Coebel had used 2,000 pounds from the proceeds of *renten* sales to cover his arrears as Receiver for the Prince of Orange's lands in south Holland; his clerk, Mangelman, who had since fled, lent 4,000 of the Common Land's money to a certain individual, and thirty or thirty-five others in The Hague received sums totalling 12,000 or 13,000 pounds. The flight of Coebel's clerk suggests that there was some truth in these charges, and it seems too that Coebel was not so careful about accounting for the sums he received as some other fiscal officials were. For example, between 1521 and 1530 Willem Goudt as Receiver for the *beden* collected *beden* with a nominal value of 2,013,201 pounds, whereas between 1552 and 1560 Coebel as Receiver for the Common Land collected *beden* with a nominal value of 2,489,000. But Goudt's accounts for the 1520s never show a deficit greater than 4,500, whereas Coebel accumulated arrears of 82,673. But no one in authority credited the insinuation that the new fiscal system was fundamentally corrupt. Even before the States had a copy of Snouckaert's charges, they were forewarned by someone (Mellink suggests Assendelft, who was no friend of Snouckaert: see below), so as to eliminate some of the irregularities at issue.[23]

The strength of the States lay in their credit rating. In the last years of Charles V's reign, the States were already endorsing promissory notes or *obligatiën* to the bankers, to be made good by future *bede* revenues (see chap. 5). The government's fiscal impotence became embarrassingly clear in the early months of Philip II's reign, when Holland consented to a 200,000-*bede*, half to be levied by the *schiltal* and half by a sale of *renten*. Perhaps because of Snouckaert's charges against Coebel, the government wanted the *schiltal* portion of this *extraordinaris bede* collected by its own fiscal bureaucracy, contrary to the practice of the last few years. As a result, the States agreed to sign an *obligatie* only for the portion to be raised through *renten*, a sum for which Coebel was still responsible; as for the rest, if it was to be collected by the King's official, he should interpose his own credit. But within a few weeks, Viglius reported that the King's Receiver-General was unable to obtain credit in Antwerp; the States were thus asked to obligate Holland for the full 200,000 pounds, with the understanding that Coebel would be the collector.[24] In 1557, when Philip II was forced to declare a partial repudiation of his debts, the "faith and credit" (*krediet en geloove*) of the States must have seemed all the more solid by contrast.

Savoy asked the Marquis of Vere at this time to arrange a
200,000-pound forced loan from private persons in Holland,
but the Stadtholder replied, on the advice of Assendelft and
Councillor Cornelis Suys, that it would be much better to rely
on "the credit of the States," by asking them to agree to a sale of
renten for 200,000 and to give their *obligatie* for this amount.[25]
Hollanders were still nervous about dealing with the "great
purses" of Antwerp,[26] especially Gaspar Schetz, Philip II's loan
broker, who was the second-generation head of one of the great
banking houses.[27] But Schetz was helpful to the States in presenting Savoy with a 10,000-pound gratuity—he accepted their
obligatie so the money could be transmitted to the Governor-
General immediately—and in 1561 Schetz himself received a
gratuity of 1,100 pounds for helping the States to arrange a
favorable exchange rate in settling provincial debts.[28] Deputies
remained wary of such transactions, but men with money to
lend and institutions with a strong credit rating will find ways of
accommodating each other.

From Coebel's accounts one cannot tell what the state of the
Common Land's treasury may have been at a given moment,
since he routinely entered as income all payments that were
due, regardless of whether the money had been received.[29]
There must have been cash on hand because the States periodically gave Coebel instructions on how to use it,[30] and there is
reason to believe that the sums available grew larger as time
went on. At the beginning of Philip's reign, the approximately
100,000 pounds in revenue from the impost and land tax was
barely enough to pay annual interest on provincial *renten*.
Coebel had instructions to pay "outlanders" (non-Hollanders)
first, to avoid trouble, but there were still occasional reports of
Hollanders having their property seized in Zeeland or elsewhere for non-payment of interest on Holland *renten*.[31] But
Coebel was able to reduce the province's indebtedness as interest rates receded from peak levels of the early 1550s; thus he
sold heritable annuities (*losrenten*) at the rate of 1:12 to redeem
life annuities (*lijfrenten*) sold at 1:6. Before long he was able to
find buyers for *losrenten* at 1:16, to redeem those sold at 1:12. In
addition, two tenth-pennies levied by the States (1561, 1564)
brought in enough to redeem almost half the outstanding capi-

tal. Thus annual *renten* interest charged to the impost and land tax accounts declined from a high of 134,000 in 1555/1556 to 59,685 in 1566/1567.[32] But since rates for the impost and land tax were maintained at the same level, the State gradually built up a positive cash balance. In the years just before the Revolt, the surplus was used mainly for further redemptions of *renten,* including full repayment to a single *rentenier* who had subscribed 64,000 pounds for a new issue of 100,000 to which the States consented in 1565.[33]

Gratuities were of course another way in which the States could employ their ready cash. According to Snouckaert's list of complaints (1555), when Coebel was asked to make payments on the order of the Court of Holland, he would say that he was not answerable to the Court or that "what money he had in his office had to go to Brussels for gratuities (*propeynen*) at the court, and that gratuities took precedence."[34] Certain kinds of gratuities were quite traditional. In the early years of Charles V's reign it was customary for the States to reward prominent individuals at court, sometimes upon recommendation of the Stadtholder, by writing these expenses into the small levies or *omslagen* that the Receiver for the Common Land collected for the needs of the States. There were also special levies for prominent figures like the Regent or the Stadholder.[35] Now that there was a steady flow of cash into Coebel's office, the States could make such payments without any special levies. For example, the deputies decided in February 1559 to raise 10,000 pounds for Savoy by having Coebel sell that amount in *renten* "under the mass of what his Majesty has asked for" in the nine-years' *bede.* Gaspar Schetz advanced the money, as noted above, and just to make things legal, the States voted to add a clause about Savoy's gratuity, retroactively, to their consent to the pertinent portion of the nine-years' *bede.*[36]

Most interesting is the possibility that the States could now make payments of this kind under the table without any of the King's auditors knowing about them. *Omslagen* were audited by committees that included auditors from the Chamber of Accounts in The Hague, and the committees that audited Coebel's receipts for the impost and land tax always included one member from this body and one from the Council of Holland, as

well as deputies from the States. But when the States decided
(1557) to spend 1,200 pounds on a gift for Viglius, President of
the Council of State, Coebel was instructed to account for this
and a few smaller payments to court figures "apart," and not in
the presence of commissioners from the Council or the Chamber of Accounts. About a year later, when Coebel reported that
he was behind on his installment payments to Viglius and the
others, he was told to make a budget summary for the Advocate
and the six great cities, and not to let it come into anyone else's
hands. It seems the payments in question were later slipped into
one of the accounts for the impost and land tax in 1564/1565,
but by this time whatever Viglius had done for the States in
1557 had been long forgotten.[37]

There are not many references to such behind-the-scenes
payments, but this is not a matter on which one would expect
the official records of the States to be very informative. The
truth probably lies somewhere between Coebel's boasting (as
reported by Snouckaert) about all the gratuities he paid, and
the relative silence of the *Resolutiën van de Staten van Holland*
(RSH). Cornelis Suys, President of the Council of Holland, was
presented with a stained-glass window by the States in 1560,
and one can only speculate about the extent to which Suys and
his colleagues, who went nearly three years without receiving
any salary from the government, were amenable to being influenced by further largesse from the States. If an official who
took money from someone other than his master was not un-
equivocally condemned in sixteenth-century Europe, those who
made such payments clearly believed they were buying influence and preferred to keep the relationship confidential. Thus
Charles V's government no doubt had good reason for assigning a handsome payment in 1540 to Aert van der Goes, Advocate and chief spokesman of the States, in one of the accounts of
the Receiver for the *beden* to which deputies of the States were
not privy.[38] One must likewise assume that the States of Holland
had good reason for their payment to Viglius in 1557. By noting the difference between paymaster and recipient in these
two cases, one can perhaps form a just estimate of how the fiscal
ground had shifted in the Low Countries. Obviously the King's
debts did not call into question his sovereignty of the Nether-

lands, but there is much truth in the old adage that he who pays the piper calls the tune.

THE LEADERSHIP OF WILLIAM OF ORANGE

In any discussion of political development, one must keep in mind the distinction between bureaucratic processes and individual leadership. The former can be incremental and is to some degree predictable in its effects, but the latter is more like the spirit which blows where it will. For an understanding of Holland's fiscal strength under Philip II, it is of some importance to know that the committees appointed by the States to audit Coebel's accounts frequently included major buyers of provincial *renten*, like Haarlem's Meester Gerrit Hendrikszoon van Ravensberg.[39] But the solid credit rating of the States did not in itself guarantee that any of the deputies would have a clear vision of Holland's interests within the Habsburg state or the capacity to persuade others to work for common goals. Indeed, just as there was a crisis of authority at the center of government under Margaret of Parma, at the provincial level the strong figures that marked earlier decades of Holland's history were not to be found in the early years of Philip II's reign.

The Marquis of Vere (d. 1558), hereditary Admiral of the Netherlands, had been named Stadtholder of Holland in the hope that by combining both offices he could put to rest the Hollanders' long resistance to the authority of the admiralty. But he kept mainly to his own territory in Zeeland and was understandably preoccupied, as Admiral, by the continuing depradations of French and Scottish privateers. He was regularly consulted by the government about Holland's affairs, but he seems to have relied heavily on the advice of Assendelft. One never sees him, like Hoogstraten, visting individual towns or remonstrating with their deputies at meetings of the States.[40]

Among its many Stadholders Holland had never had such a potentate as William of Orange, Vere's successor. Hendrik van Nassau and his son Reynier, both of whom served briefly as Stadholders in Holland, had been Princes of Orange before him, and Hendrik had built the magnificent palace in Brussels where William entertained distinguished visitors with *éclat*. But

William was the first to combine in one person both the Netherlands and the German lands and titles of the Nassau family.[41] The freedom of action that this German background provided him is evident both in his marriage (1561) to a Lutheran princess, Anna of Saxony, against the will of the Netherlands government, and in his decision to attend in his own right an assembly of the princes of the Empire at Naumburg after Margaret had refused to appoint him as the representative for the Netherlands.[42] In Holland he was referred to as "his grace," and Amsterdam's *vroedschap* instructed the city's deputies on one occasion to vote with the majority of the States, "in order to win the good will of the Prince of Orange."[43] But precisely because of his many commitments in Germany and in Brussels, William of Orange was too preoccupied to give much time to his northern stadtholderates—Holland, Zeeland, and Utrecht. There is also no indication that deputies in the States spontaneously looked to him for guidance. They were still mindful of the unexpected defeat that the States had suffered when Philip II granted a blanket tax-exemption to the "three personages," Orange, Egmont, and Hornes. Periodically, the deputies reviewed documents pertaining to their efforts to sue for reversal of the King's decision, and Coebel was instructed to be sure to collect for the tenth penny on properties held by Orange that may not have been included in the 1556 decree.[44]

Lamoraal van Egmont was an important man in the province, but he was also involved in a serious quarrel with the States over navigation rights in the Maas delta. The delta was divided lengthwise by the adjacent islands of Voorne and Putten, both of which were part of Holland. One of the requirements for Holland's middleman role in the Baltic trade was an easy transit from its inland waterways to Antwerp and its outports in Zeeland. Vessels crossing the Maas delta from, say, Rotterdam to Antwerp had to pass between the islands or sail around them by going upstream as far as Dordrecht. But the channel that ran past Dordrecht was becoming impassable.[45] The Bernis channel between Voorne and Putten was also becoming so shallow that the Geervliet toll station at its lower end took in hardly any revenue. Thus only a new channel known as the Spoeye, where a new toll station had been built, was now used by vessels.

In his capacity as Prince of Gavre, Egmont had title to a stretch of bottom land adjoining Putten, including the Spoeye, and by 1555 he announced his intention to have this land diked in to make a polder, in keeping with privileges granted in 1479 to the previous owners. His lawyers denied the Hollanders' contention that the Spoeye was a public waterway, alleging that the water level was at times only a foot deep. The States sent delegations to Antwerp in hopes of gaining that important city's support ("Jacob the land-measurer" was paid thirty pounds for a map brought to Antwerp). They also tried to interest Egmont in a "friendly" solution, out of court, but to no avail. Egmont was ordered not to dike in his land pending a decision, but in 1562 the case was still being argued before the Secret Council.[46] One can hardly imagine a sharper conflict between the rights of a single great landholder and the common interests of a seafaring province. All in all, the early years of Margaret of Parma's regency did not seem a propitious moment for rapprochement between the States and the great lords.

Next to the Stadholder, the head of the Council of Holland was the leading figure in the province. Unlike his predecessor (Everaerts) and successor (Suys), Assendelft was called First Councillor, not President, perhaps because, being a nobleman, he had not remained at the law faculty of Orleans long enough to take a degree.[47] But during Mary of Hungary's long regency, Assendelft had been indispensable to the government as a constant source of information and especially as a man having sufficient authority to mediate disputes among the towns represented in the States. He often spoke for the nobles in the States, and the fact that he served in two capacities at once—representing both the prince and the nobles of Holland—seems to have been a source of strength rather than an occasion for comment.[48] The measure of his status in Holland is that it was not affected by the scandal that touched his family. As a student in Orleans, Assendelft had made his innkeeper's daughter pregnant, and then married her—something that few noblemen would have done. But Catherine Le Chasseur was never at home among the elite families of The Hague's *binnenhof*, and in 1541 she and two accomplices were convicted in the capital crime of counterfeiting. At the Council of Holland's request, the Secret Council permitted her execution to be carried out in private, "for the honor of the house of Assendelft."[49]

In April 1555, while attacking Coebel and the management of funds by the States, Snouckaert also presented the Secret Council with a list of over 500 charges of impropriety by Assendelft and his protégé, Cornelis Suys.[50] The bill of particulars is apparently no longer extant, but to judge from their replies, Suys was accused of unlawful dealings with his kinsmen among Holland's town magistrates, and Assendelft was charged with numerous counts of profiteering and tax evasion. Suys acknowledged his kinship by marriage with Aert Coebel and with Adriaan Sandelijn, Amsterdam's pensionary, but he rejected the notion that officers of the prince must be indifferent to personal considerations: "everyone is obliged to help his friends find good positions for which they are suited." He also denied any improper favoritism. For example, his silver service was bought with his own money, not given him by Amsterdam, as Snouckaert charged, in return for information on discussions within the Council about Amsterdam's magistrates.[51] Assendelft in his reply poured scorn on the social pretensions of Snouckaert, this "knight by decree" (*ridder bullatus*), "what they call a carriage knight," who claimed the title by letter patent without having been "dubbed by Emperor or King." Within the Council the factionalism undoubtedly lying behind this whole episode is evident in Snouckaert's contention that Assendelft slighted him in the distribution of commissions— that is, the investigations that were a main part of the Council's business and for which Councillors were paid "for their troubles" by the contending parties. Assendelft claimed that another of the charges proved that Snouckaert had been his secret enemy for many years. There may have been bad blood going back to the period between 1535 and 1545 when Snouckaert, along with Guilleyn Zeghers, was evidently trusted by the government more than other Councillors were in the sensitive matter of defending orthodoxy. Whatever the origins of this dispute, neither Suys nor Assendelft suffered any ill consequences, and Snouckaert, who continued his charges against the two, was forced to resign.[52]

Assendelft's death marks in many ways the end of an era for

the Council. In his study of Holland's noble families in this period, Van Nierop calls attention to those who were important enough to be summoned to the *ridderschap*, the college of nobles with a vote in the States. These men typically received their knightly titles by being dubbed and thus were entitled to be called "lord," whereas lesser men, including some who might be described as professional bureaucrats cultivating an aristocratic style of life, had only letters patent. Assendelft belongs in the former category, whereas Suys, Snouckaert, and Zeghers belong in the latter. After about 1550, *ridderschap* nobles were no longer interested in official posts, whether as members of the Council or as bailiffs exercising police powers in rural districts.[53]

At the same time, the Council was becoming more exclusively identified with its judicial function, as distinct from the political and administrative functions especially visible in Assendelft's correspondence. De Schepper's work on the Grand Council of Mechelen shows an enormous increase in the volume of litigation in the Low Countries during the Habsburg era.[54] After Assendelft's death the Council of Holland continued its political correspondence with the authorities in Brussels, but letters were exchanged with great frequency only during a terrible grain crisis in the early months of 1557. In more personal terms, Suys's few extant letters to Viglius bear no comparison with Assendelft's steady stream of reports to Hoogstraten and Mary of Hungary on all manner of topics, including the appointment of magistrates and officials. By contrast, there is preserved in The Hague a folio of correspondence for this period between the Council of Holland and the Secret Council. This correspondence records cases before the Secret Council referred to the provincial body for its opinion.[55] In effect, the Council of Holland was undergoing an evolution that had long since taken place in the more southerly provinces closer to the centers of wealth, power, and litigation. Already by the beginning of Charles V's reign, the Council of Flanders occupied itself wholly with judicial matters and, unlike the Council of Holland, was supposed to be excluded from the eminently political task of choosing magistrates from among nominations submitted by the towns.[56] By the end of Charles's reign, the Council of Holland was less aristocratic, more closely allied with burgher elites (see chapter 5), and more strictly judicial in its functions. These developments point to a loss of independent political influence; thus, it is easier to understand how the States could successfully resist most of the Council's claims to the right of overseeing their fiscal decisions. Philip II's government needed an authoritative voice in Holland no less than Charles V's government did, but Suys and the Council were no longer able to provide it.[57]

For some issues, the government seemed to rely less on the Council than on Sheriff Willem Dirkszoon Baerdes of Amsterdam. When Baerdes was first appointed (1544), the office was still held in pawn by the city government, but he continued in office after Mary of Hungary redeemed the government's right of appointment in 1550. Through his contacts with the merchant community, Baerdes was a constant source of reliable information on the vital grain trade. As need required, he could describe trading practices on the Torun grain exchange in Poland or explain how current prices in Lisbon were affecting grain markets in the Netherlands.[58] He was not able or perhaps not willing to enforce the government's commands for Amsterdam to "communicate" its precious grain to other cities during the terrible shortage of 1557,[59] but in more normal times he used the powers of his office to regulate the flow of grain out of the city according to a price-trigger mechanism first put into place by Mary of Hungary. If this meant restricting the activities of his merchant contacts, he also did them an important service by helping persuade the government to take action against the "monopolists" of the southern Netherlands who bought up fields of rye in Poland before the crop was even sown.[60] Baerdes was the man to whom the government sometimes turned first for general information about the province. For example, in 1558 Savoy wanted a troublesome mercenary army moved from Amersfoort to England by a route that would cause least inconvenience to the King's lands. Contacted by the Governor-General, Baerdes provided four alternatives, commenting on the advantages and disadvantages of each; without naming his source, Savoy passed these alternatives on to the Council, asking them to name an "expert person" to advise the English ambassador.[61] To be sure, as Woltjer points out, Baerdes had not had anyone executed for the crime of heresy since 1553. Yet when informed about a fugitive preacher making his way through Holland, he took measures that would inspire confidence in any ruler, including having "two of my secret informants spend two nights outside the Haarlem gate, with a description of [the fugitive's] appearance."[62]

Baerdes's effectiveness was limited, however, by the bitter feud that seems to have begun as soon as he accepted appointment from the Queen (1550). Friction between locally elected magistrates and a sheriff appointed by the prince was commonplace in Holland's towns,[63] but the struggle in Amsterdam had an intensity and a duration that suggests deep-seated animosity. The shift (after 1538) from one ruling faction to another had been accompanied by recriminations against leaders of the former regime with whom Baerdes had close ties; moreover, his initial appointment as Sheriff (1542) seems to have been a peace offering from the current magistrates to those who were now excluded from power.[64] In any event, after 1550, Baerdes was refused admission to meetings of the *vroedschap;* he was not allowed to appoint a deputy, and when he finally did so, the burgomasters contested the appointment for years. Worst of all, in 1553 Baerdes, his wife, and daughter were acccused of heresy by two informants who came forward with the support of Meester Hendrik Dirkszoon and of the pastor of the Old Church, Floris Engelbrechtszoon. After many years of litigation, the tables were turned: the two key witnesses were convicted of bearing false accusations, and their two sponsors were convicted of having suborned them. The leading witness, a woman of mean estate, was executed; Dirkszoon got off with four years of house arrest in The Hague, the pastor with perpetual banishment from Amsterdam.[65]

There is little doubt that officials in both Brussels and The Hague favored the Sheriff, not his accusers. Sent to Amsterdam to place Dirkszoon and the pastor under arrest as quietly as possible, Vere reported that he had gotten a promise that nominations for the college of *schepenen* would be made "in the presence of Assendelft, or of the Sheriff," but he feared that nothing less than the King's "absolute power" was required to break the power of Dirkszoon's friends among the burgomasters and the *vroedschap*.[66] The Council in The Hague sought but did not obtain permission to put the pastor under torture, and when asked to investigate further in subsequent years, they insisted there was no other way to get at the truth.[67]

This vindictive campaign against the Sheriff diminished not only his political effectiveness, but also that of Amsterdam's magistrates. Relative to Holland's other towns, Amsterdam grew steadily larger and wealthier as time went on,[68] but its continuing economic strength somehow did not translate into a leadership in the States like that exercised by its deputies during the Guelders wars of the 1520s or the Baltic crises of the 1530s (see chaps. 3 and 4). Amsterdam had much to bargain with in its dealings with a penurious government—the city carried a surplus forward from year to year in its accounts—but the ongoing feud with Baerdes seems to have narrowed the magistrates' vision of what to bargain for.

In February 1557, asked to endorse a 50,000 pound *obligatie* in the city's name, the magistrates wanted the office of the sheriff to be included among the parcels of domain-that would be placed in their keeping for the duration of the loan. Savoy wrote Vere that "for several reasons" he was unwilling to place the sheriff's office into their hands, not even for 50,000 pounds. When Amsterdam insisted on precisely this condition, dragging out the negotiations, Savoy raised the stakes by ordering Vere to delay the election of magistrates beyond the customary January term, on the grounds that privileges granted by Mary of Hungary had not been renewed in Philip's reign. Finally, in April 1558, the magistrates signed off on the *obligatie* in return for renewal of the city's election privileges and the keeping of certain parcels of domain, not including the sheriff's office.[69] In 1564 the magistrates finally persuaded Margaret of Parma to surrender control of the sheriff's office, for a cash payment of 20,000 pounds. But the certain knowledge that Baerdes would be removed when his current three-year contract expired prompted his supporters in the town to file a grievance or *Doleantie* with the government, charging the burgomasters with nepotism, misappropriation of tax revenue, and other abuses. The seventy burghers (henceforth known as *Doleanten*) who signed this grievance included many of the city's prominent merchants, and it was on this account to be taken seriously. It seems to have been well received in Brussels where Margaret of Parma was especially interested in hearing more about those allegedly misappropriated revenues.[70] Thus if the magistrates did gain their partisan objective, they did so at the price of their credibility, both at home and in Brussels.

Even in regard to the Baltic trade, Amsterdam's Dirkist magistrates were not so prominent in discussions in the States as their predecessors had been.[71] For one thing, they apparently did not have the kind of contacts in the Baltic region that Cornelis Bennink enjoyed in earlier decades. In 1561, when France sent an envoy to Copenhagen, Philip II and his government heard about this potentially dangerous connection not from Amsterdam, but from William of Orange, who had learned of it on one of his trips to Germany.[72] The same year, the States decided, with Margaret's approval, to send an envoy to protest an increase in the rates of the Sound Toll. The initial choice fell on Meester Pieter Bicker, a wealthy Amsterdammer, but not a magistrate. But since the government apparently felt that a man of greater dignity should be sent, Bicker was replaced by Meester Philips Coebel, a member of the Secret Council, and brother of Holland's Receiver for the Common Land.[73] Finally, as mentioned earlier, when Amsterdam's grain merchants sought relief from the monopolistic practices of "great purses" seeking to control eastern grain markets, they approached the Netherlands government through Baerdes, not the magistrates.[74] Amsterdam's burghers were in a sense bound to become less important in the formal dealings between their government and the Baltic states than they once had been, if only because the placement of diplomacy on a more regular basis required the employment of important nobles or at least high officials like Philips Coebel rather than mere businessmen like Pieter Bicker. But one might also infer from what has been said that there was something less than close collaboration between Amsterdam's magistrates and the resident community of grain merchants. In fact, just as there is a curious absence of brewers among Delft's magistrates at this time, there were no grain merchants among Amsterdam's leading *Dirkisten*, except for Klaas Doedeszoon, who died in 1558.[75] It is also worth noting that while many magistrates lived along Warmoes Straat, they lived at the upper end of the city's most fashionable street, whereas merchant-burghers and foreign grain dealers were concentrated at the lower end where the open-air grain market was held. Conversely, one finds men from the lower end of Warmoes Straat among signatories of the *Doleantie*, in effect supporting Sheriff Baerdes.[76]

In any case, Amsterdam was not the only city where one can detect a certain estrangement between the magistrate elite and the substantial population of comfortable-to-wealthy men who were their natural constituents. This stratum, known as the *rijkdom*, provided recruits for a town's military guilds (the *schutters*), and at the upper levels for the magistracy. But there seems to have been a tendency for ruling elites to have become more tightly oligarchical as time went on—this was certainly true for Amsterdam's *Dirkisten*—and in the iconoclastic crisis of August 1566, many a town government was afraid to call on its *schutters* to stop the mobs rampaging through the churches. In an interesting study of the relations between magistrates and wider elites in Holland's towns, Christopher Grayson finds that "the crisis of authority in the Netherlands from 1564 to 1567 was not confined to the center."[77] Another way of putting the matter is to say that the magistrates of this era understood more about lawsuits and debt servicing than they did about commerce. As time passes, the pages of the *Resolutiën van de Staten van Holland* (RSH) are more and more filled with petitions for tax rebates, instructions to Coebel about the sale of *renten* or the repayment of debt, payment orders for services rendered to the States, and summaries of lawsuits sustained by the States before the Grand Council or the Secret Council. This development obviously reflects the devolution of fiscal responsibility in the Low Countries to the provincial states, and it virtually demanded the services of magistrate-deputies who were trained in the law and who were themselves major investors in the public debt. But the men who had these qualifications were necessarily somewhat detached from the business concerns of their constituents, and they had no special expertise in dealing with a political or religious crisis that threatened the foundations of the social order.

On many occasions during these years, it was the noble deputies who provided leadership in the States. Speaking first in the States, the nobles had long been accustomed to framing proposals or counter-proposals in fiscal negotiations with the government, and during Charles V's reign what the States finally agreed to was often compounded of elements from proposals by the nobles and the towns, especially Dordrecht and Amsterdam. Under Philip II, and perhaps a bit earlier, nobles attended sessions of the States in greater numbers, as if exchanging participation in this body for the government offices that their ancestors had held. For example, the son of Assendelft and the nephew of his fellow-Councillor Arent van Duvenvoirde, Lord of Warmond, frequently attended meetings of the States, but were not officials.[78] Also, possibly because of new techniques for drainage and dike-building, the age-long process of reclaiming land for cultivation was vigorously taken up again around mid-century, overseen by officials acting for the crown as well as urban investors.[79] But nobles great and small had always been the natural leaders of reclamation projects and still were. Egmont and Brederode had major interests in the Zijpe and elsewhere in north Holland. To the south, Egmont at least had plans for his holdings on Putten, as noted earlier, and Heyman van der Ketel, a son of Meester Vincent Corneliszoon van Mierop, diked in some land in the Maas delta that later bore his name.[80] Thus the landed interest for which the nobles in the States spoke was a relative bright spot in Holland's economy during a period when commerce and manufacturing were periodically damaged by war in Germany, war with France, friction with England, and troubles in the Baltic. Finally, the fact that the countryside was now shouldering proportionately more of the tax burden (see chapter 5) likely gave greater weight to the single vote of the college of nobles who alone represented the countryside. It is probably in this sense that Verhofstad speaks of the "moral authority" of the nobles in the States.[81] All in all, it is not surprising if the urban members of the States were sometimes willing to "follow the nobles," as Amsterdam's *vroedschap* once instructed its deputies to do.[82]

To sum up, with a partial exception for the nobles in the States, no person or group played a leading role in Holland's affairs, as Hoogstraten or Assendelft or Amsterdam's magistrates in the era of Cornelis Bennink and Ruysch Janszoon had once done. This situation began to change in March 1563, when Orange and Egmont withdrew from the Council of State and travelled together to Holland. En route, they evidently discussed Egmont's dispute with the States over the Spoeye. On 6 April the States voted to accept Orange's offer of mediation. On 7 May, the deputies agreed to terms proposed by Egmont: he would keep the channel open, and Holland would compensate him for whatever losses he suffered, as determined by arbiters who were experts on dikage, including Orange and the Marquis of Vere. Each side would continue to argue its case before the Secret Council, with the understanding that they could at any time conclude the suit by mutual agreement. On 22 May, when Orange's role as mediator was again affirmed, the States determined that Egmont and Hendrik van Brederode would be summoned to all future *dagvaarten*.[83] Meanwhile, Orange had been building up a clientele in Holland, as great lords did. For example, Assendelft's brother, Dirk van Assendelft, was the long-time Sheriff of Orange's town of Breda in northern Brabant. Orange arranged for Cornelis Suys to become *ambachtsheer* of Rijswijk, near The Hague (1557), and he was also instrumental in Suys's appointment as President of the Council of Holland (1559). Aert Coebel, it will be recalled, served as *rentmeester* for some of Orange's lands in south Holland even while serving the States as Receiver for the Common Land.[84] The only sour note came from the patrician feud in Amsterdam; Margaret asked Orange to mediate the factional dispute, but the *vroedschap* refused to bear the costs of his visit to the city since it had come at the behest of certain "private persons," that is, the *Doleanten*. From the tone of this comment in the *vroedschap* resolutions it sounds as if the *Doleanten* too had been added to Orange's long list of friends.[85]

Meetings of the States were not very frequent during the troubled final years of Margaret of Parma's regency, but one sees the deputies calling on Orange to present their case for diplomatic initiatives to keep the Sound open, postponing their response to the government's request for a *bede* until his return, and petitioning Margaret to instruct him to reside in Holland for the winter of 1565/1566.[86] To show their appreciation to the Stadtholder, the States offered him a 30,000-pound gratuity, the same amount Hoogstraten had demanded for himself in the 1520s. When Orange indicated that he did not want the money, the States insisted on giving him 10,000 anyway, assigned to the impost and land tax account for 1566/1567. The Prince's advisers later suggested he could use the rest of the money, and an additional 20,000 pounds was assigned to the same account. Two years later, when this account was audited, both payments to Orange were disallowed for "certain reasons." By this time, Orange was in Germany, the exiled leader of a rebellion.[87]

Earlier chapters of this book have suggested that the States of Holland could work their will against powerful government officials only in collaboration with the great lords. Thus the States went to IJsselstein and others to have Castre removed, despite Hoogstraten's objections (1528); they rewarded members of the Council of State for their decision to remand the *congie* dispute to the Grand Council of Mechelen (1531); and they persuaded IJsselstein and Hoogstraten to refuse the Queen's order to lead their *bandes d'ordonnance* against Meynert van Ham, meaning that troops destined for the unpopular expedition to Copenhagen would have to be used instead (1536). One might even suggest that Mary of Hungary was able to assert real authority in the Netherlands only because alliances of this sort, joining the power of the purse in the states and the political influence of the great nobles, were temporary rather than permanent. But under Margaret of Parma there was a new constellation of relationships in the Council of State, and hence in the provinces as well. Individually, men like Egmont and Orange asserted their personal authority more forcefully than ever so that, as Vermij observes, the government had the novel experience of seeing the influence of the high nobility as "ruinously competitive with royal authority."[88] As a group, joined together against Granvelle, these men commanded an allegiance never before enjoyed by subjects of a Habsburg or Burgundian ruler. Under Orange's leadership, Holland was being drawn into a national movement of opposition, first against Granvelle, then against the *placards*.

HOLLAND'S RESISTANCE TO THE PLACARDS

As in other parts of the Netherlands,[89] the continuing enforcement of the *placards* against heresy brought numerous protests
in Holland, sometimes with overtones of violence. In April
1557 two Anabaptists, including one burgher, were held in
Haarlem's St. John's gate prison under sentence of death by the
town *gerecht*. One or both became known to the populace because of sermons preached through the prison window, attract-
ing large crowds. On the night of 25 April, around midnight,
Sheriff Pieter van Soutelande ordered his deputies to bring the
prisoners to the town hall, whence they were to be led out to the
scaffold on the main square the next day. Despite the lateness of
the hour, a numerous and angry company attended the deputies, causing the Sheriff to have the prisoners brought inside his
own house. At first light he set off with them for the town hall,
but this time a crowd estimated by the Sheriff at 300 gathered
again, many kissing the prisoners and bidding them adieu en
route. Ouside the town hall, the square was so full that it took
strenuous efforts by the Sheriff and all members of the *gerecht*
to form the "ring" within which the executions were to take
place. When the excutioner had done his work, one of the
bystanders grabbed a board from the pile meant for burning
the bodies of the victims and threatened the Sheriff. Soutelande
drew his sword, and when (according to the Sheriff's testimony) someone cried out, "Strike them dead!" all the magistrates scattered to the safety of the town hall, leaving Soutelande alone to face the crowd.[90] Savoy's instinct was to have a
member of the Grand Council deputed to investigate the Sheriff's complaints about this incident as well as about the generally
lax attitude of the magistrates toward enforcement of the law.
But at Viglius's suggestion the matter was referred to Vere and
the Council of Holland. Four months later, Savoy reminded
Vere and the Council that they had not reported on what happened in Haarlem. In reply, the Council said that inquiries by
one of the Councillors had not turned up reliable evidence that
any crime had been committed, since the claim about "seditious
words" was supported only by one of the Sheriff's servants.
Savoy had to be content with scolding Haarlem for giving the

prisoners access to a window; the magistrates replied that they had no cells without windows.[91]

Sometimes it was not possible to tell the difference between old-fashioned anticlericalism and new-style heresy, as at Oudewater where women and children made a show of barring the town gate to the inquisitor and deputy procurator who had come to arrest the vice-curate.[92] In Enkhuizen, on the night of 26 July 1557, the *schutters,* "having made good cheer all day," marched with fife and drum to the house of Sir Balthasar Platander, pastor of the Old Church. When one of their officers received no reply after striking the door three times with his staff, the men smashed in the door with a beam, but the pastor had fled. According to the complaint that reached Savoy, it was the intention of the culprits to "help [the pastor] out of this world," because they blamed him for the fact that Ruard Tapper, chief Inquisitor for the Netherlands, had removed from his post a popular but suspect preacher at the New Church, Cornelis Coelthuyn.[93] As described in reports from the Council of Holland, this episode has overtones of a counter-ritual enactment of the way the minions of the law sometimes sought out accused persons in their homes at night.[94] But Procurator General Christiaan de Waert could not confirm the more serious allegations during his inquiry in the city. The *schutters* did indeed stove in the pastor's door, but neither he nor the pastor of the New Church believed there was any heresy involved. Rather, as the *schutters* claimed, they were amusing themselves in the way the men of such companies sometimes did. Later, the Council wrote Philip II urging him not to "reform" the light sentence Enkhuizen's *gerecht* had meted out to the offenders, noting that criminal sentences were not easily corrected (the accused was not allowed to appeal a conviction), and that lawless behavior was common when *schutters* convened among themselves.[95]

The most serious incident took place in Rotterdam on 28 March 1558 when three men and two women Anabaptists, arrested early in the month, were to be executed in front of the town hall. Perhaps mindful of what had happened at Haarlem, the magistrates took the precaution of enclosing the "ring" within which the hangings were to take place with a double row of stakes. A large crowd watched as the first victim, a man, dangled at the end of a rope. Thinking he was dead, the executioner tried to light a pile of straw under his feet, but at this point the unfortunate man's legs moved. At this "there came a great outcry from the people, who were mostly from outside the city," or so Rotterdam's deputies claimed in their initial report to the Council of Holland. A woman's slipper flew into the ring, and before long the stakes were broken down, the victim was cut down, and the bailiff and the magistrates sought shelter in the tower of the town hall; "to save their lives" they had to release the other four prisoners still in their keeping, while a mob rummaged through the building, smashing doors and windows and burning records. This time the Council reported directly to Philip II who demanded an additional report from the Count of Boussu (substituting for his brother-in-law, Vere, who was ill) and Johan van Cruningen, lord of nearby Heenvliet. Because the escaped Anabaptists (including the man who was nearly dead) had not been recaptured, the Council and the two lords acted jointly to interrogate and punish leaders of the mob, some of whom were arrested in Delfshaven and Zwartewaal. One man who had heaved a stone to break down the town hall door was executed, as was another who had helped "a crippled woman prisoner" to escape, and several others were severely punished.[96]

Both the Council and the two lords strictly instructed Rotterdam's magistrates to take greater precautions next time, by closing the town gates and assembling the *schutters* at the place of execution. In fact there was not to be a next time for Rotterdam's magistrates, and there do not seem to have been any further executions for heresy by any town government in Holland prior to 1566, except in The Hague where a kinsman of David Joris is reported to have been "punished according to the placards" in 1564.[97] Meanwhile, the States kept up their defense of the principle of *de non evocando*, by joining in suits by various towns to prevent their burghers from being tried against their will outside the province.[98]

That there were Mennonite communities in various localities was common knowledge. In 1562 a repentant Anabaptist in Amsterdam, Jan Janszoon Mandemaker, gained clemency by giving the names of fifty-two Mennonites and three other sectarians of his acquaintaince, many of whom were still living in Amsterdam. Margaret of Parma transmitted this list to the Council in The Hague and instructed Suys to contact one of Amsterdam's burgomasters "discreetly" and to bring Jan Janszoon to The Hague for further questioning. Instead, another Councillor going to Amsterdam on other business contacted Sheriff Baerdes; fourteen persons were arrested as a result. Questioned on this matter some years later, the Council acknowledged that all fourteen had somehow escaped, but had no further information.[99] When the *placards* against heresy were reissued in Holland in 1564, deputies in the States expressed alarm at their apparent novelty, not understanding that the text was made up from "extracts" of earlier *placards* or that the wording did not mean that persons found in possession of forbidden books would not have an opportunity to exculpate themselves.[100]

The Council itself was somewhat more zealous about enforcing the *placards* than town governments were, but not much.[101] Margaret of Parma repeatedly asked the Council to investigate reports she was receiving from unnamed informants, but seldom did she receive a reply that she would likely consider satisfactory.[102] In March 1561 Frans van Boschuysen, Sheriff of the island of Texel, submitted to the Council a detailed plan, requiring two caravels and four oared barges, to seize numerous "sectarians" who had taken refuge on the neighboring island of Vlieland. Margaret liked the plan and ordered the receiver of domain revenues for north Holland to give the Procurator General 600 pounds to put it into effect. Instead, the Council consulted further with Boschhuysen and with Amsterdam's Sheriff Baerdes, then reported to William of Orange that the plan was unwise because many of those being sought would already be at sea for the sailing season and because there was already "murmuring" on Vlieland.[103] In January 1562 Andries Dirkszoon, pastor of Enkhuizen's New Church, was summoned to Hoorn and detained there by the Dean of West Friesland on charges that he "preached against the Pope" at nighttime gatherings. One night some burghers of Enkhuizen called up to the prisoner's window and had him jump onto a bed they had brought; after preaching again in Enkhuizen, Dirkszoon escaped to

Emden, as Cornelis Coelthuyn had done a few years earlier. Margaret wanted a report from the Council because Orange had informed her that the Sheriff of Enkhuizen dared not lay hands on the culprits, "which makes us think that things are not as they should be in Enkhuizen." When the Procurator General found that those accused had "alibis" for the night in question, they were released.[104]

In the summer of 1564 Margaret received two private reports on the state of religion in Holland, probably from trusted noblemen, including an assurance that the Council was "doing their duty" in regard to heresy. In fact, it was about this time that Jan Gerritszoon Ketelboeter was burned in The Hague as a "stubborn Anabaptist," the first person to be executed for heresy by the Council since 1552.[105] Finally, in January 1565 the Council accepted the word of Medemblik's magistrates that none of their burghers were "infected" with heresy. Margaret replied that she would be happy to believe this report but could not because her "informations" told her otherwise. Thus she ordered the Council to check again.[106]

From this correspondence one may infer a pattern of tension between Regent and Council that both sides understood without wishing to acknowledge. The Council often found ways of not doing what the Regent ordered, while avoiding a direct refusal, and Margaret kept up the pretense of treating the Councillors as loyal executors of her will, while manifestly doubting some of what they told her. If there was anyone in Holland whom Margaret could trust fully on the delicate matter of enforcing heresy law, it would surely have been the new bishops—Niklaas van Nieuwland, Bishop of Haarlem, and Willem Lindanus, dean of the chapter in The Hague and Bishop-elect of Roermond. In fact, however, neither of these men was entirely suitable for her purposes. Nieuwland had a drinking problem, and at his previous post as auxiliary bishop of Utrecht, he had been popularly known as "Nick the drunk" (*dronken Klaasje*). He was appropriately critical of Church officials who took fees for granting petitions, but he apparently did not support the draconian policies that were a test of loyalty in Philip's eyes. Early in 1564 he asked permission to grant remission to repentant heretics in the West Friesland district, in effect a reversion to milder policies tried during the 1530s. With reluctance, Margaret approved his request, noting that Philip II had determined not to let any of his provincial councils have authority to grant remission.[107]

After his unfortunate experience in Friesland, Lindanus lived quietly in The Hague. He accepted a new commission as inquisitor for Holland only after it became apparent that the town of Roermond, where he had been appointed Bishop (1562), would not admit him within its gates. The terms of his commission authorized him to interrogate suspected heretics, with the understanding that on his recommendation accused persons would be arrested by the local officer of justice and tried by the Council of Holland.[108] In 1564 one of Margaret's informants told her that Lindanus was "held in meager esteem" in Holland. His activity as inquisitor has left no trace in the correspondence between Brussels and The Hague, but he probably had something to do with the two trials that ended in executions in The Hague in 1564, one by the city government and one by the Council. By 1565 there was evident friction between Lindanus and the Council. In March, Margaret ordered the Council to make sure the chapter allowed Lindanus the income from his benefice even when he was absent from The Hague, since his absence was in the service of Church and King. There was also a three-cornered exchange of letters between Margaret of Parma, Lindanus, and the Council concerning two stained-glass artists from The Hague, Meinert Pieterszoon and Joris Janszoon. The two had been arrested for heresy at Lindanus's recommendation by the Bailiff of The Hague, and when the *schepenen* of the town voted to acquit them, the Bailiff appealed their verdict to the Council. Margaret wanted to know in April 1565 why the Council had not proceeded against the two prisoners, and in November she was still asking. The Council insisted that, although these men admitted being communicants of the "upright church of Christ" and would not produce evidence that their children had been baptized, there was no evidence that they had committed overt acts against the *placards* and they should therefore be tried by Church courts for their heretical opinions. Lindanus countered that there was no point in turning such stiff-necked heretics as these over to the Church courts, which lacked the power to impose a death sentence. There were unfortunately lots of Anabaptists, and what was needed was honest enforcement of the *placards* by the secular courts.[109]

Lindanus did agree to compile a list of complaints of dereliction of duty by the Council and lesser courts in Holland and Zeeland, a copy of which was sent to the Council in April 1565. Many of the incidents he raised go back several years, like the smashing-in of the pastor's door in Enkhuizen (1557), or the escape of fourteen Anabaptists in Amsterdam. He also entered on slippery ground by associating himself with those for whom charges of heresy were a partisan weapon against their adversaries, as when he alleged that the punishment of the pastor of Amsterdam's Old Church (one of Sheriff Baerdes's accusers) had deterred many honest Catholics from coming forward with accusations. In the case of the small town of Medemblik where Lindanus repeated Margaret of Parma's contention that heresy was rife, the Council was able to reply that such accusations were part of an ongoing feud among the town's few patrician families.[110]

Elswhere, Lindanus had gotten his information wrong, or else the local authorities whom the Council consulted before responding had found a clever retort; for instance, the chamber of rhetoric in Capelle (Zeeland) had indeed put on a scurrilous play on Shrove Tuesday, but the object of their merriment was "the pants of Priapus," not "the pants of St. Francis." As to Lindanus's question whether "the number of people in church and at Easter mass [in Holland] does not diminish continually," the Council reported that recent inquiries in Hoorn and West Friesland, an area thought to be suspect, produced reliable information that "the Catholic religion grows more than declines"; in Hoorn itself, there were 500 more communicants than the previous year. It might be noted that one of Margaret of Parma's private informants had made a similar observation about Catholicism in north Holland in 1564. Finally, the fact that the Council waited ten months before submitting its formal reply, despite the King's interest in Lindanus's charges, suggests that no one in Brussels took the matter too seriously.[111]

Orthodox zealots like Lindanus were at most an irritant in the delicate play of evasion conducted by Margaret of Parma and the officials and magisitrates to whom she communicated her instructions. The Regent undoubtedly knew that her correspondents were ignoring the *placards* as far as they dared, but, given the tenor of Philip's instructions, confirmed once again in the letters from Segovia Wood, she had no choice but to pretend that she was writing to people who would obey her. In Holland, men in responsible positions had no desire to undermine the authority of their sovereign lord, the King of Spain, but neither were they so foolish as to persist in the enforcement of laws that the King's subjects deemed unlawful. That crowds were breaking through the "ring" of punishment, that visible emblem of the majesty of the law, shows clearly enough what people thought of the idea that religious dissent was punishable by death. J. J. Woltjer has identified opposition to the death penalty for religious offenses as the key political question in the Netherlands after 1560. He rejects the claim that Orange seized on this issue opportunistically, as if something more important were at stake, and he points out that even a figure like Hippolytus Persijn, erstwhile hammer of heretics in Friesland, had concluded by 1565 that heresy should no longer be punished by death. But Philip II, in the privacy of his study in far-off Madrid, could not distinguish between maintainance of the Catholic religion and maintainance of the *placards*.[112]

No one, it seems, contested the principle that the sovereign prince had residual powers (*potestas absoluta*) to override existing laws and privileges. Philip II's problem was that he chose to exercise this authority on an issue for which there was almost no support. Had he chosen to override the tax exemptions of Holland's "three personages," he would have had the States fully behind him. Instead, by confirming the privileges of Orange and the others, he showed the States how powerless they were without the cooperation of these great lords. When he revealed himself unremitting in his insistence on the *placards,* both the provincial states and, in a quieter way, the King's officials rallied to the position taken by Orange and others in the Council of State. It was, finally, by demanding obedience to this unpopular law that the King made his subjects aware of their strength.

Conclusion

It has not been the aim of this book to argue that Holland somehow ripened into revolt against Philip II, like an apple about to fall off a tree. Revolt is by definition sudden, often unexpected, certainly in this period of history, and no one could have predicted the chain of events that led to the crisis: the organized wave of iconoclasm that spread from Flanders through Holland in the late summer of 1566, the terrified inaction of town governments as mobs rampaged through their churches, and Philip's decision to send Alba with an army of 10,000, despite assurances from Margaret of Parma that noble and burgher elites had now rallied to the support of the government.[1] Further, while the emphasis here has been on the development of provincial institutions, centering on the States, another book could be written on contemporaneous processes by which the Netherlands provinces were being knitted together into a single realm. If fiscal history has a centrifugal tendency, because of the autonomy the provincial states demanded as their tax burdens increased, the judicial system of the Netherlands was a powerful agent of centralization. By mid-century, even the provinces that had been acquired by Charles V and were not required to send deputies to the States General,[2] were showing a dramatic increase in appeals to the Grand Council of Mechelen,[3] and presumably to the Secret Council as well. Bondholders might wish the revenues by which debt was funded to be managed in The Hague rather than Brussels, but wealthy litigants care more about getting a verdict that is final and decisive than about where the verdict is rendered. The point is that in a highly articulated polity like the Habsburg Netherlands, a strengthening of provincial institutions does not preclude a similar development at the center of government. In this sense too, the growing autonomy of provincial institutions is not in itself a prelude to revolt.

It has also not been the purpose here to claim that the States of Holland, with its majority of burgher deputies, was politically self-sufficient within the framework of the Habsburg state. In their ongoing debates with government commissioners, the States by themselves could successfully assert their will on fiscal issues (e.g., how a subsidy was to be raised or who was to collect it), but not much else. Significant political victories for the States were possible only through collaboration with the great lords who were themselves an important part of the government. Thus the close relationship between the States and William of Orange during the final years of Margaret of Parma's regency was not wholly without precedent. As for the Revolt, it is common knowledge that the success of the rebel cause depended at times on decisive action by Orange, overruling the hesitations and quarrels of the States. For example, the Spanish siege of Leiden was relieved (October 1575) only after Orange, disregarding the adamant opposition of local interests, ordered the dam at Leidschendam broken through, allowing flood waters to carry the Dutch flotilla to the walls of Leiden.[4] One can indeed speak of Holland as a burgher republic in the middle of the seventeenth century, but only in a qualified sense during the early decades of the Revolt, and not at all in the Habsburg period.

Rather, it has been the argument here that the county of Holland showed noticeably greater unity and cohesion by the 1560s than it did at the beginning of the century. The change resulted from the pressure of external events, from the growth of provincial institutions and responsibilities, especially in the fiscal sphere, and from a common political consciousness centered on the idea of defending the privileges of the province and of its component members. Each of these points deserves a final comment.

Enemies on the landward side were of no small importance in causing Holland's fractious communities to establish important patterns of cooperation among themselves. From the time of its absorption by the Dukes of Burgundy (1425) until the first military campaigns of the Revolt, Holland faced only two major threats from the east: the first during the Utrecht War of 1481–1484; the second, less intense but more prolonged, in the incursions from Guelders, from the 1490s until the conquest of

Utrecht in 1528. Coinciding with a grain shortage that was even worse than that of 1557, the Utrecht War compelled Holland to raise a level of subsidies that would not be seen again until the 1520s. Of particular interest is a sale of *renten* in excess of 200,000 pounds, for which "the common land" assumed responsibility, and which was funded by domain receipts entrusted to the States. To be sure, the fact that Amsterdam sold its quota "apart" was a breach of corporate solidarity, but even this limited assertion of the principle of provincial responsibility for debt seems to have been without precedent among the Low Countries parliaments at this time. The Guelders wars revealed and eventually surmounted a latent hostility between towns in the southern and northern parts of the province. Amsterdam had many grievances against Dordrecht (and its ally, Gouda) over the inland waterways, and it is not surprising if the northern towns at times refused to consider an attack along the Maas valley as their problem. They changed their tune, however, as it became evident that Guelders could attack equally well down the Rijn through the bishopric of Utrecht or across the Zuider Zee. By the 1520s, the States were willing to respond enthusiastically if promised an attack on the enemy and if their deputies participated in the management of war subsidies.

Yet because Holland was a seafaring province, its interests were most vitally affected by anything that threatened the massive flow of goods along its inland waterways, outbound toward the Baltic and inbound in the direction of Antwerp. Though comparisons of this sort are inherently difficult, there is a *prima facie* case that no other Low Countries province depended so much on a single strand of economic activity as Holland did on the Baltic trade. Even as a Burgundian province, Holland had gone to war against Lübeck in the 1430s to preserve its position in the Baltic, and it is not surprising if the States displayed a singular unanimity in responding to any threat to Holland's Baltic trade during Charles V's reign. They fitted out war fleets against Lübeck in 1511 and again in 1533, and by "making friends" with the great lords, they warded off several efforts to impose an export duty on Baltic grain that would have been disastrous for Holland. At the same time, under Philip II the States were somewhat less vigilant for the interests of the Baltic trade, perhaps because the crucial city of Amsterdam now had a new ruling faction in which the grain traders apparently had less influence than they did in the ruling party ousted in 1538. It did make a difference who the deputies were and to whom they listened at home.

So long as a parliamentary body retained the power of the purse, one would expect it in the normal course of things to develop some sort of bureaucratic apparatus of its own, as well as a greater sense of its dignity. For the parliaments of the Low Countries provinces, this natural tendency was accelerated by the enormous war debts that the government accumulated and by the imperious practical need to convert bankers' loans at up to twenty-two percent into funded or long-term debt that could be supported at much lower rates. The fact that Antwerp's bankers came to trust no one but the provincial states to sign short-term obligations—not the King, not his fiscal officials, not the great lords of his council—was another powerful inducement for the states to develop their own fiscal competency.

In Holland, one may distinguish three phases in the States' assuming collective responsibility for debt. First, during the Utrecht War, the States took on both the responsibility for the *renten* debt and the management of the domain receipts by which it was to be funded; indeed, the office of Receiver for the Common Land dates from this period, though it was not yet controlled by the States. Second, during the Guelders wars, the States allowed the *ordinaris bede* revenues, which they themselves granted, to be pledged as surety for new issues of *renten*. But since these receipts were controlled by the Emperor's Receiver for the *beden,* not by anyone answerable to the States, funds allocated for the redemption of *renten* were seldom used for this purpose, and interest payments on old *renten* became a chronic burden on the *ordinaris bede*. Finally, during the last two Habsburg-Valois wars, the States agreed to much larger issues of *renten,* funded by the impost and land tax that the States themselves granted and managed. Moreover, during this period Amsterdam was forced to end its proud isolation, so that the debt was truly the responsibility of "the common body of the land." The outcome of these different ways of managing debt make it clear why Antwerp's bankers preferred to deal with the States. The Utrecht War debt was not paid off until 1529, and two-thirds of the *renten* sold on the *ordinaris bede* between 1515 and 1533 were still outstanding in 1566. By contrast, the first *renten* funded on the impost and land tax were retired within a few years, and the huge debt accumulated between 1552 and 1559 was about half paid off by 1566.

This new form of debt creation served the Habsburg state well by raising vast amounts of money during the 1550s, but in the long run it effected a dramatic shift in the relative position of the central government and its provinces. Although Holland guaranteed short-term notes in Philip II's reign to "strengthen the credit of his majesty," the province contributed almost nothing to the government's needs once the war with France was over, on the grounds that its tax-paying capacity was fully absorbed in servicing the debt created during the war. As a result, the province not only maintained a superior credit rating, at a time when the government could not even pay the salaries of its officials, but showed a positive cash flow, which could be used either for additional debt retirement or for gratuities to helpful officials. By this time, the office of Receiver for the Common Land was fully controlled by the States, which could instruct Aert Coebel to make certain payments under the table so as not to be noticed by government officials who sat on the auditing committees. The Council of Holland, somewhat against its will, was induced to place the enforcement apparatus of the Hof van Holland at the disposal of the States, for collecting the revenues they controlled. No wonder, then, that in these years the deputies took to calling themselves "mighty lords."

Finally there is the question of political consciousness. Vermij detects a growing provincial patriotism in Holland, and the term *patria*, popularized by the humanists, is used even earlier in discussions in the States, as when the deputies voted a birthday gift for Erasmus "ratione communis patriae." But in the absence of careful study of how this term and related words are used, in which many different kinds of sources would have to be consulted, one cannot be sure what sixteenth-century Netherlanders meant when they said "fatherland." Erasmus himself was more a Netherlander and less a rootless cosmopolitan than has commonly been thought. His usage of *patria*, which has been studied, refers sometimes to Holland where he was born, and sometimes to Brabant where he lived much of his adult life.[5] Others may have used the term of the Habsburg Netherlands as a whole or at least the "patrimonial lands" which Charles V inherited from his Burgundian ancestors.

Much better documented in the sources used here is the concept of privilege. The fierce attachment of communities to special privileges granted by their rulers is an old theme in the history of the Low Countries and can be seen, for example, in October 1541, when Amsterdammers rioted against the official who dared attempt to collect a *congie*, despite the freedom from duty on grain exports that Maximilian I had granted to the city in 1495. During the Revolt, the official justification for rebellion against the King was, again, the defense of privileges.[6] Under Charles V and Philip II this commonplace theme was refined or sharpened in two important ways: first, by a continuing growth in the number of privileged communities; second, by the ways in which the government chose to exercise or not exercise its power to quash privileges in the name of the common good.

By the beginning of Charles V's reign, Holland's important towns already had more privileges tucked away in locked chests than they could use or keep track of. For example, Amsterdam at one point consulted no fewer than six lawyers to see if, in one of its disputes with the government, it was worth citing a privilege granted by Count Floris V (d. 1299).[7] In the countryside, however, the traditional process of recognizing corporate entities by granting them privileges continued. By about 1450, a few of Holland's villages had already obtained permission to sell *renten* on the "body" of the village, just as the towns had been doing. By the time of the 1514 *Informatie*, roughly two-thirds of Holland's approximately 180 villages had contracted debts of this kind. The *Informatie* also shows that a few villages had governments organized in the manner of towns, with the right to levy excise taxes on their inhabitants. In succeeding decades it was more common for villages to be granted the privilege of having a *vroedschap*. During Philip's reign, the Council of Holland, when consulted by the Secret Council, routinely recommended approval of petitions to have a *vroedschap*. Indeed, the political and social logic of entrusting power to a closed corporation of wealthy men was the same for a village as for a town. As the Council of Holland remarked, "reason demands that the affairs of the common lands and the villages are more taken to heart by those who have a notable amount of property, and are taxed the highest."[8]

Two episodes from the 1560s illustrate the importance of privileges for rural folk. The *waterschap* of Woerden consisted of five villages located on the border between Holland and Utrecht. In the spring of 1564, the *dijkgraaf* (count of the dike) and *heemradschap* (polder board) undertook to build a stone bridge across the Rijn at Bodegraven and erected two dams in the river to serve as foundations. Three of the villages complained to the Council of Holland, on the grounds that a privilege of 1395, confirmed by the Council in 1555, required that a majority of the five villages give their consent in such cases. These villages had not consented and said that they would nonetheless be expected to help pay for the bridge. Despite the Council's order that the *dijkgraaf* cease construction, the work continued. On 3 May 1564, 200 men from the three villages came to Bodegraven, in arms and with fife and drum, and smashed the two dams meant as foundations for the bridge. Erich von Braunschweig, as Lord of Woerden, lodged a criminal complaint, alleging that what the villagers had done was especially serious because of "the bearing of arms" (*portus armorum*). The Council of Holland, for its part, did not believe the villagers had committed a crime, since the *dijkgraaf* had clearly violated their privileges. Braunschweig's judicial officers seized one of the leaders of this demonstration, Hendrik Huygeszoon, and sent him to The Hague, but the Council released him, albeit after requiring him to post a huge bond (4,000 pounds).[9]

In January 1566, 500 men marched out in arms from the village of Assendelft to a point on the dike road to Edam where they smashed a sluice that had just been stopped up at the direction of Sebastiaan Craanhals, *dijkgraaf* of the important "hoogheemraadschap of the water-draining sluices." Having surrounded Craanhals for several hours, using threatening words, some of the party went on to Assemburg castle, hereditary seat of the Assendelft family, where they scaled the outer tower and committed minor acts of vandalism (the head of the house at this time was Niklaas van Assendelft, son and heir of the Assendelft so often mentioned above). The same group then crossed a lake to the town of Beverwijk where they seized and harassed the Sheriff who was also Assendelft's judicial officer for his lands. They dragged him through the muddy streets and made him return a "pot and kettle" that they said he had seized illegally. When one of the leaders threatened the Sheriff with a drawn sword, Cornelis Willem Gerritszoon intervened: "Don't kill him yet, let me read him something first." He then drew out and read aloud "a document [*cedulle*] which he said was a privilege." A few months later the Sheriff arrested Gerritszoon in Dordrecht on a warrant issued by Niklaas van Assendelft. But the Council of Holland demanded the right to try him on the grounds that he had committed *lèse majesté* by his actions against Craanhals, who, unlike the Sheriff of Woerden, was an officer of the King.[10]

The Council's very different treatment of Hendrik Huygeszoon and Cornelis Willem Gerritszoon suggests that it may have been considered lawful for villagers to bear arms in defense of privileges, so long as the privileges were duly recognized and so long as they did not mistreat an officer of the King in the process. Also, Braunschweig, though vociferous in his support of the King and of orthodox religion, seems to have made enemies all around by his obstreperous behavior.[11] What is important here is not the difference between the two cases but their resemblance: villagers marched out in battle array to defend their privileges, making a show of force without shedding blood. Town militias had been engaging in the same ritual of combat, usually if not always in defense of privileges, for over a hundred years. These incidents prove, then, that villages were learning to behave like towns. They also suggest wide diffusion of the the concept of organized society as a federation of privileged bodies.

The only other concept of organized society known in this period was the one derived from Roman law in which the will of the sovereign prince had the force of law. *Divide ut imperas* was also a Roman maxim, and one can imagine a government of the Netherlands exploiting its "absolute power" to make the crown the arbiter between competing towns or social groups. For example, a government of this sort might have shown Holland's towns the benefits of allegiance to the prince by quashing the staple privileges of Dordrecht and the tax exemptions of the "three personages." Instead, without any settled policy at the center, the government and its organs acted in such a way as to make the towns believe that privileges were indeed the final political reality in the Netherlands. Thus Dordrecht was vindicated in almost all respects by the Grand Council of Mechelen, and the "three personages" received a boon from Philip II. Equally if not more important, the government's determination to override privileges that conflicted with its heresy legislation had the effect of drawing towns and nobles together in a common predicament, despite their differences. In Holland, heresy flourished most in commercial towns like Amsterdam and Delft and in enclaves of feudal jurisdiction like Cruningen's Heenvliet or Buren's Hazerswoude and Benscop. There were many conflicts between the towns and the feudal enclaves, and the government was sometimes helpful to the towns, as in its efforts to end the practice of private truces in time of war. Yet the government's most persistent effort to assert its authority came in one of the few areas where towns and privileged enclaves had something in common, that is, the protection of their judicial autonomy.

In a legal brief on behalf of Dordrecht at the outset of Charles V's reign, Oem van Wijngaerden could quibble about whether Holland was a "body," but no one seems to have had any doubts forty or fifty years later. Moreover, like the Netherlands as a whole, Holland was an articulated polity in which, for instance, privileges like *de non evocando* could have meaning at different levels. The obvious role for the States in this setting was to make themselves the defenders of any local privilege that came under challenge. This concept of things is sometimes evident in the discussions, as when the men of Delft, apropos of heresy law, said that "we must all support one another in our privileges" (1527), or when, on grounds that the privileges of "members" of the States deserved protection (1560), Amsterdam and the nobles voted to support three other cities whose rights at Leidschendam were threatened by the actions of a local landowner.[12] The various unifying forces described here do not mean that Holland's internal tensions disappeared. In fact, as towns and villages became more conscious of their privileges, conflicts of one sort or another were perhaps more frequent than ever. There is, however, an important difference between the fractiousness of a territory ruled by a prince and the self-ordered fractiousness of a republic. Holland under Habsburg rule traversed a considerable part of the distance from the former to the latter. By the reign of Philip II, it was a body politic, if not yet a republic.

Abbreviations

ACB   "Ambtenaren Centraal Bestuur," Rijksarchief van Zuid-Holland, The Hague.

AFR   Tracy, James D. *A Financial Revolution in the Habsburg Netherlands: "Renten" and "Renteniers" in the County of Holland, 1515–1566* (Berkeley, Los Angeles, London, 1985).

AGN   van Houtte, J. A., Editor, *Algemene Geschiedenis der Nederlanden*. 11 vols. Utrecht, 1949–58.

AHN   *Acta Historica Neerlandica.*

AJ   Andries Jacobszoon. "Prothocolle van alle die reysen . . . bij mij Andries Jacops gedaen. . . ." 2 vols. Gemeente Archief, Amsterdam.

ARS/KAW-CRH   *Academie Royale des Sciences de Belgique/ Koninklijke Academie van Wetenschapen van België, Commission Royale d'Histoire.*

ASR   "Stadsrekeningen," Extant from 1531, Gemeente Archief, Amsterdam.

Aud.   "Papiers d'Etat et de l'Audience," Algemeen Rijksarchief, Brussels.

AVR   *Resoluties van de vroedschap van Amsterdam, 1490–1550.* Eds. P. D. J. van Iterson and P. H. J. van der Laan. Gemeente Archief van Amsterdam, 1986.

BMHGU   *Bijdragen en Mededelingen van het Historisch Genootschap te Utrecht.*

BMGN   *Bijdragen en Mededelingen betreffende de Geschiedenis van de Nederlanden.*

Blok Blok, P. S. *Geschiedenis eener Hollandse Stad.* 4 vols. The Hague, 1910–1918.

BVGO Bijdragen en Mededelingen voor Vaderlandsche Geschiedenis en Oudheidkunde.

BGN Bijdragen tot Geschiedenis der Nederlanden.

CC "Chambre des Comptes." Algemeen Rijksarchief, Brussels.

GRK "Graafelijkheids Rekenkamer," Rijksarchief van Zuid-Holland, The Hague.

GVR "Goudsche Vroedschapsresolutiën betreffende Dagvaarten der Staten von Holland ende Staten Generaal (1501–1572)," ed. M. Rollin Couquerque, A. Meerkamp van Emden, *BMHGU*, 37 (1916): 61–81; 38 (1917): 98–357; 39 (1918): 306–407.

HB Pirenne, Henri. *Histoire de Belgique.* 7 vols. Brussels, 1902–1932.

HH "Hof van Holland." Rijksarchief van Zuid-Holland, The Hague.

HVH "Historie van Holland." Koninklijke Bibliotheek, The Hague.

HVR "Haarlem Vroedschapsresolutiën." Gemeentearchief, Haarlem.

LeGlay LeGlay, André Joseph. *Correspondance de l'Empereur Maximilien Ier et de Marguerite D'Autriche.* Paris, 1839.

Lanz Lanz, K. *Correspondenz des Kaisers Karls V, aus dem Königlichen Archiv und der Bibliotheque de Bourgogne zu Brüssel.* 3 vols. Leipzig, 1844–1846.

Leiden *dagvaarten* Secretarie, Nr. 1218. Stadsarchief, Leiden.

Lille B   "Comptes des Receveurs Generaux," Ar-
             chives du Département du Nord, Lille (mi-
             crofilm copies, Algemeen Rijksarchief,
             Brussels).

NAGN   Blok, D. P., et al., eds. *Algemene Geschiedenis
          der Nederlanden.* 15 vols. Haarlem, 1977–
          1983.

RSH   *Resolutiën van de Staten van Holland.* 278 vol-
         umes. N. p., 1524/43–1793.

Sandelijn   Andriaan Sandelijn, "Memoriaelboek."
             4 vols. Gemeente Archief, Amsterdam.

SH   "Staten van Holland voor 1572." Rijksar-
        chief van Zuid-Holland, The Hague.

Ter Gouw   Ter Gouw, J. *Geschiedenis van Amsterdam.*
            8 vols. Amsterdam, 1879–1893.

VKAW-KL   Verhandelingen der Koninklijke Akademie
             van Wetenschapen, Letteren en Schoone
             Kunsten van Belgie, Klasse der Letteren.

Notes

INTRODUCTION

1. For the contributions of American scholars to these areas, it may suffice to cite the names of Joseph Strayer (for medieval English and French constitutional history), Gene Brucker (Renaissance Florence), and Thomas Brady (south German free cities).

2. *AFR* argues that the forms of public debt created by Low Countries provinces represent a stage of development intermediate between the debts of medieval cities and the first national debt, created by the English parliament at the end of the seventeenth century.

3. Nannerl Keohane, *Philosophy and the State in France* (Princeton, 1980), 232–235, 384–388, 407–419; cf. Montesquieu, *Spirit of the Laws*, Bk. 9.

4. Hans Conrad Peyer, "Die Entstehung der Eidgenossenschaft," in *Das Handbuch der Schweizer Geschichte* (Zurich, 1972), 1:161–238.

5. H. G. Koenigsberger, "The Italian Parliaments from Their Origins to the End of the Eighteenth Century," *Standen en Landen* 70 (1977):101.

6. Hans Nabholz, et al., *Die Geschichte der Schweiz*, 2 vols. (Zurich, 1932), 1:174–184. See also François Gilliard, "Gouvernés et Gouvernants dans la Confédération Helvétique, des Origines à la Fin de l'Ancien Régime," *Recueils de la Société Jean Bodin* 25 (1965): 139–162.

7. For general surveys, see *NAGN*, vols. 4–6; Pirenne, vols. 3–4; Pieter Geyl, *The Revolt of the Netherlands*, 2d ed. (London: 1958); and Geoffrey Parker, *The Dutch Revolt* (Ithaca: 1977). The Revolt began in 1568, with William of Orange's unsuccessful invasion from Germany, but the rebels did not control any territory until the towns of Holland and Zeeland adhered to the revolt in 1572.

8. Johannes Althusius, *Politica Methodice Digesta*, ed. Carl Friedrich (Cambridge: 1932), 122–136.

9. W. P. Blockmans, "De Representatieve Instellingen in het Zuiden, 1384–1483," and P. H. P. Leupen, "De Representatieve Instellingen in het Noorden, 1384–1482," *NAGN* 4: 156–163, 164–171; A. Th. van Deursen, "Staatsinstellingen der Noordelijke Nederlanden, 1579–1780," *NAGN* 5: 350–387.

10. Pieter Geyl, *Orange and Stuart, 1641–1672* (London: 1969); on

the two most important Grand Pensionaries, see Jan Den Tex, *Olden-barneveld*, 2 vols. (Cambridge, 1973), and H. H. Rowan, *John de Witt* (Princeton, 1978).

11. K. H. D. Haley, *The Dutch in the Seventeenth Century* (New York, 1972), 64–74; Keohane cites the view of René-Louis de Voyer de Paulmy, Marquis d'Argenson, that the Dutch regime "has many arms, but lacks a head" (386).

12. Van Deursen, in *NAGN* 5: 350–353; the quotation is from Willem Bentinck, lord of Rhoon.

13. Ibid., 350–355. In 1645 the States General considered dissolving the Union among the provinces that traced back to 1579, now that the long war against Spain was concluded. H. Wansink, "Holland and Six Allies: the Republic of the Seven United Provinces," *Britain and the Netherlands* (1971) 4:133–155, concludes that "at the end of the eighteeenth century the Republic was not markedly more unified than at the end of the sixteenth" (155).

14. Van Deursen, in *NAGN* 5:352-354; G. de Bruin, "De Souvereiniteit in de Republiek: een Machtsprobleem," *BMGN* 94 (1979): 27–40.

15. Pirenne, vol. 3; K. J. W. Verhofstad, S.J., *De Regering der Nederlanden in de Jaren 1555–1559* (Nijmegen, 1937). "Verwerperlijk archaïsch" is W. P. Blockmans's characterization for the traditional view of provincial particularisms: "Breuk of Continuiteit? De Vlaamse Privileges van 1477 in het Licht van het Staatvormingsproces," in Blockmans, *Het Algemeen en de Gewestelijke Privileges van Maria van Burgondië voor de Nederlanden, 1477 = Standen en Landen* 80 (Heule, 1985): 119.

16. On the historiography of the Revolt, see J. W. Smit, "The Present Position of Studies Regarding the Revolt of the Netherlands," *Britain and the Netherlands* 1 (1960): 11–29; and Heinz Schilling, "Der Aufstand der Niederlanden–bürgerliche Revolution oder Elitenkonflikt?" *Geschichte und Gesellschaft* 2 (1976): 177–231.

17. *AFR.*

18. J. J. Woltjer, "Dutch Privileges, Real and Imaginary," *Britain and the Netherlands* 5 (1975): 19–35.

19. Tracy, "The Taxation System of the County of Holland under Charles V and Philip II, 1519–1566." *Economisch- en Sociaal-Historisch Jaarboek* 48 (1984): 72–117.

20. Haley, 64–71; the fullest account of the social and economic history of the Republic is J. G. van Dillen, *Van Rijkdom en Regenten: Handboek tot de Economische en Sociale Geschiedenis der Nederlanden tijdens de Republiek* (The Hague, 1970).

1: TOWNS AND PRINCES IN LATE MEDIEVAL HOLLAND

1. For the history of Holland's waterways, the fundamental work is A. H. Beekman, *Holland, Zeeland en Westfriesland in 1300* (The Hague, 1916–1920; the three parts bound together in this volume originally appeared separately); this book is text volume 4, corresponding to map number 5 in map volume 1 of *Geschiedkundige Atlas van Nederland*, 3 volumes of maps (The Hague, 1913–1938); 15 volumes of text (The Hague, 1916–1938).

2. The best works in English are: William Te Brake, *Medieval Frontier: Culture and Ecology in Rijnland* (College Station, 1985), and Audrey Lambert, *The Making of the Dutch Landscape* (London, 1971).

3. S. J. Fockema Andreae, "Embanking and Drainage Authorities in the Netherlands during the Middle Ages," *Speculum* 27 (1952): 158–167; C. Dekker, "The Representation of Freeholders in the Drainage Districts of Zeeland West of the Scheldt during the Middle Ages," *AHN* 7 (1975): 1–30.

4. H. P. H. Jansen, "Holland's Advance," *AHN* 10 (1978): 1–20; Lambert, 154–178. Most of the Dutch scholars now working on Holland's medieval history are represented in the memorial volume for Prof. Jansen: D. E. H. de Boer and J. W. Marsilje, eds., *De Nederlanden in de Late Middeleeuwen* (Utrecht, 1987).

5. For Holland's political history in the fourteenth century, see J. F. Niermeyer, "Hennegouwen, Holland, en Zeeland onder Willem III en Willem IV van Avesnes," and "Het Sticht Utrecht en het Graafschap Holland," *AGN* 3:63–80, 287–297, and H. P. H. Jansen, "Holland, Zeeland, en het Sticht," *NAGN* 2: 293–307.

6. P. J. Blok, "De Financiën van het Graafschap Holland," *BMGN*, 3d. ser., 3 (1886): 36–130.

7. H. P. H. Jansen, *Hoekse en Kabeljauwse Twisten* (Bussum, 1966). Michiel Brokken, *Het Ontstaan van de Hoekse en Kabeljauwse Twisten* (Zutphen, 1982) presents a more detailed and more nuanced account, in which the dispute over the Dordrecht staple is seen as less important than local rivalries and constitutional issues.

8. J. F. Niermeyer, "Hennegouwen, Holland, en Zeeland onder het Huis Wittelsbach," *AGN* 3: 104–107.

9. Klaus Spading, *Holland und die Hanse im 15en Jahrhundert* (Weimar, 1973), 1–12; H. A. H. Boelmans-Kranenburg, "Visserij van de Noordnederlanders," in *Maritieme Geschiedenis der Nederlanden*, ed. G. Asaert, et al., 4 vols. (Bussum, 1976–1978), 1: 290–294.

10. N. W. Posthumus, *De Oosterse Handel van Amsterdam* (Leiden, 1953), and *Geschiedenis van de Leidsche Lakenindustrie* (3 vols. The

Hague, 1908–1933) vol. 1; J. C. van Loenen, *De Haarlemse Brouwindustrie voor 1600* (Amsterdam, 1950).

11. Niermeyer, "Hennegouwen, Holland, en Zeeland onder het Huis Wittelsbach," *AGN* 3: 110–111.

12. A. G. Jongkees, "Strijd om de Erfenis van Wittelsbach, 1417–1433," *AGN* 3: 226–252; H. P. H. Jansen, *Jacoba van Beieren* (The Hague, 1967), 54–91; J. Scheurkogel, "Opstand in Holland," in De Boer and Marsilje, *De Nederlanden in de Late Middeleeuwen*, 363–378. For a sample of "Hoek historiography," see below, note 13.

13. Jan Wagenaar, *Vaderlandsche Historie*, 21 vols. (Amsterdam, 1749–1759), 3: 475–479: the Duke of Burgundy's foreign garrisons and the "perpetual fines" he imposed on Hollanders who had supported Jacoba were "tangible signs of an arbitrary regime" ("tastelyke blyken van een willkeurige regeringe"), a yoke from which Hollanders would finally gain freedom during the Revolt.

14. Richard Vaughan, *Philip the Good* (New York: 1970), 303–331; J. Bartier, "Filips de Goede en de Vestiging van de Bourgondische Staat," *AGN* 3: 253–271; W. P. Blockmans, "Vlaanderen, 1384–1482," *NAGN* 4: 217–220.

15. Wagenaar, *Vaderlandsche Historie*, 4: 39; E. A. M. E. Jansen, *De Opkomst van de Vroedschap in Enkele Hollandse Steden* (University of Leiden, 1927). Cf. Niermeyer, "Hennegouwen, Holland, en Zeeland onder het Huis Wittelsbach," *AGN* 3: 108. Duke Albert introduced a guild regime in Dordrecht to weaken the authority of Hoek patricians. For urban constitutions in the southern Netherlands, see H. van Werveke, "De Steden. Rechten, Instellingen, en Maatschaapelijke Toestanden," *AGN* 2: 374–416, and R. van Uytven, "Het Stedelijk Leven, 1100–1400," *NAGN* 2: 187–253.

16. For the organization of the Hof van Holland see the introduction to A. S. de Blécourt and E. M. Meijers, *Memorialen van het Hof van Holland, Zeeland, en Westfriesland van de Secretaris Jan Roosa*, 3 vols. (Haarlem: 1929); J. van Rompaey, "De Bourgondische Staatsinstellingen," *NAGN* 4: 152–153.

17. Wagenaar, *Vaderlandsche Historie*, 3: 486; P. H. D. Leupen, "De Representatieve Instellingen in het Noorden, 1384–1482," *NAGN* 4: 164–165; W. P. Blockmans, "De Representatieve Instellingen in het Zuiden, 1384–1482," *NAGN* 4: 156–163; H. de Schepper, "De Burgerlijke Overheden en hun Permanente Kaders, 1480–1579," *NAGN* 5: 323–328. See also the important collection of texts edited by W. Prevenier and J. G. Smit, *Bronnen voor de Geschiedenis der Dagvaarten van de Staten en Steden van Holland voor 1544*, vol. 1 (The Hague, 1987).

18. Paul Rosenfeld, "The Provincial Governors from the Minority

of Charles V to the Revolt," *Standen en Landen* = *Anciens Pays et Assemblées d'Etat*, 17 (Leuven, 1959): 1–63; Vaughan, *Philip the Good*, 127–204. T. S. Jansma, "Holland en Zeeland onder de Bourgondische Hertogen, 1433–1477," *AGN* 4: 313–316, 322–328.

19. J. A. van Houtte, R. van Uytven, "De Financiën," *NAGN* 4: 118–120; Van Houtte, *An Economic History of the Low Countries* (New York, 1977): 110–113; John Gilissen. "Les États Généraux en Belgique et aux Pays Bas sous l'Ancien Régime," *Recueils de la Société Jean Bodin* 24 (1966): 401–438.

20. Tracy, "The Taxation System of the County of Holland," *Jaarboek voor Economisch- en Sociaal-Geschiedenis* 48 (1984): 71–81; Vaughan, *Philip the Good*, 193–194; H. P. H. Jansen, "Holland en Zeeland, 1433–1482," *NAGN* 4: 272–273; Jansma, "Holland en Zeeland onder de Bourgondische Hertogen," *AGN* 3: 313–316.

21. Spading, *Holland und die Hanse im 15en Jahrhundert*, 1–19; Jansen, "Holland en Zeeland, 1433–1482," *NAGN* 4: 277–279; Vaughan, *Philip the Good*, 65–77, 92–94, 141–163.

22. Ter Gouw, 3:25–55; J. C. A. De Meij, "Oorlogsvaart, Kaapvaart, en Zeeroof," *Maritieme Geschiedenis der Nederlanden*, 1: 311–315; on the composition of Holland's war fleet, see Raimond van Marle, *Le Comté de Hollande sous Philippe le Bon (1428–1467)* (The Hague, 1908), 79–80, citing Baron Fr. de Reiffenberg, *Mémoire courennée en réponse à cette question proposée par l'Académie Royale des Sciences et Belles Lettres de Bruxelles: Quel a été l'état de la population, des fabriques et manufactures, et du commerce dans les Provinces des Pays Bas, pendant les XVe et XVIe siècles?* (Brussels, 1820), 231.

23. Richard Vaughan, *Charles the Bold* (London, 1973), 183–184; see also pp. 1–40, 84–100.

24. Vaughan, *Charles the Bold*, 185–189, 205–210, and *Valois Burgundy* (London, 1975), 106–107; Gilissen, 416.

25. J. Bartier, "Karel de Stoute," *AGN* 3: 272–298; *AFR*, 14–17; Isaak Le Long, *Historische Beschryving van de Reformatie der Stad Amsterdam* (Amsterdam, 1729), 379–382; Vaughan, *Charles the Bold*, 414–415; M. Mollat, "Récherches sur les Finances des Ducs Valois de Bourgogne," *Revue Historique* 219 (1958): 285–321.

26. Jansen, "Holland en Zeeland, 1433–1482," *NAGN* 4: 284–5; R. Fruin, "De Verpondingen van 1496 en 1515 en haar Voorbereiding," in his *Verspreide Geschriften*, ed. P. J. Blok, et al., 10 vols. (The Hague, 1900–1904), 6: 141–143; Ter Gouw, 3: 100–108. Aud. 650: 486ᵛ, quotes from an *assiètte* or quota for a *bede* of 500,000 crowns in 1473, in which Holland, West Friesland and Zeeland combined were assessed for 127,000 or as much as Flanders.

27. Jansen, "Holland en Zeeland, 1433–1482," *NAGN* 4: 282–284; Ter Gouw, 3: 130.

28. Jongkees, "Het Grote Privilege van Holland," in *Het Algemeen en de Gewestelijke Grote Privileges van Maria van Bourgondië;* see also W. P. Blockmans's contribution to the same volume, "Breuk of Continuiteit? De Vlaamse Privileges van 1477 in het Licht van het Staatvormingsproces," 97–144. *HB* 3: 7–17; Blok, 2: 25–28; De Schepper, "De Burgerlijke Overheden en hun Permanente Kaders, 1480–1579," *NAGN* 5: 324.

29. F. W. N. Hugenholz, "Crisis en Herstel van het Bourgondisch Gezag, 1477–1493," *AGN* 4: 1–10, and "The 1477 Crisis in the Burgundian Duke's Dominions," *Britain and the Netherlands,* 2 (1962): 33–46; Jansen, "Holland en Zeeland, 1433–1482," *NAGN* 4: 288–291; Ter Gouw, 3: 130–149; Wagenaar, *Vaderlandsche Historie,* 4: 185–197, 220–233; R. van Uytven, "Crisis als Cesuur 1482–1494," *NAGN* 5: 422–423; *AFR,* 57–58.

30. Hugenholz, "Crisis en Herstel," *AGN* 4: 11–22. For two different views of the Bread and Cheese War, see F. W. N. Hugenholz, "Het Kaas- en Broodvolk," *BMHGU* 81 (1967): 201–247, and J. Scheurkogel, "Het Kaas- en Broodspel," *BMGN* 99 (1979): 189–211.

31. J. E. A. L. Struick, *Gelre en Habsburg, 1492–1528* (Arnhem, 1960), 8–26; Blok, 2: 25–27: coached by his advisers, Philip omitted from his oath many of the concessions included in Mary of Burgundy's "Great Privilege" of 1477; thus was the principle of majority rule restored to the States of Holland, at least as far as the government was concerned. Jongkees, "Het Grote Privilege van Holland," 180–181.

32. Struick, 39–52; Wiesflecker, *Kaiser Maximilian I,* 2: 140–146.

33. The best account of the Guelders wars is found in Struick, *Gelre en Habsburg.*

34. Posthumus, *De Oosterse Handel van Amsterdam* (Leiden, 1953); *De Uitvoer van Amsterdam* (Leiden, 1971); Ter Gouw, 3: 110–130.

35. Richard W. Unger, *Dutch Shipbuilding before 1800* (Assen, 1978), 1–5; Posthumus, *De Uitvoer van Amsterdam,* 186, Table 15, lists the value of goods exported to various destinations (including Norway) between 1543 and 1545.

36. James D. Tracy, "Habsburg Grain Policy and Amsterdam Politics: the Career of Sheriff Willem Dirkszoon Baerdes, 1542–1566," *Sixteenth Century Journal* 18 (1983): 309–310; H. de Haan, *Moedernegotiatie en Grote Vaart* (Amsterdam, 1977).

37. Aksel E. Christensen, *Dutch Trade to the Baltic around 1600* (Copenhagen, 1941), 29–45.

38. Lambert, 142, 170–172, 185–186; Geraerdt Brandt, *Historie*

der Vermaerde Zee- en Koop-Stadt Enkhuizen (Hoorn, 1740), 21; J. A. van Houtte, "Nijverheid en Handel," *NAGN* 4: 101–108. H. A. H. Boelmans-Kranenburg considers the estimate of 250 *busses* "exaggerated:" "Visserij van de Noordnederlanders," in *Maritieme Geschiedenis der Nederlanden,* vol. 1, ed. G. Asaert, et al. (Bussum, 1976), 290.

39. Posthumus, *Geschiedenis van de Leidsche Lakenindustrie,* vol. 1; W. P. Blockmans, et al. "Tussen Crisis en Welvaart: Sociale Veranderingen, 1300–1500," *NAGN* 4: 51.

40. J. C. van Loenen, *De Haarlemse Brouwindustrie voor 1600* (Amsterdam, 1950); C. C. J. Pinske, "Het Goudse Koutbier," in *Gouda Zeven Eeuwen Stad* (Gouda, 1972), 91–128; GVR 20 (February 1509, 13 April 1537); see also an undated petition from Gouda's brewers to the Stadtholder, Hoogstraten, Aud. 1524, 18–19; M. A. Timmer, "Grepen uit de Geschiedenis der Delftsche Brouwnering," *De Economist* 70 (1920): 358–373, 415–430; J. J. Woltjer, "Een Hollands Stadsbestuur in het midden van de 16e eeuw: brouwers en Bestuurders te Delft," in De Boer and Marsilje, *De Nederlanden in de Late Middeleeuwen,* 261–279.

41. F. Ketner, "Amsterdam en de Binnenvaart door Holland in de 15e Eeuw," *BVGO* 4 (1943): 169–200; 5 (1944): 33–59.

42. Aud. 650: 486; *GRK* 3425 (Holland's portion of a 1523 *extraordinaris bede* of 608,000 was 81,607, or 13.33%). Leo Noordegraaf, *Hollands Welvaren? Levens-Standaard in Holland, 1450–1650* (Bergen, 1985): 76, cites a long list of authors who agree on Holland's prosperity under Charles the Bold.

43. Noordegraaf, 20–22, 32–34, 41–43, 77–81.

44. P.A. Meilink, *Archieven van de Staten van Holland voor 1572,* 53.

45. R. Fruin, ed., *Informacie:* of 171 villages surveyed, 148 had sold *renten* by 1514, including eighteen for the Utrecht War.

46. Posthumus, *Geschiedenis van de Leidsche Lakenindustrie,* 1: 195–213.

47. E. Coornaert, *Un Centre industriel d'autrefois. La Draperie-sayerie d'Hondschoote, XIVe–XVIIe siècles* (Paris, 1930); Posthumus, *Geschiedenis van de Leidsche Lakenindustrie,* 1: 245–259, 368–371 (tables on cloth production). For complaints by Leiden that its merchants have no credit, see *AJ,* 10 September, 29 December 1523, 28 January 1524.

48. Pinske, "Het Goudse Kuitbier;" *GVR,* 20 February 1509.

49. Woltjer, "Een Hollands Stadsbestuur;" Van Loenen, *De Haarlemse Brouwindustrie,* 15–21, 45–62. In the sixteenth century Haarlem contributed stained-glassed windows to churches in towns in Waterland, West Friesland, and Friesland where much Haarlem beer was consumed: *HVR,* 20 March 1521 (Purmerend), 8 June 1521 (Medem-

blik), 8 April 1522 (Enkhuizen), and 13 April 1529 (Workum, in Friesland).

50. Fruin, *Informacie.*

51. Fruin, *Informacie.* Haarlem reports that its overseas shipping is only a fraction of what it was fourteen years previously.

52. I. Prins, *Het Failissement der Hollandsche Steden: Amsterdam. Dordrecht, Leiden en Haarlem in het Jaar 1514* (Amsterdam, 1922); W. Downer, "De Financiële Toestand van de Stad Leiden omstreeks 1500," (typescript at the Leiden Stadsarchief 1951); J. C. Overvoorde and J. N. Oerburgt, *Het Archief van de Secretarie van de Stad Leiden, 1252–1575* (Leiden: 1937), Regestenlijst, for prolongation of Leiden's dept-postponement, no. 1262, 1271, 1301, 1315, 1337, 1404, 1447, 1502, 1551, 1679, 1770, 1932; cf. no. 1390, 1400.

53. Fruin, *Informacie;* J. C. Naber, *Een Terugblik: Statistische Bewerking van de Resultaten van de Informatie van 1514* (reprint, Haarlem, 1970), Bijlage 10.

54. Fruin, *Informacie;* Naber, *Terugblik.*

55. Fruin, *Informacie;* Naber, *Terugblik.*

56. W. S. Unger, "De Sociale en Economische Struktuur van Dordrecht in 1555," *De Economist* 63 (1913): 947–984.

57. C. Hoek, "Delfshaven, de Rivierhaven van Delft," in *De Stad Delft: Cultuur en Maatschappij tot 1572* (Delft, 1980), 100–104. Fruin, *Informacie:* Rotterdam itself reports sixty-three herring *busses*, Schiedam another twenty. Christensen, 111–121, chooses a Delft merchant (active after 1560) to study the organization of Dutch commerce in the Baltic.

58. Noordegraaf, *Hollands Welvaren*, 80–81; Christensen, 29–39: on the earliest Sound Toll registers, from 1497 and 1503.

59. Jansen, "Holland's Advance"; Jan De Vries, *The Dutch Rural Economy in the Golden Age, 1500–1700* (New Haven, 1974), 86.

2: THE STATES OF HOLLAND AND THE HABSBURG
GOVERNMENT

1. Otto Hintze, "Typologie der ständischen Verfassung des Abendlands," *Historische Zeitschrift* 141 (1929/1930): 229–248; A. R. Myers, *Parliaments and Estates in Europe to 1789* (London, 1979), 34-48. See also *Gouverants et Gouvernés* = *Recueils de la Société Jean Bodin* vols. 22–27 (Brussels, 1965–1968), and Antonio Marongiu, *Medieval Parliaments: A Comparative Study*, tr. S. J. Woolf (London, 1968).

2. J. E. A. Jolliffe, *The Constitutional History of Medieval England*, fourth edition (London, 1961), Chapters 3 and 4, passim; Hintze, "Typologie der ständischen Verfassung des Abendlands."

3. Jan Dhondt, "Les Assemblées d'État en Belgique avant 1795," *Recueils de la Société Jean Bodin* 24 (1966): 325–400; Jolliffe, 349–350.

4. H. G. Koenigsberger, "The Powers of Deputies in Sixteenth-Century Assemblies," *Estates and Revolutions* (Ithaca, 1971), 176–210; Marongiu, *Medieval Parliaments*, 228–232.

5. AJ, 14 October 1523, 15 October 1523, 25 October 1523, 19 April 1524. H. G. Koenigsberger, "The Parliament of Piedmont during the Renaissance, 1460–1560," in *Estates and Revolutions*, 19–79; Antonio Marongiu, *Il Parlamento in Italia nel Medio Evo e nell'Eta Moderna* (Milan, 1962), 398, citing Armando Tallone, editor of the series, *Parlamento Sabaudo;* for the period of interest here, see *Parta Prima, Patria Cismontana*, vols. 6 and 7 (Bologna, 1932–1933), and *Parte Seconda, Patria Oltramontana*, vol. 2 (Bologna, 1937).

6. H. G. Koenigsberger, "The States General of the Netherlands before the Revolt," in *Estates and Revolutions*, 125–143; R. Wellens, *Actes des États Genéraux des Anciens Pays Bas*, vols. 1 (1464–1477), 2 (1478–1493), 3 (1493–1506) (Heule, 1974–).

7. Otto Brünner, *Land und Herrschaft*, 128–146, 231–240, 414–440.

8. Herbert Helbig, *Das Wettinische Ständestaat* (Münster/Cologne, 1955), 464–476; Blickle, *Landschaften im Alten Reich* (Munich, 1973), 3–48.

9. W. Prevenier, *De Leden en de Staten van Vlaanderen, 1384–1405* = *VKAW-KL* 43 (Brussels, 1961), 19–23, 57–84.

10. See Chapter 1, note 29. Brünner, *Land und Herrschaft*, 414–440. For criticism of various aspects of Brünner's views, see R. Folz, "Les Assemblées d'états dans les principautés Allemandes (fin XIVᵉ–debut XVIᵉ siècle)," *Recueils de la Société Jean Bodin* 25 (1965): 166–169; Gerhard Oestreich, "The Estates of Germany and the Formation of the State," in his *Neostoicism and the Early Modern State* (Cambridge, 1982), 197; and W. P. Blockmans, "Typologie van de Volksvertegenwoordiging in Europa tijdens de Late Middeleeuwen," *Tijdschrift voor Geschiedenis* 87 (1974): 484–485.

11. *AFR*, 57–58; Leiden *dagvaarten*, 13 May 1535, 4, 18 November 1538.

12. Floris Oem van Wijngaerden, "Register van tgeene Gedaen . . . Is in Diverse Dagvaarten," no. 29 of a 33-point memorandum that begins on fol. 22, and fol. 34ᵛ–36 (Gemeentearchief Dordrecht).

13. P. D. J. van Iterson, P. H. J. van der Laan, *Resoluties van de Vroedschap van Amsterdam, 1490–1550* (Amsterdam, 1986), 39, 44. See Chapter 1, Table 1.

14. On sources for the medieval concept of the corporation, see

Brian Tierney, *Foundations of the Conciliar Theory* (Cambridge, reprint 1968), 106–117, and Otto Gierke, *Geschichte des Deutschen Körperschafts-recht* = vol. II of his *Das Deutsche Genossenschaftsrecht* (Berlin, 1873), especially 485–489, 553–558. (The Low Countries *waterschappen,* not discussed by Gierke, may have been a model for other corporate bodies in this region.) The "corporatist" interpretation of medieval history proposed by E. Lousse, *La Société de l'Ancien Régime* = *Standen en Landen* 6 (Leuven, 1943) is rightly criticized by Jan Dhondt, " 'Ordres' ou 'Puissances:' l'Exemple des États de Flandre," in *Estates or Powers,* ed. W. P. Blockmans = *Standen en Landen* 79 (Heule, 1977), 27–53, and by Blockmans himself, "Typologie van de Volksvertegen-woordiging in Europa," 484–485.

15. AJ, 27 May 1524: when the nobles refuse to pay in a new tax, Amsterdam asks clarification of "wye aan tlichaem oft corpus van hollant behooren oft niet / en oft de adelen een lit vant voors. corpus zyn oft niet" ("who belongs to the body or corpus of Holland or not; and if the nobles are a member of the aforesaid corpus or not").

16. AJ, 25 January, 8–10 February, 8 June 1524, 15–20 June 1525: deputies from small cities voice their opinions, but these opinions did not count as votes. AJ, 23 August 1523, the small cities ought to be summoned, because "frequentior senatus" means "breeder last." Even in later years Assendelft would still cite the opinions of the small cities in his reports on the meetings, e.g., to Hoogstraten, 18 September 1542 (Aud. 1646:3).

17. See Chapter 3, notes 50, 51.

18. Blockmans, "Typologie van de Volksvertegenwoordiging in Eu-ropa," and *De Volksvertegenwoordinging in Vlaanderen in de Overgang van Middeleeuwen naar Nieuwe Tijd (1384–1506)* = *VKAW-KL* 90 (Brussels, 1978): 195–206. The figures for *dagvaarten* for the States of Holland are based on *RSH,* AJ, and *GVR.*

19. For contrasting views on the parliamentary "liberties" of Ara-gon, see Carlos Lopez de Haro, *La Constitucion y Libertades de Aragon* (Madrid, 1926), and Ralph E. Giesey, *If Not, Not; The Oath of the Ara-gonese and the Legendary Laws of Sobrarbe* (Princeton, 1968). F. L. Carsten, *Princes and Parliaments in Germany* (Oxford, 1959), 1–6.

20. See the literature cited above, note 5.

21. Carsten, 3, 258–259 on the preeminence of urban deputies in the Estates of Württemberg and in the Rhineland Duchies of Julich and Berg.

22. Ricardo Garcia Carcel, *Cortes del Reinado de Carlos V* (Valencia, 1972) reproduces sixteenth-century editions of the laws or *furs* (cf. the Castilian term *fueros*) promulgated by the Valencia *corts* of 1528, 1533,

1537, 1542, 1547, and 1552. The only other session during Charles's reign was in 1535: Joan Regla, *Appoximacio a la Historia del Pais Valencia* (Valencia, 1978), 87–88.

23. Cited by Oestreich, *Neostoicism and the Early Modern State,* 192. See also H. G. Koenigsberger, "Composite States, Representative Institutions, and the American Revolution," *Bulletin of the Institute of Historical Research,* 62 (1989): 135–153.

24. Marongiu, *Medieval Parliaments,* 196–206, and *Il Parlamento in Italia,* 294–297. Koenigsberger, "The Parliament of Piedmont during the Renaissance," 63–79, disputes the common view that parliamentary irresponsibility paved the way for Emmanuel Philibert's triumph.

25. Carsten, *Princes and Parliaments in Germany,* 6–25; for fuller information, see Walter Grube, *Der Stuttgarter Landtag, 1457–1957* (Stuttgart, 1957), "Erstes Buch," 12–193.

26. Esteban Sarasa Sanchez, *Las Cortes de Aragon en la Edad Media* (Zaragoza, 1979).

27. Blockmans, "Typologie van de Volksvertegenwoordiging in Europa," 491–492.

28. For the development of committees in the States of Holland, see the forthcoming dissertation of J. W. Koopmans, "De Staten van Holland, 1544–1584" (University of Groningen). I am grateful to Mr. Koopmans for sharing with me a draft of his chapter dealing with the organization of the States.

29. Of the six great cities, Amsterdam was farthest from The Hague, about forty miles, presuming the deputies traveled by way of Haarlem.

30. John B. Henneman, *Royal Taxation in Fourteenth-Century France* (Princeton, 1971); Martin Wolfe, *The Fiscal System of Renaissance France* (New Haven, 1972), 30–41.

31. Wladimiro Piskorski, *Las Cortes en el Periodo de Transito de la Edad Media a la Edad Moderna, 1188–1520,* tr. C. Sanchez-Albornoz (Barcelona, 1977), 150–170, 188–193. This book is a reprint of the 1930 edition, based on the Russian original of 1897. See also Steven Haliczer, *The Revolt of the Comuneros* (Madison, 1981).

32. Barthélemy Amadée Pocquet du Haut-Jussé, "A Political Concept of Louis XI: Subjection instead of Vassalage," in *The Recovery of France in the Fifteenth Century,* ed. P. S. Lewis (New York, 1971), 196–215; J. W. Allen, *A History of Political Thought in the Sixteenth Century* (London, reprint 1960), 271–285.

33. Stanford E. Lehmberg, *The Reformation Parliament, 1529–1536* (Cambridge, 1970); Michael A. Graves, *The Tudor Parliaments* (London, 1985), 77–81; Carstens, 430–437.

34. Carsten, 11, 24–25; *AFR,* 19–21; Oestreich, 192–195.

35. *AFR,* 18–26, 43, 99: the German estates which took over princes' debts did not issue instruments of indebtedness; the French and Spanish monarchies did issue instruments similar to the Netherlands *renten,* but these were not guaranteed by parliamentary bodies.

36. Stanford E. Lehmberg, *The Later Parliaments of Henry VIII,* 92–95, 175–180; G. R. Elton, "Taxation for War and Peace in Early Tudor England," in J. M. Minter, ed. *War and Economic Development* (Cambridge, 1975), 47: "Though 'everybody knows' that the principle [of redress of grievances before granting of supply] existed in the medieval history of the English parliament, it is in fact hard to find it there." I owe these references to my colleague at Minnesota, Prof. Lehmberg.

37. *RSH,* 29 March 1531.

38. Margaret of Austria to Charles V, July 1530, in Gordon Griffiths, *Representative Government in Western Europe in the Sixteenth Century* (Oxford, 1968), 354.

39. *HB,* 2: 133–149. Jongkees, "Het Groot Privilege van Holland en Zeeland van 1477," 189–190, 216–235: paragraph 19 of the 1477 Great Privilege for Holland, requiring consent of the States for war, was not renewed after 1494, except for clauses relating to feudal military service.

40. Wallace Notestein, *The House of Commons, 1604–1610* (New Haven, 1971), 264–265.

41. Carsten, 26. For military unions between the States of Holland and the quarters of Antwerp and 's Hertogenbosch (Brabant), see Chapter 3, notes 55, 79.

42. Carcel, *Cortes del Reinado de Carlos I,* fol. IV^v; see Sebastian Garcia Martinez, *Bandolerismo, Pirateria, y Control de Moriscos en Valencia durante el Reino de Felipe II* (Valencia, 1977), 21–25. For provisions made by the States of Holland for defense of the Zuider Zee, see *AJ,* 25 October 1523, 10 February, 19 April. 28 August 1524.

43. Marongiu, *Il Parlamento in Italia,* 294–297. Cf. Chapter 3, note 61.

44. The first six volumes of *RSH* were published separately in 1751. Between 1791 and 1798 they were reissued, together with 277 more volumes, covering the period to 1795. For Brabant there is only the "Roet Boek van de Staten van Brabant (1506–1572)," Algemeen Rijksarchief, Brussels, Collection "Staten van Brabant," nr. R 199/16.

45. Six volumes of the series *Handelingen van de Leden en van de Staten van Vlaanderen = KAW-CRH, Publications in Quarto* have now appeared,

edited by W. Prevenier (1384–1405, vol. 58, Brussels, 1959), A. Zoete (1405–1419, vols. 72:1, 72:2, Brussels, 1981–1982), and W. P. Blockmans (1467–1477, vol. 64, Brussels, 1971, and 1477–1506, vols. 67:1 and 67:2, Brussels, 1973). A seventh volume covering the period from 1419 to 1467, also edited by Prof. Blockmans, is in press.

46. W. Prevenier, J. G. Smit, *Bronnen voor de Geschiedenis der Dagvaarten van de Staten en Sieden van Holland,* vol. 1 (The Hague, 1987).

47. *AVR, GVR, HVR.*

48. The fullest study of the office of town pensionary is J. Melles, *Ministers aan de Maas: Geschiedenis van de Rotterdamse Pensionarissen, 1508–1795* (The Hague, 1962). See Chapter 5, Table 4.

49. The travel diaries of Jacobszoon and Sandelijn have been used by Ter Gouw and others, but the Leiden *dagvaarten* seems to have escaped notice (Stadsarchief Leiden, Secretarie, nr. 1218). It is a loosely bound collection of annual notebooks, each beginning in October; the consecutive pagination is in a later hand. Folios 1–48 are in the same hand; Willem Pieterszoon uyten Aggar is present for every meeting described, and on fol. 45 he says "I, Willem Pieters uyten Aggar," undertook a journey for the city. The rest of the manuscript is in a different hand, and "Jacob de Milde, pensionaris" is present for all the meetings described.

50. Aud. includes correspondence between the Council of Holland and leading government figures; Assendelft's letters alone number in the hundreds.

51. R. van Uytven, "1477 in Brabant," and "De Blijde Inkomst van Maria van Bourgondie, 29 Mei 1477, Text en Eigentijds Commentar," in Blockmans, *Het Algemeen en de Gewestelijke Privileges van Maria van Bourgondie voor de Nederlanden,* 253–285, 286–372. On names for and conceptions of unity in the Habsburg Netherlands, see Johan Huizinga, "Uit de Voorgeschiedenis van Ons Nationaal Besef," in *Verspreide Opstellen over de Geschiedenis van Nederland,* ed. W. E. Krul (Alphen aan den Rijn, 1982), 53–68, and J. J. Poelhekke, "Het Naamloze Vaderland van Erasmus," *BMGN* 86 (1971): 90–123

52. M. Gachard, *Collections des Voyages des Souverains des Pays-Bas,* vol. 2 = *Academie Royale des Sciences, des Lettres et de Beaux-Arts de Belgique, Commission Royale d'Histoire, Publications in Quarto* 15:2 (Brussels, 1874), 15–16. For Charles's reception in Amsterdam, see *HVH,* 176–177ᵛ.

53. Gachard, *Collection des Voyages,* 2: 27–30, 158–67, 269–274, 293–301, 310–330, 374–396.

54. Jane de Iongh, *Margaretha van Oostenrijk* (Amsterdam, 1947),

and *De Koningin: Maria van Hongarije, Landvoogdes der Nederlanden* (Amsterdam, revised 1966).

55. Paul Rosenfeld, "The Provincial Governors from the Minority of Charles V to the Revolt," *Standen en Landen* 17 (1959): 1–63. On rivalries among these families during Charles's minority, see Andreas von Walther, *Die Anfänge Karls V* (Leipzig, 1911). On the Brederodes, see H. A. Enno van Gelder, "De Hollandse Adel," *Tijdschrift voor Geschiedenis* (1930), as cited by A. C. Duke, "The Time of Troubles in the County of Holland, 1566–1567," *Tijdschrift voor Geschiedenis* 82 (1969): 316.

56. Jan van Rompaey, *De Grote Raad van de Hertogen van Bourgondie en het Parlement van Mechelen = VKAW–KL*, no. 73 (Brussels, 1973); J. Th. de Smidt, et al., *Chronologische Lijst van de Geëxtendeerde Sententiën en Procesbundels Berustende in het Archief van de Grote Raad te Mechelen 1465–1555*, 4 vols. (Brussels, 1966–1987).

57. Van den Bergh, *Correspondentie van Margaretha van Oostenrijk, 1506–1528* = vols. 2 and 3 of *Gedenkstukken tot Opheldering der Nederlandsche Geschiedenis*, 3 vols. (Leiden: 1842–1847); K. Lanz, *Correspondenz des Kaisers Karls V, aus dem Königlichen Archiv und der Bibliotheque de Bourgogne zu Brüssel*, 3 vols. (Leipzig: 1844–1846). Cf. Aud. 47–70: Lanz published only a few letters from these twenty-four packets of correspondence between Charles V and Mary of Hungary. The letters printed in Manuel Fernandez Alvarez, *Corpus Documental de Carlos V* (5 vols, Salamanca, 1973–1981) have little direct bearing on the Low Countries.

58. Margaret of Austria to Charles V, 23 October 1524, in Lanz, *Correspondenz des Karls V*, no 59, 1: 146–148; Charles V to Mary of Hungary, 3 January 1531, Lanz, no. 156, 1: 417–418; Mary of Hungary to Charles V, 28 January 1532, Aud. 52; Charles to Mary, 23 October 1535 (Aud. 52), and 2 March 1536 (Aud. 52); Mary to Charles, 21 April 1536, Lanz, Letter 633, 2: 600. De Iongh, *De Koningin: Maria van Hongarije*, 180–182, 194–195.

59. Michel Baelde, *De Collaterale Raden onder Karel V;* on Schore, see 309–310.

60. H. de Schepper, "De Grote Raad van Mechelen, Hoogste Rechtscollege van de Nederlanden?" in H. de Schepper, ed., *Miscellanea Consilii Magni* (Amsterdam, 1980), 171–192. See below, note 69.

61. See the introduction to vol. 1 of Blécourt and Meijers, *Memorialen van het Hof van Holland . . . van de Secretaris Jan Roosa*. Paul van Peteghem, "Centralisatie in Vlaanderen onder Karel V," (dissertation, University of Ghent, 1980), describes the personnel and functions of the Council of Flanders.

62. A. Kluit, *Historie der Hollandsche Staatsregering tot aan het Jaar 1795*, 5 vols. (Amsterdam, 1802–1805), 5: 529–531, a list of thirty-seven bailiffs and sheriffs in 1420. By 1552 there were 105 local judicial officers responsible for the posting of government ordinances or *plakkaten:* Council of Holland to Mary of Hungary, 15 January 1552 (Aud. 1646:2).

63. On the *Blijde Inkomst*, see note 51 above; Powicke, *The Reformation in England* (Oxford, reprint 1965), 35–37; Koenigsberger, "The Parliament of Piedmont," 29; Hintze, "Typologie der ständischen Verfassung des Abendlands," 231–232.

64. P. Leupen, *Philip of Leiden, a Fourteenth-Century Jurist* (The Hague, 1981), 91–103. There is need for a study of Meester Vincent Corneliszoon van Mierop; see the references in Chapter 5.

65. Aud. 650: 527–528. On the collection in which this document is found, see *AFR*, 73; Koenigsberger, "Patronage and Bribery during the Reign of Charles V," in *Estates and Revolutions* (Ithaca, 1971), 170, citing AJ, 9 December 1535.

66. *RSH*, 25 February 1543. On contemporary notions of absolute power among professors of civil law at French universities, see Allen, *A History of Political Thought in the Sixteenth Century*, 280–285.

67. In addition to the incident cited in note 66, see the minute of 28 June 1528 by the Audiencer, Laurens Du Blioul, in Griffiths, *Representative Government in Western Europe*, 351–352, on Margaret of Austria's decision to force through a *bede* not accepted by the States of Brabant. The third case occurred when Charles V occupied Ghent (1540) and compelled its acceptance of a *bede* already endorsed by the other three Members of Flanders: see N. Maddens, "De Opstandige Houding van Gent tijdens de Regering van Karel V, 1515–1540," *Appeltjes uit het Meetjesland 28* (1977) 203–239; Van Durme, *Antoon Perrenot, Kardinaal van Granvelle*, 377–379. Folkert Postma, *Viglius van Aytta als Humanist en Diplomaat (1507–1549)* (Zutphen, 1983) covers Viglius's career up to the point he assumed his post in the Secret Council, and Dr. Postma (University of Groningen) is at work on a sequel. R. Fruin and H. T. Colenbrander, *Geschiedenis der Staatsinstellingen in Nederland*, 40.

68. Niklaas Everaerts, *Consiliorum Opus* (Leuven, 1571), 5–6, 97–102.

69. Sandelijn, 15 December 1549: Holland should pursue its claim to exemption from the Antwerp toll in the Grand Council of Mechelen, because both the Secret Council and the Council of Finance were "quite suspect" in regard to the Emperor's toll revenues. Cf. 13 October 1548, 9 October 1551 and 27 January 1553: the Grand Council

judged in Holland's favor (1548) on the important issue of grain export fees, but the States could not get the verdict engrossed because Mary of Hungary wished the Secret Council to "examine" it first.

70. Council of Holland to the Secret Council, *HH* 381, 20 February 1560: the Council and the Chamber disagreed over a challenge to the privileges of the island of Voorne. On differences over the enforcement of heresy laws between the Council and Charles V's prosecutor, the Procurator General, see Tracy, "Heresy Law and Centralization under Mary of Hungary: Conflict between the Council of Holland and the Central Government over the Enforcement of Charles V's Placards," *Archiv für Reformationsgeschichte* 73 (1982): 284–307.

71. See the last three letters of Charles V to Mary of Hungary cited in note 58.

72. For example, Maximiliaan van Egmont, Count of Buren, joined the officials of his town of Leerdam under house arrest, rather than authorizing them to pay a novel tax: For references, see chapter 5, note 71.

73. Assendelft to Hoogstraten, 24 January 1535 (Aud. 1529), and 30 September 1535 (Aud. 1527): Hoogstraten and the Regent each wanted to have direct reports from the Council of Holland, and each could be upset to hear about something through the other.

74. See chapter 7, notes 34–35. Alain Derville, "Pots de vin, cadeaux, racket, patronage: essai sur les mécanismes de décision dans l'état Bourguignon," *Revue du Nord* 56 (1974): 341–364, and "Les Pots-de-Vin dans le dernier tiers du XVe siècle (d'après les comptes de Lille et St. Omer)," in W. P. Blockmans, ed., *Het Algemeen en de Gewestelijke Privileges van Maria van Bourgondië voor de Nederlanden*, 449–471.

75. AJ, 2 October 1525, 19 October 1526, 23 June 1539.

76. AJ, 1 January 1536.

77. AJ, 22 October 1531; Assendelft to Hoogstraten, 18, 26 January 1537 (Aud. 1530) and 28 January 1537 (Aud. 1532).

78. AJ, 23–24 February 1536, *RSH* 5, 25 February 1536.

79. *RSH*, 25 August 1531; AJ, 16 June 1530, 4–8 February 1536.

80. Whether there were precisely seventeen separate provinces is a matter for discussion: H. de Schepper, "De Burgerlijke Overheden en hun Permanente Kaders," *NAGN* 5: 315–316. The provinces of Friesland (1523), Utrecht and Overijssel (with Drenthe, 1527), Groningen (with Twente, 1536) and Gelderland (1543) were added under Charles V.

81. Mary of Hungary to Charles V, 8 February 1536, and Charles to Mary, 2 March 1536, in Lanz, Letters 627, 631, 2: 657–659.

82. Lille B 2301, 2309, 2315, 2320, 2328, 2504: total receipts aver-

aged 1,229,555 pounds between 1521 and 1525, but the income for 1552 was 5,021,015. In wartime years (as in 1552) receipts were swollen by *extraordinaris beden*, which the states granted only grudgingly in peace time.

83. Aud. 837:53ᵛ–57ᵛ, 312–315, shows repayment of 499,747 in loans ("deniers prins a frait") for the period 1521–1530, not counting sales of *renten* and anticipations of *bede* payments, meaning that the government paid back an average of 50,000 per year. Aud. 1407:1 shows an annual debt of roughly 3,800,000 pounds for the period 1554–1556.

84. Tracy, "Taxation System in the County of Holland," 80–81.

85. Aud. 867:116–123, a summary of domain income and the expenditures charged against that income for 1527.

86. H. Soly, "De Aluinhandel in de Nederlanden in de 16e Eeuw," *Belgische Tijdschrift voor Filologie en Geschiedenis / Revue Belge de Philologie et d'Histoire* 52 (1974): 800–857.

87. AJ, 13 February, 21 November 1523, 31 December 1523, 9 February 1525, 31 July 1527, 6 April 1528.

88. Hugo de Schepper, *Belgium Nostrum, 1500–1650: Over Integratie en Desintegratie van het Nederland* (Antwerp, 1987).

89. States of Holland petition to Margaret of Hungary (1524? Aud. 1524: 61–2); Council of Holland to the Council of Finance, 14 March 1542 (Aud. 1533).

90. Aud. 868:120–128, an anonymous and undated memorandum (ca. 1540) proposing important changes in the existing system of taxation.

91. Fritz Blaich, *Die Reichs-Monopolgesetzgebung im Zeitalter Karls V* (Stuttgart, 1967).

92. On disputes between large and small brewers, see J. C. van Loenen, *De Haarlemse Brouwindustrie voor 1600* (Amsterdam, 1950), 37–44; Aud. 1441:4, nos. 1 and 5, document a similar dispute involving the government and the brewers of Delft.

93. Mary of Hungary to the Sheriffs of Dordrecht, Delfshaven, and Rotterdam, 5 December 1552 (Aud. 1656:2); Council of Holland to Emmanuel Philibert of Savoy, 28 November 1556 (Aud. 1419:1).

94. Tracy, "Herring Wars: Sea Power in the North Sea in the Reign of Charles V," under consideration by a journal.

95. Anneke Geitz, "De Staten van Holland en hun Personeel," 27–29.

96. Geitz, 33; see P. A. Meilink, *Archieven van de Staten van Holland voor 1572*, nos. 1706–1789 (The Hague, 1927) for an inventory of *omslag* accounts.

97. AJ, 27 January, 13 February, 7, 8 March, 14 August, 10 September 1523, 31 May, 13 August 1524; Henk F. K. van Nierop, *Van Ridders tot Regenten*, 179–185. The States tried in vain to obtain the papers of Albrecht van Loo, and Aert van der Goes's record was preserved only because his son succeeded him (Sandelijn, 18–19 April 1555; Meilink, *Archieven van de Staten van Holland voor 1572*, 1–5). Cf. Blok, *Geschiedenis eener Hollands Stad*, 2: 25–28.

98. Tracy, "The Taxation System of the County of Holland," 79–80; Blockmans, "Breuk of Continuiteit? De Vlaamse Privileges van 1477," 114.

99. Leiden *dagvaarten*, 20 August 1532.

100. AJ, 31 December 1530–2 January 1531, 16 August 1531.

101. Oem van Wijngaerden, "Register van tgeene gedaen is," 65–75, Delft's brewers contested the monopoly claimed by Dordrecht for the distribution of beer in rural south Holland; H. A. Diederiks, "Amsterdamse Binnenscheepvaart-politiek in de 16e Eeuw," *Amstelodamum* 56 (1969): 111–115, the inland shippers' guild of Haarlem disputed the right claimed by their Amsterdam counterparts to have preference given to Amsterdam ships, provided the ship-type and the freight charges were the same.

102. B. van Rijswijk, *Geschiedenis van het Dordtsche Stapelrecht*, 64, 80–82. See also the capsule history of the staple controversy in Matthys Balen Janszoon, *Beschryving der Stad Dordrecht* (Dordrecht, 1677), 441–516.

103. AJ, 11–27 October 1527.

104. Rijswijk, 83–95; Council of Holland to Mary of Hungary, 7 November 1539 (Aud. 1528); report by Pieter Venyck, secretary to the Emperor, 27 March 1542 (Aud. 1533); Dordrecht to Lodewijk van Schoer, 11 April 1543 (Aud. 1656:1).

105. For commodities exported from Amsterdam, see Posthumus, *De Uitvoer van Amsterdam*, 181–192. *GRK* 4921 contains accounts of the Gouda toll from 1 May 1541 through 30 April 1544, accounts which were deposited with officials in The Hague because of a law-suit.

106. *GRK* 4921, the Gouda toll account; Stadsarchief Leiden, Oude Secretarie 1264:58e (1557 report on traffic through the Sparendam lock); Fruin, *Informacie op het Staet van Hollant*. See above, note 101.

107. F. Ketner, "Amsterdam en de Binnevaart door Holland"; on the Sparendam lock and its rebuilding in 1518, Stadsarchief Leiden, Oude Secretarie 1263:206–208, 214–232; *HVR*, 18, 22, 26 June; 3, 12, 17, 21 July; 7 August 1518.

108. J. C. Overvoorde, J. N. Oerburgt, *Archief van de Secretarie van*

de Stad Leiden, 1253–1575 (Leiden, 1937), Regesten, nos. 1317 (14 May 1519, a placard issued at the request of Gerrit Geerloofs, toll-farmer of Gouda), 1818 (26 October 1553); A. J. Enschede, *Inventaris van het Oud-Archief van de Stad Haarlem* (Haarlem, n.d.), Regesten, 26 June 1536: passages specifically prohibited are at Billerdam, Heiligen Weg (site of Amsterdam's *Overtoom*), Zevenhove, and Goe Jan Verwellersluis, between Gouda and Oudewater. See also Enschede, Privileges, no. 253 (1516): Amsterdam and Leiden are prohibited from attempting to escape tolls at Gouda and Sparendam (1516).

109. On the duties and privileges of the *ambachtsheer*, see van Nierop, *Van Ridders tot Regenten*, 119–126.

110. The distinction between a *waaiersluis* and an *opwindende sluis* is explained by C. Hoek, "Delfshaven, de Rivierhaven van Delft." See Fockema Andreae, *De Hoogheemraadschap van Rijnland*.

111. 1) From the early fifteenth century through much of the sixteenth century, there were disputes between Haarlem and Amsterdam concerning an overhaul or *overtoom* that permitted direct connections between the Amstel and the Haarlemmermeer, bypassing the IJ and Haarlem. 2) From 1520 through 1545, Haarlem, Gouda, and Dordrecht disputed efforts to open a sluice gate in the Billerdam south of Amsterdam, which would have opened another direct connection to the Haarlemmermeer. 3)Between 1492 and 1555 there were various efforts to build a sluice through the Leidschendam (between Delft and Leiden), to put a windlass on top, or to dig a new channel northward from Delft via Nootdorp; all were blocked by Haarlem, Gouda, and Dordrecht, joined at times by Leiden. 4)In 1492, 400 men from Gouda and Dordrecht smashed an *overtoom* at Hildam on the Rotte (built by Rotterdam so its barges could reach the Oude Rijn without passing through Gouda) as well as the new sluice in the Leidschendam. 5) Between summer 1517 and spring 1518, men from Haarlem twice appeared in arms on the IJ dike to prevent the building of a new lock they thought would have been too narrow, and prejudicial to their shipping. 6)In 1562 Hendrik van Brederode sent men to sink a ship at Vreeswijk on the Lek, opposite his town of Vianen, just at the point where the city of Utrecht was cutting a new opening in the Lek dike. 7) In May 1564 men from the villages of Hermelen, Camerijk and Zegwert in the *Land van Woerden* marched out—with banners, fife and drum—to smash a dam and stone bridge being built at Bodegraven by the Dike-Count of the *Land van Woerden*, without their approval. 8) Dordrecht to Gouda, 2 January 1565 (Stadsarchief Haarlem, Loketkast 7.5.6. nr. 1) proposes joint action to oppose Schoonhoven's request for

permission to travel with small ships and barges through Goe Jan
Verwellersluis, as had already been permitted to Woerden and Oude-
water. References and further details will be provided in Tracy, "Armed
Non-Rebellion: the Assertion of Corporate Privileges in the Habsburg
Netherlands," an article in preparation.

112. Delft argues in its defense of the Nootdorp channel (no. 3 in
note 111) that "waterways are public and that all prohibitory injunc-
tions tend to cause inconvenience for some users, or to make navigation worse than it formerly was . . .[;] moreover according to common
law each is entitled to make use of his own so as to make a profit." Cf.
the statement from one of Niklaas Everaert's briefs that "de jure
gentium omnibus libera per mare & flumina competit navigatio"
(*Conciliorum Opus*, 3: 7–8), and Everaert's opinion on the inequity of
the Dordrecht staple.

113. T. S. Jansma, "De Betekenis van Dordrecht en Rotterdam
omstreeks het Midden der Zestiende Eeuw," *De Economist* 93 (1943):
212–250.

114. Pirenne, *Histoire de Belgique*, 3: 259–272. W. Brulez, "Brugge
en Antwerpen in de 15e en 16e Eeuwen. Een Tegenstelling?" *Tijdschrift voor Geschiedenis* 83 (1970): 15–37, relativizes Pirenne's sharp
contrast between the dynamic, free trade of Antwerp and the stagnat-
ing, regulated trade of Bruges. Van der Wee, "De Overgang van de
Middeleeuwen naar Nieuwe Tijd," 20–22, 29–30, traces the continuing prosperity of the southern Netherlands in this period to the development of specialized luxury products and services, with less emphasis on the so-called new cloth industries. E. C. G. Brünner, *De Orden op
de Buitennering van 1531* (Utrecht, 1918), 79–80.

115. Brünner, *De Orden*, 65–78, 126. *RSH*, 7 June 1529, 24 February 1530, 6 July, 2 August 1531, 5 February 1532; *AJ*, 31 October
1528, 7 June 1529, 5 March 1530. Overvoorde and Oerburgt, *Het
Archief van de Secretarie van de Stad Leiden*, Regesten, 1677, 1685, 1706;
Brünner, *De Orden*, 155.

116. Klaus Spading, *Holland und die Hanse in 15en Jahrhundert* (Weimar, 1973), x, stresses the "progressive" character of Holland's economy in this era; W. van Ravensteyn, *Onderzoekingen over de Economische
en Sociale Ontwikkeling van Amsterdam*, 45–51, argued that Amsterdam
was already different from other Holland towns in the Middle Ages,
since its involvement in the transit trade, rather than in any particular
industry, meant that its guilds were not guilds in the conventional
sense. Other scholars have been more impressed by the traditional
features of Holland's economy. W. S. Unger, "De Hollandse Graanhandel en Graanhandelspolitiek in de Middeleeuwen," *De Economist*

(1916): 480–482, treats Hollanders' arguments for free trade as a matter of self-interest, not as a precocious statement of liberal economic doctrine. T. S. Jansma, "Hanze, Fugge, Amsterdam," *BMGN* 91 (1976): 6, rejects the notion that Holland in its economic development was, prior to about 1550, superior to its Baltic rival, Lübeck. Pirenne, *Histoire de Belgique*, 3: 228–238; *Early Democracies in the Low Countries*, tr. J. V. Saunders (New York, 1971), 162–171, 187–215.

117. For Amsterdam's defense of "free trade" in various contexts, see AJ, 9 March 1527 (Amsterdam and Dordrecht protested restrictions on the sailing dates for the herring fleet on the grounds that "alle neringhe ende hanteringhe van coopmanschap behoort vry te wesen ende nyet gerestringeert tot enige sekere conditien"), 11 April 1537; *RSH*, 5 August 1545, 15 December 1549; Meilink, "Rapporten en Betoogen nopens het Congiegeld op Granen," 90, 118. Cf. *RSH*, 24 September 1532: Amsterdam did not have a representative on the delegation sent to Brussels in connection with the ban on *buitennering*. Meilink, "Rapporten en Betoogen," 1–5; the privilege was confirmed in 1507. AJ, 18–21 June 1528.

118. Geyl, *The Revolt of the Netherlands*, 15–66.

3: THE GUELDERS WARS

1. Geoffrey Parker, *The Military Revolution, 1500–1800* (Cambridge, 1988); J. R. Hale, *War and Society in Renaissance Europe, 1450–1620* (New York, 1985), 61–63; E. F. Jacob, *Henry V and the Invasion of France* (New York, 1966), 68; Perry Anderson, *Lineages of the Absolutist State* (New York, 1974), 30–33.

2. Pocock, *The Machiavellian Moment: Florentine Political Thought and the Atlantic Republican Tradition* (Princeton, 1975).

3. Cited by Donald Wilcox, *The Development of Florentine Humanist Historiography* (Cambridge, Mass., 1969), 90.

4. "Sileni Alcibiadis," in *Adagiorum Chiliades, D. Erasmi Opera Omnia*, ed. J. Leclercq, 10 vols. (Leiden, 1703–1706) = *LB* 2: 775DE: "Justum bellum appellant, cum ad exhauriendam opprimendamque rempublicam Principes inter se colludunt." Cf. "Tributum a Mortuis Exigere," *LB* 2: 338C, and Erasmus to Antoon van Bergen, 14 March 1514, in *Opus Epistolarum D. Erasmi*, ed. P. S. Allen, 12 vols. (Oxford, 1906–1963), Letter 288, 1.55–56, 1: 553.

5. J. H. Shennan, *The Origins of the Modern European State, 1450–1725* (London, 1974), 37.

6. Budé, *De Studio Litterarum* (Paris, 1532), 13.

7. Tracy, *The Politics of Erasmus*, 67–68; AJ, 29 June–7 July 1529.

8. For example, the Emperor sought a special gift of 50,000 pounds in 1510: Maximilian to Margaret of Austria, 10 June 1510, LeGlay, Letter 213, 1:282–284; Margaret of Austria to Maximilian, July 1510, LeGlay, Letter 233, 1: 308–310; and Maximilian to Margaret of Austria, 18 August 1510, LeGlay, Letter 237, 1: 313–315.

9. See below, notes 83–90; *HVH*, 156ᵛ–157, 198ᵛ–199.

10. On the meaning of "exploicter," see Maximilian to Margaret of Austria, 21 May 1510, LeGlay, no. 206, 1: 269.

11. Struick, *Gelre en Habsburg*, 6–12. On the Zuider Zee channels, which had to be marked each year by Amsterdam's *stroommeester* or master of the current, see Ter Gouw, 4: 115–117.

12. Struick, 39–58; Wiesflecker, *Kaiser Maximilian I*, 2: 140–146, 3: 92–104; L. P Gachard, "Les Anciennes assemblées nationales de Belgique," *Revue de Bruxelles* 3 (1839): 16–17. Struick cautions against the view that Karel van Egmont should be considered a Renaissance version of Attila the Hun (6).

13. *HVH* 186–194ᵛ; J. S. Theissen *De Regering van Karel V in de Noordelijke Nederlanden* (Amsterdam, 1922), 35–48; J. J. Kalma, *Grote Pier van Kimswerd* (Leeuwarden, 1970).

14. Struick, 230–231; Cuthbert Tunstall and Edward Ponynges to Henry VIII, 25 March 1516, in J. S. Brewer, ed., *Letters and Papers Foreign and Domestic, of the Reign of Henry VIII* (Reprint: Vaduz, 1965), 2:i.

15. AJ, 17–21 November 1527, 29 April 1524. E. M. ten Cate, "Onderhandelingen van het Hof te Brussel met de Munstersche Wederdopers Aangeknoopt," *Doopsgesinde Bijdragen* (1899).

16. Hadrianus Barlandus (d. 1535), *Historia Rerum Gestarum a Brabantiae Ducibus* (Frankfurt, 1585), 169; Ludwig Duncker, *Fürst Rudolf der Tapfere von Anhalt und der Krieg gegen Herzog Karl von Geldern, 1507–1508* (Dessau, 1900), 37. For a similiar misinterpretation of events, see below, note 35.

17. See above, note 12.

18. Collection "Staten van Brabant," Algemeen Rijksarchief, Brussels.

19. Hermans, *Hollandiae Gelriaeque Bellum*, in Ant. Mathesis, *Veteris Aevi Analecta* (The Hague, 1738).

20. Cornelius Aurelius, *Cronycke van Hollandt, Zeelandt en Vrieslant* (Antwerp, 1530). R. Fruin, "De Zamensteller van de zogenaamde Divisie-Kroniek," in his *Verspreide Geschriften*, (The Hague, 1903), 7: 66–72.

21. On Snoy, see Robert de Graaf, *Reyner Snoygoudanus, a Bibliography* (Nieuwkoop, 1968).

22. An archivist's note describes the anonymous author as "een Amsterdamse schrijver en oogentuyge." In connection with a visit to Amsterdam in 1515 by Adriaan van Utrecht, the future Pope Adrian VI, the author (220) names the altar on which he said mass twice, and mentions that Adriaan "maecte costelicke boecken ende besonderling screef by seer coestelyck op dat boek van de hogen sinne"—a reference to Adrian's "Commentarius sive Expositiones in Proverbia Salamonis," a full text of which survives in manuscript but was never published in its entirety: *Dictionnaire de théologie catholique*, 15 vols. (Paris, 1909–1950), 1:461.

23. Hermans, *Hollandiae Gelriaeque Bellum*, 334.

24. "Ad Suam Bataviam," in Cornelis Aurelius, *Batavia sive de Antiquo eius Insulae Quam Rhenus . . . Facit Situ*, ed. Bonaventura Vulcanius (Antwerp, 1586), 78. Translation mine.

25. Cornelius Aurelius, *Batavia*, 84–98: letters to Hendrik van Nassau, Stadholder of Holland; Jacob Lokhorst, burgrave of Leiden; and Jan Bennink, member of the Council of Holland.

26. Snoy, *De Rebus Batavicis Libri XIII*, 187.

27. Like his kinsman, Willem Hermans, Aurelius was an early friend and correspondent of Erasmus: see Allen, *Opus Epistolarum D. Erasmi*, vol. 1; and P. C. Molhuysen, "Cornelius Aurelius," *Nederlands Archief voor Kerkgeschiedenis*, n. s. 2 (1902): 1–28. Aurelius to Snoy, in *Batavia*, 49–50, says that he wrote this treatise at Snoy's request.

28. IJsselstein to Margaret, 2 March 1512, Van den Bergh, Letter 168, 3: 13–15. Spinelly's report, 13 January 1513, in Brewer, *Letters and Papers of the Reign of Henry VIII*, 1:i, no. 1594. IJsselstein was apparently popular in Dordrecht, which had supported the war against Guelders: AJ, 29 December 1523, the *pensionaris* of Dordrecht speaks up in behalf of Hoogstraten, "prodens ita dordracensium bonum favorem ad Florentium comitem de Buren."

29. *HVH*, 143^v, 151, 169.

30. See above, note 16.

31. *HVH*, 142^v–143, 160^v, 162^v, 167.

32. Contrast *HVH*, 166^v, with Struick, *Gelre en Habsburg*, 139–146.

33. *HVH*, 162^v.

34. Velius, *Chronyk van Hoorn*, ed. Sebastian Centen (Hoorn, 1740), 196.

35. *HVH*, 164^v; cf. 185, regarding a six-week truce in Friesland ending 4 May 1517: "This truce was made to the disadvantage of our land. And it is to be supposed that some lords made this truce without the knowledge of the King of Spain [Charles], because they did not

love our land, and in order that the war in Friesland should last longer, and our portion of the land suffer more harm." Theissen, *De Regering van Karel V in de Noordelijke Nederlanden*, 48: the truce in question was concluded in conjunction with the Treaty of Cambrai (11 March 1517, between Francis I, Maximilian, and Archduke Charles), which is not mentioned by the author of the "Historie van Hollant."

36. *HVH*, 187ᵛ–188, has Nassau stationing cavalry in Schoonhoven (on the Lek) and Haarlem, and parcelling out four "banners" of infantry (about 900 men) to Edam, Monnikendam, Hoorn, and Uutdam. Aurelius, *Cronycke van Hollandt, Zeelandt en Vrieslant*, sig. Ee 5ᵛ, concurs, but also mentions that Medemblik, where the Black Band landed, had "300 foreign troops" within its walls.

37. *HVH*, 191ᵛ.

38. Tracy, *The Politics of Erasmus*, 96–107.

39. D. S. van Zuider, "De Plundering van Den Haag door Maarten van Rossum 6–9 Maart 1528," *Die Haghe* (1911): 130–152. The reference is to Hortensius, *Secessionum Civilium Ultrajectinarum et Bellorum ab Anno 1524 Historia* (Basel, 1546), and Heuterus, *Rerum Austriacarum Libri XV* (Antwerp, 1584).

40. Maximilian to Margaret of Austria, 29 April 1509, LeGlay, Letter 100, 1: 130–133. Deputies to Low Countries parliaments were not alone in harboring such suspicions: Marongiu (*Il Parlamento in Italia*, 296) notes that Duke Charles of Savoy assured the *stati* of Piedmont (1518) that the troops he was recruiting were not meant to attack his subjects.

41. Margaret of Austria to Maximilian, [April 1512], Van den Bergh, Letter 179, 3: 32–34; the same text is given in LeGlay, Letter 380, 1:504–507. See also Gachard, "Anciennes assemblées nationales de Belgique," 23–24.

42. Margaret of Austria to Maximilian, July 1510, LeGlay, Letter 233, 1: 308–310, and n.d., Letter 302, 1: 394; Maximilian to Margaret, 29 September 1512, Letter 413, 2: 40–42.

43. Margaret to Maximilian, 18 March 1512, LeGlay, Letter 377, 18 March 1512, 1:501–502; 20 August 1512, LeGlay, Letter 402, 2: 23–25; and 15 December 1512, Van den Bergh, Letter 184, 3: 58–60.

44. Struick, *Gelre en Habsburg*, 311–315; Theissen, *De Regering van Karel V in de Noordelijke Nederlanden*, 74–84.

45. Tracy, "The Taxation System of the County of Holland," Table 1, 108–109.

46. AJ, 25 October 1523, 20 November 1527 *RSH*, 18 June 1535 (Hoogstraten's *bande d'ordonnance*). *AJ*, 25 September, 3 October, 5–

12, 17 December 1523; cf. 9 December 1522, 31 March 1528; *RSH*, 31 March, 16 June 1528, 26 March, 3 April 1533, 20 September 1534; Struick, *Gelre en Habsburg*, 287. Masons earned five or six stuivers per day in Haarlem and Leiden between 1525 and 1530 (Noordegraaf, *Hollands Welvaren*, Tables 4d and 4e, 69–70).

47. AJ, 3, 9, 20, 25 October 1523.

48. Struick, *Gelre en Habsburg*, 286.

49. The Dutch word *staet* (from the French *état*) can mean a prospective or retrospective budget summary (see Aud. 650 for examples of both kinds), or, in this case, budget for a *bede*.

50. AJ, 28 December 1523; cf. 9 January 1524.

51. AJ, 18 January 1524; the burgomaster was Robrecht Jacobszoon.

52. *HVH*, 218–218; AJ, 3 October 1523.

53. AJ, 31 December 1523.

54. Margaret to Charles V, 21 February 1524, Lanz, *Correspondenz des Kaisers Karls V*, Letter 49, 1: 89–90; the ninth of Gattinara's "ten commandments for war," Henne, *Histoire de Belgique sous le Règne de Charles V*, 1: 316–322; Struick, *Gelre en Habsburg*, 288–289.

55. The other two cities with voting rights in the States of Brabant, Leuven and Brussels, were farther removed from the fighting, and had refused to pay for the war in 1512: Margaret to Maximilian, April 1512, Van den Bergh, Letter 179, 3:32–34 = LeGlay, Letter 380, 1:504–507.

56. Struick, *Gelre en Habsburg*, 289–295.

57. AJ, 19 February; 1, 13, 15 April; 12, 12, 20 May; 4, 7 June; 13 August 1524; 1, 31 May; 1 June 1525.

58. In a discussion among cities involved in the Baltic trade, the men of Antwerp said that a Baltic war would be "worse for us [meaning all those assembled] than three French wars": AJ, 18 January 1524.

59. AJ, 28 December 1523. Cf. Theissen, *De Regering van Karel V in de Noordelijke Nederlanden*, 35–48: Duke Albert of Saxony received Holland's claim to Friesland in payment for a campaign he had conducted for Maximilian; his son, Duke George, sold it back to the Habsburg government in 1515.

60. AJ, 7, 11 March 1523.

61. *HVH*, 217ᵛ–218ᵛ. AJ, 15, 20, 25 October 1523; cf. 25 September 1523.

62. H. F. K. van Nierop, *Van Ridders tot Regenten*, 45–46; *AFR*, 48, 76, 86–87.

63. Using *RSH*, *AJ*, and *GVR*, one can find eighteen occasions between 1522 and 1530 when the towns were divided on a government

proposal. Dordrecht voted initially with the government seventeen times, Haarlem fourteen, Amsterdam twelve, Leiden four, Delft three, and Gouda two. Cf. Mary of Hungary to Assendelft, 20 September 1554 (Aud. 1646:3): the Regent finds it strange that those resisting a new *bede* request include the men of Dordrecht, "qui sont accoustumez a donner example aux aultres."

64. *HVR*, 17 January 1519: Stadtholder Hendrik van Nassau reminds Haarlem's deputies of the "contract" their city had made with the Duke of Saxony, in order to obtain a favorable rate of *gratie*. The city had two-thirds *gratie* on its *ordinaris bede* at this time: Tracy, "Taxation System of the County of Holland," 79–80.

65. For the Ieper poor law of 1525, see J. A. van Houtte, *An Economic History of the Low Countries* (New York, 1977), 128–129, and [William Marshal], *The Forme and Maner of Subvention for Pore People at Hypres* (London, 1535; reproduction Amsterdam, 1974), a translation of the Ieper ordinance. For discussion in the States of Holland, see AJ, 18–27 February 1529; *RSH*, 4 September, 20 November 1527 (copies of the Ieper ordinances are distributed), 3 March 1528, 16 March 1529.

66. See Chapter 5, notes 100, 101.

67. *GVR*, 7 April 1524; AJ, 10 September, 9 December 1523, 28 January, 14 February, 1 April 1524.

68. *GVR*, 28 September 1528, 6 November 1529, 8 January, 11 July 1530, 7 January 1531, 27 January, 3 July 1533, 13 April 1537; AJ, 1–6 December 1527, 14 January 1531.

69. See Chapter 1, note 28. Assendelft to Hoogstraten, 22 February 1540, Aud. 1528, two cities have still not consented to a levy of 2,000 pounds for gratuities (bribes), "ende zal niettemin den ommeslach terstont hebben voertganck als geconsenteert . . . by tmeerderdeel"; Council of Holland to Mary of Hungary, 26 May 1544, Aud. 1646:1, the nobles have not agreed to a special tax that bears on the countryside, and people will "murmur" because one of the four cities which agreed, Delft, is now exempt from all *beden* because of a recent fire, and thus the majority is questionable.

70. *AFR*, 52, note 84.

71. Ruysch Janszoon's importance is suggested by the fact that a *dagvaart* of the States was postponed because he forgot to come: AJ, 3 November 1523; Elias, *De Vroedschap van Amsterdam*, I, *sub nomine*.

72. On *décharges*, see the references in *AFR*.

73. AJ, 7 March, 20 October 1523.

74. AJ, 25 October 1523. The *Audienceur* was head of the government chancery.

75. AJ, 3, 20 October, 21–29, 31 December 1523, 25–28 January, 8, 10, 14 February, 9 April 1524. Hoogstraten pledged his credit to the service of the state on numerous occasions and claimed he had not always been reimbursed: *AFR*, 113–114.

76. *HVH*, 219.

77. AJ, 6–11, 27 June 1525; cf. 23 March 1528.

78. AJ, 21 November 1523, 5 May, 19 June 1524; but cf. AJ, 28 January 1524, Castre conducted a raid through the Veluwe district of Guelders.

79. Struik, *Gelre en Habsburg*, 311–315; Theissen, *De Regering van Karel V in de Noordelijke Nederlanden*, 74–84. On the strategic significance of the acquisition of Friesland and Utrecht, see AJ, 21 December 1523, 9 February 1528.

80. *HVH* 249–249ᵛ; AJ, 23 September 1527. See chapter 3, note 39.

81. AJ, 22, 23 March 1528.

82. *RSH*, 13, 31 March 1528; AJ, 14–16, 17 April 1528. On Renneberg, see Leo Peters, *Wilhelm von Renneberg, ein Rheinischer Edelherr zwischen den Konfessionellen Fronten* (Kempen, 1979).

83. AJ, 1–6, 19–23 December 1527, 24 January 1528.

84. Struick, *Gelre en Habsburg*, 290–291; for efforts to breach the tax exemption enjoyed by the feudal enclaves, see Chapter 5.

85. *RSH*, 16 February, 25 July 1528. Council of Holland to Hoogstraten, 6 December 1527, and 27 February 1528, Aud. 1524; AJ, 23 March 1528; Struick, *Gelre en Habsburg*, 290–291.

86. AJ, 22 March 1528; *RSH*, 28 February, 1, 13 March 1528.

87. AJ, 22–23 March 1528; cf. 25–28 January 1524.

88. Struick, *Gelre en Habsburg*, 313–323.

89. Tracy, "The Taxation System of the County of Holland," 111, Table 3, items n–q, four sales of *renten* totalling 96,000 pounds.

90. AJ, 16–27 August, 7 September 1528; *RSH*, 12–19 September 1528.

91. AJ, 30 April 1528.

92. AJ, 1 June 1525.

93. *RSH*, 7 May, 18 July 1528; AJ, 20, 25 October, 21–29 December 1523, 10, 14–15 February 1524; Council of Holland to Hoogstraten, 9 July 1528 (Aud. 1524).

94. See Chapter 3, note 75.

95. Council of Holland to Hoogstraten 9 July 1528 (Aud. 1524). There are, however, no further references to the Treasurer of War's accounts.

96. Among the members of Amsterdam's *vroedschap* in the 1520s,

Heyman Jacobszoon van Ouder Amstel had served as castellan of Muiden in 1508 (*HVH,* 166), Goosen Janszoon Recalf had served as admiral of the Zuider Zee in 1523 (*AJ,* 13 March 1523), and Meester Pieter Colijn was one of the masters of the muster appointed by the States (see above, note 93): on these men, see the entries in J. E. Elias, *De Vroedschap van Amsterdam, 1578–1795,* 2 vols. (Amsterdam, 1963).

4: HOLLAND'S SEAFARING TRADES

1. Cornelis de Scepper to Maximilian of Burgundy, lord of Vere and Beveren, 5 June 1546 (Aud. 1659:3 / III).

2. For salient features of the westward trade, see van Houtte, *An Economic History of the Low Countries,* 176, 178–181, 184–185, 192, 195–196. For discussion in the States of Holland on protective measures, Sandelijn, 24 September; 12, 14, 23–24 October; 5, 15 November; 8, 15, 21 December 1549.

3. Rogier De Gryse, "De Gemeenschappelijke Groote Visscherij van de Nederlanden in de XVIe Eeuw," *BGN* 7 (1952): 32–54. On the size of Holland's fleet, Chapter 1, note 38; Assendelft to Hoogstraten, 18 October 1536 (Aud. 1526), and to Mary of Hungary, 12 September 1552 (Aud. 1646:3). On the size of busses, see Assendelft to Mary of Hungary, 27 July 1537 (Aud. 1532), 15 August 1547, 10 August and 14 August 1552 (Aud. 1646:3). For the 1550 *lastgelt,* CC 23336. CC 23358 (100th penny tax on goods exported from Holland, November 1543–February 1544), entries on herring exports indicate an average price of 40.5 pounds per *last.*

4. Council of Holland to Hoogstraten, 5 May 1528 (Aud. 1524), 10 April 1537 (Aud. 1530). Charles de la Roncière, *Histoire de la Marine Française,* 6 vols. (Paris, 1909–1932), 3: 432–452; Robert Kerr Hanny and Denys Hay, *The Letters of James V* (Edinburgh, 1954), 326–7, 370, 404, 407–408, 414.

5. Mary of Hungary to Assendelft, 31 July 1547 (Aud. 1646:3), and to Beveren and Scepper, 25 June 1552 (Aud. 1659:3 / III).

6. Rogier De Gryse, "De Konvooieering van de Vlaamse Vissersvloot in de 15e en 16e Eeuwen," *BGN* 2 (1948): 1–24. Besides the *dagvaarten* of the States, *RSH* records certain *dagvaarten particulier,* including those of "towns and villages engaged in the herring fishery." For *omslagen* by the States to help pay for warships, see *HTR,* 1522/3, *AJ,* 22 January 1523.

7. *GVR,* 6–22 August 1522, 28 June 1524, 2 October 1525.

8. AJ, 22 January 1523; 15, 25 June 1524; it was also alleged that warships robbed the busses they were meant to protect.

9. AJ, 6 April, 6 May 1528; cf. *RSH*, 7 May 1528. For other complaints about how safe-conducts worked to the profit of "great purses," see AJ, 13 February, 21 November, 8, 31 December 1523, 9 February 1525, 8 January 1526, 31 July 1527. Soly, "De Aluinhandel in de Nederlanden," shows the government alum monopoly working exactly this way.

10. AJ, 10 July 1536, 20 June 1537; *RSH*, 8 August 1536, 11 August 1537; Assendelft to Hoogstraten, 19 July, 21 August 1536; 18, 23 October 1537 (Aud. 1526), 16 September 1536, 8 January 1537 (Aud. 1530).

11. Council of Holland to Hoogstraten, 10 April 1537 (Aud. 1530), 20 April 1537 (Aud. 1532); Assendelft to Hoogstraten, 9 July 1537, and 23 October 1537, including a report by Secretary Vuytwyck (Aud. 1532); Hoogstraten to Mary of Hungary, 12 July and 27 July 1537 (Aud. 1532); minute of Mary of Hungary's response to deputies from Holland, 1 June 1537 (Aud. 1532); AJ, 17, 18 May; 1, 13, 20 June 1537; *RSH*, 18 April; 1, 15, 30 June, 15 July 1537. A later letter reports deputies from Schiedam saying their town has only the herring fishery to sustain it: Assendelft to Mary of Hungary, 14 August 1552 (Aud. 1646:3).

12. *Letters and Papers of the Reign of Henry VIII*, 16: Letter 150; 17: Letter 529; 19.1: Letter 345; 19.2: Letters 349 and 364; 20.1: Letter 598, Treaty of 4 April 1528 between Scotland and the Netherlands; 21.2: Letter 24, 5 September 1546 addition to the treaty, to enforce more strictly the provision that safe-conducts be respected by both sides. The Antwerp petition (Aud. 1659:3/III) can be dated prior to September 7, 1551. For other reports of hostile acts by the Scots, see Council of Holland to Beveren, 28 July 1550, and to Mary of Hungary, 25 March 1552 (Aud. 1646:2).

13. Mary of Hungary to the Council of Holland, 11 June and 5 July 1547 (Aud. 1646:1); Assendelft to Mary of Hungary, 11 June 1547 (Aud. 1646:3). *RSH*, 27 June, 19 July 1552, 14–16 March 1553; *RSH*, 11, 22, 29, 30 June, 3 July 1547.

14. *RSH*, 15, 21, 30 July, 8 September 1547, 7 August 1548, 7 June 1549; De Gryse, "De Gemeenschappelijke Groote Visscherij van de Nederlanden," 43–44; Council of Holland to Mary of Hungary, 15 and 21 July 1547 (Aud. 1646:1); Assendelft to Mary of Hungary, 21 July 1547, 5 and 15 August 1547 (Aud. 1646:3); Mary of Hungary to Assendelft, 31 July 1547, and 19 December 1547 (Aud. 1646:3); Sandelijn, 3 June 1549.

15. For Habsburg naval strategy, see Tracy, "The Herring Wars: Sea Power in the North Sea in the Reign of Charles V," under consideration by a journal.

16. P. A. Meilink, "Rapporten en Betoogen nopens het Congiegeld op Granen, 1539–1541," *BMHGU* 44 (1923): 73, 111; Richard W. Unger, *Dutch Shipbuilding before 1600* (Assen, 1978), 11.

17. AJ, 16 May 1528, 11 February 1530, 30 March 1531, 7 May 1532; Mary of Hungary to Assendelft, 14 March 1544 (Aud. 1646:3): the Queen is puzzled that the nobles join in opposing the tenth penny on commercial profits. Cf. De Vries, *The Dutch Rural Economy in the Golden Age*, 166.

18. Enschede, *Inveniaris van het Oud-Archief van Haarlem* (Haarlem, s.d.), Regesten, 26 April 1516, Charles grants Haarlem the staple for herring packing; but in light of Haarlem's refusal to pay for protection of the herring fleet (above, note 7), one must wonder how effective this regulation was. On herring exports to the Baltic, see Posthumus, *De Uitvoer van Amsterdam*, 174–192.

19. Nina Ellinger Bang, *Tabeller over Skibsfart og Varetransport gennem Øresund, 1497–1660*, 2 vols. (Copenhagen, 1906–1922), 1:2–3, 6–8, 18–33; Christensen, *Dutch Trade to the Baltic*, 29–45.

20. Spading, *Holland und die Hanse im 15en Jahrhundert*, 1–12; I. H. Kam, *Waar Was dat Huis op de Warmoes Straat?* (Amsterdam, 1968), 13; Alfred Schmidtmayer, "Zur Geschichte der bremischen Akzise," *Bremisches Jahrbuch* 37 (1937): 64–79; cf the series "Bremisches Kornhaus," 1, Stadtsarchiv Bremen, beginning with the year 1549. On the growth of Bremen's direct trade with Iberia, see Council of Holland to Hoogstraten, 24 February 1538 (Aud. 1531), and Meilink, "Rapporten en Betoogen noopens het Congiegeld op Granen," 37, 82–83. For links between Hamburg and Antwerp, see G. Asaert, *De Antwerpse Scheepsvaart in de XVe Eeuw = VKAW-KL* 72 (Brussels, 1973), 304–314.

21. G. A. IJssel de Schepper, *De Lotgevallen van Christiern II en Isabella van Oostenrijk gedurende hun Ballingschap in de Nederlanden* (Zwolle, 1870), 17–21, 46–52.

22. H. Klompmaker, "Handel, Geld- en Bankwezen in de Noordelijke Nederlanden," *NAGN*, 6: 61; AJ, 29 May 1529, 12 May 1530.

23. AJ, 12 January 1527, 7 January 1536; Henne, *Histoire de Belgique sous le Règne de Charles Quint*, 2: 184–190; sketches of both men in Michel Baelde, *De Collaterale Raden onder Karel V*, 252–253, 327–328.

24. *RSH*, 28 February 1528; AJ, 16 May 1528.

25. Meilink, "Rapporten en Betoogen nopens het Congiegeld op Granen," 5–6; *RSH*, 9 January 1527.

26. AJ, 8–11 January 1527.
27. AJ, 2 February 1527, 24 January, 18 February, 16 May 1528; *RSH*, 28 February 1528.
28. *RSH*, 3 January 1530; AJ, 29 May, 11 September 1529, 10 January 1530.
29. *GVR*, 3 March 1530; *RSH*, 3, 17 January 1530; AJ, 27 February, 27 September 1523, 28 January 1524, 29 May 1528, 15 December 1529, 10–28 January 1530; W. S. Unger, *De Tol van Iersekeroord, Documenten en Rekeningen, 1321–1572* [= *Rijksgeschiedkundige Publicatiën, Kleine Ser.*, 29 (The Hague, 1939), 129–130].
30. For the two *beden* in question, see Tracy, "Taxation System of the County of Holland," 111, Table 3, items s and t; AJ, 12, 22 May 1529, 1, 8, 11 (the quotation), 17 February, 11 March 1530.
31. AJ, 25 February 1530; *GVR*, 2 March 1530; *RSH*, 9 June 1530. See below, note 35.
32. AJ, 17 November 1528, 16 July 1530; *RSH*, 27 July 1530, 25 August 1531.
33. AJ, 14 February, 25 May, 16 June 1530. For example, the budget for an *omslag* of 4,776 pounds in 1533 included 800 pounds in "gratuities" for various officials, including Assendelft: Leiden *dagvaarten*, 29 October 1533.
34. AJ, 8, 21 February 1530; *RSH*, 18 February, 2 May, 1 July 1530; Meilink, "Rapporten en Betoogen," 25–46.
35. Meilink, "Rapporten en Betoogen," 35–64.
36. Meilink, "Rapporten en Betoogen," 49, 82–83, 114–116. For price ranges per *last* of rye, see below, note 63.
37. Meilink, "Rapporten en Betoogen," 34–65.
38. *RSH*, 5, 10–11 May, 1 July, 28 November 1530; AJ, 26 November, 21 December 1530. Both sources indicate that the grain export ban was renewed in November 1530, but again not published by the Council of Holland.
39. *RSH*, 9, 28 March 1531; AJ, 20 March 1531.
40. *RSH*, 24 April, 24 June, 5, 11 July 1531; AJ, 22 August 1534.
41. *RSH*, 5, 23 February 1536; AJ, 13 January, 4 February 1536; on Ruffault, see Baelde, *De Collaterale Raden*, 302.
42. AJ, 5 June 1535; *ASR* 1535, 35–38.
43. AJ, 1 January, 23–24 February 1536; *RSH*, 5, 12, 15, 23–25 February 1536. On the falsification of documents, see Chapter 7, for the case of the inquisitor Frans van Hulst.
44. *RSH*, 17 June 1536; cf. AJ, 4–8 February 1536: while Ruffault and his allies were pressing for a *congie*, Hoogstraten secretly wrote Aert van der Goes that Nassau, IJsselstein, and other great lords who

understood Holland's needs had arrived in Brussels. *Ingelande* was the term for the major landowners of a district who were eligible for membership on local drainage boards. See also below, note 77.

45. N. Maddens, "De Opstandige Houding van Gent tijdens de Regering van Keizer Karel, 1515–1540," *Appeltjes uit het Meetjesland*, 28 (1977): 203–239.

46. J. J. Woltjer, "Het Conflikt tussen Willem Baerdes en Hendrik Dirkszoon," *BMGN* 86 (1971): 180. For the Hendrik-Dirkisten, see also Chapter 5.

47. *RSH*, 21 November 1540, 7, 22, 25 January, 22 February, 22 April, 3 September 1541; Meilink, "Rapporten en Betoogen," 93–95, 101; ASR, 1540, 45ᵛ; 1541, 50,

48. Tracy, "Habsburg Grain Policy and Amsterdam Politics," 299–303; *RSH*, 5 September, 2 November 1541; ASR, 1541, 55, 60–60ᵛ.

49. *RSH*, 31 October, 27–28 November 1545, 11 February, 27 November 1546, 1, 13 March, 15 July, 2 August, 22 October 1547, 21 January, 26 February, 1, 5, 18 March, 16 May, 30 June, 25 July, 13, 26 October, 14 November, 12 December 1548, 9 October 1551, 10 May 1552, 27 January 1553, 11 October 1554, 20–21 February, 4 May 1555.

50. Spading, *Holland und die Hanse im 15en Jahrhundert*, 1–7.

51. Ter Gouw, 3: 347–353; Häpke, *Die Regierung Karls V und der Europäische Norden*, 98–101; Jansma, "Hanze, Fugger, Amsterdam," 6; Svend Cedergreen Bech, *Reformation og Renaissance* [= *Danmarks Historie*, ed. John Danstrup, Hal Koch, vol. 6 (Copenhagen, 1963)], 173–182.

52. Bech, *Reformation og Renaissance*, 206–436. Denmark, Norway and Sweden were joined in the 1378 Union of Kalmar; when Sweden regained its independence under Gustavus Vasa (1523), the southern province of Skåne remained for some time a part of Denmark.

53. Häpke, 92–97; AJ, 30 March, 20 August, September 1523.

54. AJ, 13 February, 30 March 1523; Häpke, 98–101.

55. Häpke, 110–115; AJ, 13 February, 5 August 1523, 25–28 January, 15 February, 11 July 1524; *GVR*, 24 May, 4 November 1524.

56. IJssel de Schepper, 196–204; AJ, 26 November 1530, 15 September, 6 November 1531; *RSH*, 8 September, 5 November 1528, 15 September, 13 November 1531; *GVR*, 12 September 1531; Assendelft to Hoogstraten, 25 September, 28 September, and 21 October 1531 (Aud. 1525).

57. Waitz, *Lübeck unter Jürgen Wullenwever*, 1: 36–88, 127–136.

58. See the French-language report on Baltic affairs, titled "news from Amsterdam," (undated, but after 6 February 1532, Aud. 1530).

59. Assendelft to Hoogstraten, 10 November 1532, 13 March 1533 (Aud. 1525). Otto Nübel, *Pompeius Occo* (Tübingen, 1972): Occo was responsible for the delivery of Fugger copper from the Vistula to Antwerp, via the Øresund and the Holland *binnenlandvaart,* and he also had close ties with Christiern II: G. W. Kernkamp, ed., "Rekeningen van Pompeius Occo aan Koning Christiaan II van Denemerken, 1520–1523," *BMHGU* 36 (n.d.): 255–329.

60. Hoogstraten to the Council of Holland, 28 June 1533 (Aud. 1446:2b); Assendelft to Hoogstraten, 13 March, 27 March 1533, 8 November 1534 (Aud. 1525). Benninck was twice sent on embassies to the Baltic as part of a Netherlands delegation, and twice accompanied Melchior Rantzau on the Netherlands portion of journeys to the Habsburg court. Elias, *Vroedschap van Amsterdam,* 1: 43.

61. Ter Gouw, 4: 215–224; instructions for Meester Abel Coulster, member of the Council of Holland, 14 May 1532, and (a letter doubtless carried by Coulster on his mission to the court) Hoogstraten to Mary of Hungary, 15 May 1532 (Aud. 1525).

62. *GVR,* 17 May 1532; *RSH,* 7, 13 May 1532; AJ, 16 July 1532; Waitz, 1:152–157.

63. Ter Gouw, 4:219–221; Waitz, 1:157–164, 174–184.

64. Waitz, 1: 184–189; *HVH* has Lübeck asking for 300,000 gold *gulden* in indemnities (316^v), but *RSH,* 4 April 1533, correctly attributes this demand to Frederik I.

65. *RSH,* 3, 20, 24, 30 April, 5, 12, 16 May 1534. Cf. Ter Gouw, 4: 222–230: the States General, meeting at Mons in December 1532, acknowledged that the war against Lübeck pertained to the Emperor's lands as a whole, and not just Holland; owing to a recent flood; however, the other provinces were unwilling to make a contribution.

66. *RSH,* 29 May 1534; Assendelft to Hoogstraten, 19 May 1533, and 5 June 1533 (Aud. 1446:2b); Council of Holland to Hoogstraten, 30 May 1533 (Aud. 1446:2b).

67. Minute of a meeting of the Council of State, June 1533, and Hoogstraten to the Council of Holland, 28 June 1533 (Aud. 1446:2b).

68. Letter patent of Charles V, acknowledging Hoogstraten's *obligation* in the amount of 35,675 pounds, 2 July 1533 (Aud. 1662:3b).

69. *RSH,* 13, 27 July, 2, 3, 10, 20 August 1533; Assendelft to Hoogstraten, 12 September 1533; *HVH,* 320–322^v. The Council of State (minute cited above, note 67) rejected Bruges's plea for exemption from the ban on accepting goods from Lübeck.

70. Assendelft to Hoogstraten, 26 October, 30 October 1533 (Aud. 1446:2a), and 26 November, 27 November 1533, 8 December 1533 (Aud. 1446:2b); minute of report to Hoogstraten by two of Merke-

ren's commanders, Maurice of Oldenburg and Walram de Haplin-court, 9 November 1533 (Aud. 1446:2a); *HVH,* 316–318ᵛ, 320–322ᵛ; Ter Gouw, 4: 226–230.

71. Ter Gouw, 4:226–232.

72. The fullest account of the Counts' War is C. Paludan-Muller, *Grevens Feide,* 2 vols. (reprint of 1853–1854 edition, Copenhagen, 1971).

73. Waitz, 2: 130–139; Assendelft to Hoogstraten, 24 January 1535 (Aud. 1529), and 11 July 1535 (Aud. 1646:3).

74. Charles V to Mary of Hungary, 3 May 1532 (Aud. 52), and 13 August 1532 (Lanz, Letter 288, 2:3); Mary to Charles, 20 August 1534 (Aud. 52), and 27 May 1535 (Lanz, Letter 402, 2:180–181); Charles to the Archbishop of Lund, 11 March 1534 (Lanz, Letter 94, 2: 94–95); the Archbishop of Lund to Charles, 1 October 1534 (Lanz, Letter 382, 2:125–130).

75. Assendelft to Hoogstraten, 29 May 1535 (Aud. 1529), and 11 July 1535 (Aud. 1646:3; Assendelft recognizes the signature of Karel van Egmont). *RSH,* 28 February, 7 April 1536; Council of Holland's instructions for Secretary Vuytwyck, 25 May 1536 (Aud. 1530).

76. *RSH,* 21 April, 24 May 1536.

77. *RSH,* 28 April, 24 May, 16 June 1536; Council of Holland's instructions for Vuytwyck, cited above, note 75.

78. Assendelft to Hoogstraten, 4 July 1536 (Aud. 1530), 11 July, 31 July and 3 August 1536 (Aud. 1526), 22 August and 24 August 1536 (Aud. 1530), 9 September 1536 (Aud. 1526), 15 October 1536 (Aud. 1532), and 18 October 1536 (Aud. 1526); Council of Holland to Hoogstraten, 11 July 1536 and 25 August 1536 (Aud. 1526); report by Secretary Vuytwyck, 4 August 1536 (Aud. 1530); Adolph of Bur-gundy to Mary of Hungary, 1 July and 27 July 1536 (Aud. 1530).

79. Extracts from Hoogstraten's instructions to La Tiloye for a mission to Charles V, dated by Lanz between 15 September and 12 November 1536. See Lanz, Letter 656, 2: 667.

5: HOLLAND FINANCES UNDER THE CONTROL OF THE
STATES

1. Aud. 868:3–18, 873:143–70, and 650:141–148, 398–400 for military budget summaries. For the wider context, see Geoffrey Par-ker, *The Military Revolution;* M. J. Rodriguez-Salgado, *The Changing Face of Empire: Charles V, Philip II and Habsburg Authority, 1551–1559* (Cambridge, 1988), 232–242; Martin Wolfe, *The Fiscal System of Renais-sance France* (New Haven, 1972), 109–118.

2. Based *AFR*, and Tracy, "The Taxation System of the County of Holland."

3. Wolfe, 76–85.

4. Assendelft to Hoogstraten, 11 July 1536, 5 January 1537 (Aud. 1530): postponing the semi-annual interest payments due at the St. John's term would be unwise because it would lead to arrests on Holland goods by *renten*-holders in Brabant and Flanders. The States sometimes instructed the Receiver for the Common Land to pay "foreigners" first (e.g., Flemings, Brabanders), to avoid seizure of goods for non-payment: *RSH*, 30 July 1544, 1 March 1547.

5. AJ, 29 December 1523: the deputies say they dare not take the (new) *staetgen* that has been shown them home to their principals; cf. Chapter 3, note 75.

6. *RSH*, 29 March 1531, Sandelijn, 6–8 March 1549. The *accord* agreed to by the States became known as the *acceptatie* when signed by the Regent; it was then copied in at the head of the account for the *bede* in question. Cf. *RSH*, 10 December 1545, a complaint by the States that the Emperor's *acceptatie* of a *bede* is not in conformity with the *accord* signed by the States.

7. The *accord* always contained a clause linking the *bede* to local defense.

8. Assendelft to Hoogstraten, 21 October 1531 (Aud. 1525).

9. Receiver General's accounts, Lille B, 2416, 2430, income items for "From the Emperor's coffers," 107,392 in 1539, 90,000 in 1540; Mary of Hungary to Charles V, 28 November 1542 (Aud. 53); see Chapter 3, note 8.

10. Tracy, "The Taxation System of the County of Holland," 76–81.

11. In the inventory for *GRK*, Goudt is listed as "Receiver General" for the *beden* in Holland bettween 1510 and 1543.

12. Tracy, "The Financial System of the County of Holland," 110, Table II, item v; *RSH*, 7, 13, 14 May, 6 August 1532; AJ, 7 May, 16, 18 July, 6 August 1532.

13. *RSH*, 16 August 1532. 18–19 June 1535; Council of Holland to Hoogstraten, 27 June 1536, and Assendelft to Hoogstraten, 4 July 1536 (Aud. 1530).

14. Assendelft to Hoogstraten, 20 November 1531 (Aud. 1525), 28 January 1537, and 28 January 1539 (Aud. 1532); Mary of Hungary to Assendelft, 27 November 1542 (Aud. 1646:3).

15. The best discussion is J. J. Poelhekke, "Het Naamloze Vaderland van Erasmus," *BMGN* 86 (1971): 90–123.

16. *RSH*, 3–5 July, 2 September, 12–13 October 1537.

17. Mary of Hungary to Guileyn Zeghers, 15 April 1543 (Aud.

1646:1); on Zeghers as a confidant of the government, see Tracy, "Heresy Law and Centralization under Mary of Hungary," 302, 305–306. I have not been able to trace a loan "for Maastricht" secured by the Holland *beden*, but in March 1543 Goudt obtained 35,000 pounds in Antwerp, which he brought to Reynier van Nassau in 's Hertogenbosch for the payment of troops: *GRK*, 3441, "Reisen en Vacatien," trips by Goudt on 12 March (to Antwerp) and 18 March (to 's Hertogenbosch), and Reynier van Nassau to Mary of Hungary, 19 March 1543 (Aud. 1660:1c).

18. Mary of Hungary to the Council of Holland, 12 May 1543 (Aud. 1646:1).

19. *AFR*, 40–43.

20. *GRK*, 3440, "Payments to Officers" (the rubric under which *décharges* are listed); Aud. 650: 293–294.

21. Mary of Hungary to [the Council of Holland], 6 January 1537, and Assendelft to Hoogstraten, 13 January 1537 (Aud. 1530); *AFR*, 43, note 51.

22. *SH*, 1602, Barthout van Assendelft's account, as Receiver of the Common Land, for *renten* sold during the Utrecht War; Geitz, "De Staten van Holland en hun Personeel, 1540–1555," 33–38. For the development of this office after 1555, see the forthcoming dissertation of J. W. Koopmans (University of Groningen).

23. *SH*, 2275, Van der Ketel's account for the *renten* sale of 60,000 pounds. For the 31,000-pound *obligatie*, see the letter of Mary of Hungary to Assendelft, 27 November 1542 (Aud. 1646:3).

24. On Van der Hove, see Geitz, "De Staten van Holland en hun Personeel, 1540–1555," 39–40. *GRK*, 3445 indicates that Van der Hove conveyed 13,118 to the Receiver for the *beden* to cover a shortage in a *morgental* to which the States had consented; cf. *RSH*, 19 September 1545. For the States' insistence that deputies be present when tenth penny accounts were examined by government auditors, see *RSH*, 5, 26 March, 9 April 1544, 21 May, 9 July, 5, 21 August 1545.

25. E.g., *GRK*, 3454: gross receipts were 105,598; disposable income (after subtraction for *gratie* and *renten* interest) was 48,581.

26. *SH*, 2277–2282. Cf. Tracy, "The Taxation System of the County of Holland," 112, Table III, items hh–ll.

27. Figures from *SH*, 2279–2282.

28. *GRK*, 3454: 94–96^v, "Décharges non couchées," twenty-one items, dated from 27 July 1552 to 18 March 1555, totalling 530,640 pounds, plus another 65,764 in outstanding *obligatiën*.

29. *AFR*, 131–138; Tracy, "The Taxation System of the County of Holland," 117. Members of the audit committee, listed at the end of

each account, include deputies from the States for sums collected by the Receiver for the Common Land (*SH*), but not for sums collected by the Receiver for the *beden.*

30. *RSH* is used here, as the most consistent and reliable source for meetings of the States. But in a comparison with AJ and the Leiden "Register van de Dagvaarten," three students in my seminar at Leiden (spring 1987) noted several *dagvaarten* that are not mentioned by Aert van der Goes because he was absent on other business: Raymond Fagel, Fiekke Krikhaar, and Sandra Slaghekke, "De Hollandse Dagvaarten, 1530–1535: Drie Bronnen Vergeleken." H. De Ridder-Symoens, "De Universitaire Vorming van de Brabantse Stadsmagistraten en Funktion-arissen: Leuven en Antwerpen, 1430–1580," *Verslagboek van de Vijfde Colloquium, "De Brabantse Stad."* ('s Hertogenbosch, 1978), 21–125).

31. Ter Gouw, 8: 345; Elias, *Vroedschap van Amsterdam,* 1: 304.

32. Ter Gouw, 3: 366–369.

33. Based on *RSH,* kept by the Advocate, who sometimes has one town or another represented by "someone I don't know," or "een quidam."

34. A list of Gouda's brewers and the number of "brews" they produced during the last year is included with a petition from Gouda which has a marginal note dated 9 August 1546 (Aud. 1656:1). Lists of officeholders are given in Ignatius Walvis, *Beschryving der Stad Gouda* (Gouda, 1713), and C. J. De Lange van Wijngaerden, *Geschie- denis en Beschrijving der Stad van der Goude,* 2 vols., (Amsterdam, 1817).

35. *GVR,* 3 October 1512, the *vroedschap* decrees that members who are deputed to represent the city at a *dagvaart* may not refuse.

36. C. C. Hibben, *Gouda in Revolt* (Utrecht, 1983).

37. Genealogies of these families are given in Matthys Balen, *Beschryving der Stad Dordrecht* (Dordrecht, 1677).

38. See Chapter 3, note 63.

39. Van Nierop, *Van Ridders tot Regenten,* 171.

40. *AFR,* 177–178; Reiner Boitet, *Beschryving der Stad Delft* (Delft, 1729), for the Sasbout family; for lists of potential officeholders in Delft, Aud. 1441:4 no. 2, discussed by J. J. Woltjer, see "Een Hollands Stadsbestuur," *De Nederlanden in de Late Middeleeuwen,* 261–279.

41. Boitet, *Beschryving der Stad Delft;* Aud. 1441:4 no. 2; D. Hoek, "Het Geslacht Duyst van Voorhout in de 16e Eeuw," *Jaarboek voor het Centraal Bureau van Genealogie* 12 (1958): 185–220.

42. A. E. D'Ailly, *Zeven Eeuwen Amsterdam,* 6 vols., (Amsterdam, 1943–1950), 1: 40–49; Ter Gouw, 3: 366–369; Blok, *Geschiedenis eener Hollandsche Stad,* 2: 93–107;

43. *HVR* has approximately 1500 pages for the years 1518–1566,

whereas P. D. J. van Iterson, P. H. J. van der Laan, *Resoluties van de Vroedschap van Amsterdam, 1490–1550* (Amsterdam, 1986) has 96 pages of text; on selling "apart," 59–62.

44. S. A. C. Dudok van Heel, "Oligarchiën in Amsterdam voor de Alteratie van 1578," in Michiel Jonker, et al., eds., *Van Stadskern tot Stadsgewest* (Amsterdam, 1984), 35–61.

45. Lists of burgomasters and other officials are printed at the end of each volume in Ter Gouw. See also A. J. M. Brouwer Ancher and J. C. Breen, "De Doleantie van een Deel ber Burgerij van Amsterdam tegen den Magistraat dier Stad van 1564 en 1565," *BMHGU* 24 (1903): 85.

46. *AFR*, Chapter 5.

47. Sources for these two tables are the same as for Table 15b in Tracy, *AFR*, 145.

48. Tracy, *AFR*, 128–129, 157–158.

49. *AFR*, 175–176, 182–183 (large purchases of *renten* by brewers in Delft, but not by investors in land).

50. For the popularity of urban *lijfrenten*, see the income entries in ASR under sales of *renten:* 1550, there is a limit of three pounds interest per *rentebrief;* 1552, the limit is set at six pounds, "so that everyone might be satisfied." Gene Brucker, *The Civic World of Early Renaissance Florence* (Princeton, 1977), 144, 270.

51. Tracy, *AFR*, 125, 134, and Appendix IIb, nos. 37, 62.

52. Van Nierop, *Van Ridders tot Regenten*, 155–185; see below, note 89.

53. See the two sources on Delft cited above, note 40.

54. Balen, *Beschryving der Stad Dordrecht, sub nomine.*

55. Van Nierop, *Van Ridders tot Regenten*, 81–105; Letter from J. J. Temminck, Archivaris, Gemeentearchief Haarlem, 16 January 1984.

56. Balen, *Beschryving der Stad Dordrecht, sub nomine.*

57. *Renten* purchases listed in *SH*, 2279 and 2280 indicate that Sybrant Meester Hendrik Dirkszoon was married to Lijsbeth Reyniersdochter Brunt, and that Dirk Hendrikszoon Opmeer was married to Neel Reyniersdochter Brunt: cf. Elias, *De Vroedschap van Amsterdam*, 1, xxxiv, xxxvi, xlii, 29, 108; Ter Gouw, 8: 337, Kam, *Waar Was dat Huis op de Warmoes Straat*, 170; Brouwer Ancher, "De Doleantie van een Deel van de Amsterdamse Burgerij," 82. The father of these women was very likely Meester Reynier Brunt, Procurator General of Holland from 1523 to 1536 (de Blécourt and Meijers, *Memorialen van het Hof van Holland*).

58. Cf. the Council of Holland's refusal to publish grain export bans without consulting the States: Chapter 4, notes 26, 41.

59. Enforcement of taxes decreed by the States is discussed in Chapter 7.

60. De Vries, *The Dutch Rural Economy*, 41–43; For sums paid by the clergy, see AJ, 21 November 1523, 19 June 1525; *RSH*, 9–10 February, 19 June 1525, 18 October, 14 November 1533, 1 January 1534 (Aud. 1446:2b), 31 August 1537 (Aud. 1532); Assendelft to Mary of Hungary, 23 October 1546, 20 May, 2 June 1551 (Aud. 1646:3). Cf. *RSH*, 19 August 1543, deputies "curse" the clergy and the nobles and the great lords for not bearing the cost of war.

- 61. J. C. Naber, *Een Terugblik*, 34, finds a total of 239,297 *morgen* counted in the 1515 *schiltal*. Taking in each case the average of two accounts from the 1540s and 1550s, one may estimate 268,926 *morgen* under the *schiltal* (*SH*, 1792, 2210), and 36,680 *morgen* outside it (*SH*, 2281, 2283), or twelve percent of the total.

62. *GRK*, 3422, folio 19.

63. Asperen, Heukelom, IJsselstein, Leerdam, Vianen, Woudrichem, and Zevenbergen.

64. *RSH*, 7 March 1543, imposition of the hundredth penny.

65. *Nieuw Nederlandsch Biographisch Woordenboek*, 1: 136 (Hendrik van Nassau); 3: 324–339 (the Egmonts); 9: 416 (Montmorency); 10: 121, 128–32 (the Brederodes).

66. Charles V to Reynier van Nassau, 10 May 1542 (said to be in the Emperor's own hand), 10 June 1542, 19 August 1543, 23 September 1543, 1 November 1543, 9 November 1543 (Aud. 1660:1c); Rosenfeld, "The Provincial Governors," 5–6.

67. On Maximiliaan van Egmont, see *Biographie Nationale de Belgique* 6: 488–490.

68. The exempt areas were supposed to contribute in certain *extraordinaris beden* of 1523 and 1524, but apparently did not; cf. Aud. 873:120, sums not paid by Egmont's villages, 1520–1530.

69. E.g. *RSH*, 14–16 March, 9–17 April 1553; the account for this *bede* is *SH*, 2278, but for the *acceptatie* see *GRK*, 3453.

70. *RSH*, 9 August 1555, 26 August 1556.

71. Council of Holland to Mary of Hungary, 3 February 1544, and Mary of Hungary to the Council of Holland, 12 March 1545 (Aud. 1646:1); statement by Witte Aertszoon van der Hoeve as collector for Leerdam, 9 September 1545 (Aud. 1656:1). *RSH*, 6 August, 19 September, 6 December 1545, 6 November 1546, 14 March 1547, 21 January 1548.

72. *RSH*, 27 January, 15 February 1553, 4 May 1555; the Emperor's Procurator-General in Holland at this time was Christiaan de Wairt (1549–1558; de Blécourt and Meijers). Cf. *RSH*, 30 October

1553, and Geitz, "De Staten van Holland en hun Personeel," 46–49, the States dismissed their own Procurator before the Court of Holland, Joost Jacobszoon de Bye, because he too refused to take action in this case.

73. *RSH*, 2 November 1553, 1 October 1554; Assendelft to Mary of Hungary, 26 October 1555 (Aud. 1646:3).

74. *RSH*, 22 August, 7 September, 17 October 1556.

75. Mary of Hungary to the Council of Holland, 12 December 1542, and to Amsterdam, 14 March 1543 (Aud. 1646:1); *RSH*, 7 March 1543; Ter Gouw, 4: 115–117; Mary of Hungary to Amsterdam, 24 April 1543 (Aud. 1656:1), 8 February, 13 July 1544 (Aud. 1652:5a).

76. Mary of Hungary to Assendelft, 11, 12 January 1543 (a draft and a corrected draft of the same letter), 30 November 1543 (Aud. 1646:3), *RSH*, 7 March 1543, 5 August 1545 (1,200 pounds collected). For Delft, Amsterdam, and Leiden, included in Meilink, "Gegevens aangaande Bedrijfscapitalen," the total was 1,111. Aud. 650: 355, 357, 382.

77. For discussion of the wine tax proposal in the States of Holland, see Sandelijn, 14 November, 4 December 1548, 14, 22–23 November, 8, 15 December 1549; *RSH*, 22–23, 29 October, 1, 24 December 1549, 19 March 1550.

78. *RSH*, 20 July 1550; cf. CC 23336, Maximilien Dublioul's account for the first two years of the wine tax. See Chapter 2, note 104.

79. *RSH* and Sandelijn, entries for 2 August 1552, 28 May 1554; Aud. 650: 316–317, summary of receipts for the first four years.

80. That is, the *congie,* the hundredth penny on exports (1543–1545, the tenth penny on mercantile inventories (1543–1545), the wine tax, a 200th penny on all goods imported into the Netherlands (1552), and a 50th penny on all goods exported "westward" (1552–1554). For accounts of the latter two levies, see CC 23456, 23474–23477. For a summary of *bede,* income from Holland during these years, see Tracy, "The Taxation System of the County of Holland," 108–109.

81. On the political influence of the twelve abbots who made up Brabant's first estate, see P. J. Gorissen, "De Prelaten van Brabant . . . en Hun Confederatie."

82. See Chapter 2, note 9.

83. For the argument that cities prosper by allowing free trade, see AJ, 5 January 1536, 11 April 1537; Meilink, "Rapporten en Betoogen nopens het Congiegeld," 90, 108. There was a legal tradition that viewed certain restrictions on commercial activity, like the Dordrecht

staple, as contrary to natural law (AJ, 11, 15, 17 October 1527; Niklaas Everaerts, *Consiliorum Opus*, 8–10). Typical of such arguments was Amsterdam's contention that the hundredth penny on exports was "outside all natural laws and reason, and contrary to various privileges of the city and province" which the ruler had sworn to uphold at his accession: to the Council of Holland, 2 March 1544 (Aud. 1656:4a).

84. See accounts for *beden* of 100,000 e.g., GRK, 3441. AJ, 25 June 1536; cf. Mary of Hungary to the Council of Holland, 3 June 1544 (Aud. 1646:1), the countryside in Holland is not taxed as heavily as in Brabant and Flanders.

85. *AFR*, 85, and Tracy, "The Taxation System in the County of Holland," 89. For the account of this *bede*, see *SH*, 2208, *GRK*, 3445. *RSH*, 2 March 1543, says the nobles gave their consent, but cf. Council of Holland to Mary of Hungary, 26 May 1544 (Aud. 1646:1). Mary of Hungary to Pieter Moens Willemszoon (Goudt's successor as Receiver for the beden), [?] April 1543 (Aud. 1656:1), and Council of Holland to Mary of Hungary, 20 June 1544 (Aud. 1646:1). For another *bede* in which the countryside made up for urban rebates, see Sandelijn, 29–30 January 1552; *RSH*, 22, 29–30 January, 6, 12, 26 February 1552; Assendelft to Mary of Hungary, 23 January 1552, and Assendelft and Cornelis Suys to Mary of Hungary, 31 January 1552 (Aud. 1646:2); *GRK*, 3451.

86. The assumptions are: 1) that rural tenth penny income was 70.77 percent of the total, as in 1557; 2) that the rural portion of a *schiltal* assessment was 42.25 percent of the total; and 3) that the rural share of *gratiën* was 20 percent for *ordinaris beden*, and 10 percent for *extraordinaris beden*. Calculation is based on Tables 1–3 of Tracy, "The Taxation System of the County of Holland," using net income figures for *beden* levied according to *schiltal*. Not counted are 39,240 pounds from a hearth tax in which there is no way of gauging actual contributions from town and country, and two small levies on property outside the *schiltal* (*SH*, 2283, 2284), whose collection must be regarded as uncertain.

87. Council of Holland to Mary of Hungary, 17 August 1549 (1646:2). Cf. *SH*, 1792, the account which includes the *morgental* referred to in this letter.

88. Henk Schorl, *'T Oge: Het Waddeneiland Callensoog onder het Bewind van de Heren van Brederode en hun Erfgenamen* ([Haarlem], 1979), 67–72; Archief van Het Hoogheemraadschap van Rijnland, Leiden, 7192, "Receuil van Stukken betreffende de Grote Sluis te Sparendam," nos. 13/2 and 14 (for a comparable description of the wooden sluice as rebuilt in 1518, see Stadsarchief Leiden, Oude Se-

cretarie, 1263:206); on draining by windmill-pumps, see below, note 89. On reclamation projects in the years before the Revolt, see De Vries, *The Dutch Rural Economy*, 192–196, and Van Nierop, *Van Ridders tot Regenten*, 128–130.

89. For the drainage of a small lake near Alkmaar, undertaken by Lamoraal van Egmont and Hendrik van Brederode, see Council of Holland to the Secret Council, 12 May, 10 June 1564, 18 September 1565 (*HH*, 381).

90. *RSH*, 14 November 1548, 12 October, [?] November 1549, 9 October 1551, investments by Baudoin de Lannoy and Maximilian of Burgundy; for investments by the Antwerp merchant Arnoldus Rosenberger, see the testimony collected in Alkmaar (May 1568) under orders from Alba's Council of Troubles (Algemeen Rijksarchief, Brussels, "Raad van Beroerten," item no. 109 [sec. 110]).

91. J. P. A. Louman, " 'Roerende dat Heycoopwater en Amstellant': Een Hollands-Utrechts Waterstaatsgeschil en de Instelling van het Hoogheemraadschaap van Amstellant, 1520–1527," *Hollandse Studiën* 12 (1982): 121. Heyman Jacobszoon became *ambachtsheer* of Ouder Amstel in 1531: Elias, *De Vroedschap van Amsterdam*, 1: 67.

92. J. J. Schilstra, *Wie Water Deert: Het Hoogheemraadschap van de Uitwaterende Sluizen, 1544–1969* (Wormerveer, n.d.), 21; report from Egmond Binnen, "Raad van Beroerten," 109 (110). For the landed interests of Amsterdam's leading magistrates, including Buyck and Mattheuszoon, see *AFR*, 181–184.

93. Wealth inventories in the archives of Amsterdam's orphan bureau (*weeskamer*) often include private *renten* secured on houses in the city and on land in the countryside.

94. See the instructions entered at the head of accounts for the *morgental* in the 1550s, *SH*, 2293–2295. *GRK*, 3453, *accord* and *acceptatie* for a tenth penny, as part of a 300,000 pound *bede* in 1553 (cf. *SH*, 2278). According to J. Kuys and J. T. Schoenmaker, *Landpachten in Holland, 1500–1650* (Amsterdam, 1981), 27–29, sixteenth-century lease contracts required the *pachter* or lessee to assume the burden for the *bede* payments by the *schiltal*, tenth penny taxes, and dike maintainence taxes. The only exceptions the authors find are in West Friesland and in the *vroonlanden* which were part of the prince's domain. Cf. Council of Holland to Mary of Hungary, 19 August 1549 (Aud. 1646:2), *pachters* of domain land will not pay the current levy of two stuivers per *morgen* unless the Chamber of Accounts promises them it will be deducted from their lease obligation, as in previous *beden*.

95. A hearth tax was tried in 1552, but yielded only about forty

percent of what was expected: *SH,* 2277; *RSH,* 4–5 April, 2 August 1552; Sandelijn, 5 July 1552.

96. Assendelft to Mary of Hungary, 28 December 1543 (Aud. 1646:3). For riots over *accijnsen,* AJ, 1:160, reporting a July 1524 "upstal" in The Hague, in which "de gemeene buerluyden" accused the magistrates of bad governance and demanded lower excise taxes. AJ, 15–20 June 1525, the States refuse a *bede* request on the grounds that "if one further troubles the commons or imposes exactions on them, it is to be feared there will be riots, such as occurred at Utrecht, Antwerp, and 's Hertogenbosch." The social inequity of *accijnsen* was a commonplace: *Institutio Principis Christiani,* ed. Otto Herding, in *Des. Erasmi Opera Omnia,* 4:1 (Amsterdam, 1974), 190–191.

97. *RSH,* 5, 22 February, 5, 18, 19, 27 March, 7 April 1544; Council of Holland to Mary of Hungary, 26 May 1544 (Aud. 1646:1). Cf. LTR, HTR for 1520.

98. Cf. *SH,* 2295 with LTR and ASR for 1556.

99. Mary of Hungary to Leiden, 5 December 1547 (Aud. 1656:1) ordering the city to honor the exemption from excises and tolls enjoyed by Antoine Carlier as a Councillor of Holland. Carlier was not a "Councillor Ordinary" (he does not appear on de Blécourt and Meijer's list), but he is named as "General of the Mint" (in Leiden) in some accounts for the purchase of Holland *renten* (e.g., *SH,* 2282), and was presumably a "Councillor Extraordinary," without salary.

100. AJ, 10 September 1523, 18, 25 January, 30 April 1524, 14 May 1526.

101. In a *bede* of 100,000 pounds (e.g. *GRK,* 3441), Delft's quota was 8,517; the next highest were Leiden (8,067) and Amsterdam (8,017). For an example of Delft's demands for equality in taxation, see AJ, 10 September 1523.

102. Assendelft, Vincent Corneliszoon, and Joost Sasbout to Hoogstraten, 14 October 1538 (Aud. 1527); Assendelft to Mary of Hungary, 23 February (Aud. 1646:3), and 26 May 1544 (Aud. 1646:1).

103. AJ, 15–21 September 1538, Haarlem and Leiden reject a *bede* proposal because both had to levy a *capitale impositie* on their burghers for the last *bede;* proposals by Delft, *GVR,* 12 October 1523, AJ, 21 October 1528.

104. AJ, 9 July 1523; *RSH,* 2 August 1543; Aud. 650:488ᵛ, from a memorandum of [1542] on new ways to raise revenue: "Par assiette capitale selon la valeur et puissance des biens des subgectz. Lon entend quil seroit fort difficile a conduire."

105. De Vries, *The Dutch Rural Economy,* 50–55. Assendelft's fear of rebellion in northern Holland was acute during the Anabaptist move-

ment of the 1530s (see chap. 6). Assendelft to Mary of Hungary, 5 August 1547, 10 August 1552 (Aud. 1646:3). See Chapter 1, note 12.
106. Council of Holland to Hoogstraten, 10 March 1535 (Aud. 1646:1), and Assendelft to Hoogstraten, 24 August 1536 (Aud. 1530); Schorl, *Het Waddeneiland Callensoog*, 46–48.
107. Assendelft to Hoogstraten, 5 January 1537 (Aud. 1530); Council of Holland to Mary of Hungary, 26 May, 20 June 1544 (Aud. 1646:1).

6: "NO MORE FOR THE BUTCHER'S BLOCK": HABSBURG
HERESY LAWS AND HOLLAND'S TOWNS

1. Recall the riot against collection of the grain tax in Amsterdam in 1541 (chap. 4), and the armed demonstrations by towns whose participation in the privileged *binnenlandvaart* was threatened by the opening of new channels (chap. 2).
2. For the importance of the distinction between burghers and mere residents, see notes 74 and 75 below.
3. The old view that the northern Netherlands spawned an autonomous "sacramentarian" movement in the 1520s is questioned by J. J. Woltjer, *Friesland in Hervormingstijd* (Leiden, 1962), 102.
4. Ernest McDonnell, *The Beguines and Beghards in Medieval Culture* (New Brunswick, 1954); L. Philippen, *De Begijnhoeven. Oorsprong, Inrigtingen, Geschiedenis* (Antwerp, 1918).
5. R. R. Post, *The Modern Devotion* (Leiden, 1968) supersedes Albert Hyma, *The Devotio Moderna* (Grand Rapids, 1924).
6. The town of Amersfoort (Utrecht province) has a well-preserved *hofje* dating from the fifteenth century which is still in use.
7. C. Ligtenberg, *Armenzorg in Leiden tot het Einde van de XVIᵉ Eeuw* (The Hague, 1908); C. A. van Manen, *Armenpflege in Amsterdam in ihrer Historischer Entwicklung* (Leiden, 1913).
8. For a splendid parish history, D. P. Oosterbaan, *De Oude Kerk van Delft gedurende de Middeleeuwen* (The Hague, 1973).
9. Laurentius Knappert, *De Opkomst van het Protestantisme*, 46–56; H. van Druten, *Geschiedenis van de Nederlandsche Bijbelvertaling*, 2 vols. (The Hague and Rotterdam, 1895–1897), vol. 1; F. J. Dubiez, *Op de Grens tussen Humanisme en Hervorming* (Nieuwkoop, 1962).
10. *De Imitatione Christi*, ed. Paul Hagen (The Hague: Nijhoff, 1935); three of the mystical treatises of the Hollander Hendrik van Mande are printed as appendices in Willem Moll, *Johannes Brugman en het Godsdienstig Leven onzer Vaderen in de 15ᵉ Eeuw*, 2 vols. (Amsterdam, 1854), 1: 259–313.

11. Alfons Auer, *Die vollkommene Frömmigkeit eines Christen* (Düsseldorf, 1954) remains the best study of Erasmus's *Enchiridion*.

12. See Chapter 5, note 60.

13. Overvoorde and Oerburgt, *Archief van de Secretarie van de Stad Leiden,* "Regesten," 7 January 1519, 24 October 1520; Enschede, *Inventaris van het Oud-Archief van de Stad Haarlem,* "Contracten," 16 May 1516. Cf. Margaret of Austria's instruction for an embasssy to Charles V in Spain, 9 July 1525: Lutheranism sprouts from "contempt for the extortions which men of the Church practice in the laity in many places"; in Paul Fredericq, *Corpus Documentorum Inquisitionis Haereticae Pravitatis Neerlandicae,* 5 vols. (Ghent, 1889–1902), 5: 34–35.

14. For the 1525 riot in 's Hertogenbosch, see Aelbertus Cuperinus *Chronike,* in C. R. Hermans, *Verzameling van Kronyken,* 1: 90–91; cf. AJ, 1:160, and 15–20 June 1525.

15. Ter Gouw, 5: 174–195; P. Scheltema, *Inventaris van het Amsterdamsche Archief,* 3 vols. (Amsterdam, 1866–1874), 1:45–46, 87; R. R. Post, *Kerkgeschiedenis van Nederland in de Middeleeuwen,* 2 vols. (Utrecht, 1957), 2: 79–85.

16. R. R. Post, *Kerkelijke Verhoudingen in Nederland voor de Reformatie* (Utrecht, 1954), 205–206; Ter Gouw, 5: 177–181.

17. Post, *Kerkelijke Verhoudingen,* 37–55: in 1500, the diocese of Utrecht had about 600,000 faithful, with 1,500 secular priests with cure of souls, and another 3,500 without cure of souls; in 1950 the same diocese had about 600,000 faithful and 800 parish priests.

18. Erasmus to Willibald Pirckheimer, 28 August 1525, in Allen, *Opus Epistolarum,* 6:155, Letter 1603, 1: 27–29: "Maxima populi pars apud Hollandos, Zeelandos, Flandros scit doctrinam Lutheri, et odio plusquam capitali fertur in monachos."

19. For the one exception, see J. Hof, *De Abdij van Egmond van de Aanvang tot 1573* (The Hague, 1973).

20. Rogier, *Geschiedenis van het Katholicisme in Noordelijke Nederland,* 69–76; Post, *Kerkelijke Verhoudingen,* 327–341. On Franciscan preachers, see Moll, *Johannes Brugman;* Johannes Hopfer, *Johannes Kapistran,* 2 vols. (Heidelberg, 1964–1965); Iris Origo, *The World of San Bernardino* (New York, 1962); André Godin, *Le Homiliaire de Jean Vorier* (Geneva, 1971).

21. John Harthan, *The Book of Hours, with a Historical Survey and Commentary* (New York, 1977); Oosterbaan, *De Oude Kerk van Delft,* 225.

22. Frederik Pijper, *Het Middeleeuwsch Christendom. De Vereering der Heilige Hostie* (The Hague, 1907); Post, *Kerkgeschiedenis van Nederland,* 294.

23. R. R. Post, "Het Sacrament van Mirakel te Amsterdam," *Studia Catholica* 30 (1955): 241–261; Ter Gouw, 5:166–174; A. J. Kölker, *Alardus Amstelredamus en Cornelius Crocus, Twee Amsterdamse Priester-Humanisten* (Nijegen, 1963), 60–66, 95–107, 158.

24. Kölker, *Alardus Amstelredamus en Cornelius Crocus.*

25. Moll, *Johannes Brugman,* 1: 129–146, citing the seventeenth-century historian Geraert Brandt.

26. Ter Gouw, 4: 201–206, 353–356, 360–362; on Jan Bennink and Imme van Diemen, see Elias, *De Vroedschap van Amsterdam, sub nomine;* de Blécourt and Meijer (Bennink was Councillor Extraordinary, 1513–1518 and Councillor Ordinary, 1518–1534); and Louman, "'Roerende dat Heycoopwater en Amstellant.'" See also below, note 75.

27. *HVH* 295ᵛ–298.

28. Ter Gouw, 4: 197–203; the text of the sentence by the city court is given in J. G. van Dillen, *Bronnen tot de Geschiedenis van het Bedrijfsleven en het Gildewezen van Amsterdam* (3 vols., The Hague, 1929–1974), 1: 95–96, and confirms the account in *HVH.*

29. A. F. Mellink, *Documenta Anabaptistica Neerlandica,* vol. 5, *Amsterdam 1531–1536* (Leiden, 1985), no. 302.

30. On Netherlands Protestant humanists, see Johannes Lindeboom, *Het Bijbelsch Humanisme in Nederland* (Leiden, 1913), 152–157 (Willem de Voldersgracht, or Gnaphaeus); J. Prinsen, *Geraard Geldenhouwer Noviomagus* (The Hague, 1908); D. Frielinghaus, *Ecclesia et Vita. Eine Untersuchung zur Ekklesiologie des Andreas Hyperius* (Göttingen, 1956); H. F. Wijnman, "Wouter Deelen, de Eerste Professeur in het Hebreeuwsch te Amsterdam," *Jaarboek Amstelodamum* 27 (1930): 43–65; and below, notes 34, 53.

31. Trijn Hillebrandsdochter was the sister of Dirk Hillebrantszoon Otter, the future Dirkist burgomaster, and both the husband of Geert Garbrandsdochter (Willem Klasszoon Koeck) and her brother (Egge Garbrandszoon Paf) were among the seven "sincere" *schepenen* elected for 1536, in the wake of the Anabaptist uprising of 1535 (see below, n. 90). Engel Corsdochter was married to Heyman Jacobszoon van Ouder Amstel, a leading figure in the more tolerant ruling faction which preceded the Dirkisten. On all these individuals, see Elias, *De Vroedschap van Amsterdam, sub nomine.*

32. *Dictionnaire de Théologie Catholique,* 7:2, 2049; G. Grosheide, *Bijdragen tot de Geschiedenis der Anabaptisten in Amsterdam* (Hilversum, 1938), 272–277.

33. Fredericq, *Corpus Documentorum,* nos. 72 and 73, 4: 101–105, commissions for Hulst and Lauwerijns, 23 April 1522, and no. 154, 4:

219–220, exerpt from AJ for 23 August 1523, Wijngaerden's interview with Charles V; De Hoop Scheffer, *Geschiedenis der Kerkehervorming*, 144; Erasmus to Lauwerijns, Allen, *Opus Epistolarum*, Letter 1299, 14 July 1522, 5: 84–87, with a warning about Niklaas Baechem, on whom see also Letter 1153, 1, 15–18, 4: 362.

34. A. Eckhof, *De Avondmaalsbrief van Cornelis Hoen* (The Hague, 1917). Bart Jan Spruyt (Universities of Utrecht and Leiden) is preparing a dissertation on Hoen.

35. AJ, 31 December 1521; Erasmus to Peter Barbirius, 17 April 1523, Letter 1358: 26–28, 5:276.

36. Fredericq, *Corpus Documentorum*, 4: nos. 125–127; Scheltema, *Inventaris van het Amsterdamsche Archief*, 1: 34, 69; Grosheide, *Geschiedenis der Anabaptisten in Amsterdam*, 272–277.

37. Fredericq, *Corpus Documentorum*, 4: nos. 120, 123, 136, 149; De Hoop Scheffer, 174–194.

38. Fredericq, *Corpus Documentorum*, 4: nos. 151–153, 156, 157, 161–164, 167, 169–172, 188, 197. Note that while this controversy continued, with Hulst in Gorinchem, Hoogstraten was also there, arousing the suspicion of the States by raising an army which then failed to invade Guelders (chap. 3).

39. De Hoop Scheffer, 334–337; Fredericq, *Corpus Documentorum*, 4: no. 164; 5: no. 520; *RSH*, 2 October 1527, 17–18 November 1528; Post, *Kerkgeschiedenis van Nederland*, 94–95, a 1434 concordat between Duke Philip the Good and the Bishop of Utrecht included the privilege *de non evocando* for the Duke's subjects.

40. A. C. Duke, "The Face of Popular Religious Dissent in the Low Countries," *Journal of Ecclesiastical History*, 26 (1975):41–67; De Hoop Scheffer, 256–278.

41. Fredericq, *Corpus Documentorum*, 4: nos. 175, 214, 215, 226, 244, 248, 353. For examples of similar punishments for cursing and blaspheming, see "Justitieboek," Rechterlijk Archief, Gemeeente Archief Amsterdam, entries for 21 September 1537 and 7 July 1539.

42. F. van der Haeghen, et al., *Bibliographie des Martyrologes Protestants Neerlandais*, 2 vols. (The Hague, 1890), 2: 81–91, 271–304; J. W. Gunst, *Johannes Pistorius Woerdensis* (Hilversum, 1925); J. C. van Slee, *Wendelmoet Claesdochter van Monnikendam* (The Hague, 1917).

43. For the quotation, see AJ, 8–14 March 1526.

44. Fredericq, 4: nos. 247, 278; 5: nos. 544, 580; De Hoop Scheffer, 338–339.

45. Fredericq, 4: no. 151, extract from *HVR;* cf. no. 214, Amsterdam makes the same claim of independence vis-à-vis the Court of Holland.

46. Prisoners from little Monnikendam were brought to The Hague over the objections of the magistrates: Fredericq, 5: nos. 447, 497, 498, 544, 548, 555, 580. With the "great cities" the Council was apparently more circumspect: the Leiden printer Jan Zeverszoon was summoned four times to appear in The Hague, and apparently never did; see also 4: nos. 183, 201, 212, 213; 5: no. 430. For the Council's intervention in the trial of David Joris in Delft, see De Hoop Scheffer, 223–238; R. H. Bainton, *David Joris* (Leipzig, 1937).

47. AJ, 10–16 December 1526, 17–22 March, 6–8, 8–14, 17–19 April, 22 April–1 May, 3–8, 10–12, 13–23 May 1527. Many of these passages are exerpted in Fredericq, vol. 5. The sentence against Zijvertszoon is printed in Wagenaar, *Amsterdam in Zijn Opkomst, Aanwas, en Geschiedenis,* 4 vols. (Amsterdam, 1760), 1: 235.

48. On Lauwerijns, see above, note 33.

49. Dubiez, 99–103, establishes that Amsterdam's crippled book dealer is not the same man as the Leiden printer mentioned in note 46.

50. AJ, 18–21 June 1528; *RSH,* 8 July 1528.

51. Fredericq, 5: 581, 582, 589, 592, 662, and 684 = Council of Holland to Hoogstraten, 1 February 1528 (Aud. 1524).

52. H. J. Elias, *Kerk en Staat in de Zuidelijke Nederlanden onder de Regering der Aartshertogen Albrecht en Isabella, 1595–1621* (Antwerp 1931), 12–35.

53. Sartorius is mentioned as penitent in the letter cited in note 51, but cf. "Memoire pour M. le Tresorier" [Vincent Corneliszoon], *ACB,* 93, between letters dated 15 December 1536 and 2 January 1536, and *Nieuw Nederlands Biographisch Woordenboek* 2: 1263.

54. AJ, 1 April 1528.

55. Tracy, "Heresy Law and Centralization," 289–290.

56. A. F. Mellink, "Pre-Reformatie en Vroege Reformatie," *NAGN,* 6:151, and *Documenta Anabaptistica,* 5: 253, from no. 302, "Memorie vant ghundt dat vuyt diverse informatien tot Amsterdam bevonden werdt," January 1536.

57. That the Netherlands Reformation was radicalized by the removal of moderate leadership through persecution is a commonplace among historians, e.g., Cornelius Krahn, *Dutch Anabaptism* (The Hague, 1968), 133.

58. A. F. Mellink, *De Wederdopers in de Noordelijke Nederlanden* (Groningen, 1954), and *Amsterdam en de Wederdopers in de Zestiende Eeuw* (Nijmegen, 1978); Grosheide, *Bijdragen tot de Geschiedenis der Anabaptisten in Amsterdam;* Krahn, *Dutch Anabaptism;* James M. Stayer, *Anabaptists and the Sword* (Lawrence, 1972); P. Kawerau, *Melchior*

Hoffman als Religiöser Denker (Haarlem, 1957); W. J . Kühler, *Geschiedenis der Nederlandsche Doopsgezinden in de Zestiende Eeuw* (Haarlem, 1932).

59. The important collections of sources by C. A. Cornelius, *Geschichte des Münsterschen Aufruhrs*, 2 vols. (Leipzig, 1855–1860) and G. Grosheide, "Verhooren en Vonnissen der Wederdopers, betrokken bij de Aanslag op Amsterdam," *BMHGU* 41 (1920): 1–197, have now been superseded by the series *Documenta Anabaptistica Neerlandica*, of which vols. 2 and 5, edited by A. F. Mellink, are pertinent here: *Amsterdam (1531–1536)* (Leiden, 1985), and *Amsterdam (1536–1578)* (Leiden, 1980).

60. Charles V to Mary of Hungary, 3 January 1531, Lanz, Letter 156, 1:417–418; Jane de Iongh, *De Koningin: Maria van Hongarije, Landvoogdes der Nederlanden* (Amsterdam, 1966), 57–63, 79–83. In 1542 her confessor, Peter Alexander, was jailed on a heresy charge. See Mellink, "Pre-Reformatie en Vroege Reformatie," 157. On Nicolaus Olah, see the entry by L. Domonkos in Peter Bietenholz, ed., *Contemporaries of Erasmus*, 3 vols. (Toronto: 1985–1987), 3: 29–31.

61. "Erste Memoriaalboek van Jan de Jonge," 87–91ᵛ, *placard* of 7 October 1531 (*HH*, no. 29, Rijksarchief van Zuid Holland, The Hague).

62. Mellink, *Documenta Anabaptistica*, 5, nos. 1, 302.

63. Unlike the rest of Hoogstraten's correspondence, which is part of Aud. (at the Algemeen Rijksarchief in Brussels), *ACB* is found at the Rijksarchief van Zuid-Holland in The Hague.

64. Assendelft to Hoogstraten, 3 May 1533, 23 February 1534 (Aud. 1446:2b); 30 November 1534, 29 December 1534, 14 February, 12 March 1535 (Aud. 1529).

65. Woltjer, *Friesland in Hervormingstijd*, 91–102.

66. Assendelft to Hoogstraten, 8 November 1534 (Aud. 1529). For correspondence between Erasmus and members of the Council, see Allen, *Opus Epistolarum*, Letters 1092, 1186, 1188, 1238, 1469, 1653 (Niklaas Everaerts), 2645 and 2844 (Joost Sasbout), and 2734 (Assendelft). For the gift, see AJ, 19–21 August 1532; *RSH*, 16 August 1532; and Allen, *Opus Epistolarum*, 9: 55.

67. Mellink, *Documenta Anabaptistica*, 5, nos. 37, 38, 39 and 302, which recount charges against four priests favored by the magistrates; minute of Hoogstraten's comments to Assendelft and Vincent Corneliszoon, dated 20 November 1533 in his wife's town of Culemborg (Aud. 1446:2b); Assendelft to Hoogstraten, 13 September and 30 October 1533 (Aud. 1446:2b); De Hoop Scheffer, *Geschiedenis der Kerkhervorming in Nederland*, 505–512.

68. Mellink, *Documenta Anabaptistica*, 5, no. 15, and *De Wederdopers in de Noordelijke Nederlanden*, 101–105.

69. Mellink, *Documenta Anabaptistica*, 5, no. 148. See nos. 276, 277 and 307 for additional prophecies, and nos. 113, and 312 for an indication of debates among the Anabaptists about violence; for the wider context, see Stayer, *Anabaptists and the Sword*, 267–269.

70. Council of Holland to Hoogstraten, 30 May 1533, and Jan de Jonge to Hoogstraten, 23 November 1533 (Aud. 1446:2b); Council to Hoogstraten, 10 March 1535 (Aud. 1646:1); Assendelft to Hoogstraten, 5 June 1533, and 7 February 1534 (Aud. 1446:2b). Hendrik Goetbeleet, one of the leaders of the May 1535 uprising in Amsterdam (see Mellink, *Documenta Anabaptistica*, 5, *sub nomine*) is probably the man of the same name who served as an officer among the *knechten* sailing with the Baltic war fleet of 1533: Assendelft to Hoogstraten, 27 November 1533 (Aud. 1446:2b).

71. Brunt to Hoogstraten, 20 March 1534, *ACB*, 92, Anabaptists are heading for Cromeniedijk (Kennemerland), meaning to take ship for Münster, instead of presenting themselves for penitence; Assendelft to Hoogstraten, 26 December 1539, Jan de Haes (one of the suspect priests in Amsterdam in 1534, above, note 67) found a post as vice-curate in the village of Middelie.

72. *HVH*, 324–326.

73. Mellink, *De Wederdopers in de Noordelijke Nederlanden*, 30–38.

74. *HVH*, 337–347.

75. Sheriff Jan Hubrechtszoon had been removed in February 1534, but his successor, Heyman Jacobszoon van Ouder Amstel, was not much better from the government's point of view: Mellink, *Documenta Anabaptistica*, 5, no. 16. On Sheriff Klaas Gerritszoon Mattheus, see Ter Gouw, 4: 255–259, and Brunt to Hoogstraten, 21 November 1534, *ACB*, 92. The draper who calmed the crowd was Joost Buyck, the future Dirkist magistrate, who left his own account of these events; "Nieuwe Maren of Verhall van hetgeen voorgevallen is binnen Amsterdam, 1534–1536," printed in full in P. Scheltema, *Amstel's Oudheid*, 6 vols. (Amsterdam, 1855–1872), 2: 55–76, and partially in Mellink, *Documenta Anabaptistica*, 5. On relations between town magistrates and those next below them in the social hierarchy, known loosely as "the well-to-do" (*het rijkdom*), see Christopher Grayson, "The Common Man in the County of Holland, 1560–1572: Politics and Public Order in the Dutch Revolt," *BMGN* 95 (1980): 35–63.

76. Council of Holland to Hoogstraten, 10 November 1534, to Assendelft, 23 November 1534, and to Mary of Hungary, 24 January 1535 (Aud. 1529); Assendelft to Hoogstraten, 11 November 1534, 29

December 1534, 24 January 1535 (Aud. 1529); Brunt to Hoogstraten, 29 December 1534, 30 January 1535 (Aud. 1529). Mellink, *De Wederdopers in de Noordelijke Nederlanden*, 156–168.

77. Knappert, *De Opkomst van het Protestantisme in eene Noord-Nederlandsche Stad*, 148–155.

78. Council of Holland to Mary of Hungary, [?] January 1535 (Aud. 1504:2). This important letter, not previously cited, is transcribed by Leo Schulte-Noordholt in a seminar paper for the University of Leiden: "De Twee 'Bekeringen' van Jannetgen Thijsdochter," (Spring 1987). For Jannetgen Thijsdochter's confession, see Mellink, *Documenta Anabaptistica*, 5, no. 76.

79. Mellink, *Documenta Anabaptistica*, 5, nos. 87–91, and *Amsterdam en de Wederdopers*, 45–49.

80. Mellink, *Geschiedenis der Wederdopers in de Noordelijke Nederlanden*, 71–72, 86–91.

81. Mellink, *Documenta Anabaptistica*, 5, nos. 111, 123, and *Amsterdam en de Wederdopers*, 53–75.

82. Woltjer, *Friesland in Hervormingstijd*, 105–106; Mellink, *Amsterdam en de Wederdopers*, 76–86; Ter Gouw, 4: 383–405; Grosheide, *Geschiedenis der Anabaptisten in Amsterdam*, 307 ff; Krahn, *Dutch Anabaptism*, 166–175.

83. Johan De Cavele, *Daagraad van de Reformatie in Vlaanderen* = *VKAW-KL* 76 (Brussels, 1975), 33–34; Woltjer, *Friesland in Hervormingstijd*, 105–121; Assendelft to Hoogstraten, 24 June 1534 (Aud. 1646:3).

84. Tracy, "Heresy Law and Centralization," 291–293. The quotation is from the Council of Holland's instructions for Meester Abel van Coulster on a mission to Hoogstraten, dated 17 Febraury 1534, in Mellink, *Documenta Anabaptistica*, 5, no. 16.

85. Mellink, *Documenta Anabaptistica*, 5, nos. 61, 69–71.

86. Assendelft to Hoogstraten, 14 February, 12 March 1535 (Aud. 1529); Brunt to Hoogstraten, 15 March 1535 (*ACB*, 93).

87. Instructions for Guilleyn Zeghers, 27 May 1534, and Mary of Hungary to the Council of Holland, 1 June 1534 (*ACB*, 92). Council of Holland to Hoogstraten, 22 June 1534 (Aud. 1646:1) and 28 July 1534 (Aud. 1529); Assendelft to Hoogstraten, 24 June 1534 (Aud. 1646:3).

88. Council of State's instructions to Brunt, for the Council of Holland, 23 January 1535 (*ACB*, 92); "Instructions pour M. le Tresorier" (Vincent Corneliszoon), after 15 December 1535 (*ACB*, 93).

89. Queen's instructions for Hoogstraten in Holland, 7 April 1535 (*ACB*, 93); Brunt before the Secret Council, 5 May 1535, with marginal notes giving the Council's answers (Aud. 1529).

90. Ter Gouw, 4: 279–284; Mellink, *Amsterdam en de Wederdopers*, 80–82. The new *schepenen* for 1536 included Egge Garbrandszoon Paf and Willem Klaaszoon Koeck (see above, n. 31) and Klass Doedeszoon, Klaas Gerrit Mattheuszoon, and Pieter Kantert Willemszoon (see chap. 5, table 6).

91. For the attack on Hazerswoude, see Kühler, *Geschiedenis der Nederlandsche Doopsgezinden*, 188–189; Mellink, *Amsterdam en de Wederdopers*, 84–86.

92. Tracy, "Heresy Law and Centralization," 300–301.

93. Assendelft to Hoogstraten, 12 April 1537 (Aud. 1530); Council of Holland to Hoogstraten, 15 April 1537; Mary of Hungary to Lodewijk van Schore, 6 October 1537, and Council of Holland to Schore, 9 November 1537 (Aud. 1532).

94. Tracy, "Heresy Law and Centralization," 302–303.

95. Assendelft to Hoogstraten, 24 March 1536 and 27 May 1536 (Aud. 1530).

96. For trials in Delft and Haarlem, see Assendelft to Hoogstraten, 27 December 1538, 12 February 1539 (Aud. 1532), and 1 January 1539 (Aud. 1528); Sheriff, burgomasters and *schepenen* of Haarlem to the Council of Holland, 30 May 1539, and Assendelft to Hoogstraten, 19 June 1539 (Aud. 1532).

97. Tracy, "A Premature Counter-Reformation," 162–165; Mellink, *Amsterdam en de Wederdopers*, 76–86; Grosheide, *Bijdragen tot de Geschiedenis der Wederdopers in Amsterdam*, 307 ff.

98. See the letter from officials in Haarlem cited above, note 96.

99. "Derde Mermoriaalboek van Jan de Jonge," 15–20 (22 September 1540); "Eerste Memoriaalboek van Jan van Dam," 89–92 (18 December 1544), 201–204 (30 June 1546); "Tweede Memoriaalboek van Jan van Dam," 55ᵛ–56, renewal of the *placards* mentioned above (7 June 1549), 180–190 and 190–201ᵛ (29 April 1550). Council of Holland to Mary of Hungary, 15 November 1550, and Mary of Hungary to the Council, 23 November 1550 (Aud. 1646:2).

100. For capsule sketches, see Baelde, *De Collaterale Raden*, 288–289, 328–329, 240–241.

101. On the Regensburg Colloquy of 1541 and events leading up to it, see Peter Matheson, *Cardinal Contarini at Regensburg* (Oxford, 1972), and Cornelis Augustijn, *De Godsdienstgesprekken tussen Rooms-Katholieken en Protestanten van 1538–1541* = *Verhandelingen Uitgegeven door Teylers Godgeleerd Genootschap*, n.s., 30 (Haarlem, 1967).

102. Mary of Hungary to the Marquis of Bergen, 5 March 1542 (Aud. 1533).

103. Mellink, "Pre-Reformatie en Vroege Reformatie," 157; Mary of Hungary to the Council of Holland, 22 October 1546, and the Council to Mary, 29 October 1546 (Aud. 1646:1).

104. On two or possibly three "scandalous" *rederijker* plays performed in Amsterdam, see Mellink, *Documenta Anabaptistica*, 5, no. 16, p. 21, and nos. 37 and 39, paragraphs 8 and 24. Assendelft to Hoogstraten, 11 November 1534 (Aud. 1529); Mary of Hungary to Leiden, 26 May 1546 (Aud. 1656:1); Goudriaan to Mary of Hungary, 20 June 1646 (Aud. 1646:3); Mary of Hungary to Assendelft, 4 April 1551 (Aud. 1656:2).

105. "Criminele Sententieboek," "Hof van Holland," Rijksarchief van Zuid Holland, The Hague.

106. Le Cocq to the Privy Council, 8 February 1545 (Aud. 1533).

107. Duke, "The Face of Popular Religious Dissent," 46; Council of Holland to Mary of Hungary, 24 July 1544 (Aud. 1646:1); Woltjer, "Het Conflict tussen Willem Baerdes en Hendrik Dirkszoon," 183–190.

108. AJ, 20–24 April, 5–15 July, 21–30 October 1534; *RSH*, 1: 291 (May 1537).

109. *RSH*, 15 September, 6 November 1544, 9 April 1545; Mary of Hungary to the Council of Holland, 4 March 1545 (Aud. 1646:1).

110. On the Cruningen family, see Van Nierop, *Van Ridders tot Regenten*, 20–24. On Engel Willemszoon, see W. Moll, *Angelus Merula, de Hervormer en Martelaar des Geloofs (1530–1557)* (Amsterdam, 1855), and R. Fruin, "Het Proces van Angelus Merula," *Verspreide Geschriften*, 1: 229–265. *RSH*, 10 July 1553, 21 March, 1 October 1554, 5 February 1555; "Tweede Memoriaalboek van Jan van Dam," 90–93ᵛ (2 June 1553). Council of Holland to Mary of Hungary, 3 April 1554, 16 April 1554, and Mary to the Council, 16 June 1554 (Aud. 1646:2). *Clarissimi Theologi D. Ruardi Tapperi Apotheosis*, ed. F. Pijper, in *Bibliotheca Reformatoria Neerlandica*, 1 (The Hague, 1903), 567–636. The treatise, published anonymously in 1568, has been attributed to Hendrik van Geldorp, on whom see J. H. De Muinck Keizer, *Hendrik van Geldorp* (Croningen, 1893).

111. See the correspondence about the pastor of Rotterdam, at war with the magistrates and deemed unqualified by the Council of Holland, who was offered rewards by both if he would resign his post, but would not do so for anything less than a canonry in Utrecht: Assendelft to Hoogstraten, 7 November 1538 (Aud. 1527), 9 November 1539 (Aud. 1532), 16 November 1539 (Aud. 1528), 20 December 1539 (Aud. 1530), and 8 February 1540 (Aud. 1528); Hoogstraten to Assendelft, 25 November 1539 (Aud. 1532).

7: HOLLAND UNDER PHILIP II, 1556–1566

1. Recent studies include Peter Pierson, *Philip II of Spain* (London, 1975); Geoffrey Parker, *Philip II of Spain* (London, 1977); Miguel de Ferdinandy, *Philipp II* (Wiesbaden, 1977); and Robert van Roosbroeck, *Filips II, Koning van Spanje, Soeverein der Nederlanden* (The Hague, 1983).

2. J. J. W. Verhofstad, *De Regering der Nederlanden*, 82–107.

3. Ibid., 118–159; *AFR*, 99–107.

4. R. Fruin, "Het Voorpsel van de Tachtig-Jarige Oorlog," in his *Verspreide Geschriften*, 1 (The Hague, 1900), 276–288; Verhofstad, *De Regering der Nederlanden*, 28–30; and G. Janssens, "De Eertse Jaren van Filips II, 1555–1566," *NAGN*, 6: 189–190.

5. Margaret of Parma to Philip II, 13 June 1562, in L. P. Gachard, *Correspondance de Marguerite d'Autriche avec Philippe II*, 2 vols. (Brussels, 1867–1870), Letter 165.

6. Philip II to Margaret of Parma, 24 August 1559, and Margaret of Parma to Philip, 4 October 1559, in Gachard, *Correspondance de Marguerite d'Autriche*, Letters 7, 8. What the King says is, "Je n'entens aucunement dissimuler."

7. The number of Calvinist and Anabaptist communities in Flanders ca. 1560 is graphically represented in S. Groenveld, *De Kogel door de Kerk?*, 61. For a case study, see Charlie R. Steen, *A Chronicle of Conflict: Tournai, 1559–1567* (Utrecht, 1985), 23–26. I am not aware of any official notice of Calvinism in Holland prior to the complaint in Lindanus's 1565 report (see below, note 110) that "Anabaptists and Calvinists are increasing daily."

8. P. Th. van Beuningen, *Willem Lindanus als Inquisiteur en Bisschop* (Assen, 1966), 43–99; Woltjer, *Friesland in Hervormingstijd*, 91–97; Margaret of Parma to Philip II, 17 March, 23 April, and 27 August 1560, Gachard, *Correspondance de Marguerite d'Autriche*, Letters 29, 40, 60.

9. M. Dierickx, S.J., *De Oprichting der Nieuwe Bisdommen in de Nederlanden onder Filips II, 1559–1570* (Antwerp, 1950) = *L'Erection des Nouveaux Diocèses aux Pays Bas, 1559–1570* (Brussels, 1967).

10. Dierickx, *Oprichting der Nieuwe Bisdommen*, 15–37, 45–75, 92. N. M. Sutherland, "William of Orange and the Revolt of the Netherlands: a Missing Dimension," *Archiv für Reformationsgeschichte* 74 (1983): 203–209, argues that Orange's breach with the Netherlands government traces to his fears of a "Catholic crusade," which were revived by formation of the Catholic "triumvirate" in France in March 1561, including the Duke of Guise and the Constable, Anne de Montmorency. She mentions the bishoprics only in passing, and does not cite the work

of Dierickx (above, n. 9), which has led to a scholarly consensus that the bishoprics were indeed the rock of division in the Council of State.

11. Dierickx, *Oprichting der Nieuwe Bisdommen*, 12–14, 39–40, 161–176; cf. Rogier, *Geschiedenis van het Katholicisme*, 1: 212–246, 402, 414. Dierickx rather skirts the issue raised by Rogier's contention that most of Philip II's new bishops were "servile." See Fruin, "Voorspel van de Tachtig-Jarige Oorlog," 312–320.

12. Geoffrey Parker, *The Dutch Revolt* (Ithaca, 1977), 51–54.

13. Ibid., 62–67; John Lothrop Motley, *The Rise of the Dutch Republic*, 3 vols. (New York, 1859), 1: 448–485.

14. *RSH*, 15 July 1560, 17 January, 10 March 1562, 8 January 1564; See *GRK*, 3457–3462, the *ordinaris bede* accounts for the period 1560–1567. Assignations on the *ordinaris bede* at this time included interest on the *renten* sold between 1515 and 1533 (about 22,000 pounds), money for warships, and wages for the garrison of Vredenburg castle in Utrecht.

15. Minute by Suys, enclosed with Council of Holland to Margaret of Parma, 23 December 1560 (*HH*, 381); Council of Holland to the Council of Finance, with identical letters to Viglius and Margaret of Parma, 6 July 1562 (*HH*, 381); Council to Margaret, 5 May 1563 (*HH*, 381); and Suys to Viglius, an autograph in Latin, 12 May 1563 (Aud. 1417/11).

16. The one *extraordinaris bede* granted by the States between 1560 and 1565 was a sale of *renten* (100,000) in 1565: see below, note 33.

17. For troubles with England, see *RSH*, 4 July 1560, 11 March 1562, 1 May 1565. Margaret of Parma to the Council of Holland, 23 May 1564 (Aud. 1704/1), Hollanders are not to resort to Emden (East Frisia) to buy English cloth. For problems in the Baltic, see *RSH*, 24 July 1563, 6 February 1564, 2 May, 14 September, 17 November 1565. Charles E. Hill, *Danish Sound Dues and the Command of the Baltic* (Durham, 1926), 63–68; Sven Cedergreen Bech, *Reformation og Renaissance* = *Danmarks Historie*, ed. John Danstrup, Hal Koch, (Copenhagen, 1963), 6: 364–446.

18. *SH*, 2343 and 2344, for the two tenth-pennies; the amounts entered as income were 266,593 and 278,855.

19. The Dominican cloister was where the accounts of the Receiver for the Common Land were heard, until the new office was built.

20. *RSH*, 21 May 1556, 4 May 1557, 17 August 1557, 23–24 June 1558, 28 September 1558, 5 May 1560.

21. *RSH*, 3 May 1557, 26–28 February, 6, 25 April, 18–19 May, 28 September 1558, 7 April, 14 July 1559, 27 October 1561, 10 March, 19 December 1562. For resistance by the Council of Holland to the

States' summoning themselves to meet, see Council of Holland to the Secret Council, 17 March 1561 (*HH*, 381); Margaret of Parma to the Council of Holland, 5 November and 10 December 1562, and the Council to Margaret, 28 November 1562 (Aud. 327).

22. P. A. Meilink, "Remonstrantie van het Hof van Holland en de Rekenkamer nopens de Administratie van de Ontvanger-Generaal A. Coebel en de Staten van Holland," *BMHGU* 45 (1924): 157–183.

23. *Bede* figures from *GRK*, 3417–3434 (for Goudt) and *SH*, 2277–2288 (for Coebel); Mellink, "Remonstrantie van het Hof van Holland," 164.

24. Sandelijn, 12 December 1555. 6 January 1556; all of the income for this *bede* was in fact collected by Coebel: see *SH*, 2283.

25. On Philip II's financial problems at this time, see Modesto Ulloa, *La Hacienda Real de Castilla en el Reinado de Felipe II* (Madrid, 1977), 759–831. Vere to Savoy, 24 February 1557 (Aud. 325); cf. *AVR*, 5 June 1557 (Amsterdam is asked for a 50,000-*obligatie* "to strengthen the credit of his majesty"), and 15 July 1562 (request for a 200,000-*obligatie* "on the faith and credit" of the States of Holland).

26. Cf. the disquiet caused when Arent van Dale, a well-known Antwerp merchant-banker, purchased a large Holland *rente* on the secondary market: *RSH*, 26 February, 29 September 1556.

27. On Gaspar Schetz, see the references in Baelde, *De Collaterale Raden*, 307–308. For disputes between Schetz and the States of Holland, see *RSH*, 21 June, 6 October, 2 November 1558, 3 February 1559, 5 March 1560, and *AVR*, 27 January 1557,

28. *RSH*, 2 April, 5 May 1560, 27 October 1561, 12 March 1562.

29. One account might show Coebel paying out 38,000 less than he took in, another might show him paying out 66,000 more than he took in; these totals were combined and carried forward without regard to the distinction between *beden* owed to the prince, and impost and land tax revenue for the debts of the Common Land: cf. *SH*, 2282, 2294.

30. *RSH*, 27 July 1559; cf. 3 February 1559, orders to Coebel for the use of 25,000 in cash

31. *RSH*, 4–5 August 1558, 6–7 September 1559, 17–19 January 1560.

32. *AFR*, 93–99. When he was looking for investors who would accept conversion of their *renten* to a lower rate, instead of demanding to have the cash back, Coebel was instructed to try this approach "with rentiers, since they have nothing else to do with their money to make a profit, unlike the merchants" (*RSH*, 5 March 1560).

33. *SH*, 2289 (the sale of *renten*), 2304 (impost and land tax account for 1565/1566), and 2344 (tenth penny levied in 1564). The *rentenier*

was Duke Erich von Braunschweig, currently lord of Woerden in Holland.

34. Meilink, "Remonstrantie van het Hof van Holland," 169.

35. See column 7, "Gratuities," in Table 4, Tracy, "The Financial System of the County of Holland," 115–117.

36. *RSH*, 10–11 February, 30–31 March, 7–9 April 1559; *SH*, 2283.

37. *RSH*, 23–24 February, 4–5 May 1557, 5 March 1560; *SH*, 2303: 1,200 for Viglius, and 300 each for Philibert de Bruxelles and Albrecht van Loo, the same names and amounts indicated in discussions in the States in 1557. Cf. *RSH*, 6 June 1561, wine for Viglius.

38. *RSH*, 6 June 1560, Coebel is to pay for a "glass" given to the President [Suys]. *GRK*, 3440, under "Mandamenten," payment of 300 pounds to Aert van der Goes for his "services" to the Emperor, according to a payment order dated 30 September 1540.

39. E.g., *RSH*, 10 June 1558, Coebel is instructed to give his account for the sale of *losrenten* at 1:12 to redeem *lijfrenten* at 1:16 to Mr. Gerrit Hendrikszoon and the other commissioners, so they can notify the deputies when to meet to close the account. In this account (*SH*, 2347), Mr. Gerrit himself is listed as having purchased four *renten* with a total value of 4,800 pounds.

40. Aud. 1659/3 has extensive correspondence on naval affairs in the early 1550s, between Brussels and Vere and his two deputies, Wackene and Scepper. Occasional letters to and from Vere occur in the folios devoted to correspondence with Holland and Zeeland in 1555–1558, Aud. 325 and 326.

41. For the history of the two branches of the family down to 1554, see Felix Rachfahl, *Wilhelm von Oranien und der Niederländische Aufstand*, 2 vols. (Halle, 1906–1907), 1: 7–126.

42. Rachfahl, 2: 85–128; Fruin, "Voorspel van de Tachtig-Jarige Oorlog," 318–320.

43. *RSH*, 27–28 June 1560, *AVR*, 10 December 1561.

44. On the taxation of Orange's fisheries in south Holland, see *RSH*, 5–6 May, 1–3 June 1559, 4–9 February 1561, 12 August 1562; on Holland's suit against the three personages, see *RSH*, 10 April 1557, 19 December 1562.

45. Council of Holland to the Secret Council, 17 December 1562 (*HH*, 381).

46. Sandelijn, 5–9 August, 28 October, 25–26 November 1555, 9 May 1556; *AVR*, 25 September 1556; *RSH*, 3 January, 11 October 1556, 4 January 1562. "Jacob the land-measurer" was perhaps Jacob van Deventer, whose map of Holland, printed in Abraham Ortelius,

Theatrum Orbis Terrarum (Antwerp, 1570) shows the Spoeye as the main channel, and Bernis as much narrower.

47. Letters to the Council under Assendelft's leadership are addressed, "To the First Councillor and the Other Councillors," not "To the President and the Council."

48. When Mary of Hungary issued a *placard* renewing the obligation of military service by the Emperor's vassals, Assendelft declined to give an opinion, lest he incur "the indignation of the nobles here." Assendelft to Hoogstraten, 16 September 1536 (Aud. 1530).

49. F. A. Holleman, *Dirk van Assendelft, Schout van Breda, en de Zijnen* (Zutfen, 1953), 10–17 239–247; unsigned letter to Mary of Hungary, 25 February 1541, Zeghers's notes on a meeting of the Secret Council on the Assendelft case, at Binche on 18 March, and Mary of Hungary to the Council of Holland, 6 April 1541 (Aud. 1533).

50. Assendelft recommended Suys for promotion to the post of Councillor Ordinary (with salary) to replace Abel van Coulster, instead of the son-in-law to whom Coulster wished to resign his office. Assendelft to Lodewijk van Schore, 19 March 1543 (Aud. 1646:3). Suys got the job.

51. Suys's reply to articles presented by Snouckaert, dated 1 October 1555 (Aud. 1646:2).

52. Assendelft's reply to Snouckaert's charges, 7 December 1555 (Aud. 1646:3). Like Guilleyn Zeghers (see chap. 5), Snouckaert was evidently trusted by Brussels in the sensitive matter of preserving orthodoxy, for it was he whom the Council proposed, in place of the inquisitor Ruard Tapper, for the task of culling the Council's library for forbidden books: Mary of Hungary to the Council of Holland, 22 October 1546, and the Council to Mary, 29 October 1546 (Aud. 1646:1). Assendelft's letters make no comment on Snouckaert, but show a definite coolness towards Zeghers: he declined to support Zeghers's candidacy for Councillor Ordinary, as well as the candidacy of one of his friends, and made fun of Zeghers for purchasing the right to call himself "lord" of Wassenhove. Assendelft to Hoogstraten, 12 September 1535 (Aud. 1529), 22 February 1539 (Aud. 1531), and 8 February 1540 (Aud. 1528).

53. Van Nierop, *Van Ridders tot Regenten*, Chapter 2, "Deugd en Afkomst," and Chapter 6, "Ambachtheren en Ambtenaren."

54. Hugo de Schepper, *Belgium Nostrum, 1500–1650: Over de Integratie en Desintegratie van het Nederland* (Antwerp, 1987).

55. *HH*, 381, the folder of correspondance between the Council of Holland and the Secret Council. Aud. has five folders of correspon-

dence with Holland for this period, but Aud. 325, covering the period from January through June 1557, is almost entirely occupied with the grain shortage, and Aud. 326–330 (1557–1566) has correspondence on Zeeland and Utrecht as well as Holland (the three provinces had the same Stadtholder). For Suys's Latin letters to Viglius, in an elegant humanist hand, see Suys to Viglius, 6 January 1550 (Aud. 1646:2), and 12 May 1563 (Aud. 1417/11).

56. Paul van Peteghem, "Centralisatie in Vlaanderen onder Karel V," 257–276.

57. Boussu to Savoy, 24 January 1559 (Aud. 326), a complaint that, with both the Stadtholderate and the Presidency of the Council vacant, there was no one in Holland "who dares speak for the service of his majesty, to push [the States] forward." For Suys as commissioner to the States of Holland, see Margaret of Parma to Suys, 10 May 1560 (Aud. 326), 20 June 1560 and 28 December 1560 (Aud. 1704/1), and 23 January 1561 (Aud. 327); Suys to Margaret, 1, 11 January 1561 (Aud. 327). For examples of Assendelft's success as a mediator of disputes within the States, see Assendelft to Mary of Hungary, 5, 15 August 1547 (Aud. 1646:3), and 10, 14 August 1552 (Aud. 1646:3).

58. Baerdes to Viglius, n.d. [probably 1553–1554] (Aud. 1441/1), to Suys, 13 February 1563 (Aud. 328), and to Margaret of Parma, 18 November 1565 (Aud. 329) and 14 January 1566 (Aud. 330).

59. *AVR*, 4 February 1557; Philip II to the Council and the Council's reply, 30 November 1557 (Aud. 1704/1), 16 December 1557 (*HH*, 381); Council to Margaret of Parma, 18 January, 18 February, 9 March 1563, and to the Prince of Orange, 18 February 1563 (*HH*, 381); Margaret of Parma to the Council, 24 February 1563 (Aud. 328) and 16 March 1563 (Aud. 1704/1); *AVR*, 16 February, 5, 6, 8, 16 March. 14 July 1563; Council to Orange, 14 May 1565 (Aud. 329), and Margaret to the Council, 5 September 1565 (*HH*, 381).

60. Tracy, "Habsburg Grain Policy and Amsterdam Politics," 314–318.

61. Aud. 326, leaf 49, undated memo in Baerdes's distinctive hand, outlining the four alternatives, and leaves 61–62, copy of Savoy to the Council of Holland, 10 June 1568.

62. Woltjer, "Het Conflikt tussen Willem Baerdes en Hendrik Dirkszoon," 189. On the pursuit of Adriaan van Heemstede of Zierikzee, see Council of Holland to Margaret of Parma, 23 December 1560 (*HH*, 381), and 11 January 1561, enclosing a copy of Baerdes's letter to Orange of 22 December (Aud. 327).

63. In 1539 the magistrates of Delft presented the Council of Holland with certain "articles" against Sheriff Jan de Heuter: Gemeentear-

chief Delft, Eerste Afdeling, "Memoriaalboek" of the burgomasters, entries for 11, 15 November 1539. For Sheriff Wouter Bekesteyn's quarrel with the magistrates of Haarlem, see Council of Holland to the Secret Council, 10 January 1550, and to Mary of Hungary, 15 November 1550 (Aud. 1646:2), an unsigned letter to Assendelft, 24 March 1551 (Aud. 1646:3). There were also disputes of this kind in smaller towns like Schoonhoven (Council of Holland to Vere, 18 November 1557, *HH*, 381) and Medemblik (Council of Holland to the Grand Council of Mechelen, 10 April 1564, *HH*, 381).

64. Ter Gouw, 4: 279–284, 414–416; Tracy, "Habsburg Grain Policy and Amsterdam Politics."

65. Aud. 1441:3, no. 13, undated memorandum [1554 or 1555] listing Baerdes's complaints against the magistrates; *AVR*, 6 May, 29 July 1556, 21 October 1557, 9 January, 27 August, 6 October, 3 November, 15 December 1558, 7 February 1560. Woltjer, "Het Conflikt tussen Willem Baerdes en Hendrik Dirkszoon," 190–195.

66. Vere to Philip II, 9 December 1557 (Aud. 325).

67. Council of Holland to Margaret of Parma, 27 September 1559, and to the Secret Council, 19 June 1560, and 27 October 1561 (*HH*, 381); Margaret to the Council, 2 January 1562, and the Council to Margaret, 17 April 1562, with a copy of the Council's sentence against Engelbrechtszoon, dated 16 April (Aud. 327; as this letter makes clear, it was episcopal officials in Utrecht who denied permission for the pastor to be tortured); and Council of Holland to the Grand Council of Mechelen, 15 May 1564 (*HH*, 381).

68. De Vries, *The Dutch Rural Economy*, 89–90.

69. *AVR*, 6 April, 5, 7 June, 8, 9, 14 August 1557, 27 March, 12, 23 April 1558; Savoy to Vere, 4 June 1557 (Aud. 325). *ASR* shows a surplus for every year from 1544 through 1564, ranging from a low of 6,306 for 1549 to a high of 66,798 in 1563. For both 1557 and 1558 the surplus was around 25,000.

70. Brouwer-Ancher, "De Doleantie van een Deel der Burgerij van Amsterdam;" Margaret of Parma to Amsterdam, 29 January 1565, and to the Council of Holland, 3 September 1565 (Aud. 329).

71. On Amsterdam's role in providing warships to protect the returning grain ships during the famine of 1557, see the following from Aud. 325: Council of Holland to Savoy, 18 and 20 February; Amsterdam to the Council, 20 February; Vere to Savoy, 21 February, 3, 15, 17, 29 March, 25, 28 April, 15, 22 May; Savoy to Vere, 12 March, 16 April, 3, 22 May, 4 June; Wackene and Quarré to Savoy, 1 May; and Quarré to Berlaymont, 4 May. See also *RSH*, 8, 19, 31 March, 13, 16, 27 April, 2–5 May 1557; for the sale of *renten*, see *SH*, 2285.

72. Philip II to Margaret of Parma, 15 June 1561, Gachard, *Correspondance de Marguerite d'Autriche*, Letter 112; Margaret of Parma to William of Orange, 15 June 1561, G. Groen van Prinsterer, *Archives ou Correspondance Inédite de la Maison Orange-Nassau*, (Leiden, 1835), 1:109–114.

73. *RSH*, 15 July, 26 October 1561, 24 July 1563; *AVR*, 21 March 1561. Elais, *De Vroedschap van Amsterdam*, 1: 176–177.

74. See above, note 60.

75. Woltjer, "Een Hollands Stadsbestuur in het Midden van de 16e Eeuw;" Tracy, "A Premature Counter-Reformation," 158–159.

76. Names of the *Doleanten* are given in Brower-Ancher, "De Doleantie van een Deel der Amsterdamse Burgerij," and names of those who paid taxes in 1563 on the roughly one hundred houses on either side of the street are given in Kam, *Waar Was dat Huis op Warmoes Straat?* By dividing the street arbitrarily in the middle, according to the modern house numbers Kam uses, one obtains the following picture:

	below no. 100	above no. 100
Dirkist magistrates	7	15
Doleanten	14	5

77. Christopher Grayson, "The Common Man in the County of Holland, 1560–1572: Politics and Public Order in the Dutch Revolt," *BMGN*, 95 (1980): 45. The *Doleanten* were correct in charging the Dirkist government with nepotism in the choice of junior magistrates. See Tracy, "A Premature Counter-Reformation," 160–162.

78. See the references in Van Nierop, *Van Ridders tot Regenten*, for Niklaas van Assendelft, lord of Assendelft, Arend van Duvenvoirde (d. 1579), lord of Duvenvoirde, and Gijsbrecht van Duvenvoirde, lord of Warmond (d. 1580).

79. Schorl, *Het Waddeneiland Callensoog*, 67–72, describes the work done in north Holland in the 1550s by the Brabant dikage expert Andries Vierlingh; see also the modern edition of his *Tractaet van Dyckagie*, ed. J. Hullu, A. G. Verhoeven (The Hague, 1920 = *Rijksgeschiedkundige Publicatiën, Kleine Serie*, no. 20).

80. Much of Schorl's discussion in *Het Waddeneiland Callensoog*, 67–130, deals with works relating to the Zijpe in the middle decades of the sixteenth century. *RSH*, 17 November 1562, presents a request from the tenants of "Heyman van der Ketels land," on the Moerdijk near Lage Zwaluwe.

81. Verhofstad, *De Regering der Nederlanden,* 74.

82. *AVR,* 30 June, 31 July 1556.

83. *RSH,* 6 April, 7, 22 May, 25 June, 29 September, 22 October, 2 December 1563, 9 April 1564, 2 May, 13 July 1565, 30 April 1566. Orange also offered to mediate the quarrel between the States and the Count of Hornes as Admiral of the Netherlands: *RSH,* 18 July, 2, 5 December 1563, 12 July 1565.

84. Holleman, *Dirk van Assendelft, Schout van Breda;* Rienk Vermij, "'s Konings Stadhouder in Holland, Oranjes Trouw aan Filips II," *Utrechtse Historische Cahiers* 2/3 (1984): 43: *RSH,* 14 September 1565; see above, note 44.

85. Margaret of Parma to the Council of Holland, 29 January 1565; *AVR,* 7 May 1565.

86. *RSH,* 29 January, 10 February 1564, 2 May, 20 November, 1 December 1565.

87. *RSH,* 27 January, 15 July 1566; *SH,* 2305.

88. Vermij, "'s Konings Stadhouder in Holland," 40.

89. See Woltjer, *Friesland in Hervormingstijd,* and De Cavele, *Dagraad van de Reformatie in Vlaanderen.*

90. Soutelande's complaint to the Stadtholder and the Council, 18 April 1557 (Aud. 1704:1), and the reply of Haarlem's magistrates, 15 May 1557 (Aud. 1704:2).

91. Savoy to Vere and the Council, 25 September 1557 (Aud. 1704:1), and to Haarlem, 17 October 1557 (Aud. 1715:1); Council of Holland to Charles Count of Lalaing [Hoogstraten's nephew], 1 October 1557, and Lalaing to the Council, 17 October 1557 (Aud. 1704:1).

92. Information on the Oudewater incident is contained in Savoy's letter to Vere and Lalaing's to the Council, cited in note 91.

93. On Coelthuyn's activity in Enkhuizen, see Geraerdt Brandt, *Historie der Vermaerde Zee- en Koop-Stadt Enkhuizen,* ed. S. Centen (Hoorn, 1740), 107–115.

94. On the ritual element in sixteenth-century popular protest, see Natalie Zemon Davis, "The Rites of Violence," in *Society and Culture in Early Modern France* (Palo Alto, 1975), 152–187.

95. Savoy to Vere and the Council, 25 September 1557, Council of Holland to Lalaing, 1 October 1557, and Lalaing to the Council, 17 October 1557 (Aud. 1704:1); Council to Savoy, 20 December 1557, and to Philip II, 10 January 1558 (*HH,* 381); copy of Lindanus's 1565 report, with replies by the Council entered in the margin at the appropriate point, under "Enkhuizen" (Aud. 1397:8).

96. Council of Holland to Philip II, 28 March, 30 March, 31 March 1558 (Aud. 1715/1), 11 April 1558, and [January] 1559 (*HH,* 381);

Council to Vere, 29 March 1558 (*HH*, 381); Boussu and Cruyningen to Philip II, 19 April 1558 (Aud. 326).

97. Margaret of Parma to Suys, 8 July 1564, and Suys to Margaret, 24 July 1564 (Aud. 328).

98. *RSH*, 19–20 June 1556, 24 February, 16 March 1557, 16–19 September 1558, 17–19 January, 19–20 November 1560. In one of the cases the States sided with Klaas van Berendrecht, Sheriff of Leiden, whose harassment of the Jewish-Christian physician Andries Salomonszoon was being challenged by Salomonszoon before the Grand Council of Mechelen: Jeremy D. Bangs, "Andries Salomonsz, a Converted 'Rabbi and Doctor' in Leiden (1553–1561)," *Jewish Social Studies* 40 (1978): 271–286. At the same time, the States backed Delft in demanding that an inquisitor show his commission from the King before summoning a burgher to The Hague: *RSH*, 3 July 1557, 9 January 1564.

99. Margaret of Parma to the Council of Holland, and to Suys, both dated 15 July 1562 (Aud. 327); Mellink, *Documenta Anabaptistica*, 2: nos. 254, 255. Lindanus's report, under "Amsterdam" (Aud. 1397/8).

100. *RSH*, 17 April 1564.

101. Council of Holland to Philip II, 27 May 1558 (*HH*, 381), responding to the King's order that a confessed Anabaptist whom Dordrecht had already put to torture twice be tortured again by the Council: apart from the fact that the Council was busy with other matters, like the recent "tumult" in Rotterdam, "it is also very harsh, begging your majesty's leave, that one should torture for the third time a prisoner who has already been sharply examined twice."

102. Margaret of Parma to the Council of Holland, 15 July 1560 (Aud. 326), and 8 February 1561 (Aud. 327); Rijksarchief van Zuid-Holland, *HH*, no. 138, "Criminele Sententiën," 371ᵛ.

103. Council of Holland to Margaret of Parma, 31 March 1561, enclosing a copy of Boschhuysen's letter to the Council, 29 March 1561, and Margaret to the Council, 10 April 1561 (Aud. 1704/1); Council to William of Orange, 28 May 1561 (*HH*, 381).

104. Margaret of Parma to the Council of Holland, 29 January 1562 (Aud. 327); Lindanus's report, under Enkhuizen (Aud. 1397/8); Brandt, *Historie van Enkhuizen*, 121–124 (in December 1562, ten men received light sentences from the city court for their part in this affair).

105. Aud. 328, leaves 198, 214, unsigned reports to Margaret, in French, [June] 1564 and 8 July 1564; *HH*, no. 138, "Criminele Sententiën," 385.

106. Council of Holland to Margaret of Parma, 15 January 1565, Margaret to the Council, 24 January 1565, and Medemblik to the Council, 12 January 1565 (Aud. 329).

107. Fruin, "Het Proces van Angelus Merula," 257; Nieuwland to Margaret of Parma [March 1564], and Margaret of Parma to Nieuwland, 17 March 1564 (Aud. 328).

108. Van Beuningen, *Willem Lindanus als Inquisiteur en Bisschop,* 112–131; Lindanus to Margaret of Parma, October 1562, and 10 November 1562, and Margaret to Lindanus, 27 October 1562 (Aud. 327); ? to Suys, 21 February 1563 (Aud. 1704/1).

109. Comment in the first of the anonymous memoranda cited in note 105; Margaret of Parma to the Council of Holland, 31 March 1565, 16, 27 November 1565 (Aud. 329); the Council to Margaret, 6 April, 30 June, 31 July, 3 September 1565 (*HH*, 381), and 27 August 1565 (Aud. 329); Margaret to Lindanus, 20 July, and Lindanus to Margaret, 24, 29 July 1565 (Aud. 329).

110. Lindanus's report, with replies by the Council, Aud. 1397/8; on Medemblik, see above, note 106.

111. On Lindanus's report, see Margaret of Parma to Philip II, 12 April 1565, and Philip to Margaret, 13 May 1565, in M. R. C. Bakhuizen van den Brink, J. S. Theissen, *Correspondance Française de Marguerite d'Autriche,* 3 vols. (Utrecht, 1925–1942), 1: Letters CCCLXXIV, CCCLXXVIII: Council of Holland to Margaret, transmitting its reply to the charges, 17 February 1566 (Aud. 1397/8).

112. J. J. Woltjer, "De Vredemakers," *Tijdschrift voor Geschiedenis* 89 (1976): 299–321.

CONCLUSION

1. Parker, *The Dutch Revolt,* 64–116.

2. The "non-patrimonial" provinces were Friesland, Utrecht, Overijssel, Guelders, and Groningen.

3. Hugo de Schepper, *Belgium Nostrum.*

4. Christopher Hibben, *Gouda in Revolt,* 149–152.

5. Vermij, " 's Konings Stadhouder in Holland," 46; Poelhekke, "Het Naamloze Vaderland van Erasmus."

6. J. J. Woltjer, "Dutch Privileges, Real and Imaginary," *Britain and the Netherlands* 5 (1975): 19–35.

7. *AVR,* 15 July 1562.

8. Council of Holland to the Secret Council, 20 July 1562 (the quotation), 4 September 1565 (*HH*, 381).

9. Aud. 328, leaves 168–169, complaint by Erich von Braunschweig, and Council of Holland to Margaret of Parma, 27 June 1564 (*HH*, 381).

10. Council of Holland to Margaret of Parma, 2 March 1566, 8 April 1566, and Margaret to the Council, 27 June 1564 (*HH*, 381).

11. For Braunschweig's brutal suppression of the Lutheran Reformation in Woerden in September 1566, see Nico Plomp, *Woerden 500 Jaar Stad* ([Haarlem: Gottmer], 1977), 100–103.

12. *RSH*, 12 September 1560; AJ, 18–21 June 1528.

Glossary

acceptatie	The *accord* (q.v.) for a *bede* (q.v.), once signed and approved by the Regent in the name of the prince.
accijnsen	Excise taxes, especially on beer, wine, and grain that were the chief source of revenue for the towns.
accord	Formal agreement by the States to levy a *bede*.
Advocate	Official spokesman of the States.
bede	A subsidy granted by the States; the *ordinaris bede* was routinely granted for a term of years, and *extraordinaris beden* were sought by the government for special needs.
binnen(land)vaart	The inland waterway through Holland, from the IJ to the Scheldt estuary, especially the approved route marked out by comital toll stations.
blijde inkomst	The ceremony by which each new Duke of Brabant was acclaimed by the populace after having sworn to uphold the privileges of the land.
Chamber of Accounts	Board of auditors in The Hague, whose duty it was to watch over the prince's revenues in Holland.
Council of Finance	The organ of the central government to which the prince's revenue officers reported.
Council of Holland (Raad van Holland)	Provincial court of justice in The Hague, which at least through the reign of Charles V handled many administrative and political matters as well.

Council of State	After 1531, the most important advisory body to the Regent, especially on matters of foreign policy.
Court of Holland (Hof van Holland)	A collective name for the judicial apparatus of the prince in The Hague, headed by the Council of Holland.
dagvaart	A meeting of the States.
de non evocando	A privilege dating from the fifteenth century, by which Hollanders were not to be "evoked" for trial outside their province, except in certain reserved cases.
Dirkisten	Ruling faction in Amsterdam, 1538–1578, led by Meester Hendrik Dirkszoon.
Doleantie	List of grievances against the Hendrik-Dirkisten (q.v.) presented to the central government in 1564 by seventy burghers in Amsterdam, henceforth known as the *Doleanten*.
Gemeen land	The common territory; here, the County of Holland as a corporate entity, represented by the States.
gerecht	Town court, consisting of the *schepenen* (q.v.) plus one or two of the burgomasters, presided over by the Sheriff.
Grand Council of Mechelen	Traditional supreme court of the Netherlands, first established by Duke Philip the Good, then reestablished in 1504.
gratiën	Rebates on the *bede* quotas owed by towns or villages, used especially as an inducement to obtain consent to a *bede* from the great cities.
great cities	Cities with voting rights in the provincial states; in Holland, these were: Amsterdam, Delft, Dordrecht, Gouda, Haarlem, and Leiden.
Hof van Holland	See Court of Holland.

(Hoog)heemraadschap Polder board, usually appointed by the prince from along the chief landowners of the district, with power to tax landowners to finance improvements; members of these boards were known as *heemraden*.

joyeuse entrée See *blijde inkomst*.

Laesa Majestas The Roman law term for treason; the death penalty for heresy was justified by the contention that heresy was *Laesa Majestas divina*, or treason against God.

last (a) the charge or instructions given to deputies by their principals; (b) a measure of volume equal to about eighty-five bushels.

lastgelt A tax on the volume of the herring catch.

mogende heren "Mighty lords," a title that deputies to the States of Holland began to give themselves ca. 1550.

morgental A tax on acreage, without reference to the value of the land.

obligatie Promissory note, which could be signed by great nobles, or by fiscal officials, or by the States of Holland.

omslagen Taxes levied by the States for their own purposes (e.g., the salary of the Advocate, gratuities for government officials), and collected by the Receiver for the Common Land (q.v.).

placards (or *plakkaten*) Decrees issued by the Regent in the name of the prince; used here with special reference to heresy laws.

Privy Council Principal advisory body to the Regent prior to 1531; its responsibilities were then divided between the Council of State and the Secret Council.

Raad van Holland See Council of Holland.

Receiver for the *bede*	Official appointed by the Council of Finance to collect the prince's *bede* revenue in Holland.
Receiver for the Common Land	Revenue official appointed by the prince, but more and more under the control of the States.
Rekenkamer van Holland	See Chamber of Accounts.
renten (private)	Loans secured by real property, paying annual interest until and unless the principal was repaid.
renten (States of Holland)	Instruments of debt issued by the States, secured by (a) domain revenues placed in the keeping of the States, 1481–1484; or (b) revenue from the *ordinaris bede*, 1515–1533; or (c) revenue from an impost and land tax collected and disbursed by the States (after 1542).
renten (urban)	Instruments of debt sold "on the body" of the town, secured by revenue from the more important *accijnsen*.
Rijkdom	The wealthy burghers; these men would be members of the *schutters* guilds (q.v.), and ranked just below the office-holding elite in a town's social hierarchy.
schepenen	College of judges appointed for each town by the prince, for a one-year term.
schiltal	Assessment of wealth on which the *ordinaris bede* was based, last revised in 1514/5.
Schutters	Town militia companies; members included the *Rijkdom* (q.v.), or prominent burghers.
Schout	The town Sheriff, except in rare cases appointed by the prince.

staet(gen)   Budget for a *bede*, approved by the States at
                      the time of consent.

vroedschap   Town council, with members chosen by co-
                      optation and serving for life.

Bibliography

MANUSCRIPT SOURCES

Amsterdam—Gemeente Archief:

Andries Jacobszoon, "Prothocolle van alle die reysen ... bij mij Andries Jacops gedaen," 2 vols. (= *AJ*).
Adriaan Sandelijn, "Memoriaelboek," 4 vols. (= Sandelijn).
"Stadsrekeningen" (= *ASR*).
"Vroedschapsresolutiën" (= *AVR;* for the years 1490–1550, see the edition by Van Iterson and Van der Laan).

Brussels—Algemeen Rijksarchief:

"Papiers d'Etat et de l'Audience" = *Aud.*
"Chambre des Comptes" = *CC.*
"Raad van Beroerten (Conseil des Troubles)."
"Roet Boek van de Staten van Brabant," Collection Staten van Brabant.

Dordrecht—Stadsarchief:

Floris Oem van Wijngaerden, "Register van tgeene gedaen ... is in diverse dagvaarten."

Haarlem—Gemeente Archief:

"Tresoriers Rekeningen."
"Vroedschapsresolutiën," extant from 1518.

The Hague—Koninklijke Bibliotheek:

"Historie van Holland" (anonymous chronicle, 1477–1534).

The Hague—Rijksarchief van Zuid-Holland (derde Afdeling):

"Ambtenaren Centraal Bestuur" = *ACB.*
"Graafelijkheids Rekenkamer" = *GRK.*

"Hof van Holland" = *HH*.
"Staten van Holland voor 1572" = *SH*.

Leiden—Stadsarchief:

"Oude Secretarie."
"Tresoriers Rekeningen."

PUBLISHED PRIMARY SOURCES

Aurelius, Cornelius. *Cronycke van Hollandt, Zeelandt en Vrieslant.* Antwerp: J. Doesburg, 1530.

———. *Batavia sive de Antiquo eius Insulae Quam Rhenus . . . Facit Situ.* Ed. B. Volcanius. Antwerp: Plantin, 1586.

Barlandus, Hadrianus. *Historia Rerum Gestarum a Brabantiae Ducibus.* Frankfurt: Johannes Wechelus, 1585.

Bakhuizen van den Brink, M. R. C., and Theissen, J. S., *Correspondance Française de Marguerite d'Autriche,* 3 vols. (Utrecht: 1925–1942).

van den Bergh, Ph. C. *Correspondentie van Margaretha van Oostenrijk, 1506–1528.* Vols. 2 and 3 of *Gedenkstukken tot Opheldering der Nederlandsche Geschiedenis.* 3 vols. Leiden: Luchtmans, 1842–1847.

Brewer, J. S., ed. *Letters and Papers, Foreign and Domestic, of the Reign of Henry VIII.* 21 vols. Vaduz: Kraus reprint, 1965.

Brouwer Ancher, A. J. M., and J. C. Breen. "De Doleantie van een Deel der Burgerij van Amsterdam tegen den Magistraat dier Stad van 1564 en 1565." *BMHGU* 24 (1903): 59–200.

Budé, Guillaume. *De Studio Litterarum.* Paris: Badius, 1532.

Calendar of Letters, Despatches, and State Papers Relating to the Negotiations Between England and Spain.

Cornelius, C.A. *Geschichte des Münsterschen Aufruhrs.* 2 vols. Leipzig: T. O. Weigel, 1855–1860.

Cuperinus, Aelbertus. *Chronike.* In C. R. Hermans. *Verzameling van Kronyken . . . betrekkelijk de Stad en Meierij van 's Hertogenbosch.* 3 vols. 's Hertogenbosch, 1848, vol. I.

van Dillen, J. G. *Bronnen tot de Geschiedenis van het Bedrijfsleven en het Gildewezen van Amsterdam.* 3 vols. The Hague: Nijhoff, 1929–1974.

Eckhof, A. *De Avondmaalsbrief van Cornelis Hoen.* The Hague, 1917.

D. Erasmi Opera Omnia. Ed. J. Leclerq. 10 vols. Leiden: Leclerc, 1703–1706.

Erasmus, Desiderius. *Opus Epistolarum D. Erasmi Rotterdami.* 12 vols. Ed. P. S. Allen. Oxford: Clarendon, 1906–1963.

Everaerts, Niklaas. *Consiliorum Opus*. Leuven: J. Masius, 1571.

Fernandez Alvarez, Manuel. *Corpus Documental de Carlos V*. 5 vols. Salamanca: University of Salamanca, 1973–1981.

Fredericq, Paul. *Corpus Documentorum Inquisitionis Haereticae Pravitatis Neerlandicae*. 5 vols. Ghent: J. Vuylsteke, 1889–1902.

Fruin, R., ed. *Informacie op het Staet van Holland in 1514*. Leiden: Sijthoff, 1866.

Gachard, L. P. "Les Anciennes assemblées nationales de Belgique." *Revue de Bruxelles* 3 (1839): 1–79.

———. *Correspondance de Marguerite d'Autriche avec Philippe II*. 2 vols. Brussels: C. Muquardt, 1867–1870.

———. *Collection des Voyages des Souverains des Pays-Bas*. Vol. 2 = *ARS/KAW-CRH*, Publications in Quarto, 15:2 (Brussels, 1874).

Godin, André. *Le Homiliaire de Jean Voirier*. Geneva: Droz, 1971.

Griffiths, Gordon. *Representative Government in Western Europe in the Sixteenth Century*. Oxford: Clarendon, 1968.

Groen van Prinsterer, G. *Archives ou Correspondance Inédite de la Maison Orange-Nassau*. 14 vols. Leiden: S. and J. Luchtmans, 1835–47; Utrecht: Kemink et Fils, 1857–1861.

Grosheide, G. "Verhooren en Vonnissen der Wederdopers, betrokken bij de Aanslag op Amsterdam." *BMHGU* 41 (1920): 1–197.

van der Haegen, F., et al. *Bibliographie des Martyrologes Protestants Neerlandais*. 2 vols. The Hague: Nijhoff, 1890.

Hanny, Robert Kerr, and Denys Hay. *The Letters of James V*. Edinburgh: H. M. Stationery Office, 1954.

van Heel, D. "Merkwaardige Beslagen van Lindanus en het Hof van Holland," *Bijdragen voor de Geschiedenis van het Bisdom Haarlem* 52 (1935): 307–346.

Hermans, Willem. *Hollandiae Gelriaeque Bellum*. In Ant. Mathesius, *Veteris Aevi Analecta*. The Hague: G. Block, 1738.

Heuterus, Pontus. *Rerum Austriacarum Libri XV*. Vol. 3 of *Opera Historica Omnia*. Leuven: J. Coppenius, 1649.

Hortensius, Lambertus. *Secessionum Civilium Ultrajectinarum et Bellorum ab Anno 1524 Historia*. Basel: Oporinus, 1546.

De Imitatione Christi. Ed. Paul Hagen. The Hague: Nijhoff, 1935.

van Iterson, P. D. J., and P. H. J. van der Laan. *Resoluties van de Vroedschap van Amsterdam, 1490–1550*. Amsterdam: De Bataafsche Leeuw, 1986.

Kernhamp, G. W. "Rekeningen van Pompeius Occo aan Koning Christiaan II van Denemerken, 1520–1523." *BMHGU* 36 (n.d.): 255–329.

Lanz, K. *Correspondenz des Kaisers Karls V, aus dem Königlichen Archiv und der Bibliotheque de Bourgogne zu Brüssel* (= Lanz). 3 vols. Leipzig: F. A. Brockhaus, 1844–1846.

LeGlay, André Joseph Ghislain. *Correspondance de l'Empereur Maximilien Ier et de Marguerite d'Autriche* (= LeGlay). 2 vols. Paris: J. Renouard, 1839.

[Marshal, William]. *The Forme and Manner for Subvention of Pore People at Hypres.* London, 1535; reprint Amsterdam: Theatrum Orbis Terrarum, 1974.

Meilink, P. A. "Gegevens aangaande Bedrijfskapitalen in den Hollandschen en Zeeuwschen Handel in 1543," *Economisch- en Sociaal-Historisch Jaarboek* 9 (1922): 263–277.

———. "Rapporten en Betoogen nopens het Congiegeld op Granen, 1539–1541." *BMHGU* 44 (1923): 1–124.

———. "Remonstrantie van het Hof van Holland en de Rekenkamer nopens de Administratie van de Ontvanger-Generaal A. Coebel en de Staten van Holland." *BMHGU* 45 (1924): 157–183.

Mellink, A. F., ed. *Documenta Anabaptistica Neerlandica.* 5 vols. to date. Leiden: Brill, 1975–1988.

Ortelius, Abraham. *Theatrum Orbis Terrarum.* Antwerp, 1570; reprint Amsterdam: N. Israel, 1964.

Pijper, F. *Bibliotheca Reformatoria Neerlandica.* 10 vols. The Hague: Nijhoff, 1903–1904.

Prevenier, W., and J. G. Smit. *Bronnen voor de Geschiedenis der Dagvaarten van de Staten en Steden van Holland voor 1544.* Vol. 1. The Hague: Nijhoff, 1987.

Resolutiën van de Staten van Holland (= *RSH*). 278 vols. N.p., 1524/43–1793.

Rollin-Couquerque, M., and A. Meerkamp van Embden. "Goudse Vroedschapsresolutiën betreffende Dagvaarten van de Staten van Holland." *BMHGU* 37 (1916): 61–81; 38 (1917): 98–357; 39 (1918): 306–407.

Scheltema, P. *Amstel's Oudheid.* 6 vols. Amsterdam: J. Scheltema, 1855–1872.

de Smidt, J. Th., et al. *Chronologische Lijst van de Geëxtendeerde Sententiën en Procesbundels Berustende in het Archief van de Grote Raad te Mechelen, 1465–1555.* 4 vols. Brussels: Koninklijke Commissie voor de Uitgave van Oude Wetten en Verordeningen van België, 1966–1987.

Snoy, Reynier. *De Rebus Batavicis Libri XIII.* Ed. J. Brassica. Frankfurt: D. Augrius, C. Schleichius, 1620.

Tallone, Armando, ed. *Parlamento Sabaudo, Parte Prima, Patria Cismon-*

tana. Vols. 6 and 7. Bologna: N. Zanichelli, 1932–1933. *Parte Seconda, Patria Oltramontana.* Vol. 2. Bologna: N. Zanichelli, 1937.

Theissen, J. S., ed. *Correspondence Française de Marguerite d'Autriche, Duchesse de Parma, avec Philippe II.* 3 vols. Utrecht: Kemink en Zoon, 1925–1942.

Unger, W. S. *De Tol van Iersekeroord, Documenten en Rekeningen, 1321–1572* (= *Rijksgeschiedkundige Publicatiën,* Kleine Ser., 29.) The Hague: Nijhoff, 1939.

Velius, Theodoricus. *Chronyk van Hoorn.* Ed. S. Centen. Hoorn: Centen, 1740.

Vierlingh, Andries. *Tractaet van Dyckagie.* Eds. J. Hullu and A. G. Verhoeven. (= *Rijksgeschiedkundige Publicatiën,* Kleine Ser., 20.) The Hague, 1920.

Wellens, R. *Actes des États Genéraux des Anciens Pays Bas.* Vol. 1 *1464–1477*); vol. 2, *1478–1493;* vol. 3, *1493–1506.* Heule: 1974– .

SECONDARY WORKS

Algemene Geschiedenis der Nederlanden (= NAGN). Ed. D. P. Blok, et al. 15 vols. Haarlem: Fibula van Dishoek, 1977–1983.

Algemene Geschiedenis der Nederlanden (= *AGN*). Ed. J. A. van Houtte. 11 vols. Utrecht: W. de Haan, 1949–1958.

Allen, J. W. *A History of Political Thought in the Sixteenth Century.* Reprint. London: Methuen, 1960.

Althusius, Johannes. *Politica Methodice Digesta.* Ed. Carl Friedrich. Cambridge: Harvard University Press, 1932.

Anderson, Perry. *Lineages of the Absolutist State.* New York: New Left Books, 1974.

Asaert, G. *De Antwerpse Scheepsvaart in de XVᵉ Eeuw* = *VKAW-VL* 72. Brussels: Paleis der Academiën, 1973.

Auer, Alfons, *Die vollkommene Frömmigkeit eines Christen.* Düsseldorf: Patmos, 1954.

Augustijn, Cornelis. *De Godsdienstgesprekken tussen Rooms-Katholieken en Protestanten van 1538–1541* = *Verhandelingen Uitgegeven van Teylers Godgeleerd Genootschap* 30 (Haarlem, 1967).

Baelde, Michel. *De Collaterale Raden Onder Karel V en Filips II, 1531–1578* (= *VKAW-KL*) 27. Brussels, 1965.

Bainton, R. H. *David Joris.* Leipzig: M. Heinsius' Nachfolger, 1937.

Balen Janszoon, Matthys. *Beschryving der Stad Dordrecht.* Dordrecht: S. Onder de Linde, 1677.

Bang, Nina Ellinger. *Tabeller over Skibsfart og Varetransport gennem*

Øresund, 1497–1660. 2 vols. Copenhagen: Nordisk Forlag, 1906–1922.

Bangs, Jeremy D. "Andries Salomonsz, a Converted 'Rabbi and Doctor' in Leiden (1553–1561)." *Jewish Social Studies* 40 (1978): 271–286.

Bartier, J. "Filips de Goede en de Vestiging van de Bourgondische Staat." *AGN* 3: 253–271.

———. "Karel de Stoute." *AGN* 3: 272–298.

Bech, Sven Cedergreen. *Reformation og Renaissance.* Vol. 6: *Denmarks Historie.* Ed. John Danstrup and Hal Koch. Copenhagen: Politiken, 1963.

Beekman, A. H. *Holland, Zeeland en Westfriesland in 1300.* The Hague: Nijhoff, 1916–1920 (= text vol. 4 of *Geschiedkundige Atlas van Nederland*).

van Beuningen, P. Th. *Willem Lindanus als Inquisiteur en Bisschop.* Assen: Van Gorcum, 1966.

Biographie Nationale de Belgique. 44 vols. Brussels: Thiry van Buggenhout, E. Bruylant, 1866–1985.

Blaich, Fritz. *Die Reichs-Monopolgesetzgebung im Zeitalter Karls V.* Stuttgart: Gustav Fischer, 1967.

de Blécourt, A. S., and E. M. Meijers. *Memorialen van het Hof van Holland, Zeeland, en Westfriesland van de Secretaris Jan Roosa.* 3 vols. Haarlem: H. D. Tjenk Willink en Zoon, 1929.

Blickle, Peter. *Landschaften im Alten Reich.* Munich: Beck, 1973.

Blockmans, W. P., ed. *Het Algemeen en de Gewestelijke Privileges van Maria van Burgondië voor de Nederlanden* (= *Standen en Landen,* 80; Heule: 1985); includes "Breuk of Continuiteit? De Vlaamse Privileges van 1477 in het Licht van het Staatvormingsproces," 97–144.

———, ed. *Estates or Powers* = *Standen en Landen* 79 (Heule: 1977).

———. "De Representatieve Instellingen in het Zuiden, 1384–1483." *NAGN* 4: 156–163.

———, et al. "Tussen Crisis en Welvaart: Sociale Veranderingen, 1300–1500." *NAGN* 4: 42–86

———. "Typologie van de Volksvertegenwoordiging in Europa tijdens de Late Middeleeuwen." *TG* 87 (1974): 483–502.

———. "Vlaanderen, 1384–1482." *NAGN* 4: 217–220.

———. *De Volksvertegenwoordiging in Vlaanderen in de Overgang van Middeleeuwen naar Nieuwe Tijd (1384–1506).* Brussels: Paleis der Academiën, 1978.

Blok, P. J. "De Financiën van het Graafschap Holland." *BMGN* 3d ser., 3 (1886): 36–130.

―――. *Geschiedenis eener Hollandse Stad.* 4 vols. The Hague: Nijhoff, 1910–1918.

Boelmans-Kranenburg, H. A. H. "Visserij van de Noordnederlanders." In G. Asaert, et al., eds. *Maritieme Geschiedenis der Nederlanden.* 4 vols. Bussum: 1976–1978. 1: 290–294.

de Boer, D. E. H., and J. W. Marsilje, eds. *De Nederlanden in de Late Middeleeuwen.* Utrecht: Aula, 1987.

Boitet, Reiner. *Beschryving der Stad Delft.* Delft: R. Boitet, 1729.

Brandt, Geraerdt. *Historie der Vermaerde Zee- en Koop-Stadt Enkhuizen.* Ed. S. Centen. Hoorn: J. Duyn, 1740.

Brokken, Michiel. *Het Ontstaan van de Hoekse en Kabeljauwse Twisten.* Zutphen: Walburg, 1982.

Brucker, Gene. *The Civic World of Early Renaissance Florence.* Princeton: Princeton University Press, 1977.

de Bruin, G. "De Souvereiniteit in de Republiek: een Machtsprobleem." *BMGN* 94 (1979): 27–40.

Brulez, W. "Brugge en Antwerpen in de 15ᵉ en 16ᵉ Eeuwen. Een Tegenstelling?" *Tijdschrift voor Geschiedenis* 83 (1970): 15–37.

Brünner, E. C. G. *De Orden op de Buitennering van 1531.* Utrecht: A. Oosthoeck, 1918.

Brünner, Otto. *Land und Herrschaft. Grundfragen der Territorialen Verfassungsgechichte.* Brünn: R. M. Rohrer, 1942.

Carcel, Ricardo Garcia. *Cortes del Reinado de Carlos V.* Valenica: [n.p.], 1972.

Carsten, F. L. *Princes and Parliaments in Germany.* Oxford: Clarendon, 1959.

Cate, E. M. ten. "Onderhandelingen van het Hof te Brussel met de Munstersche Wederdopers Aangeknoopt." *Doopsgesinde Bijdragen.* 1899.

de Cavele, Johan. *Dagraad van de Reformatie in Vlaanderen.* (= *VKAW-KL*, no. 76; Brussels: 1975).

Christensen, Aksel E. *Dutch Trade to the Baltic around 1600.* Copenhagen: E. Munksgaard, 1941.

The Contemporaries of Erasmus. Eds. L. Domonkos and Peter Bietenholz. 3 vols. Toronto: University of Toronto Press, 1985–1987.

Coornaert, E. *Un Centre industriel d'autrefois. La Draperie-sayerie d'Hondschoote, XIVᵉ-XVIIᵉ siècles.* Paris: Presses Universitaires de France, 1930.

D'Ailly, A. E. *Zeven Eeuwen Amsterdam.* 6 vols. Amsterdam: Scheltema & Holkema, 1943–1950.

Davis, Natalie Zemon. "The Rites of Violence." In *Society and Culture in*

Early Modern France. Palo Alto: Stanford University Press, 1975, 152–187.

Dekker, C. "The Representation of Freeholders in the Drainage Districts of Zeeland West of the Scheldt during the Middle Ages." *AHN* 7 (1975): 1–30.

Derville, Alain. "Les Pots-de-Vin dans le dernier tiers du XVe siècle (d'après les comptes de Lille et St. Omer)." In W. P. Blockmans, ed. *Het Algemeen en de Gewestelijke Privileges van Maria van Bourgondië voor de Nederlanden,* 449–471.

———. "Pots de vin, cadeaux, racket, patronage: essai sur les mécanismes de décision dans l'État Bourguignon." *Revue du Nord* 56 (1974): 341–364.

van Deursen, A. Th. "Staatsinstellingen in de Noordelijke Nederlanden, 1579–1780." *NAGN* 5: 350–387.

De Vries, Jan. *The Dutch Rural Economy in the Golden Age, 1500–1700.* New Haven: Yale University Press, 1974.

Dhondt, Jan. "Les Assemblées d'État en Belgique avant 1795." *Recueils de la Société Jean Bodin* 24 (1966): 325–400.

———. "'Ordres' ou 'Puissances': l'Exemple des États de Flandre." In W. P. Blockmans, ed. *Estates or Powers,* 25–57.

Dictionnaire de Théologie Catholique. 15 vols. Paris: Letouzey & Ane, 1909–1950.

Diederiks, H. A. "Amsterdamse Binnenscheepvaart-politiek in de 16e Eeuw." *Amstelodamum* 56 (1969): 111–115.

Dierickx, M., S. J. *De Oprichting der Nieuwe Bisdommen in de Nederlanden onder Filips II, 1559–1570.* Antwerp: Standaard, 1950.

van Dillen, Johannes Gerard. *Van Rijkdom en Regenten: Handboek tot de Economische en Sociale Geschiedenis der Nederlanden tijdens de Republiek.* The Hague: Nijhoff, 1970.

Downer, W. "De Financiële Toestand van de Stad Leiden omstreeks 1500." Typescript at the Leiden Stadsarchief. 1951.

van Druten, H. *Geschiedenis van de Nederlandsche Bijbelvertaling.* 2 vols. The Hague and Rotterdam: D. A. Daamen, 1895–1897.

Dubiez, F. J. *Op de Grens tussen Humanisme en Hervorming.* Nieuwkoop: de Graaf, 1962.

Dudok van Heel, S. A. C. "Oligarchiën in Amsterdam voor de Alteratie van 1578." In Michiel Jonker, et al., eds. *Van Stadskern tot Stadsgewest.* Amsterdam: 1984. Pp. 35–61.

Duke, A. C. "The Face of Popular Religious Dissent in the Low Countries." *Journal of Ecclesiastical History* 26 (1975): 41–67.

———. "The Time of Troubles in the County of Holland, 1566–1567." *Tijdschrift voor Geschiedenis* 82 (1969): 316–337.

Duncker, Ludwig. *Fürst Rudolf der Tapfere von Anhalt und der Krieg gegen Herzog Karl von Geldern, 1507–1508.* Dessau: Dünnhaupt, 1900.

van Durme, Maurice. *Antoon Perrenot, Bisschop van Atrecht, Kardinaal van Granvelle, Minister van Karel V en Filips II (1517–1586).* Brussels: Paleis der Academiën, 1953.

Elias, H. J. *Kerk en Staat in de Zuidelijke Nederlanden onder de Regering der Aartshertogen Albrecht en Isabella, 1595–1621.* Antwerp: DeSikkel, 1931.

Elias, J. E. *De Vroedschap van Amsterdam, 1578–1795.* 2 vols. Amsterdam: N. Israel, 1963.

Elton, G. R. "Taxation for War and Peace in Early Tudor England." In J. M. Minter, ed. *War and Economic Development.* Cambridge: Cambridge University Press, 1975.

Enschede, A. J. *Inventaris van het Oud-Archief van de Stad Haarlem.* Haarlem, n.d.

de Ferdinandy, Miguel. *Philipp II.* Wiesbaden: Pressler, 1977.

Fockema Andreae, S. J. *Het Hoogheemraadschap van Rijnland.* Leiden: E. IJdo, 1934.

———. "Embanking and Drainage Authorities in the Netherlands during the Middle Ages." *Speculum* 27 (1952): 158–167.

Folz, R. "Les Assemblées d'états dan les principautés Allemandes (fin XIVᵉ–debut XVIᵉ siècle)." *Recueils de la Société Jean Bodin* 25 (1965): 163–191.

Frielinghaus, D. *Ecclesia et Vita. Eine Untersuchung zur Ekklesiologie des Andres Hyperius.* Göttingen, 1956.

Fruin, R. "De Verpondingen van 1496 en 1514 en haar Voorbereiding." *Verspreide Geschriften* 6: 138–175.

———. *Verspreide Geschriften.* Ed. P. J. Blok, et al. 10 vols. The Hague: Nijhoff, 1900–1904.

———. "Het Proces van Angelus Merula," *Verspreide Geschriften* 1:229–265.

———. "Het Voorspel van de Tachtig-Jarige Oorlog." *Verspreide Geschriften* 1: 266–449.

———. "De Zamensteller van de zogenaamde Divisie-Kroniek." *Verspreide Geschriften* 7: 66–72.

———, and H. T. Colenbrander. *Geschiedenis der Staatsinstellingen in Nederland tot den Val der Republiek.* The Hague: Nijhoff, 1901.

Garcia Martinez, Sebastian. *Bandolerismo, Pirateria, y Control de Moriscos en Valencia durante el Regno de Felipe II.* Valencia: University of Valencia, 1977.

Geitz, Anneke. "De Staten van Holland en hun Personeel, 1540–1565," Doctoraal Scripsie, University of Groningen, 1982.

Geschiedkundige Atlas van Nederland. 3 maps vols. and 15 text vols. The Hague: Nijhoff, 1913–1938.

Geyl, Pieter. *Orange and Stuart, 1641–1672.* London: Weidenfeld and Nicholson, 1969.

———. *The Revolt of the Netherlands.* 2d ed. London: E. Benn, 1958.

Gierke, Otto. *Das Deutsche Genossenschaftsrecht.* Vol. 2: *Geschichte des Deutschen Körperschaftsrecht.* Berlin: Weidmann, 1873.

Giesey, Ralph E. *If Not, Not: The Oath of the Aragonese and the Legendary Laws of Sobrarbe.* Princeton: Princeton University Press, 1968.

Gilissen, John. "Les États Généraux en Belgique et aux Pays Bas sous l'Ancien Régime." *Recueils de la Société Jean Bodin* 24 (1966): 401–438.

Gilliard, François. "Gouvernés et Gouvernants dans la Confédération Helvétique, des Origines à la Fin de l'Ancien Régime." *Recueils de la Société Jean Bodin* 25 (1965): 139–162.

Gorissen, Pieter. "De Prelaten van Brabant onder Karel V (1515–1544) en Hun Confederatie (1534–1544)." *Standen en Landen* 6 (1953): 1–127.

de Graaf, Robert. *Reyner Snoygoudanus, a Bibliography.* Nieuwkoop: De Graaf, 1968.

Graves, Michael. *The Tudor Parliaments.* London: Longman, 1985.

Grayson, Christopher. "The Common Man in the County of Holland, 1560–1572: Politics and Public Order in the Dutch Revolt." *BMGN* 95 (1980): 35–63.

Groenveld, Simon, et al. *De Kogel door de Kerk?* [Zutfen]: Walburg, 1979.

Grosheide, G. *Bijdragen tot de Geschiedenis der Anabaptisten in Amsterdam.* Hilversum: J. Schipper, 1938.

Grube, Walter. *Der Stuttgarter Landtag, 1457–1957.* Stuttgart: Klett, 1957.

de Gryse, Rogier. "De Gemeenschappelijke Groote Visscherij van de Nederlanden in de XVIᵉ Eeuw." *BGN* 7 (1952): 32–54.

———. "De Konvooieering van de Vlaamse Vissersvloot in de 15ᵉ en 16ᵉ Eeuwen." *BGN* 2 (1948): 1–24.

Gunst, J. W. *Johannes Pistorius Woerdensis.* Hilversum: "De Blaeuvoet," 1925.

de Haan, H. *Moedernegotiatie en Grote Vaart.* Amsterdam: SUA, 1977.

Hale, J. R. *War and Society in Renaissance Europe, 1450–1620.* New York: St. Martin's, 1985.

Haley, Kenneth H. D. *The Dutch in the Seventeenth Century.* New York: Harcourt Brace Jovanovich, 1972.

Haliczer, Steven. *The Revolt of the Comuneros.* Madison: University of Wisconsin Press, 1981.

Häpke, Rudolf. *Die Regierung Karls V und der Europäische Norden.* Lübeck: Max Schmidt, 1914.

de Haro, Carlos López. *La Constitución y Libertades de Aragón.* Madrid: Reus, 1926.

Harthan, John. *The Book of Hours, with an Historical Survey.* New York: Crowell, 1977.

Helbig, Herbert. *Das Wettinische Ständestaat.* Münster/Cologne: Böhlau, 1955.

Henne, Alexandre. *Histoire de Belgique sous le Règne de Charles V.* Vols. 1–2. Brussels: Rozez, 1865.

———. *Histoire du Règne de Charles Quint en Belgique.* 10 vols. Brussels: Flatau, 1858–1860.

Henneman, John B. *Royal Taxation in Fourteenth-Century France.* Princeton: Princeton University Press, 1971.

Hibben, Christopher. *Gouda in Revolt.* Utrecht: HES Publishers, 1983.

Hill, Charles E. *Danish Sound Dues and the Command of the Baltic.* Durham, NC: Duke University Press, 1926.

Hintze, Otto. "Typologie der ständischen Verfassung des Abendlands." *Historische Zeitschrift* 141 (1929–1930): 229–248.

Hoek, C. "Delfshaven, de Rivierhaven van Delft." In *De Stad Delft: Cultuur en Maatschappij tot 1572.* Delft, 1980.

Hoek, D. "Het Geslacht Duyst van Voorhout in de 16ᵉ Eeuw." *Jaarboek voor het Centraal Bureau van Genealogie* 12 (1958): 185–220.

Hof, J. *De Abdij van Egmond van de Aanvang tot 1573.* The Hague, 1973.

Holleman, F. A. *Dirk van Assendelft, Schout van Breda en de Zijnen.* Zutfen: W. J. Thieme, 1953.

Hoop Scheffer, J. G. de. *Geschiedenis der Kerkehervorming in Nederland van haar Ontstaan tot 1531.* Amsterdam: G. Funke, 1873.

Hopfer, Johannes. *Johannes Kapistran.* 2 vols. Heidelberg, 1964–1965.

van Houtte, J. A. *An Economic History of the Low Countries.* New York: St. Martin's, 1977.

———. "Nijverheid en Handel." *NAGN* 4: 87–111.

———, and R. van Uytven. "De Financiën." *NAGN* 4: 112–127.

Hugenholz, F. W. N. "Crisis en Herstel van het Bourgondisch Gezag, 1477–1493." *AGN* 4: 1–10.

———. "Het Kaas- en Broodvolk." *BMHGU* 81 (1967): 201–247.

———. "The 1477 Crisis in the Burgundian Duke's Dominions." *Britain and the Netherlands* 2 (1962): 33–46.

Huizinga, Johan. "Uit de Voorgeschiedenis van Ons Nationaal Besef." In W. E. Krul, ed. *Verspreide Opstellen over de Geschiedenis van Nederland.* Alphen aan den Rijn: Sijthoff, 1982.

Hyma, Albert. *The Devotio Moderna.* Grand Rapids: Eerdmans, 1924.

IJssel de Schepper, G. A. *De Lotgevallen van Christiern II en Isabella van Oostenrijk gedurende hun Ballingschap in de Nederlanden*. Zwolle: de Erven J. J. Tijl, 1870.

de Iongh, Jane. *De Koningin: Maria van Hongarije, Landvoogdes der Nederlanden*. Revised ed. Amsterdam: Querido, 1966.

————. *Margaretha a van Oostenrijk*. Amsterdam: Querido, 1947.

Jacob, E. F. *Henry V and the Invasion of France*. New York: Collier, 1966.

Jansen, E. A. M. E. *De Opkomst van de Vroedschap in Enkele Hollandse Steden*. University of Leiden, 1927.

Jansen, H. P. H. *Hoekse en Kabeljauwse Twisten*. Bussum: C. A. J. van Dishoeck, 1966.

————. "Holland en Zeeland, 1433–1482." *NAGN* 4: 271–291.

————. "Holland's Advance." *AHN* 10 (1978): 1–20.

————. "Holland, Zeeland, et het Sticht." *NAGN* 2:282–323.

————. *Jacoba van Beieren*. The Hauge: Kruseman, 1967.

Jansma, T. S. "De Betekenis van Dordrecht en Rotterdam omstreeks het Midden der Zestiende Eeuw." *De Economist* 93 (1943): 212–250.

————. "Hanze, Fugger, Amsterdam." *BMGN* 91 (1976): 1–22.

————. "Holland en Zeeland onder de Bourgondische Hertogen, 1433–1477." *AGN* 3: 313–343.

Janssens, G. "De Eerstse Jaren van Filips II, 1555–1566." *NAGN* 6: 186–201.

Jolliffe, J. E. A. *The Constitutional History of Medieval England*, 4th ed. London: Adam and Charles Black, 1961.

Jongkees, A. G. "Het Groot Privilege van Holland." In *Het Algemeen en de Gewestelijke Grote Privileges van Maria van Bourgondië*. Ed. W. P. Blockmans, pp. 145–235. Heule, 1985.

————. "Strijd om de Erfenis van Wittelsbach, 1417–1433." *AGN* 3: 226–252.

Kalma, J. J. *Grote Pier van Kimswerd*. Leeuwarden: De Tille, 1970.

Kam, I. H. *Waar Was dat Huis op de Warmoes Straat?* Amsterdam: Privately published, 1968.

Kawerau, P. *Melchior Hoffman als Religiöser Denker*. Haarlem: Bohn, 1954.

Keohane, Nannerl. *Philosophy and the State in France*. Princeton: Princeton University Press, 1980.

Ketner, F. "Amsterdam en de Binnenvaart door Holland in de 15ᵉ Eeuw." *BVGO* 4 (1943): 169–200, and 5 (1944): 33–59.

Klompmaker, H. "Handel, Geld- en Bankwezen in de Noordelijke Nederlanden." *NAGN* 6: 58–74.

Kluit, A. *Historie der Hollandsche Staatsregering tot aan het jaar 1795.* 5 vols. Amsterdam: Wouter Brave, 1802–1805.

Knappert, Laurentius. *De Opkomst van het Protestantisme in eene Noord-Nederlandsche Stad.* Leiden: C. van Doesburgh, 1908.

Koenigsberger, H. G. "Composite States, Representative Institutions, and the American Revolution." *Bulletin of the Institute of Historical Research* 62 (1989): 135–153.

———. "The Italian Parliaments from Their Origins to the End of the Eighteenth Century." *Standen en Landen* 70 (1977): 97–118.

———. *Estates and Revolutions.* Ithaca: Cornell University Press, 1971.

———. "The Parliament of Piedmont during the Renaissance, 1460–1560." *Estates and Revolutions,* 19–79.

———. "Patronage and Bribery during the Reign of Charles V." *Estates and Revolutions,* 166–175.

———. "The Powers of Deputies in Sixteenth-Century Assemblies." *Estates and Revolutions,* 176–210.

———. "The States General of the Netherlands before the Revolt." *Estates and Revolutions,* 125–143.

Kölker, A. J. *Alardus Amstelredamus en Cornelius Crocus, Twee Amsterdamse Priester-Humanisten.* Nijmegen: Dekker and Van de Vegt, 1963.

Koopmans, J. W. "De Staten van Holland, 1544–1584." Ph.D. dissertation, University of Groningen, forthcoming.

Krahn, Cornelius. *Dutch Anabaptism.* The Hague: Nijhoff, 1968.

Kühler, W. J. *Geschiedenis der Nederlandsche Doopsgezinden in de Zestiende Eeuw.* Haarlem: H. D. Tjenk Willink en Zoon, 1932.

Kuys, J., and J. T. Schoenmaker. *Landpachten in Holland, 1500–1650.* Amsterdam: Historisch Seminarium, Universiteit van Amsterdam, 1981.

Lambert, Audrey. *The Making of the Dutch Landscape.* London: Seminar Press, 1971.

de Lange van Wijngaerden, C. J. *Geschiedenis en Beschrijving der Stad van der Goude.* 2 vols. Amsterdam: Van Cleef, 1817.

Lehmberg, Stanford E. *The Later Parliaments of Henry VIII, 1536–1547.* Cambridge and New York: Cambridge University Press, 1977.

———. *The Reformation Parliament, 1529–1536.* Cambridge: Cambridge University Press, 1970.

Leupen, P. *Philip of Leiden, A Fourteenth-Century Jurist.* The Hague: Leiden University Press, 1981.

———. "De Representatieve Instellingen in het Noorden, 1384–1482," *NAGN* 4: 164–171.

Ligtenberg, C. *Armenzorg in Leiden tot het Einde van de XVI⁽ᵉ⁾ Eeuw.* The Hague: Nijhoff, 1908.

Lindeboom, Johannes. *Het Bijbelsch Humanisme in Nederland.* Leiden: A. H. Adriani, 1913.

van Loenen, J. C. *De Haarlemse Brouwindustrie voor 1600.* Amsterdam: Universiteitspers, 1950.

Le Long, Isaak. *Historische Beschryving van de Reformatie der Stad Amsterdam.* Amsterdam: Van Septeren, 1729.

Louman, J. P. A. "'Roerende dat Heycoopwater en Amstellant': Een Hollands-Utrechts Waterstaatsgeschil en de Instelling van het Hoogheemraadschap van Amstellant, 1520–1527." *Hollandse Studiën* 12 (1982): 115–166.

Lousse, E. *La Société de l'Ancien Régime* (= *Standen en Landen*) 6 (Leuven: 1943).

Maddens, N. "De Opstandige Houding van Gent tijdens de Regering van Keizer Karl, 1515–1540." *Appeltjes uit het Meetjesland* 28 (1977): 203–239.

van Manen, C. A. *Armenpflege in Amsterdam in ihrer Historischer Entwicklung.* Leiden: Sijthoff, 1913.

Maritieme Geschiedenis der Nederlanden, Ed. G. Asaert, et al. 4 vols. Bussum: De Boer, 1976–1978.

van Marle, Raimond. *Le Comté de Hollande sous Philippe le Bon (1428–1467).* The Hague: Nijhoff, 1908.

Marongiu, Antonio. *Medieval Parliaments: A Comparative Study.* Trans. S. J. Woolf. London: Eyre and Spottiswoode, 1968.

———. *Il Parlamento in Italia nel Medio Evo e nell' Eta Moderna.* Milan: Giuffre, 1962.

Matheson, Peter. *Cardinal Contarini at Regensburg.* Oxford: Oxford University Press, 1972.

McDonnell, Ernest. *The Beguines and Beghards in Medieval Culture.* New Brunswick, 1954.

de Meij, J. C. A. "Oorlogsvaart, Kaapvaart, en Zeeroof." *Maritieme Geschiedenis der Nederlanden* 1: 307–335.

Meilink, P. A. *Archieven van de Staten van Holland voor 1572.* The Hague: Algemene Landsdrukkerij, 1927.

Melles, J. *Ministers aan de Maas: Geschiedenis van de Rotterdamse Pensionarissen, 1508–1795.* The Hague: Nijgh & Van Ditmar, 1962.

Mellink, A. F. *Amsterdam en de Wederdopers in de Zestiende Eeuw.* Nijmegen: Socialistische Uitgeverij Nijmegen, 1978.

———. "Pre-Reformatie en Vroege Reformatie, 1517–1568." *NAGN* 6: 146–165.

————. *De Wederdopers in de Noordelijke Nederlanden.* Groningen: J. B. Wolters, 1954.

Molhuysen, P. C. "Cornelius Aurelius." *Nederlands Archief voor Kerkgeschiedenis* n.s. 2 (1902): 1–28.

Moll, Willem. *Johannes Brugman en het Godsdienstig Leven onzer Vaderen in de 15ᵉ Eeuw.* 2 vols. Amsterdam: Portielje, 1854.

————. *Angelus Merula, de Hervormer en Martelaar des Geloofs (1530–1557).* Amsterdam: Portielje, 1855.

Mollat, M. "Récherches sur les Finances des Ducs Valois de Bourgogne." *Revue Historique* 219 (1958): 285–321.

Motley, John Lothrop. *The Rise of the Dutch Republic.* 3 vols. New York: Harper and Brothers, 1859.

de Muinck Keizer, J. H. *Hendrik van Geldorp.* Groningen, 1893.

Myers, A. R. *Parliaments and Estates in Europe to 1789.* London: Thames and Hudson, 1979.

Naber, J. C. *Een Terugblik: Statistische Bewerking van de Resultaten van de Informatie van 1514.* Reprint. Haarlem, 1970.

Nabholz, Hans, et al. *Die Geschichte der Schweiz.* 2 vols. Zurich: Schulthess, 1932.

Niermeyer, J. F. "Hennegouwen, Holland, en Zeeland onder het Huis Wittelsbach." *AGN* 3: 92–124.

————. "Hennegouwen, Holland en Zeeland onder Willem III en Willem IV van Avesnes."*AGN* 3: 63–91.

————. "Het Sticht Utrecht en het Graafschap Holland in de Dertiende Eeuw." *AGN* 3: 269–305.

van Nierop, Henk F. K. *Van Ridders tot Regenten: De Hollandse Adel in de Zestiende en de Eerste Helft van de Zeventiende Eeuw.* The Hague: De Bataafsche Leeuw, 1984.

Nieuw Nederlandsch Biographisch Woordenboek. Ed. P. C. Molhuysen, et al. 10 vols. Leiden: Sijthoff, 1911–1937.

Noordegraaf, Leo. *Hollands Welvaren? Levens-Standaard in Holland, 1450–1650.* Bergen: Octavo, 1985.

Notestein, Wallace. *The House of Commons, 1604–1610.* New Haven: Yale University Press, 1971.

Nübel, Otto. *Pompeius Occo.* Tübingen: Mohr, 1972.

Oestreich, Gerhard. *Neostoicism and the Early Modern State.* Cambridge and New York: Cambridge University Press, 1982.

Oosterbaan, D. P. *De Oude Kerk van Delft gedurende de Middeleeuwen.* The Hague: Voorhoeve, 1973.

Origo, Iris. *The World of San Bernardino.* New York: Brace and World, 1962.

Overvoorde, J. C., and J. N. Oerburgt. *Het Archief van de Secretarie van de Stad Leiden, 1253–1575.* Leiden: Gemeente-Archief, 1937.

Paludan-Muller, C. *Grevens Feide.* 2 vols. Reprint of 1853–1854 ed. Copenhagen: Selskabet for Utgivelse of Kilder til Dansk Historie, 1971.

Parker, Geoffrey. *The Dutch Revolt.* Ithaca: Cornell University Press, 1977.

———. *Philip II of Spain.* London, 1977.

———. *The Military Revolution, 1500–1800.* Cambridge: Cambridge University Press, 1988.

van Peteghem, Paul. "Centralisatie in Vlaanderen onder Karel V." Ph.D. dissertation, University of Ghent, 1980.

Peters, Leo. *Wilhelm von Renneberg, ein Rheinischer Edelherr zwischen den Konfessionellen Fronten.* Kempen, 1979.

Peyer, Hans Conrad. "Die entstehung der Eidgenossenschaft." In *Das Handbuch der Schweizer Geschichte* 1: 161–238. Zurich: Berichthaus, 1972.

Philippen, A. *De Begijnhoeven. Oorsprong, Inrigtingen, Geschiedenis.* Antwerp, 1918.

Pierson, Peter. *Philip II of Spain.* London: Thames and Hudson, 1975.

Pijper, Frederik. *Het Middeleeuwsch Christendom. De Vereering van de Heilige Hostie.* The Hague: Nijhoff, 1907.

Pinske, C. C. J. "Het Goudse Koutbier." In *Gouda Zeven Eeuwen Stad.* Gouda, 1972.

Pirenne, Henri. *Early Democracies in the Low Countries.* Trans. J. V. Saunders. New York: Norton, 1971.

———. *Histoire de Belgique* (= *HB*). 7 vols. Brussels: H. Lamertin, 1902–1932.

Piskorskĩ, Wladimiro. *Las Cortes en el Período de Tránsito de la Edad Media a la Edad Moderna, 1188–1520.* Trans. C. Sanchez-Albornoz. Barcelona: El Albir, 1977.

Plomp, Nico. *Woerden 500 Jaar Stad.* [Haarlem: Gottmer], 1977.

Pocock, John. *The Machiavellian Moment: Florentine Political Thought and the Atlantic Republican Tradition.* Princeton: Princeton University Press, 1975.

Pocquet du Haut-Jussé, Barthélemy Amadée. "A Political Concept of Louis XI: Subjection instead of Vassalage." In P. S. Lewis, ed. *The Recovery of France in the Fifteenth Century.* New York: Harper and Row, 1971, 196–215.

Poelhekke, J. J. "Het Naamloze Vaderland van Erasmus." *BMGN* 86 (1971): 90–123.

Post, R. R. *Kerkelijke Verhoudingen in Nederland voor de Reformatie.* Utrecht: Het Spectrum, 1954.

———. "Het Sacrament van Mirakel te Amsterdam." *Studia Catholica* 30 (1955): 241–261.

———. *Kerkgeschiedenis van Nederland in de Middeleeuwen.* 2 vols. Utrecht: Het Spectrum, 1957.

———. *The Modern Devotion.* Leiden: Brill, 1968.

Posthumus, N. W. *Geschiedenis van de Leidsche Lakenindustrie,* 3 vols. The Hague: Nijhoff, 1908–1933.

———. *De Oosterse Handel van Amsterdam.* Leiden: Brill, 1953.

———. *De Uitvoer van Amsterdam.* Leiden: Brill, 1971.

Postma, Folkert. *Viglius van Aytta als Humanist en Diplomaat (1507–1549).* Zutphen: Walburg, 1983.

Powicke, Maurice. *The Reformation in England.* Oxford: Oxford University Press, 1965.

Prevenier, W. *De Leden en de Staten van Vlaanderen, 1384–1405* = VKAW-KL. Brussels: Paleis der Academiën, 1961.

Prins, I. *Het Failissement der Hollandsche Steden: Amsterdam, Dordrecht, Leiden en Haarlem in het Jaar 1514.* Amsterdam: Van Looy, 1922.

Prinsen, J. *Geraard Geldenhouwer Noviomagus.* The Hague: Nijhoff, 1908.

Rachfahl, Felix. *Wilhelm van Oranien und der Niederländische Aufstand.* 2 vols. Halle: Niemeyer, 1906–1907.

van Ravensteyn, W. *Onderzoekingen over de Economische en Sociale Ontwikkeling van Amsterdam gedurende de 16ᵉ en het Eerste Kwart der 17ᵉ Eeuw.* Amsterdam: Van Looy, 1906.

Reglá, Joan. *Approximació à la História del Pais Valencià.* Valencia: Eliseu Climent, 1978.

de Reiffenberg, Baron Fr. *Mémoire couronnée en réponse à cette question proposée par l'Académie Royale des Sciences et Belles Lettres de Bruxelles: Quel a été l'état de la population, des fabriques et manufactures, et du commerce dans les Provinces des Pays Bas, pendant les XVᵉ et XVIᵉ siècles?* Brussels: Academie Royale des Sciences, 1820.

de Ridder-Symoens, H. "De Universitaire Vorming van de Brabantse Stadsmagistraten en Funktionarissen: Leuven en Antwerpen, 1430–1580." *Verslagboek van de Vijfde Colloquium, "De Brabantse Stad."* 's Hertogenbosch, 1978: 21–125.

van Rijswijk, B. *Geschiedenis van het Dordtsche Stapelrecht.* The Hague: Nijhoff, 1900.

Rodriguez-Salgado, M. J. *The Changing Face of Empire: Charles V, Philip II and Habsburg Authority.* Cambridge: Cambridge University Press, 1988.

Rogier, L. J. *Geschiedenis van het Katholicisme in de Noordelijke Neder-landen in de 16ᵉ Eeuw.* 2 vols. Amsterdam: Urbi et Orbi, 1947.

van Rompaey, Jan. "De Bourgondische Staatsinstellingen." *NAGN* 4: 136–155.

————. *De Grote Raad van de Hertogen van Bourgondie en het Parlement van Mechelen. VKAW-KL* no. 73. Brussels: Paleis der Akademiën, 1973.

de la Roncière, Charles. *Histoire de la Marine Française.* 6 vols. 2d ed. Paris: Plon, 1909–1932.

van Roosbroeck, Robert. *Filips II, Koning van Spanje, Soeverein der Neder-landen.* The Hague: Kruseman, 1983.

Rosenfeld, Paul. "The Provincial Governors from the Minority of Charles V to the Revolt." *Standen en Landen* 17 (1959): 1–63.

Rowen, Herbert H. *John de Witt.* Princeton: Princeton University Press, 1978.

Sánchez, Esteban Sarasa. *Las Cortes de Aragón en la Edad Media.* Zaragoza: Guara, 1979.

Scheltema, P. *Inventaris van het Amsterdamsch Archief.* 3 vols. Amster-dam: Stadsdrukkerij, 1866–1874.

de Schepper, Hugo. *Belgium Nostrum, 1500–1650: Over de Integratie en Desintegratie van het Nederland.* Antwerp: De Orde van den Prince, 1987.

————. "De Burgerlijke Overheden en hun Permanente Kaders, 1480–1579." *NAGN* 5: 311–349.

————. "De Grote Raad van Mechelen, Hoogste Rechtscollege van de Nederlanden?" in *Miscellanea Consilii Magni,* 171–192. Amsterdam, 1980.

Scheurkogel, J. "Het Kaas- en Broodspel." *BMGN* 99 (1979): 189–211.

————. "Opstand in Holland," in De Boer and Marsilje, *De Neder-landen in de Late Middeleeuwen,* 363–378.

Schilling, Heinz. "Der Aufstand der Niederlanden—bürgerliche Revo-lution oder Elitenkanflikt?" *Geschichte und Gesellschaft* 2 (1976): 177–231.

Schilstra, J. J. *Wie Water Deert: Het Hoogheemraadschap van de Uitwater-ende Sluizen, 1544–1969.* Wormerveer, n.d.

Schmidtmayer, Alfred. "Zur Geschichte der bremischen Akzise." *Brem-isches Jahrbuch* 37 (1937): 64–79.

Schorl, Henk. *'T Oge: Het Waddeneiland Callensoog onder het Bewind van de Heren van Brederode en hun Erfgenamen (= Hollandse Studiën),* vol. 11. [Haarlem: Gottmer], 1979.

Shennan, J. H. *The Origins of the Modern European State, 1450–1725.* London: Hutchinson, 1974.

van Slee, J. C. *Wendelmoet Claesdochter van Monnikendam*. The Hague, 1917.

Smit, J. W. "The Present Position of Studies Regarding the Revolt of the Netherlands." *BN* 1 (1960): 11–29.

Soly, H. "De Aluinhandel in de Nederlanden in de 16ᵉ Eeuw." *Belgische Tijdschrift voor Filologie en Geschiedenis/Revue Belge de Philologie et d'Histoire* 52 (1974): 800–857.

Spading, Klaus. *Holland und die Hanse im 15en Jahrhundert*. Weimar: Böhlau, 1973.

Stayer, James M. *Anabaptists and the Sword*. Lawrence, KS: Coronado, 1972.

Steen, Charlie R. *A Chronicle of Conflict: Tournai, 1559–1567*. Utrecht: HES Publishers, 1985.

Struick, J. E. A. L. *Gelre en Habsburg, 1492–1528*. Arnhem: S. Gouda-Quint, D. Brouwer & Zoon, 1960.

Sutherland, N. M. "William of Orange and the Revolt of the Netherlands: A Missing Dimension." *Archiv für Reformationsgeschichte* 74 (1983): 201–231.

Te Brake, William. *Medieval Frontier: Culture and Ecology in Rijnland*. College Station: Texas A & M University Press, 1985.

Ter Gouw, Johannes. *Geschiedenis van Amsterdam* (= Ter Gouw). 8 vols. Amsterdam: Scheltema & Holleman, 1879–1893.

Tex, Jan Den. *Oldenbarneveldt*. 2 vols. Cambridge: Cambridge University Press, 1973.

Theissen, J. S. *De Regering van Karel V in de Noordelijke Nederlanden*. Amsterdam: Meulenhoff, 1922.

Tierney, Brian. *Foundations of the Conciliar Theory*. Reprint ed. Cambridge: Cambridge University Press, 1968.

Tilmans, Karin. *Aurelius en de Divisiekroniek van 1517*. Hilversum: Verloren, 1988).

Timmer, M. A. "Grepen uit de Geschiedenis der Delftsche Brouwnering." *De Economist* 70 (1920): 358–373, 415–430.

Tracy, James D. *A Financial Revolution in the Habsburg Netherlands: "Renten" and "Renteniers" in the County of Holland, 1515–1566* (= AFR). Berkeley, Los Angeles, London: University of California Press, 1985.

———. "Habsburg Grain Policy and Amsterdam Politics: The Career of Sheriff Willem Dirkszoon Baerdes, 1542–1566." *Sixteenth Century Journal* 18 (1983): 293–319.

———. "Heresy Law and Centralization under Mary of Hungary: Conflict between the Council of Holland and the Central Government over the Enforcement of Charles V's Placards." *Archiv für Reformationsgeschicte* 73 (1982): 284–307.

———. *The Politics of Erasmus: A Pacifist Intellectual and His Political Milieu.* Toronto: University of Toronto Press, 1978.

———. "A Premature Counter-Reformation: The Dirkist Government of Amsterdam, 1538–1578." *Journal of Religious History* 13 (1984): 150–167.

———. "The Taxation System of the County of Holland under Charles V and Philip II, 1519–1566." *Economisch- en Sociaal-Historisch Jaarboek* 48 (1984): 72–117.

Ulloa, Modesto. *La Hacienda Real de Castilla en el Reinado de Felipe II.* Madrid: Fundacion Universitaria Espanola Seminario "Cisneros," 1977.

Unger, Richard W. *Dutch Shipbuilding before 1800.* Assen: Van Gorcum, 1978.

Unger, W. S. "De Hollandse Graanhandel en Graanhandelspolitiek in de Middeleeuwen." *De Economist* 66 (1916): 461–507.

———. "De Sociale en Economische Struktuur van Dordrecht in 1555." *De Economist* 63 (1913): 947–984.

van Uytven, R. "Crisis als Cesuur, 1482–1494." *NAGN* 5: 420–435.

———. "De Blijde Inkomst van 1477, Text en Eigentijds Commentar." In W. P. Blockmans, ed., *Het Algemeen en de Gewestelijke Privileges van 1477,* pp. 286–372.

———. "1477 in Brabant." In W. P. Blockmans, ed., *Het Algemeen en de Gewestelijke Privileges van 1477,* pp. 253–285.

———. "Het Stedelijk Leven, 1100–1400." *NAGN* 2: 187–253.

Vaughan, Richard. *Charles the Bold.* London: Longman, 1973.

———. *Philip the Good.* New York: Barnes and Noble, 1970.

———. *Valois Burgundy.* London: Allen Lane, 1975.

Verhofstad, K. J. W., S.J. *De Regering der Nederlanden in de Jaren 1555–1559.* Nijmegen: Berkhout, 1937.

Vermij, Rienk. "'s Konings Stadhouder in Holland, Oranjes Trouw aan Felips II." *Utrechtse Historische Cahiers* 2/3 (1984): 37–63.

Wagenaar, Jan. *Amsterdam in Zijn Opkomst, Aanwas, en Geschiedenis.* 4 vols. Amsterdam: Isaak Tirion, 1760.

———. *Vaderlandsche Historie.* 21 vols. Amsterdam: n.p., 1749–1759.

Waitz, George. *Lübeck unter Jürgen Wullenwever und die Europäische Politik.* 3 vols. Berlin: Weidmann, 1855–1856.

von Walther, Andreas. *Die Anfänge Karls V.* Leipzig: Dunker & Humblot, 1911.

Walvis, Ignatius. *Beschryving der Stad Gouda.* Gouda: Johan & Andries Endenburg, 1713.

Wansink, H. "Holland and Six Allies: The Republic of the Seven United Provinces." *BN* 4 (1971): 133–155.

van der Wee, H. "Geld- Kredit- en bankwezen in de Zuidelijke Nederlanden," *NAGN* 6: 98–108.

van Werveke, H. "De Steden. Rechten, Instellingen, en Maatschaapelijke Toestanden." *AGN* 2: 374–416.

Wiesflecker, Herman. *Kaiser Maximilian I: Das Reich, Österreich und Europa an der Wende zur Neuzeit.* 5 vols. Munich: R. Oldenbourg, 1971–1986.

Wijnman, H. F. "Wouter Deelen, de Eerste Professeur in het Hebreeuwsch te Amsterdam." *Jaarboek Amstelodamuer* 27 (1930): 43–65.

Wilcox, Donald. *The Development of Florentine Humanist Historiography.* Cambridge: Harvard University Press, 1969.

Wolfe, Martin. *The Fiscal System of Renaissance France.* New Haven: Yale University Press, 1972.

Woltjer, J. J. "Het Conflikt tussen Willem Baerdes en Hendrik Dirkszoon." *BMGN* 86 (1971): 178–199.

——. "Dutch Privileges, Real and Imaginary." *Britain and the Netherlands* 5 (1975): 19–35.

——. "Een Hollands Stadsbestuur in het midden van de 16ᵉ eeuw: brouwers en bestuurders te Delft." In de Boer and Marsilje. *Holland in de late Middeleuwen,* 261–279.

——. *Friesland in Hervormingstijd.* Leiden: Universiteitspers, 1962.

——. "De Vredemakers." *Tijdschript voor Geschiedenis* 89 (1976): 299–321.

van Zuider, D. S. "De Plundering van Den Haag door Maarten van Rossum, 6–9 Maart 1528." *Die Haghe.* 1911: 130–152.

Index

313